W9-BPJ-190

THE LAST ARMADA

THE LAST ARMADA

Queen Elizabeth, Juan del Águila, and Hugh O'Neill:
The Story of the 100-Day Spanish Invasion

DES EKIN

PEGASUS BOOKS
NEW YORK LONDON

THE LAST ARMADA

Pegasus Books LLC
80 Broad Street, 5th Floor
New York, NY 10004

ISBN: 978-1-60598-944-0

10 9 8 7 6 5 4 3 2 1

Printed in the United States of America
Distributed by W. W. Norton & Company, Inc.

Dedication

For Grace

Contents

A detail from this extraordinary sixteenth-century map depicts Ireland's southwest coast and 'The Spanish Sea'. With west topwards, it shows O'Sullivan Beare's territory (top) and Baltimore, Castlehaven and Cork (to the right of the words 'The', 'Spanish' and 'Sea' respectively). Kinsale lies just to right of the ship: the black castle of 'Barry Óg' is Rincorran.

'Truly I think that when the Devil took our Saviour Jesus Christ to the pinnacle of the Temple and showed him all the kingdoms of the world, he kept Ireland hidden … to keep it for himself. For I believe that it is the Inferno itself, or some worse place.'

– Don Juan del Águila, Spanish commander

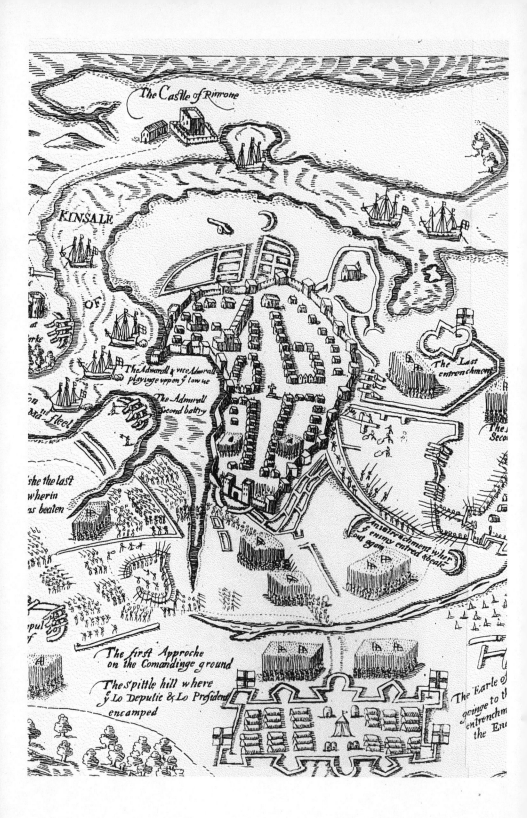

The Castle of Rincrone

KINSALE

OF

rke

on
d ye fleet

The Admirall & vice Admirall
playinge vppon ye towne

The Admirall
Second battry

The Last
entrenchment

The
Seco

she the last
wherin
as beaten

An intrenchment wher
ye enimy entred & beate
ye out gard

The first Approche
on the Comandinge ground

The spittle hill where
ye Lo Depulie & Lo President
encamped

The Earle of
goinge to the
entrenchme
the Ene

PREFACE

It is one of the great adventure stories of history – a siege drama that deserves to rank alongside the Battle of the Alamo and the heroic defence of Rorke's Drift against the Zulu nation.

At 6pm on 21 September 1601, one of the strangest invasion forces in history sailed into the southern Irish harbour of Kinsale, a place its commander had never wanted to go. Battered by punishing storms and towering waves, it had lost contact with its best ships, most of its troops and some of its most important supplies. Although its ostensible purpose was to fight its way through Ireland and conquer England from the west, the expedition included hundreds of women and children. Its ranks contained scores of petrified young soldiers who had no idea how to shoot a gun. It had 1,600 saddles but no horses to put under them.

This was the last of the great armadas of the Elizabethan era – and the last Spanish armada ever to attempt an invasion of England through Ireland.

As the boats dislodged the 1,700 weary troops and the seasick civilians onto shore, the open-mouthed townspeople also saw a gaggle of nuns in their wimples and veils (and perhaps an occasional starched cornette) trip delicately across the rock and shingle. They were followed by a succession of bizarre religious figures. There was a much-feared Jesuit secret agent who was wanted by the English for allegedly organising a murder plot against Queen Elizabeth. There was a Franciscan friar who'd been appointed as Archbishop of Dublin – a city he would never visit, and a See he never saw. There were two more bishops, and a confusion of priests and friars. In this strange guns-and-rosaries expedition, the clerics enjoyed huge power. They immediately tried to order the veteran soldiers around. Even when it came to military matters, they felt they knew best.

As the townspeople soon found out, this wasn't even purely a Spanish expedition. The ships – an odd mix of serious warships and requisitioned merchant vessels hauling cargos like salt and hides – carried a multinational mix of Spanish, Italians, Portuguese, Irish insurgents, and even a few English dissidents. Yet this oddball force was destined to be the most successful Spanish invasion ever mounted against England. Unlike the renowned Great Armada of 1588, this expedition actually established a bridgehead on English-controlled territory and captured a string of key ports.

The *maestro de campo general* or overall land commander of the expedition was an intriguing veteran named Don Juan del Águila. Today, he is relatively unknown. And yet Águila was the commander responsible not only for this last Spanish invasion of Ireland at Kinsale, but also, a few years earlier, for the last Spanish 'invasion' of England: a daring incursion into Cornwall from his base in Brittany.

Águila held out in the walled city of Kinsale for a hundred days, enduring a crippling siege imposed by English commander Charles Blount. Pinned down in one of the least defensible towns in Europe, the Spaniards shivered and starved under the relentlessly pounding English artillery and the equally pitiless Irish weather.

Monstrous guns hurled down fire and death from the hills into the narrow streets. Cannonballs tore breaches in their walls. Besieged from sea and land, the invaders had been reduced to eating dogs, cats and knackered horses – indeed, those were described as 'treats' and 'the best victuals within the town'. Their troops died in their hundreds from hypothermia, malnutrition and dysentery.

Yet they held out and never surrendered.

There were bitter disappointments for the invaders: the locals initially gave them little help, despite confident promises; reinforcements despatched from Spain failed to get through to the town; and a huge relieving force of Irish insurgents from the north of the island proved unable to smash the siege and unite with their beleaguered allies. Still, even after the Irish rebel force was routed at the Battle of Kinsale, and all hope of success had been dashed forever, the surviving invaders still clung grimly on, declaring their determination to die before surrendering the town.

With both sides battle-wearied, and neither relishing the idea of a bloody hand-to-hand fight through Kinsale's narrow and claustrophobic streets, Águila eventually came to terms with his English counterpart. The proud Spaniard sailed home, undefeated, with his sword still at his side and his colours still flying. An honourable man, he insisted on one particular condition that almost broke the deal: although the English wanted to arrest and hang the Irish 'traitors' who'd fought on the Spanish side, he refused to hand them over.

—If you so much as mention such disgraceful terms again, he told Blount in haughty Castilian fury, you should return to your sword.

He said he would fight to the death rather than betray his comrades. Blount dropped his demand and the Irish sailed off to Spain with Águila.

This is the story of the Last Armada, an astonishing tale of courage, endurance and heroism (on all sides) that has long been lost in a mist of myth, legend and self-serving propaganda. One eminent nineteenth-century historian has described Águila's defence of Kinsale as 'the most brilliant example of combined pluck, skill and endurance' in Irish history.

On a global level, the siege and battle at this remote port on the western fringe of civilisation altered the balance of world power and changed history – with consequences that we are still living through today. Spain suffered a major reputational defeat at Kinsale. At sea, its proud navy was outclassed by a superior English fighting fleet. On land, its supposedly invincible infantry was shown to be as vulnerable as any other force. These reversals, combined with the final proof that Ireland would never be an easy back-door route to England, created a much more decisive turning point than the celebrated defeat of the Great Armada of 1588. It led to England's expansion as a naval power and Spain's decline.

The impact in Ireland was even more dramatic. After Kinsale and the departure to Europe of the leading Gaelic noblemen, England finally enjoyed total control over its first colony. Determined to avoid another rebellion from the north, they flooded the northern Gaelic heartland of Ulster with their own people – English and Scots planters. This was intended to guarantee peace but the actual effect, as we know only too well, was almost exactly the opposite. This experimental human mélange of assertive Anglican colonists, uncompromising Scots Calvinists and disempowered and resentful Catholic Irish was to prove a volatile mix.

I first became interested in this story while researching my book *The Stolen Village*, the true-life account of the 1631 slave raid by North African pirates on the fishing port of Baltimore, County Cork. I am a journalist by profession – not an academic and certainly not a qualified historian – so I was surprised and intrigued to learn that Baltimore had become Spanish territory for several weeks in 1601 under this Last Armada. I couldn't help wondering: what had life been like for them, these men from the lands of sunshine, fighting through the rigours of this bitterly cold northern winter?

When I began my researches, I became fascinated by the personalities involved at Kinsale. There was Juan del Águila, a grizzled veteran fighter with nothing to lose. He had been in deep trouble with the Spanish authorities, and was gambling his career on this last throw of the dice. There was the English commander Charles Blount, scandal-hit after an affair with a lethal *femme fatale*, and equally desperate in his need for rehabilitation after being caught up on the fringes of an abortive palace coup in London. And there were the Irish commanders: Hugh O'Neill, a complex figure whose decision to withdraw his troops at a crucial moment before a planned link-up with the Spaniards remains an intriguing mystery; and Red Hugh O'Donnell, a man of action whose dramatic mental breakdown in the aftermath of the Battle of Kinsale ruled out all chances of the insurgent forces regrouping and retaliating.

I have spent several years researching this story, poring over every relevant line of the main original English and Irish sources; reading a great deal of the extensive Spanish *legajos*, or bundles of correspondence; peering over the shoulders of the well-informed Venetian ambassadors; and tapping into some obscure 1600s histories to gain angles and insights which rarely make their way into mainstream books.

One important point: this is a post-Good Friday Agreement book. I am not interested in bitter recriminations, laments or partisan rants about what ought not to have happened in the past. Rather, I view the Kinsale saga as a bit like those beautiful Georgian houses that line Dublin's squares. A generation ago, many were torn down and viewed as hated symbols of Ireland's colonisation. Now, they are cherished and protected because we all appreciate that they are part of our shared history. The story of Kinsale – where Irish people fought with equal commitment on either side – belongs to us all.

I wanted to make this story come alive again – as an exciting and vibrant tale of human endurance under pressure; of epic personality clashes; of a Spanish commander whose courage went unrewarded by his unforgiving King; and of an English commander who gained hero status from his victory at Kinsale, but threw it all away for his forbidden love of a married woman.

It is a tale from the era of Shakespeare, with all the elements of a Shakespearean tragedy, and yet it is also a contemporary story of politics and intrigue, of human weaknesses and strengths, that speaks clearly to us across the centuries. I hope you find it as captivating as I do.

A NOTE
ON THE TEXT

This is a work of nonfiction. Nothing has been made up or 'novelised'. Everything is attributable to an identified source.

Reading this book, you will notice that sometimes I use standard 'curly' quotation marks and sometimes Continental-style quotation dashes. This is a deliberate technique. Words in quotation marks are a direct quote, faithfully reproduced but sometimes edited back. Quotation dashes signify an indirect quote: that is, an honest and accurate reflection of what was said, but not using the actual words. In fact, sometimes I will use modern phrases to convey the same meaning. I find this helps to lighten the leaden plod of indirect testimony in official accounts, which were never intended for easy reading and rapidly become wearisome. However, both types of quotes are fully sourced and attributed. No dialogue has been invented.

I have modernised spellings for easier accessibility. Dates are kept in the Old Style (OS) Julian Calendar used by the English at the time.

For simplicity, I generally refer to the participants by their second names rather than their titles. For instance, in repeated references, Charles Blount, Lord Mountjoy, is 'Blount' rather than 'Mountjoy', and so on. No disrespect is intended. Similarly, Juan del Águila is simply 'Águila'. I am aware that this isn't actually his surname (any more than 'da Vinci' is Leonardo's) but if Dan Brown can get away with it, so can I.

Des Ekin

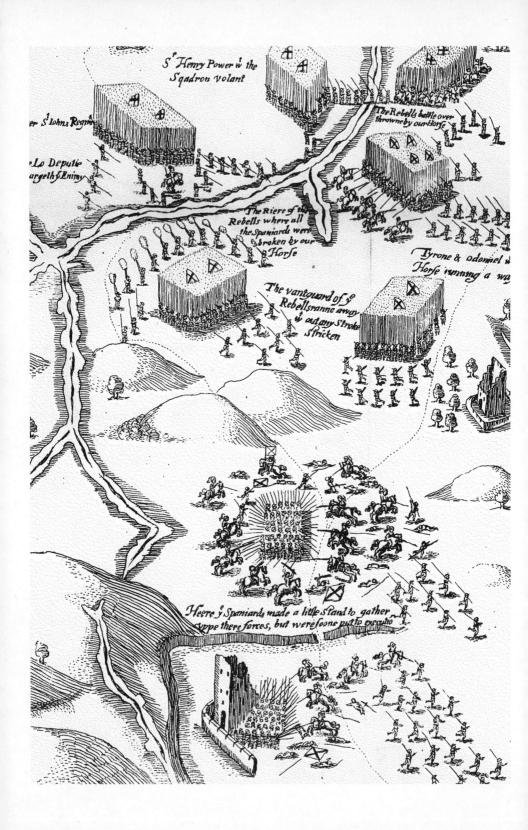

S.r Henry Power w.th the
Sqadron Volant

er S.t Iohns Regim

e Lo Deputie
argeth y.e Enimy

The Rebells battle over
throwne by our Horse

The Riere of the
Rebells where all
the Spaniards were
broken by our
Horse

Tyrone & odonnel w
Horse running a wa

The vantguard of y.e
Rebells ranne away
w.th out any stroke
stricken

Heere y.e Spaniards made a little stand to gather
vppe there forces, but were soone put to execution

CHAPTER ONE

Tinker, Tailor
... Soldier

Somewhere between Bristol and London

29 December 1601

Five days after the Battle of Kinsale

L IKE THE shadow of a storm cloud scudding across a troubled sky, the cloaked rider thundered through the heartland of England in his headlong race to the court of Queen Elizabeth. Sweat flew like sea-spume from the lathered flanks of his galloping horse. Mud and turf sods splattered from its hooves as its rider coaxed the gasping animal to greater speed.

Richard Boyle – a dark, wolfish and fiercely ambitious man of thirty-four – barely paused to glance at the darkened windows of the wealthy merchants' homes as he clattered across the cobbles of each sleeping town. What he carried in his satchel was more valuable than all their gold. He had information – crucial information that would upset carefully laid plans and elevate some powerful politicians while consigning other courtiers to oblivion. It would destroy many careers at court and advance others – including, he hoped, his own.

Boyle was well aware of the power he possessed and of the need to keep his information secret until it reached the right ears. At each staging point on the Queen's postal route from Bristol to London, he would ignore the curious queries from stable masters. Instead, he would thrust forward a document signed by his superior officer, General George Carew, and by the Queen's all-powerful Secretary of State, Robert Cecil, declaring that he was on a mission of national importance.

And indeed, it was an epic trip – possibly a record-breaking one. Boyle had left Cork, on the southern coast of Ireland, at 2am on Monday, 28 December. A favourable breeze had carried his ship swiftly into Bristol harbour. Now, on the Tuesday evening, he was on the last leg of the gruelling 122-mile trip from Bristol to London. The post horse relay network set up earlier in Elizabeth I's reign was remarkably efficient. As the fastest means of travel imaginable, 'posting' was used by Shakespeare as a word to describe flashing speed. But even in summer – when the roads were dry and in good shape – a hurrying post-boy would usually cover ten miles per hour. Seventy miles in a day was considered a good speed for urgent packages. Boyle was chalking up that distance, plus half as much again, and then some, in the middle of a particularly wet and cold winter, all by himself, on a single day – and this was just the culmination of a total journey on sea and land of more than 420 miles.

Although weary and wet to the bone, Boyle didn't care about the rigours of the road. He knew how important it was that his version of events – or more correctly, the version of his boss Carew – should reach the Queen's ears first.

George Carew, now based in Ireland, had long been an ally of Secretary Robert Cecil in London – united against a highly placed cadre of rivals in a bitter power struggle that had torn Elizabeth's court asunder. Even now, a messenger from the rival camp was rushing from Cork to the Queen's palace to disclose the same tale, with a different twist. The news itself was important. But even more important was who told it to her first.

By late on Tuesday evening, Boyle's sensitive nose was catching the first traces of the human stench that signified he was approaching London. Already Europe's third largest city, the metropolis contained 200,000 people jam-packed into the 450 acres within the city walls. Boyle was familiar with London – he'd been involved in intrigues at the royal court before. Once, after being accused of corruption, he'd thrown himself personally at the mercy of Queen Elizabeth. The bold move had paid off, slapping down his enemies and elevating Boyle to the position of Clerk of the Council of Munster.

He knew his way around the city. Just down the river was the newly built Globe Theatre, where the Lord Chamberlain's Men were playing to packed houses. Perhaps Boyle felt a pang of regret that his faraway posting had prevented him from seeing the new play everyone was talking about – the one featuring Hamlet, Prince of Denmark.

Sparks flying from his horse's iron shoes, he clattered along the stony roads towards Westminster, the political capital of England. He swung into the private courtyard of Secretary Cecil's mansion on the Strand – which, as its name suggests, was at that time situated right on the riverbank. After handing his horse to a groom, he entered the jaw-dropping splendour of London's most lavish private house and was eventually greeted by an extraordinary figure.

Robert Cecil did not look like the most powerful man in England. So short in stature that the Queen privately mocked him as 'my pygmy', he was further plagued by a spinal deformity that gave him a slight hunch. His oversized head seemed perpetually cocked to one side. His large, expressive eyes, combined with his squat frame, gave him an unfortunate resemblance to a wide-eyed frog. His rivals had nicknamed him The Toad.

'Here lieth The Toad at London', read the spiteful notes they would post outside his house. Others viciously mocked his 'wry neck, a crooked back, and splayed foot'. But Cecil had the last laugh. As Secretary of State he occupied a role we'd now describe as Prime Minister, and he was possibly the first to use that role in the modern sense, bypassing and even surreptitiously overruling the Queen in what he regarded as the national interest. A popular lampoon jibed: 'Little Robert runs up and down / he ruleth both court and crown.'

Cecil controlled a vast matrix of influence. Inspired by his mentor, the notorious spymaster Francis Walsingham, he had built up a formidable intelligence network and knew exactly what was stirring in every nest of dissent. At times he'd intervene; at other times he would sit back and silently let things develop. That was his style. No one ever knew exactly what The Toad was thinking – not even the Queen herself.

Over supper, Boyle wasted no time revealing his news. Cecil already knew the full background – that a Spanish invasion force of nearly four thousand troops had landed in the southwest of Ireland the previous September and had taken the harbour town of Kinsale. English defenders had rapidly besieged the town, but had themselves been surrounded by a relieving force of Irish rebels. A harsh winter had taken its toll on all three forces. Cecil knew that his beleaguered English troops were exhausted, hungry and running low on supplies. Everything depended on whether the outer ring of rebels could link up with the besieged Spanish in Kinsale and, between them, crush the English. The Queen's forces had better artillery and cavalry, but the Spanish forces included seasoned fighters with the determination of men who had their backs to the sea. With both sides now roughly equal in number, the result was almost a coin-toss.

Boyle revealed that just a few days earlier, on Christmas Eve, the meta-phorical coin had been thrown with disastrous results for the Irish relieving force. They had launched a surprise dawn thrust in a bid to link up with the Spaniards in Kinsale. But in atrocious weather conditions, they ended up in disarray. The Irish had decided to retreat and regroup, temporarily giving up their hilltop advantage and gambling that the English forces would be too fatigued to follow.

It had been exactly the wrong call. The English commander, a thirty-eight-year-old military tactician named Charles Blount, had realised that his enemies were headed towards wide-open terrain where they could not deploy their traditional fighting technique – an ambush followed by a retreat into the safety of dense woodland or mountain glen. His cavalry pursued and forced the Irish to make a stand in the open.

The battle that followed lasted only a few hours. It had been a rout, a catastrophe for the insurgents and their Spanish allies. By Christmas Day, around a thousand Irish lay dead, and most of the rest had begun trudging home in defeat.

As he related his good news to Robert Cecil, Boyle must have been struck by the Secretary's reaction. It was not one of pure delight. On the contrary, Cecil seemed anxious and worried. The two men talked long into the night. Despite Boyle's weariness, they did not retire until 2am. The English victory had eased one threat to the realm, but it had created another.

These were dark days at Elizabeth's court. Less than a year ago, Cecil had uncovered a treasonous plot to topple the Queen. A group of headstrong young courtiers, led by Robert Devereux, the charismatic Earl of Essex, had tried to spark off a full-scale palace revolution in the streets of London. The revolutionaries had planned to arrest the Queen and usurp her power by forcing her to declare King James VI of Scotland as her successor.

Essex had once been a war hero and a national idol. But his adoring public had drawn the line at insurrection, and as the Earl rode through the streets calling for popular support he had been shunned and ignored by a sceptical citizenry. The great revolution had fizzled out in a whimper as Essex and some of his fellow plotters had been tried and executed. But interrogations had shockingly revealed that hundreds of highly placed nobles and courtiers had been involved to some degree in the conspiracy. There were clearly a large number of moles in the highest ranks of the Elizabethan court who had sympathised with Essex's aims. Some were still in positions of power, awaiting the right moment to act. The Queen was far from safe.

Shortly before he met his death, Essex himself had admitted that his conspiracy was 'a leprosy, that had infected far and near'. And after a painstaking analysis of the plot, the loyal courtier Francis Bacon also warned that 'the dregs of these treasons … do yet remain in the hearts and tongues of some misaffected persons'.

Who were these 'misaffected persons'? Who were the moles? It was Cecil's job to find out. Some of the confessions he'd read were political dynamite – so potentially devastating that they'd had to be suppressed in the interests of national stability.

Cecil would have been especially troubled by the testimony of an executed ringleader named Sir Charles Danvers. Danvers gave credible testimony that a senior military figure had been involved in the conspiracy at an early stage. Entrusted with the command of thousands of English soldiers, he had treasonously offered to lead up to five thousand of his troops to Scotland to join King James's army in a demonstration of power against the Queen.

This military figure had been closely linked to the leading conspirators, including those who'd been executed. He was a friend of the ringleader, Essex. He was the illicit lover of Essex's married sister, a ravishing society beauty named Penelope Rich, who herself had been deeply involved in the plot. Now this same military man was encamped outside the town of Kinsale, with thousands of English soldiers under his command.

How would this man react to the changed situation? He could cut a deal with the defeated Irish commander Hugh O'Neill, as Essex had once done. He could forge a treasonous agreement with the Spanish commander who still held the town of Kinsale. Either move could give him enough power to become a kingmaker. Such temptation would be difficult to resist.

For months Cecil had harboured deep concerns about the loyalty of this top military man – so much so that he had asked his friend General George Carew to spy upon him and keep the Secretary closely informed. Their exchanges were so sensitive that the potential traitor could not even be named. Instead, they used a numerical code – the man was '2026' when Carew wrote to Cecil, and '2047' in the Secretary's replies.

In a typical coded letter, Cecil refers to '2047' guardedly, informing Carew 'how far his unworthy friends [ie Essex and his fellow plotters] have wounded him here and what impression it hath taken'. In a cryptic phrase that Carew would immediately have understood, he adds '... and what it is like to be his domestic fortune'. For his part, Carew openly casts doubt on the officer's loyalty. 'He is [either] a noble gentleman, and all yours,' he informs Cecil from the war zone, 'or else he is a devil.'

So no wonder Secretary Cecil was a worried man. Sitting at 2am over his guttering candle in the Strand, he had to face the very real possibility that the man who had just won the Battle of Kinsale – Charles Blount, commander of the English forces in Ireland – was the greatest and most dangerous mole of all.

Cecil's odd phrase 'his domestic fortune' was a coded reference to Blount's mistress. And at that stage, deep in the heart of the Sussex countryside, Lady Penelope Rich was reduced to pacing in frustration around the prison of her gilded mansion, waiting anxiously for news from the Irish front. At thirty-eight years of age, Penelope was still being acclaimed as one of the most beautiful women in England. With her striking combination of golden blond hair and midnight-black eyes, she could turn the heads of rich men, soldiers and poets alike. Just a smile from 'my Lady Rich' could transform the salty, red-blooded fighting men of Elizabeth's court into lovelorn moon-calves.

The swashbuckling warrior-poet Philip Sidney rhapsodised about her golden hair, about jet-black eyes that could manage to beam 'like morning sun on snow' and about cheeks of 'fair claret' set against a face of alabaster. However, he also saw another side to Penelope – a woman who was 'most fair, most cold'. His experience of loving her was 'as he who being poisoned, doth poison know'.

For, besides being one of the most radiant figures of her age, Penelope was also one of the deadliest. An independent woman, centuries before her time, she had always taken a cheerfully fluid approach to the strict rules of the repressed era into which she had been born. Monogamy, religion, the con-stant grovelling to superiors, and above all the automatic right of monarchs to rule – to her, they were all up for debate and open to challenge.

Independent, intelligent and ruthlessly ambitious, she was one of Eng-land's first female revolutionaries. She had helped to plot the palace coup that aimed to reduce the Queen to a mere puppet of Penelope's schem-ing brother, the Earl of Essex, and of his preferred monarch, King James of Scotland. Penelope had been right at the centre of the conspiracy – plotting, encouraging, and marshalling sympathisers.

According to the Earl of Essex, his sister had 'a proud spirit' and mocked him when his own revolutionary zeal had waned just before the uprising. '[She] did continually urge me on with telling me how my friends and fol-lowers thought me a coward, and that I had lost all my valour,' he testified under interrogation.

If that sounds eerily similar to the words of Lady Macbeth as she scorn-fully urged her husband to get rid of his monarch ('What? Quite unmanned in folly?'), it may not be entirely a coincidence. Essex's testimony about his sister would have been very much in the audience's minds when Shakespeare's play was staged.

That may not have been the playwright's only link with the beautiful Penelope Rich. Some, including James Joyce, have claimed that she was the mysterious 'Dark Lady' who inspired some of Shakespeare's most desperately lovelorn sonnets. 'Poor Penelope, Penelope Rich,' muses Stephen Dedalus in *Ulysses*, using a complex pun on both the forename and surname to contrast the fortunate Penelope Rich with her pitiable counterpart, Anne Hathaway, who waited like Homer's Penelope for her husband, William Shakespeare, to return home.

Now it was Lady Rich's turn to be housebound and waiting. Lucky to escape unpunished after her clear complicity in the February rising, she had been exiled to rural Sussex, where she had been placed under virtual house arrest in the custody of her unloved husband, Robert. Here, amid the excruciating boredom of the damp fields and forests, Penelope waited for her lover, Charles Blount, to finish his task in Ireland and return to England, where they would resume their former life as the scintillatingly shameful golden couple of courtly society.

For much of the past decade, Blount and Penelope had been the Elizabethan equivalent of Edward VIII and Wallis Simpson, or Taylor and Burton before their marriage – fashionably illicit lovers whose relationship was an open secret. Penelope had been compelled to marry Robert Rich in 1581, and the couple had raised four children. This minor obstacle had not prevented her carrying on a parallel 'marriage' with Charles Blount and having five more children with him. (Two other babies, one to each father, had died in infancy.) Despite the inevitable scandal, their high connections and invigorating conversation had combined with the delicious frisson of the forbidden to make Charles and Penelope welcome guests at the grandest mansions.

Luckily for the couple, the Queen didn't appear to mind. She had identified the personable Blount as a 'favourite' when he was barely out of his teens. In her eyes, he could do no wrong. Elizabeth had no objection to her favourites having flings with other women – provided, of course, they reserved their special, spiritual, ethereal love for the monarch herself.

Besides being the golden couple, Blount and Penelope had been right at the heart of society's greatest golden circle. Penelope's brother, the Earl of Essex, had for years been among the most powerful men at court. Her lover, Blount, was one of Essex's closest friends. Their circle was never boring – it had attracted poets, actors, playwrights, pirates, philosophers, adventurers, soldiers and (in the spirit of the age) men who were many of these things at once.

But now, ten months after the abortive coup, the circle had been smashed – Essex beheaded, the principal plotters executed, and many of the other leading members either imprisoned, exiled or shamed. Robert Rich, sensing a change of atmosphere, was already drawing up plans to divorce his unfaithful wife. And Charles Blount was under deep suspicion – so much so that he had contemplated abandoning his command and fleeing to France. When Essex himself had broken under interrogation and named Blount as 'an accessory' to his conspiracy, only the Queen's personal reassurances had kept him in place at the head of the English forces in Ireland.

Elizabeth had no such warm feelings towards Penelope Rich, who treated the Queen with thinly disguised contempt. However, the monarch spared her for Blount's sake. Penelope seemed to live such a charmed life that some of the more superstitious courtiers even suspected she was a witch. One poet, Thomas Campion, described her as 'Penelope ... whose sweet voice cast a spell over the Ruler of the Irish'. The man he believed was helplessly in thrall to Penelope was the English Lord Deputy, or governor, of Ireland – Charles Blount.

Richard Boyle finally collapsed into bed, satisfied that he had fulfilled his mission. Many years later he was to recall that night with justifiable pride: 'I made a speedy expedition to the court,' he wrote. 'I left my Lord President [Carew] at Shandon Castle, near Cork, on the Monday morning about two of the clock, and the next day being Tuesday, I delivered my packet and supped with Sir Robert Cecil … at his house in the Strand.'

(Some doubt the accuracy of Boyle's claim, but such epic journeys were possible. Just two years later, an English horseman was to ride the 162 miles from London to Doncaster in a single day, 132 miles the next, and nearly 100 the third day to carry news of the Queen's death to Edinburgh. And in the mid-1600s, the Duke of Ormond was to leave London at 4am on a Saturday, sail from Bristol and arrive in Waterford at 9am on Monday.)

But despite his exhaustion and his 2am bedtime, Richard Boyle was allowed to sleep for only around five hours before being jostled awake. 'By seven that morning, [Secretary Cecil] called upon me to attend him to the court,' he recalled.

The road-weary messenger had no idea he was about to be presented to the Queen in person. Boyle barely had time to dress before he was being led by Cecil through the corridors of Elizabeth's sumptuous royal court. Boyle must have been acutely conscious of his haggard appearance as he strode alongside the Secretary through the opulent corridors of the palace, glancing into the elegant rooms graced with deep Turkish carpets, lined with vividly coloured tapestries and capped with heavily moulded plaster ceilings. Scarlet-clad yeomen of the guard, their uniforms each marked with a single golden rose, paced through the corridors past huddles of courtiers, immaculate in their buttoned doublets and impractical ruffs.

Boyle was to be received in the Queen's own bedchamber. He would have been well aware of the significance of the privilege. Not so long ago, the hot-headed Earl of Essex had infamously violated the sanctity of this same bedchamber when he stormed into the room unbidden, before the Queen had had a chance to put on make-up or don her usual wig.

Eventually, Boyle and Cecil were summoned into the royal chamber. They were received by a readily recognisable figure who – even by the standards of the day – must have looked truly outlandish. Although not far from her seventieth year, the Queen still appeared to believe that she was young and attractive. It was a delusion that many of her poets and sycophants did nothing to discourage.

The reality was revealed only in despatches by foreign visitors. One French ambassador reported that she wore a massive red wig festooned with pearls, but that her face was 'long and thin' and her yellowed, broken teeth were in such bad shape that 'it is difficult to understand her when she speaks'. Even more disturbingly, she had the habit of letting the bodice of her dress lie open. 'One could see the whole of her bosom,' he wrote – not a pleasant sight since it was 'rather wrinkled'. Another ambassador said she had a thin, hooked nose and her pure white skin contrasted with her tiny, black eyes.

Boyle was gratified to find that the sixty-eight-year-old monarch remembered him. She extended a bejewelled hand for the kneeling messenger to kiss.

—Richard Boyle, she purred. I am glad that you are the happy man to bring the first news of this glorious victory.

Boyle hardly had a chance to stammer a reply before the royal interrogation began. This was to be no fleeting visit. The Queen made it clear that she wanted to know every detail of the siege and battle of Kinsale – those momentous three months that had culminated in this long-awaited triumph over her despised enemy Hugh O'Neill.

Boyle was happy to oblige. For much of the campaign, he had served under General Carew, a copious collector of information. He knew the entire saga better than most people. Settling in on the silken cushions, Boyle took a deep breath and told Queen Elizabeth the full story of the Last Armada.

CHAPTER TWO

'Haste, Haste, for Your Life'

Kinsale, Monday, 21 September 1601
The Arrival

CAPTAIN WILLIAM Saxey stared at the approaching ships and cursed his luck.

Saxey was just one of around a dozen English army officers who'd been sent to guard the small towns dotted around the southern Irish coastline in preparation for a long-anticipated Spanish invasion. His own posting, to the quiet town of Kinsale, had never been regarded as a key target, so he had been given a mere hundred men to maintain a token presence.

Suddenly, the idea of a hostile landing at the sleepy County Cork harbour didn't seem so far-fetched after all. Saxey had just received reports that a large armada of Spanish ships had passed the promontory known as the

Old Head. It was assumed that they were trying to tack their way up to the nearby port of Cork city, but, if they were, the gods of weather had other ideas. The blustery autumn winds were making the short journey next to impossible. Whatever the intention, one thing was certain: they were now headed into Kinsale.

How many soldiers were on board the ships? Six thousand? Five thousand? Fewer? Nobody knew for certain. But with Saxey's own meagre force, plus maybe another sixty volunteers from among the townsfolk, he wouldn't be able to hold them off for five minutes.

Saxey looked around the town and considered his options. Kinsale had the paradoxical qualities of being a nightmare to attack and an even worse nightmare to defend. It had a great harbour, but control of that port depended on holding two forts on either side of the sea approach. If those fortresses fell into enemy hands, Kinsale's fate would be sealed, because it could not rely on help from the sea.

Defending the landward side depended upon controlling the heights above the town. Kinsale lay in a virtual pit backed by steep hills and was wide open to attack from cannon – a child could stand up there and practically toss stones right into the streets.

The town's ancient stone walls were crumbling and dilapidated and needed reinforcing before they would be fit to defend the city against even the basic mediaeval weapons they'd been designed to withstand, never mind the heavy artillery of modern warfare. The streets were barely wide enough for two men to pass each other.

'The town is protected by only one wall, with turrets at intervals,' one expert wrote later, adding that it was inconceivable that such a place could withstand a long siege. On the plus side, Kinsale had two mills to grind corn and enough ovens to bake bread for thousands of troops.

Was it worthwhile to attempt a defence? Saxey knew only too well the deal that the Spanish were likely to offer – it was the standard arrangement of a merciless age: surrender, and we let you live; try to resist, and we will put everyone to the sword.

But there was a good reason why the Spanish should withdraw even this basic concession. They had a grudge to settle. Just two decades before, a Catholic expedition of six hundred Spaniards and Italians had occupied Smerwick in County Kerry. Pinned down by thousands of English troops, the invaders had surrendered in the belief that their lives would be spared. Instead, the English had cold-bloodedly massacred almost the entire force.

As Saxey watched the approaching Spanish ships, he must have felt a deep sense of dread. Whatever he decided to do, he might not survive to see another dawn in Kinsale.

On 21 September in any other year, Kinsale would have been settling quietly into another somnolent autumn. This was St Matthew's Day, an important date in the calendar of farmers and fisher folk. The ancient pagan festival marking the transition from summer towards winter, from light towards darkness, had been adopted by the early Christians and dedicated to the disciple Matthew. A mnemonic passed down from parent to child reminded farmers of their duties at this time of year:

> *St Matthee, shut up the bee;*
> *St Mattho, take thy hopper and sow;*
> *St Matthy, all the year goes by;*
> *St Matthie, sends sap into the tree;*
> *St Matthew brings the cold, rain and dew.*

Kinsale knew all about cold, rain and dew. It was especially prone to precipitation, in all its forms. 'The air is laden with warm moisture,' one writer noted, adding: 'Soft grey mists creep in from the sea in the autumn and cover its slopes with a grey, impenetrable mantle.' A soldier would later grumble about the constant dampness: 'There are perpetual springs from these rocks which make them slippery and very dangerous,' he complained.

Sailors, on the other hand, loved Kinsale. It was blessed with a near-perfect harbour, according to one early visitor 'one of the finest I ever saw, and one of the safest ... even at low water, it is deep enough to contain 500 sail of ship, landlocked.' Another wrote in the 1600s: 'The haven of Kinsale is one of the most famousest of Ireland; ships may sail into it, keeping in the midst of the channel, without any danger ... [at] the quay of Kinsale, ships may ride in eight or ten fathoms of water, being defended of all winds.'

The town's name celebrates its greatest assets: *Cionn tSáile*, 'the saltwater headland'. Another version of its name, according to Samuel Lewis's 1837 *Topographical Dictionary*, is Cune Sáille, Irish for 'smooth basin'. An added advantage was the strong tidal flow. Even in calm weather, with the right timing, ships rarely needed to be rowed or towed out of port.

The town was then, as now, breathtakingly beautiful. Its jumble of winding streets seems to have been thrown chaotically against the side of a steep hill overlooking the wide River Bandon as it sweeps in a dramatic meander around a promontory, into an estuary and out to sea. A female tourist in the 1800s told how it lay 'picturesquely nestled in the deep valley formed by surrounding hills. Beyond and towards the left, lay the placid waters of the pretty harbour.'

But the key to the town's success was not its looks, but its location. Anyone sailing directly due north from the bustling Spanish port of La Coruña – 'The Groyne' as the English called it – would cross 800km of open sea before making landfall around Kinsale. The English port of Bristol, 482km away from Kinsale, may have looked closer on the maps – but when the winds were blowing a certain way, Spain was more convenient than England. Kinsale became a major conduit for business between the squelchier and the sunnier regions of Europe.

The Irish and English couldn't get enough of Spain's wines, lace and metalwork. The Continentals needed Irish fish, cattle, butter, wool, leather and timber. Every year, at the fair of St James in Compostela, traders from the two centres would meet to hammer out deals which would keep everyone happy and wealthy for the next twelve months.

Such connections inevitably rubbed off both in the attitudes and genes of folk in Kinsale. Even today, the town has the strange appearance of a seaport in the Iberian Peninsula. Its narrow streets seem designed, along Mediterranean lines, to provide shade from a blazing sun, and to force cooling sea breezes throughout the centre. The fact that Kinsale actually sits on the same latitude as Newfoundland and rarely needs such air-conditioning devices gives the town a strange air of bewildered out-of-placeness, as though it has been teleported directly and mysteriously into Northern Europe from its natural home amid the olive groves.

Many of the townsfolk, too, have often shown signs of Spanish ancestry. A visitor to Kinsale in the 1700s remarked on how different the locals looked, 'with black hair and skin more brown than white … heavy cheekbones and large upper lips as though swollen'. Although to modern readers this provides an almost perfect description of a pouting Latina movie star, the visitor regarded these attributes as 'uglier' than the norm.

With some two hundred houses within its walls, Kinsale sustained a population of around 1,800 to 2,000 – much the same as today's figure. It was not great farming country, but it had another good source of food. All year round, its sturdy eight-man fishing boats plied the local waters and landed their silver hauls. In the 1700s, one visitor seeking a meal told how local children were despatched to catch 'fairly good fish' off the rocks using pins for hooks.

There were hard times, too. Violence, plague and fire had all devastated the town. 'All our men died of the pestilence,' one mayor wrote in 1548, 'and we have a wide empty town.' In 1594, just seven years before the events of our story, a blaze had gutted the entire centre. The town was only now beginning to recover. But, in truth, Kinsale's real trial by fire was just about to begin.

In imagining the town of 1601, any reader who's familiar with modern-day Kinsale will have to mentally erase many of the features that character-ise the town today. It was smaller – much smaller. Almost all the flat areas flanking the harbour and seafront are later additions reclaimed from the sea. Market Quay, now quite a bit inland, was then exactly what its name sug-gests: a waterfront. The estuary waters lapped its shores to the south and east and the Ballinacurra creek almost circled it to the west and north.

Picture the town of 1601 as a walled enclosure, roughly the shape of the continent of Africa, with the harbour along one side and its main twin-towered gate at the tip, facing inland. The wall is punctuated by more than twenty towers. Inside, there's a jumble of streets with cellared houses, some made of stone and some of wood. The main landmarks are the Norman castle of the Anglo-Irish Desmond family, a courthouse, an open market square, and St Multose's twelfth-century church, which even in the 1600s is a venerable four hundred years old. Outside the walls lies a friary, smashed by the hammer of Henry VIII in 1541 and now ignominiously used as a storehouse.

As William Saxey begins to muster his men and organise his defence, the town around him buzzes with frantic activity. Cattle are being herded into the centre from the fields outside. The wealthier townspeople are packing up their belongings and preparing to flee. However, the mayor and burgesses are keeping their options open. They make all the correct loyal noises to Saxey, but behind it all they have a Plan B – they are secretly preparing to give the newcomers a warm and hearty welcome.

John Meade, the mayor of Cork city, was a worried man. And with good reason. Cork had never been a bastion of loyalty to English rule. If the Span-iards landed here, it would be touch and go whether the citizens would fight them or embrace them.

Meade looked at the scribbled letter from his counterpart in Kinsale, warning him of the Spaniards' arrival off the Old Head, and immediately composed a report to the English commander, Charles Blount. 'A post from Kinsale came in this hour, advertising that 55 ships were seen this afternoon off the Old Head of Kinsale,' he wrote. 'They are, I expect, our enemies; and the wind serves them well for this harbour [Cork] or Kinsale.'

Meade sent that letter in the afternoon. Within a few hours, his speculation about the destination was settled. He wrote an updated note. 'The Spanish fleet of 30 ships arrived at Kinsale on 21 September and landed their men at 6pm that day,' he told Blount. He sealed the historic letter, and scribbled a frantic instruction to the messenger:

'Haste, haste, post; haste, haste, post, for your life.'

Not long afterwards, a Scottish merchant ship hauling a cargo of salt arrived in Waterford. The master, a Silvester Steene from Leith, hurried ashore and breathlessly informed the authorities about the invasion fleet. Steene had been in Lisbon when the Spanish fleet set sail in August. He claimed that fifty-five ships had left Portugal. Five of them were 'great ships' with the flagship a massive thousand tons. But the fleet also included French, Scottish and Flemish vessels, as well as four from Ireland. Steene identified the sea commanders by name – Admiral Don Diego de Brochero and his Vice-Admiral, Don Pedro de Zubiaur.

And who, demanded his interrogators, was the commander of the land forces? Steene shook his head. He had no name, just the most basic description imaginable.

—An old man, he replied. An old man whom I do not know.

CHAPTER THREE

THE MAN BORN
WITHOUT FEAR

Cadiz, Spring 1601
Four months before the invasion

THE OLD Eagle was caged in a prison cell when he was offered
one last flight to glory.

It was hard to tell exactly why Maestro de Campo Don Juan del Águila
was in jail: some said it was for taking liberties with army money during his
controversial command in western France. Some said it was because of the
notorious stubbornness that always landed him in trouble with his military
masters. Some said the former was used by the authorities as a pretext for
the latter.

It hardly mattered. But when his distinguished visitors outlined an audacious plan to invade England through Ireland, the Old Eagle had plenty of
time to listen. He would lead an expeditionary force that would sail in a

mighty armada from Lisbon, the top brass explained.

Six thousand hand-picked veteran fighters would be under his command. He would have devastating artillery. Neither would be needed when he landed in Ireland, because he would be welcomed by the cheering populace, who would steer him in a flow of jubilation towards their leaders. He didn't even need horses, because 1,600 fresh Irish mounts were to be placed at his disposal. All he needed were saddles.

The gritty old warrior was no fool and he didn't suffer fools gladly. So his irritation must have mounted as the madcap plan went from one height of fancy to another. No destination had been settled yet. It could be the west coast – Donegal, Sligo, Galway, Limerick – but, wait, then again it could be Carlingford in the east. Anyway, he didn't need to worry because he would have an old Ireland hand, a Franciscan Brother named Mateo de Oviedo, by his side to advise him on these matters.

Águila must have bitten hard on his tongue at this stage. He knew Brother Mateo's military record and it was not a distinguished one. Should he mention Smerwick at this point? The lunatic invasion the good Brother helped to inspire, the horrific massacre which he escaped?

No. He carried on listening.

Once landed, his masters continued, he would join the northern insurgent armies of Hugh O'Neill and Hugh O'Donnell, who had the entire country on their side. Their troops would swell his invasion force to 16,000, perhaps even 20,000 as other wavering lords joined the rising.

Águila listened.

The warriors for Christ would sweep across Ireland, easily quashing the few thousand troops that the Queen's commander could muster at short notice, until they reached the east coast, a mere twenty leagues from England. More ships would arrive from Spain. More veteran warriors. They would consolidate their position and gather their forces until … the final killer move: invasion of England itself. If all went well, the bells of London town would ring out to celebrate a Spanish Christmas, and a Catholic monarch would replace *La Inglesa*, the heretical Englishwoman Elizabeth Tudor, on the throne of England.

Águila had not been born yesterday. He had never been to Ireland, but he knew all about the country. During his time as Spanish commander in France he had regularly been approached by starry-eyed envoys from O'Neill and O'Donnell asking him to invade Ireland directly from Brittany. The two chieftains, aware of his military reputation, had written to him personally requesting his help.

Like many Spanish officers, Águila was deeply sceptical about assurances of popular support in Ireland. The Irish constantly professed kinship with the Spanish through ancient blood and brotherhood through religion, yet many of their chieftains – O'Neill among them – had attacked the survivors of the Great Armada as they had staggered ashore half-drowned from the wreckage. Could the Spanish trust a people like that?

Besides, the idea that the entire island of Ireland was united in rebellion was nonsense, despite what that zealot Brother Mateo might proclaim. If there was such a thing as an Irish nation seeking liberation, it had yet to emerge. Instead, there were dozens of separate clans, some pro-English, some anti-, but most of them hopping back and forward across the fence with dizzying speed. These clans spent as much time fighting each other as they spent fighting the English.

Twenty years ago, the invaders of Smerwick had been given cast-iron assurances that 'one fourth of Ireland had declared in their favour' and that 'the whole island would be with them'. That was all pie in the sky.

True, O'Neill and O'Donnell had gone further than anyone else with their 'confederacy' of insurgents, and they had chalked up some notable military successes. But they did not have the support of the major cities and towns, and large swathes of the country were hostile towards them. They said they were fighting a Catholic crusade, but most of the Catholic clergy in Ireland had declared against them.

No, Águila concluded silently, there had to be another reason why he was being sent to Ireland. It had nothing to do with invading England, at least not directly. Even helping the northern rebels was secondary to the main aim.

If invading England had been a real possibility, there would be no shortage of volunteers to lead the troops to glory. But Águila happened to know that the obvious candidate, General Antonio de Zuniga, had turned the job down. Zuniga had estimated that it would take a minimum of 8,000 troops and 1,000 cavalry just to survive in Ireland. Not possible? Then, no thanks.

Don Antonio was no fool, either. Why was he, Águila, being selected? After all, he was being pilloried for his actions in Brittany, where he had established a crucial bridgehead near Lorient, fortified it strongly, and held out for years against combined French and English forces. He had never surrendered.

A career soldier with nearly four decades of experience, Águila had fought the campaign as he saw fit, not always in accordance with the complex politics of the French wars of religion in which his country had become embroiled. His critics felt he should have been more proactive, hazarding his hard-won fortress with vainglorious attacks on other cities.

Was this a plan where Águila's supposed deficits had suddenly become regarded as virtues? Did they *want* someone who could stoically dig in and hold a position, doggedly, against all odds; who was ready to die rather than surrender? Yes, that must be it. He wasn't being sent to lead a triumphant wave of troops across Ireland. He was being sent on a near-suicide mission with a skeleton force to establish a foothold and then, like some beaten-down old streetfighter, to curl himself into a ball and take the kicks and blows for as long as it took, without giving in. Until … until what?

The answer was obvious. Until *La Inglesa* died.

The people best informed about European politics were the Venetians. Masters of intelligence-gathering, they maintained a network of well-paid informants in every royal court. One of their ambassadors, Marin Cavalli, was quick to identify the real reason for the Spanish invasion plan. Joining with the Irish rebels was a lesser aim. It was a diversion to draw English troops away from Spain's long-drawn-out conflict in the Low Countries, where Queen Elizabeth was supporting a Protestant rebellion against Spanish rule. But it was also an attempt to establish a Spanish foothold in Ireland.

'There are even greater objects,' Cavalli wrote perceptively, 'for the Queen is 68 years old, and in the natural course of events she cannot continue much longer ... and in the case of her death, this foothold in Ireland would allow the [Spanish] King either to acquire the country or to assist the Catholics, and by supporting his own nominee among the pretenders to the Crown, he can render England dependent on himself.'

In other words, the astute Venetians believed that Águila was being sent to hold the fort – literally – in expectation of the Queen's imminent death, at which stage the Spanish King, Felipe III, would announce a successor to Elizabeth and already be in a position to act to support the claim with arms.

The Spanish Council of State had already recommended a suitable candidate: the Infanta Isabella, the devoutly Catholic daughter of the late King Felipe II, and the reigning King's half-sister. Distantly descended from English royalty, she had a plausible claim to the throne. Spain was determined to block Isabella's strongest rival, the Protestant King James VI of Scotland. Although rumoured to be sympathetic to the Catholic cause for which his mother, Mary Queen of Scots, had been executed, James was mistrusted by the Spanish and regarded as 'false and shifty'.

The Venetians were in no doubt: the plan to invade Ireland was Mission Impossible. As their Ambassador to Spain, Francesco Soranzo, wrote home: 'There is little certainty of success; every certainty of failure and the destruction of these poor fellows.' They were not unique in their scepticism. A contemporary Spanish diarist named Luis Cabrera de Córdoba wrote that, while the aim of the armada was to help the Irish insurgents in their battle against the English, 'there are those who say that the effect will be very different.'

Águila could have turned down the assignment, as Zuniga had, but that wasn't his style. In his thirty-eight years as a soldier, he had never backed down from a challenge. There were other reasons why he should accept Mission Impossible. At fifty-six, he was nearing the end of his long and venerable military career. However, his reputation had been sullied by the accusations made against him. If he could pull off this mission, he could retire with honour. It was his all-or-nothing, his last throw of the dice.

Why had he been put into this position? If there was any justice, Águila would have been welcomed back from Brittany as a hero – not punished like a criminal. What he had achieved there in eight years had been remarkable. The Spanish had intervened in a convoluted French religious war, ostensibly to help the local Catholics but really to establish a string of forts along the Brittany coastline from which to attack southern England.

Águila had set up two superbly constructed fortresses, one near Lorient and the other near Brest. He had defended the first one right until the bitter end, leaving only when the political situation had shifted and he was ordered out. The other port had fallen, with horrific loss of life. However, Águila's signal achievement while in Brittany was to mastermind a military invasion of southern England, sacking and burning several towns in Cornwall before pulling out. It was one of Spain's most successful raids on England – in fact, it was to be the last Spanish invasion of England – and by right, that act alone should have earned Águila an equestrian statue in his home town of El Barraco.

El Barraco … Águila longed to retire in the little hilltop township where he had spent his childhood. He had a dream of leaving a bequest to future generations – giving hope to other children who played in those same rugged hills and valleys that he had roamed as a child.

Situated 100km from Madrid, and a thousand metres high in the Sierra de la Paramera, El Barraco lies amid a magnificent wildscape of moorland,

45

pine woods and ancient reservoirs. On the horizon are the Sierra de Gredos mountains, where the rare Spanish Imperial eagle can still be seen hovering and diving over the peaks. Águila, his family name, is also the Spanish word for 'eagle' and that seemed to be reflected in Juan's soaring, independent mindset and indomitable personality. An early portrait shows a young man whose intelligent and alert brown eyes lock the viewer's in a good-humoured yet assertive challenge. His forehead is high, his hair neatly cropped, and his chin juts out challengingly under a short, pointed brown beard.

Juan del Águila had been born into a noble family with a strong military, political and religious tradition. Its menfolk either went to war or ruled cities. Its womenfolk patronised, founded or ran convents.

The family's most famous patriarch, Nuno Gonzalez del Águila, was a colourful individual. As Lord of the castle of Villaviciosa, twenty miles from Avila, he had not only presided over a substantial estate but also held the religious role of canon and archdeacon of the cathedral. In addition, he had his hands full with his family and with a mistress, Doña Elvira Gonzales de Medina, who bore him four other children. Just before Nuno died, he sold a large chunk of his property to pass on to Elvira – a move that outraged his 'formal' family.

Even more frustratingly for them, Elvira decided to give the money to God. She established a small Carmelite convent, which developed into the Monastery of the Incarnation in Avila. Among its 140 nuns was a young sister named Teresa who, between 1535 and 1574, experienced the ecstatic visions that later elevated her to sainthood. Interestingly, the prioress who admitted her to the order was Doña Francesca del Águila, another member of the ubiquitous family.

Nuno – who was Juan del Águila's great-grandfather – had built himself a romantic turreted castle in Villaviciosa. It remains standing today, bearing the family coat of arms showing a lion rampant over an eagle.

Young Juan joined the army at age eighteen. Even though he was a noble-man, he began as a basic infantryman and was willing to work his way up through the ranks. As we'll see, that was part of the spirit of the elite Spanish regiments to which he would devote his life. During a career spanning nearly four decades, Águila saw action in almost every conceivable scenario – fighting Ottoman pirates in the Mediterranean, quashing a rebellion in Corsica, guarding the mighty galleons from the Americas, escaping across frozen polder dams in the Low Countries, and scrimmaging street by street through the embattled cities of northern Europe.

His abilities were soon noticed. '[In the Netherlands] Juan del Águila and [another commander] did signalise themselves,' wrote one contemporary. At the Siege of Antwerp, Águila arrived with his troops at a critical moment, hurled himself into the fight, and carried the day. The commanding general instantly made him a Maestro de Campo – a regimental colonel – in gratitude. He was still in his late thirties.

Águila was a harsh disciplinarian. He had to be, to survive. This was a bleak era in which a commander had to maintain order among hungry, ill-equipped men who went for months without pay. Mutinies were commonplace. Victorious troops could decide to pay themselves by looting conquered cities – once, in Antwerp, seven thousand people died in a three-day orgy of violence known as 'the Spanish fury'. Each commander walked a thin line between imposing tyranny and unleashing anarchy.

One story speaks volumes about the man's personality. After a Spanish lieutenant surrendered a key post, the enemy – hoping for a ransom – asked Águila what they should do with the prisoner.

—Do what you like with him, Águila replied crustily. But if I had him here I'd know what to do with him: hang him.

However, he said he was willing to pay a ransom for another officer who was captured while fighting.

His own courage was never questioned. After suffering serious wounds in Flanders, he was presented to King Felipe II with the words: 'Your Majesty, meet the man who was born without fear.'

Águila was lined up to lead one of the follow-up regiments for the Great

Armada's invasion of England in 1588. However, since the fleet never made landfall, he was never needed. In 1597, he was chosen as land commander for a subsequent armada, which was beaten back by bad weather.

By this stage, Águila had become a legendary figure. Spanish War Secretary Esteban de Ibarra was later to write: 'When I remember who Don Juan del Águila is, my heart is lightened and I begin to hope for great things.' Felipe II's successor, the young Felipe III, once said that the 'high opinion' he had of Águila relieved any anxieties he had about the mission to Ireland. A contemporary Spanish writer said he was one of the greatest luminaries that war had produced.

Internationally, his standing also remained high. The Venetians referred respectfully – and uncritically – to his long service in Flanders. A prominent Irish clan chieftain called him 'a wise man and a skilful commander'. But the greatest tribute to Águila was the praise of his enemies. The English commander Charles Blount described him as 'one of the greatest soldiers the King of Spain hath'. General George Carew said he was a man of quality and honour, and praised his coolness under pressure: 'He is a cold commander. I wish he were more hare-brained.'

So, with such a distinguished career behind him, why was Águila jailed at all? One source says he was imprisoned 'to answer some actions of his in Brittany'. Yet the arrests happened in 1600, several years after the events in Brittany. And towards the end of his stint there, Águila had been entrusted with the command of twelve thousand men in the 1597 Armada – hardly a job to allocate to a man with a bad military reputation. Another source, the diarist Luis Córdoba, says he was 'put in the sheriff's prison … with his wife and an army accountant, for having unfairly taken advantage of the King's revenue'. In the moral maze of Spanish politics, where corruption was rife in the highest circles, this financial offence could have been as simple a matter as failing to give kickbacks to the right people. Whatever the reason, Águila now walked out of the jail to freedom.

At the time, Águila was regarded as the right choice to lead the new expedition. One early-seventeenth-century writer said that the Spanish sent troops to Ireland 'under General Juan del Águila, a man that conceived great hopes'.

As an eminent English historian later summed it all up: 'It was [Águila] who had established the Spanish footing in Brittany, which for years had been a thorn in the side both of England and France, nor was he ever dislodged by force of arms. So high was the reputation he had won that, though at the time he was in disgrace and under arrest, he had been called out of prison to take command of the new expedition. What he had done in Brittany he intended to do in [Ireland's] Munster.'

Águila reported for duty in Lisbon in July 1601. His journey there was probably a horrific experience in itself. Famine had ravaged the area, and bubonic plague had wiped out one in ten of the population. Lisbon was 'a wilderness', according to one authority, 'with most of the population having died or fled'.

On arrival, Águila was given his own personal priest to accompany him and to hear his confessions. But Father James Archer, a militant Jesuit from Kilkenny, was no ordinary pastor. Although he had been recommended to Águila as 'a very fervent and apostolic man', he was actually high on the English authorities' most wanted list after allegations that he had conspired to kill Queen Elizabeth and participated in the kidnap of a prominent Irish nobleman. Archer had regularly slipped in and out of Ireland in disguise. While there, he would live 'in the woods and hiding places' as he encouraged the insurgent fighters. In Spain he was a legendary figure. 'Of the priests, Archer was in the best reputation with the Spaniards,' one expatriate Irishman later testified.

When Águila went to the nearby port of Santa Maria del Belém to inspect his troops, he was aghast. Both the numbers and quality were even lower than he had expected. He needed more food, more ammunition, more money and more soldiers, he wrote to King Felipe III in mid-August. And it was too late in the season to mount such an expedition.

But Felipe was determined that the force should leave before autumn.

The King's motives were complex – he had promised his father on his deathbed that he would continue the wars of religion, and he was under constant pressure from his pious wife to intervene on behalf of the Irish Catholics. He was also 'headstrong' and determined to make a grand gesture to demonstrate his maturity as an international statesman. He was, after all, only twenty-three.

CHAPTER FOUR

'FOR GOD, ALL DIFFICULTIES MUST BE OVERCOME'

Valladolid, Capital of Spain, 1601

FELIPE III, King of Spain, King of Portugal, and emperor of the greatest dominion the world had ever known, gazed with satisfaction on his royal bride as she ate and drank at table.

Queen Margaret never reached for a cup herself, which was how it should be. Instead, if she wanted to drink, she would sign discreetly to the most senior of the three ladies-in-waiting who stood by her table, each with a napkin draped precisely over their shoulder. The first lady made a signal to the second lady. The second signed to the third. The third lady signed to the *mayordomo* or steward, who signed to a page, who in turn signalled the wish to a lowly servant. Together the page and servant left the room to fetch a capped goblet on a golden tray. The page gave it to the *mayordomo*, who inspected it before allowing the page to present it to the first lady. Kneeling before the Queen, the first lady would pour a little of the liquid into the cover of the goblet and taste it via a napkin – she must never touch it with her lips – before offering the goblet and tray to her royal mistress. After the Queen had supped, the goblet was removed by the same elaborate route.

Six people to enable one woman to sip a drink. Yes, this was how it should be. It was the way things worked in Felipe's Spain, a country where the lavish opulence and overstaffing at the royal court stood in stark contrast to the grinding poverty of many of Felipe's overtaxed subjects.

Felipe was just three years out of his teens. His Queen, the Austrian daughter of the Archduke Charles, was only sixteen. Yet together they ruled over a vast empire that stretched from Peru to the Philippines.

Almost three years before, while aged just twenty, Felipe had inherited the world's first global superpower. He owned Spain, Portugal, parts of Italy, parts of North Africa, a piece of Asia, and by proxy a chunk of Europe's Low Countries. A century beforehand, the world's biggest empire had belonged to the Incas in South America. Spanning five thousand kilometres and ruling twelve million people, it was bigger than China's or Turkey's. Spain had swallowed it whole and added it to its territories.

However, decay had set in and was spreading rapidly. Felipe was well aware that he had inherited a basket-case economy. There was no industry to speak of. Nobody had seriously tried to bring farming methods out of the dark ages. Harvests had failed and famine was becoming a permanent way of life. Corruption and jobbery were rampant. One in ten people claimed noble status and refused to pay taxes. So did the hundreds of thousands of clerics who held 20 percent of the land. Just five years earlier, Spain had declared itself bankrupt for the third time, but that hadn't stopped Felipe's father, Felipe II, from splashing out millions of ducats on his splendid new palace at El Escorial.

For ordinary Spanish citizens, it was difficult to believe that Spain was taking in a fortune in gold and silver from its American colonies. Ships would arrive in Seville, their timbers groaning under the weight of New World bullion: 35 million ducats' worth in one year alone; historians now estimate that in the course of three hundred years the Spanish treasure fleets brought home the equivalent of ten trillion US dollars today. But the money all went on lavish cathedrals and unwinnable wars. And the sheer size of the cargoes made them less valuable. Ridiculously, Spain had to degrade its own coins using cheap metal imported from elsewhere in Europe. As one writer lamented: 'Spain is poor because she is rich.'

The image of the monarchy had hit an embarrassing new low when royal officials were despatched to beg door-to-door, asking householders to donate small saleable items. And yet Spain still continued its triumphal procession across the world stage, acknowledged as the richest, most powerful and most expansive empire in history. Spain was still Spain – the big dog of the global backyard. It dominated the world culturally, linguistically, financially and (it liked to think) militarily. Broke it might have been, but, for the moment at least, the rich bankers of Genoa were still ready to back Spain with loans, even though they knew that most of the cash would go to gilded palaces and costly religious conflicts. They had invested too much already, and the empire was too big to fail.

The twenty-three-year-old to whom all this wealth and power had been bequeathed was an unimposing figure: contemporary portraits show him as a pale, rusty-haired youth whose arrogantly tilted head seems to compensate for an inner nervousness. His goatee beard hides a sharp chin, both nearly smothered by an enormous ruff. He is cultivating an extravagant military moustache.

Felipe came across as an eccentric figure: amiable enough, pious to the extreme, but incapable of making his own decisions. Old Felipe II had gone to such lengths to subdue and mould his son's personality that the boy had been left with little identity he could call his own.

When it had been time to choose a wife for his son, the elder Felipe presented him with portraits of three equally acceptable sisters and instructed him to select the one he found most attractive. Young Felipe, terrified of the responsibility, said he would leave the choice up to his father. No doubt heaving an exasperated sigh, Felipe II pointed out that choosing a lifetime bedmate was a highly personal matter.

—I *have* no choice, his son stammered. Whoever seems most beautiful to Your Majesty will look the most beautiful to me.

On his deathbed the elder Felipe had fretted that his son would be too easily influenced by others. 'Ah, I fear *they* will rule *him*,' he predicted.

The shrewd old King had anticipated this problem and had recruited a group of reliable advisors to guide him. But it was too late. Felipe junior was already putty in the hands of the ambitious and deeply corrupt Don Francisco de Sandoval, a member of one of Spain's most prominent families. Sandoval – better known as the Duke of Lerma – had groomed the youngster for years. As soon as the courtiers brought him his first papers to sign, the new King gave a bored wave of the hand that signified that they should all be passed over to Lerma.

The simple gesture heralded a seismic shift in Spanish politics. For the next two decades, Lerma would hold undisputed sway as the real monarch of Spain. Felipe didn't mind. '[He] has helped me sustain the weight of state affairs,' Felipe wrote to the once powerful Council of State. 'I order that you obey the Duke in all matters.'

The Council of State was no longer allowed to approach the King directly – everything had to be filtered through Lerma. Although he loved reading and approving the paperwork, Felipe was happy to let the Duke take the decisions. This allowed the new King to devote himself to his favourite pastime: spending money.

He was very, very good at it. Within a few months he had granted more knighthoods than Felipe II had dispensed in a decade. For his own wedding to Margaret, he had embarked upon an outrageously expensive grand tour throughout Europe. Freed from the boring business of actual kingly rule, Felipe's life was enjoyably devoted to hunting, travelling and holding lavish parties. Yet he was also extremely devout. He would spend hours in prayer and ritual, and agonised over the fate of his fellow Catholics in Northern Europe. Pious and yet hedonistic, Felipe was half priest, half party animal.

As his confidence increased, Felipe began to change personality. He assumed an air of brusque arrogance. Observers in England worried that he was becoming dangerously 'headstrong'. However, attitude meant nothing without action. Felipe feared that he was still regarded as a weak and ineffective king, a shadow of his powerful father. He needed a grand gesture, a major success to show the world that he should be taken seriously.

And as he scanned the international horizon for a suitable setting, his eye settled inexorably upon Ireland.

It was not a new idea. The concept of using Ireland as 'the King of Spain's bridge into England' had been around for a long time. A famous prophesy predicted that 'he that England will win, through Ireland must come in'. Even the Great Armada of 1588 had been originally due to attack Ireland, before the plans were changed.

The old King had been keen on the idea, in theory. Irish expatriates and clerical zealots like the Franciscan Mateo de Oviedo had convinced Felipe II that he had a realistic chance of ousting the English from their first colony. Oviedo, a fifty-four-year-old theologian from Segovia, was regarded as an expert on Ireland's confusing politics. He had made several trips there and had forged close contacts with the insurgent leaders. However, his enthusiasm for their cause often blinded him to the complex realities of a dirty war, and his impatient attitude – and his belief that God would solve all practical problems – often created serious friction between him and the military commanders.

The problem for the Irish was that they weren't the only faction lobbying for Spanish intervention. The Scots Catholics were pushing for an invasion of Scotland. And many English Catholics wanted to place Felipe II's daughter, the Infanta Isabella, on the throne when Elizabeth died.

By 1596 the Spanish navy had been rebuilt to its former glory. When the English Earl of Essex made a pre-emptive strike on the Spanish port of Cadiz, Felipe II responded by sending two more armadas north in 1596 and 1597. The first, bound for Ireland, was smashed apart by storms with the loss of three thousand men. The second, featuring Don Juan del Águila as land commander, was driven home by relentless headwinds.

A year later, the old king, Felipe II, was on his deathbed when he heard news which lent his pain-racked face a fleeting smile of satisfaction. Irish insurgent forces had defeated the English at the Yellow Ford in Armagh. The Irish – for so long dismissed as opportunistic woodland raiders – had shown that they could defeat their ancient enemy on equal terms. With Spanish help, anything was now possible.

By the turn of the century, Spain had assembled an awe-inspiring fleet of 35 galleons, 70 other ships and 25,000 men. A new king was on the throne, and the Spanish were back in the game.

Felipe III had sworn to honour his father's promises to help the Irish earls, and Hugh O'Neill had promised to yield up the crown of Ireland in exchange for his support. Encouraged by Oviedo, and eager to demonstrate his strength, the new king began to demand action. In the summer of 1600 he ordered the immediate assembly of a strong army and a substantial fleet to invade Ireland. His Council of State agreed, but asked where bankrupt Spain would find the money. Felipe, however, was determined to establish his reputation. 'This is the first great enterprise the King has undertaken since his coming to the Crown,' George Carew would remark later. 'He feels himself bound in honour to see the enterprise through.'

Felipe dismissed any objection. 'As the expedition is so entirely for the glory of God,' he wrote, 'all difficulties must be overcome … I will sacrifice what I need for my own person so that it may go this year.'

But the royal cutbacks never happened, the money never materialised and it was to be another thirteen months before Felipe's command was obeyed.

At the dining table, Queen Margaret returned her husband's gaze with genuine fondness. Despite their arranged marriage, the couple had developed a true affection for each other. Yet she was increasingly finding that a third person was coming between them.

The Duke of Lerma saw Margaret's ability to influence the King as a direct challenge to his own power. He had good reason to worry. Margaret was young, but she was astute and resolute. 'She is capable of great things,' reported the Venetians. 'She would govern in a different manner to the King if she could.'

Margaret represented the interests of the powerful Austrian branch of the Habsburg family (Felipe was also a Habsburg) and was backed by two redoubtable female relatives. One was Margaret's beloved aunt, the elderly Empress Maria, who was also the aunt (and grandmother) of Felipe III. The other was Maria's daughter, a cloistered nun called Margaret of the Cross. This formidable female troika worked ingeniously to undermine Lerma's control of the King. Margaret talked politics to him in the marital bedroom, and the other two pleaded their cases during Felipe's frequent religious visits to their convent in Madrid. In effect, the convent had become an alternative royal court.

While Lerma pushed the King in one direction, the three women deftly steered him in the other. One major difference in opinion was the plight of the Catholics in England, Ireland and the Netherlands. Lerma was a realist:

his instincts were to disengage. If Spain's interests lay in making peace, religion would take second place. The women, all zealots, saw their mission as a holy crusade. The devout Felipe was not hard to persuade.

Lerma hit back, and hit back hard. At one stage he took Queen Margaret aside.

—You are forbidden to talk to the King about matters of state, he instructed. Especially in the bedroom, when you are alone.

Margaret had bristled. She was a royal Habsburg, not used to being ordered around by a mere Sandoval.

—And if I disobey?

—You will find that urgent duties will take the King away from you for increasingly lengthy periods of time.

He sacked Margaret's Austrian servants and replaced them with his spies. Then he persuaded Felipe to move the royal court from Madrid to faraway Valladolid. The pretext was the unhealthy air – the real reason was the unhealthy political atmosphere in the convent.

This made the Queen even more determined. Pale and ascetic, Margaret would spend hours in prayer. One of her most fervent prayers was that the suffering Catholic subjects of the English Jezebel should be saved from persecution. She had to persuade Felipe to send them help. She owed it to them – and to God.

The Duke of Lerma stared thoughtfully at the report on his desk. It was just a despatch on the logistics of troop movements to the Netherlands, but to Lerma it was more than that. Much more.

It was August 1601 and everything had just changed. By sheer serendipity, a mere stroke of chance, the Spanish invasion of Ireland had become possible. It might be the way to keep the female troika happy and to satisfy his own aims at the same time. The cold war at court could finally be brought to an end.

Lerma stared at the despatch, but what he was really looking at was a redrawn map of Europe as it might appear a decade from now.

Spain was mired in a horrendously expensive religious conflict in the Low Countries – a war it could never win. All Lerma's instincts told him to get out. Spain had quite enough on its plate protecting its interests in the Atlantic, America and the Mediterranean. Peace with England would pave the way to peace in the Netherlands; it would also end the relentless privateering raids that were disrupting the Spanish bullion fleets.

Taking the long view, Lerma understood that the bad blood between Spain and England was a temporary phenomenon. For centuries, the two countries had been intuitive allies, regularly cementing their friendship with royal marriages. Just a generation earlier, Elizabeth's half-sister Mary Tudor, then Queen of England, had married Felipe II, father of Spain's current monarch. Spain's fingerprints were all over modern England. Felipe II, as consort King of England, had built up Henry VIII's decaying navy – which, ironically, had later gone on to defeat his own Great Armada. And how many people in Ireland realised that King's County – which the Irish called Offaly – had been named for the Spaniard Felipe II rather than after an English monarch?

Lerma had already put out some feelers towards peace, but the English terms had been too high. A Spanish presence in Ireland would mean that Lerma could negotiate from a position of greater strength. Crucially, it would also enable Spain to act swiftly to establish a Catholic successor when Elizabeth died. It would also divert English troops from the Netherlands, and the cost would force Elizabeth closer to bankruptcy. And finally it could all be depicted (as so many invasions are) as a humanitarian intervention to protect a persecuted underclass.

Lerma turned his attention back to his report. Yes, a new window of opportunity had opened. A shift in the ever-changing allegiances in mainland Europe had meant that a fleet of ships waiting in Lisbon to carry soldiers to the Netherlands were no longer needed. The vessels were now free for other use. At last the time was ripe. Through good fortune, the stars were now lined up: Lerma, the King, the Queen, the Irish earls, and churchmen like Oviedo would all get exactly what they wanted.

The new armada would soon sail out of Lisbon ... and into history.

CHAPTER FIVE

Sailing to God or the Devil

Lisbon, August 1601

One month before the invasion

A T AROUND the same time, fortune smiled on an English galley slave named John Edie. The Cornish seaman had been captured by the Spanish in 1601 and forced into service at the oars. Smarting under the overseer's whip, Edie had seemed destined to a short and brutish life on the hell ships. But fate had other ideas.

You are in luck, *Ingleze*, his Spanish overseers had told him as they struck off his chains. We are short of good seamen. You are going to the Azores.

At the Spanish-owned island of Terceira in the mid-Atlantic, Edie's new transport ship collected a thousand veteran soldiers. This was his first inkling that major troop movements were under way.

As they entered the busy seaport of Santa Maria del Belém, at the mouth of the River Tagus near Lisbon, John Edie's eyes must have widened as he realised the scale of the operation. Several gigantic galleons were being fitted out for war. Cannon were being hoisted aboard, barrels of powder carried along gangways, stocks of salt and ship's biscuit stowed in holds. This was no minor expedition. This was an invasion fleet.

At the epicentre of this frantic storm of preparation – the hammering and caulking and shouting – was the fleet's flagship, a mighty galleon of 900 tons named the *San Andres*. It was commanded by the fleet admiral Don Diego de Brochero, a veteran naval officer. Like Edie, he was a former galley slave – he was once captured by the Turks and had spent five years chained to the oars. The 960-ton *San Felipe* would carry the Vice-Admiral Pedro de Zubiaur. A floating leviathan, the 1,300-ton *San Pedro*, completed the trinity. Their Biblical names emphasised the religious nature of the expedition.

There were three other Spanish vessels displacing 500 tons. Backing them up was an assortment of smaller warships and commandeered merchant vessels. Of the thirty-three ships in the fleet, only twenty were state vessels. As was common practice, the armada consisted of a nucleus of naval fighters augmented by whatever commercial vessels were around at the time. One witness reported 'two ships of Drogheda, one from Wexford, one Limerick' as well as vessels from France, Scotland and the Low Countries.

A typical victim was the merchantman *St Michael,* which had carried a cargo of salted hides and timber from Galway to Lisbon. On arrival, Galway merchant Andrew Lynch was told abruptly that his cargo was being requisitioned 'for the King's use' and the vessel's owner, John Clark, was informed that he would be giving his ship over to the cause. The two men were put onto separate naval vessels, and the *St Michael* carried twenty-five Spanish soldiers and a woman passenger to Ireland as part of the invasion fleet.

On the quayside at Belém, 4,464 troops were being mustered into 45 companies and grouped into two *tercios* or regiments. The seamen – anywhere between 1,000 and 1,500 sailors from Spain's Basque region – were busy checking the rigging and stowing the ships' gear. The number of fighting men was far short of the 6,000 men (that is, two normal-sized *tercios*) that O'Neill had requested and Felipe III had intended to send. The numbers had been reduced by mass desertion, sickness and corruption.

Edie had no way of knowing it, but he was witnessing a sight that would never be repeated: a full-scale naval force setting out for Ireland, intent on toppling the Queen of England from her throne. The Great Armadas of the Elizabethan era would never sail again.

At daybreak on Monday, 24 August, the mighty fleet weighed anchor. It took more than three hours for the unwieldy galleons to be towed and warped out to the harbour mouth, until at last the armada began its epic journey at 10am. Once clear of the estuary, the armada would have assumed the classic crescent formation, with the fighting ships in the centre. Although much smaller than the 130-ship Great Armada of 1588, the fleet still presented a formidable sight as it pushed northwards through the Atlantic swell. Its sheer size made it easy to spot, and by early September the English knew that the invaders were on their way.

The captive seamen noted the contrast between the obvious poverty of the soldiers and the lavish lifestyles of the grandees. 'Some of them are richly apparelled and furnished,' recalled the Scots seaman Silvester Steene. 'Five hundred, at the least, have golden chains.'

Wild rumours circulated among the captives about a vast hoard of treasure on board. Silvester Steene estimated it at anywhere between half a million and eight million ducats. John Edie said that the *San Andres* alone held nine chests of treasure, each nearly three metres long. Although these accounts were exaggerated, there was no doubt that the expedition carried a substantial war chest. One source estimates it at around 165,000 escudos, perhaps over 600,000 euro today.

In contrast, the soldiers and seamen were already malnourished, ill-equipped and shivering with cold. John Edie reported that after only a few days the mariners and troops were put on half rations. He reckoned the expedition had only enough food to last a month. Judging by the amount of preserving salt in the cargo hold, they were obviously banking on receiving large quantities of fresh beef from the Irish as soon as they arrived.

For the first few days the fleet made good progress, passing the Groyne and safely negotiating Biscay's notoriously dangerous waters. But the atmosphere on board was not quite so smooth. Admiral Brochero grumbled about the quality of his crew, which included prisoners of war and press-ganged sailors. Many of them had already fled at Lisbon. (Conditions on Spanish ships were so bad that seamen regularly jumped ship, 'barefoot and unclothed, begging for alms, many dying on the road', according to one report.)

Those who remained were openly hostile and required armed guard. Brochero was apprehensive about the return trip, when he would not have the security of four thousand troops to keep discipline among the sailors.

Meanwhile, the clerics and some of the captains became locked in bitter disputes. The Galway merchant Andrew Lynch witnessed one of these angry altercations on board one royal warship, *El Crucifijo*. The overall commander, Juan del Águila, was present at the time. Some officers were furious that the army had been reduced from a promised 6,000 to a mere 4,500. One officer dramatically brandished a muster list.

'And what is that,' he demanded, 'to invade a strange country?'

Another officer tried to calm him down.

—Don't worry, he told him. Once we arrive, we will get 6,000 Tuscan and Italian reinforcements. They will arrive by December at the latest.

The row continued as Lynch moved out of earshot.

However, Lynch was not privy to the most heated argument of all – the dispute over the fleet's destination. Astonishingly, the mission had reached a point 150km from the Irish coast without anyone having a firm idea of where they were headed. Would it be Donegal, in the extreme north? Cork or Kinsale, in the extreme south? Galway in the west, or Drogheda in the east? No one had a clue.

Even today, it remains one of the most hotly contested controversies about the Kinsale invasion.

Where did the Spanish fleet intend to land? Did they choose Kinsale or did weather conditions force them there? And in going to the extreme south of Ireland, were they ignoring the recommendations of the Irish insurgent leaders? As the old cliché has it, was their intervention 'too little, too late and to the wrong place'?

It's worth digressing briefly to examine this thorny topic. In April the previous year, the Franciscan cleric Mateo de Oviedo had sailed secretly into Donegal Bay as an official envoy of Felipe III. Accompanying him was a Spanish captain named Martin de la Cerda. As a demonstration of their seriousness, they donated a thousand arquebuses to the Irish insurgents.

They found the two leaders of the Irish insurgency waiting for them at a nearby friary. Short and wiry, Hugh O'Neill (50) was the overall commander of the rebel confederacy. Although born in County Tyrone, he had been raised in English ways and had devoted much of his early life to quelling Irish rebels on behalf of the Queen before switching loyalties and leading the uprising in the north. He was a genius at rural guerrilla fighting, but had recently built up a modernised army which was capable of challenging the English in conventional warfare. He was astute, patient and utterly ruthless.

His son-in-law Hugh O'Donnell (28) was the polar opposite. He had 'drooping branched locks' of fiery red hair and a temperament to match.

Impetuous and emotional, he had harboured a burning hatred for the English ever since they abducted him and threw him into a dungeon in Dublin Castle at age seventeen. (He escaped, but lost both big toes from frostbite during his trek to freedom across the snowbound hills.) Unlike O'Neill, who could work with anyone if it suited his interests, Red Hugh had only one ambition. And a Spanish conquest of Ireland was exactly what Oviedo and Cerda were here to discuss.

When the envoys asked where the invaders should land, O'Neill was forensically precise.

—If the force is large, O'Neill said, and I mean 6,000 men or more, it should head for the province of Munster in the south.

He explained that the south offered easier terrain, better provisioning and higher-profile targets. And with 6,000 men, the Spanish could easily hold their own until he joined them. Within Munster, O'Neill believed Cork harbour was the best option. It lay between two friendly territories, one owned by a secretly sympathetic southern chieftain named Florence Mac-Carthy (in County Cork Florence is traditionally a man's name) and the other by the openly insurgent Earl of Desmond, James FitzThomas FitzGerald. Both had agreed to support the invaders.

If the Spanish sent fewer than 2,000 men, O'Neill believed they should go north to O'Donnell's heartland of Donegal, where such a meagre force could be protected by the Irish. A medium-sized force of 3,000 to 4,000 should head for Limerick, further south on the west coast.

Today, this 'numbers formula' is often regarded as a clear and conclusive instruction from O'Neill, but it wasn't nearly that simple. Later, in November 1600, O'Neill's agent Richard Owen told the Spanish that they should invade Carlingford, Galway or Sligo. The following year Oviedo – who was essentially O'Neill's voice at the court of Felipe III – produced an entirely new numerical formula involving Cork, Waterford and Limerick.

To confuse things further, there was another Irish summit in which five other chieftains joined O'Neill and O'Donnell. Held in an atmosphere of high religious solemnity, the conference was more like a church service than a military strategy meeting. A full Mass was celebrated by sixteen priests before a word was spoken. This conference agreed that Munster should be the target. They leaned towards Limerick as a preferred destination, but Florence MacCarthy insisted on Cork city. The ensuing arguments were hot and heavy, but eventully they concluded (regardless of numbers) 'to lead the Spanish army in the river of Cork'. Oviedo seconded the motion.

The situation was complicated by deep divisions among the expatriate Irish insurgents in Spain. 'There is a difference of opinion as to the destination of the expedition among the Irish themselves,' one Spanish report noted.

Some still argued that it should go to the north of Ireland 'where most of our friends are' but others argued for a shorter voyage to Cork or Waterford, and a third faction suggested Drogheda to the east. 'The forces are ready, and only await the final decision,' the report concluded pointedly.

The land and sea commanders were at odds. Admiral Diego de Brochero advised against the entire enterprise. Juan del Águila preferred either Donegal Bay or some east-coast port facing England. Brochero vetoed the east for naval reasons. The south was more convenient for his ships, but he could tolerate Donegal. However, Oviedo and Cerda flatly refused to go north to Donegal. They insisted that Cork had been the chieftains' clear choice.

(It's ironic that for many decades, historians wrongly blamed Águila for the decision to go south. 'His selection of a point of debarkation gave early indication of his want of judgement,' declared one influential writer in the 1800s. 'Instead of making for some port in the west or northwest of the island, where the heads of all the great native families were in arms … he landed at Kinsale.' In fact, the truth was exactly the opposite: it was Águila who wanted to go north, and the clerics and Irish expatriates who insisted on going south.)

With time trickling away, the Spanish sent another envoy, Pedro de Sandoval, back to Ireland in mid-July 1601. Red Hugh told Sandoval that the situation had dramatically changed and that the fleet should stay clear of Cork. 'The armada should make for Limerick estuary or Galway,' he said. However, if it were torn apart by storms, it should head north to any point between Limerick and Lough Foyle, in the extreme north.

Meanwhile, the Spanish authorities had been vacillating. First they decided that Brochero and Águila should choose the destination. Then, under pressure from Oviedo, they did a U-turn and said Oviedo and Cerda should decide. Águila objected strongly, but the order stood. By this stage, he and Oviedo had become irresistible forces on a furious collision course. The experienced commander – who had been placed in the ludicrous position of debating military tactics with a Franciscan friar – pointed out that Cork was a strongly defended base and could not be taken without much bloodshed. Oviedo believed the city was weakly defended. Águila argued that if it had to be the Cork region, Kinsale would be a better option. Oviedo accepted the possibility of Kinsale, but stuck with Cork as his first choice. This dual option was formalised in writing just before the fleet sailed.

The captive John Edie actually witnessed the order being issued. 'The admiral [Brochero] assembled the fleet after leaving port,' he recalled, 'and told them that they must go to Ireland … if any of them were separated, they should make for Kinsale.'

Another English witness, Anthony Wells, agreed. When the fleet left Lisbon, he said, 'it was directed by the Admiral to Kinsale'.

Unfortunately, the Spanish commanders were not aware that O'Donnell had changed his mind – the emissary Sandoval did not make it back to Spain until after the armada had departed.

It is frustrating to think that the ships must have passed at some stage – the invasion fleet heading north towards the Cork-Kinsale region, and Sandoval's vessel heading south with updated instructions to avoid the area.

It was the most important message of Águila's career – and he never received it.

As the armada approached Ireland, Admiral Brochero scanned the thunderous horizon and realised that a storm was brewing. Yet the question of a destination was still under debate. Brochero reckoned they had better nail it down once and for all, before the storm hit. His subsequent report, written in his own defence, was an exercise in self-justification: 'Thirty leagues off the Irish coast, I told Don Juan del Águila to identify his chosen port, because I was merely in charge of the fleet,' he wrote humbly.

A summit meeting was held on board the *San Andres*, with a queasy Oviedo rising from his sick-bed to participate. As the rolling waves heaved and the sheets groaned overhead, the shouted arguments were heard on deck.

'[They] did not know where to land,' recalled one eyewitness, an expatriate Irish insurgent named Dermot MacCarthy. 'Some advised Connaught or Ulster, but the priests ... urged a landing in Munster ... [they said] all Munster would be theirs ... they were sure that Florence MacCarthy with all his power and friends would join them.'

Águila believed this was all hearsay and that going south would be a big mistake. As for the northern option, Oviedo painted a grim and inaccurate picture of Donegal as a bleak arctic tundra. 'It is nonsensical to say the Spaniards should have gone to [the north],' he said later, 'where you couldn't find a house to store supplies or ammunition within sixty miles ... where it is so desolate that the troops would die from starvation and cold ... we would not have had a single man left alive.'

Eventually an unhappy consensus was reached, and, like most decisions by committee, it left nobody satisfied. 'With everyone in agreement, I issued written orders to each naval captain to follow me to Kinsale,' wrote Brochero. He named the port of Castlehaven, southeast of Skibbereen and some 70km west of Kinsale, as an emergency option.

The die had been cast. The navigators rolled out their charts and set course for the harbour that the Spanish knew as *Quinsale*.

And those who had lost the argument left the meeting with their faces as thunderous as those angry black clouds that were, even now, heavily bearing down upon their fragile armada.

The storm swiped them like a giant fist, scattering the individual ships across the ocean surface like dice hurled across a table.

Águila and Brochero, in the *San Andres*, managed to battle northeast towards the Cork-Kinsale region, accompanied by the bulk of the fleet and carrying some 1,700 men. Vice-Admiral Zubiaur became hopelessly lost with his galleon, the *San Felipe,* and three other ships. Unfortunately for the invaders, they were carrying nearly seven hundred of the best troops and most of the stores and munitions.

The English, who had been awaiting the fleet, were grimly satisfied as they watched the ferocious wind whipping the waves into spume off the southwest coast of Ireland. 'If they are at sea in such weather as this,' mused one official, 'I hope most of them are with God or the Devil by now. To which of those two places I care not, [so long as] they come not hither.'

CHAPTER SIX

THE INVASION

Kinsale, Tuesday, 22 September 1601

Invasion Day

KINSALE, on a grey, squally morning in late September. Dark rain-clouds rolled in from the Atlantic, and the tail-end of a devastating storm whipped the sea into an angry, rolling boil.

Inside the town, the atmosphere was as electric as the thunder in the turbulent skies. When dawn lit up the eastern sky, the apprehensive townsfolk, red-eyed from a sleepless night, could distinguish the dim outlines of the Spanish warships, anchored more than a mile out to sea. A flotilla of small craft was battling its way through the heaving waves to the shore. Eventually, the leading boat beached on the shingle and the first Spanish soldier set foot on Irish soil.

The invasion had begun.

More boats arrived, and the air was loud with shouted commands in Spanish and Italian as hundreds of soldiers fell into ranks and formed companies. The watery sun climbed higher to reveal a quayside transformed into a parade ground, alive with colour and exotic spectacle. Twenty-five brightly decorated regimental flags rolled and snapped in the brisk, skittish wind. Aristocratic officers, resplendent in colourful doublets and puffed-out hose, barked orders to the assembled ranks of 1,700 troops. Diagonal red crosses of Burgundy declared their allegiance to the King of Spain. Swords forged from Toledo steel flashed in the weak autumn sunlight. Pikemen moved into formation, their long, spear-like weapons bristling from the ranks. Musketeers and arquebusiers fell into rank, their guns at the ready.

Inside the walls of Kinsale, the townsfolk waited in anguished uncertainty. Would the invaders demolish their walls with artillery fire? Would they choose to lob missiles over the ramparts, raining down death and carnage from the air? Or would the Spanish simply wait patiently, until starvation and plague won the war for them?

No shots rang out in anger. The two squadrons of Spanish troops began to march ... but not towards the gates. Instead, they wheeled to the side and marched *around* the walls. Past each gate they walked in grim silence: the Cork Gate, the Friars' Gate, the Blind Gate, the World's End.

The Spanish were not mounting an attack. They were putting on a parade.

Eventually the soldiers came to a halt and a grizzled old warrior stepped forward. His voice, rich with the cultured accent of his native Castile, shattered the tense silence and echoed around the old walls. Speaking in English, he said he had come not to harm them, but 'to banish fear, and win their love'. He pledged that anyone who wanted to leave could do so with no danger to themselves or their property. Even the English troops could depart in safety. Equally, those who wished to stay could rest assured that they would not be harmed.

Then, referring to himself in the third person, he gave a solemn undertaking. 'Don Juan del Águila, general to the army of Philip, King of Spain ... do promise that all the inhabitants of the town of Kinsale shall receive no injury by any of our retinue, but rather shall be used as our brethren and friends.'

It was quite a remarkable offer. By the harsh standards of the era, it would have been no surprise if Águila had killed everyone in reprisal for the Smerwick massacre – or, indeed, for the English slaughter and the Irish robbery of the shipwrecked Spanish survivors from the Great Armada. However, it was also a shrewd and sensible offer. Águila had nothing to gain from alienating the Irish, whose support was vital. And if his approach succeeded, he stood to gain control of a key port without wasting a single shot.

Even so, the episode still reflects credit on Águila. As one nineteenth-century historian later observed: 'Non-combatants and private property were never so [humanely] treated in Ireland before. Don Juan was the first military commander who ever waged war in Ireland according to the rules of modern civilised warfare.'

Standing in the ranks of officers that day was Alférez Bustamante, an ensign who specialised in deep infiltration behind enemy lines. '[We] marched around the town of Kinsale,' he wrote in his journal. 'When they saw us with two regiments lined up outside, they capitulated without resistance.'

General George Carew's secretary, Thomas Stafford, who was present for most of the Kinsale siege, agreed with the Spaniard's account. 'Upon their approach, the townsmen, not being able to make resistance [even] if they had been willing, set open their gates and permitted them, without impeachment or contradiction, to enter the town,' he wrote.

However, another English account suggests that the townsfolk were initially defiant. 'The Spaniards, on asking admission to Kinsale town, asked for it as friends, saying they were come "for the supportation of the Roman Catholic religion",' this eyewitness report read. 'But the town rejected them and stood on their guard, on which they departed.'

Shortly after – according to the same report – Águila sent an ultimatum to the Sovereign, or mayor, of Kinsale. '[He warned that] if they gave up the town, they would be favourably dealt with, but that, if it had to be taken by force, they would all be put to the sword.'

In this version of events, Águila granted safe conduct to two town officials to inspect the troops aboard the warships. The invaders showed they had provisions for a lengthy siege. They claimed to be 11,000 strong, although the Kinsale men doubted this and estimated the true number of invaders at 6,000. (This figure seems to have stuck in the minds of the English, even though it was itself a grossly inflated estimate. In fact, only around 1,700 of the 4,464 soldiers who'd set sail from Lisbon arrived on that fateful St Matthew's Day. Later, as more latecomers limped ship by ship into the harbour, the number would swell to around 3,400.)

Whichever version of events was true, the end result was the same. At some stage on Tuesday, 22 September, the ancient gates of Kinsale swung open to admit the occupying forces of King Felipe of Spain.

Once the town had been secured and Spanish guards posted on the main gates, a bizarre mixture of soldiers, civilians and animals poured from the boats onto the beaches and quays of Kinsale. Along with the cows, goats and chickens that every seafaring expedition carried to supply fresh food, the Spanish ships contained a number of lowing bulls, whose job was to haul the heavy guns around the uneven terrain. 'They have twelve cannon, besides field pieces with oxen for their carriages,' reported the Scots mariner Silvester Steene.

The former galley slave John Edie gives us a rare hint at the colour and chaos of the landing as the civilians poured ashore. 'They have 200 or 300 women and children with them,' he wrote. 'Many priests and friars are on board, also three Bishops, and one [James] Archer, a priest ... They have also brought nuns.'

In a particularly nasty assessment written shortly after the invasion, a Dublin clergyman named John Rider wrote that there were '4,000 poor sea-beaten Spaniards, 50 friars, 12 nuns, 100 priests [and] 200 whores'. He said there was 'a chanterie of priests to pray for the dead and a most damnable pestiferous stews [ie, brothel] of nuns and whores, for both their recreations'.

Ignoring such slurs, it was true that the invasion was oddly family-friendly. The Spaniards' chief pilot – one Lambert Gould – had even brought his wife and children along for the trip. John Meade, the mayor of Cork, reported: 'They have many women and children.'

The decision to send so many mothers and youngsters to a battle zone seems insane – and it was. But it illustrated the Spaniards' lack of proper intelligence from Ireland. They genuinely believed that their troops would be so welcome that they could establish their own colony of settlers right away.

Shouldering their way through this mélange of families, clerics, nuns and farmyard animals, Águila and his senior officers marched through the main gate and into the narrow, twisting streets. History doesn't record whether there was a formal changeover between Águila and the English commander, William Saxey. (One source says Saxey's men left 'before the surprise'.) Either way, the English troops left peacefully, in accordance with their orders. Saxey's superiors had considered Kinsale 'not worth preserving'.

With the departing soldiers went a number of the wealthier townsfolk – the 'persons of better sort' – clutching their possessions. As always, the poorer citizens were left to take their chances. Their last sight of their betters was the tail-end of a convoy of creaking wagons disappearing up the steep hill towards Cork.

One man who stayed was the unnamed mayor or Sovereign of Kinsale, who went out of his way to ingratiate himself with the newcomers. Carrying his ceremonial rod, he ushered them into his town and allocated their sleeping quarters. His collaboration left the English outraged. 'The Sovereign of Kinsale, with his white rod in his hand, [went] to billet and cess them in several houses, more ready than if they had been the Queen's forces,' sniffed Thomas Stafford.

Águila and his entourage occupied the best quarters – the Desmond

Castle, a squat stone 'keep' built a hundred years earlier. Located just a short but exhausting walk up a steep hill from the quayside, it commanded a clear view of the harbour and could easily be transformed into a redoubt for a final stand if the outer walls were breached. These assets outweighed its disadvantages – it was stone-cold, it was damp from seeping hill-water, and the erratic layout of its rooms reflected its original site on a rocky outcrop.

A contemporary Irish chronicler named Philip O'Sullivan recorded that the inhabitants gave the invaders a rapturous welcome. 'The townsmen, expelling the English garrison, conducted the Spanish general and his army of 2,500 foot into the town with great enthusiasm and open arms,' he reported. An English official, Sir Charles Wilmot, reported bitterly that the Spanish 'bewitch them with promises of ancient liberty, freedom of conscience and religion, and sugar them all they can'.

The helpful mayor was allowed to remain nominally in charge. 'The Sovereign still exercises his place as he did before,' Wilmot reported, 'and the people here are pleased at this.' However, the real power rested with the invaders. 'On their arrival,' wrote the Irish annalist in the *Annals of the Four Masters*, 'they took to themselves the fortifications, shelter, defence and maintenance of the town from the inhabitants.'

The locals' enthusiasm began to wane when their homes were given over to the officers. '[The Spanish] quartered their gentlemen, captains and auxiliaries throughout the habitations of wood and stone which were in the town,' the annalist added.

Despite all its many disadvantages, Kinsale had one huge asset – it was a wine-importing town. The most experienced officers chose to move into houses with deep stone cellars. They wanted to be safe in readymade shelters when the cannonballs started flying.

With the town under control, Águila's first task was to secure the harbour entrance. He had realised immediately that the defence of Kinsale depended upon the twin fortresses – Rincorran and Castle Park – that commanded the approach from the open sea. '[Kinsale] overhangs a large and excellent harbour facing to the south,' the Irish writer Philip O'Sullivan explained. 'Also overhanging the harbour are two forts, one on either side, and if these were fortified with cannon, access to the harbour could not easily be gained.'

Rincorran, which commanded the entire haven and entrance, was particularly important. 'Truly,' wrote one English military expert, 'without this fortification there can be no surety made of the town and haven of Kinsale.'

Águila moved right away to station a company of veterans – 'some of their [most] distinguished men', according to another Irish chronicler – at this vital fortress.

Águila's next priority was to link up with the insurgent Irish in the region. He was highly sceptical about promises that local warlords would march to his banner with 20,000 cheering soldiers and 1,600 prancing stallions. But he was counting on Irish support in the form of manpower, fresh meat and (above all) horses for his cavalry officers. His hopes rested on the two southern insurgent leaders, Florence MacCarthy and James FitzThomas FitzGerald, the Earl of Desmond.

The Spanish commander summoned the Sovereign to his headquarters in the castle. As a go-between, he used one of the Irish expatriates who'd sailed with him from Spain. Many of these were members of the southern Irish MacCarthy clan. They included Dermot MacCarthy, known to the Spanish as Don Dermutio; and a seasoned veteran named Cormac (Don Carlos) MacCarthy, who had fought in France with Águila.

Still clutching his white rod, the mayor scurried obediently into the room where Águila stood, his eyes worriedly scanning the bay for the naval attack he knew would soon come.

The Irish expatriate stepped forward to interpret.

—It is vitally important that we make contact with Florence MacCarthy and James FitzThomas FitzGerald, he said to the mayor, using the Irish language. Where are they?

The Sovereign was surprised that the invaders were so far behind with the news.

—I thought you knew, he blurted out. They're both locked up in the Tower of London.

CHAPTER SEVEN

'I WILL NEVER SEE MY HOMELAND AGAIN'

September 1601

Somewhere on the Atlantic

MEANWHILE, Admiral Pedro de Zubiaur was still out there, battling through shrieking winds and mountainous seas.

Zubiaur's four ships had been scattered to the four winds – swept far out into the Atlantic by the same storm which blew the others towards the Cork coast. The armada's vice-admiral had made several attempts to join his comrades before giving up. Eventually he took advantage of a northbound wind and made a spirited attempt to reach the rebel chiefs in Donegal. He reached about halfway up the western coastline before the wind shifted in the opposite direction and undid all his efforts. Doggedly, Zubiaur tried a second time before an indomitable southbound gale picked up his small flotilla and hurled it right back towards Spain.

As he limped miserably into the northwestern port of El Ferrol, near La Coruña, he knew that he would have a lot of questions to answer. Why had he allowed himself to be separated from Brochero and Águila? What on earth was he doing, back home in Spain with his galleon, the *San Felipe*, and three smaller ships, carrying nearly seven hundred of the best troops and some of the most urgently needed supplies?

'When the King heard [of his return] he was much distasted with Zubiaur,' the seventeenth-century naval historian William Monson wrote, 'and commanded him upon his allegiance to hasten with all speed to Ireland as he was formerly directed.'

It wasn't quite that simple. Zubiaur's ships had been so badly battered that they would need lengthy repairs. The entire episode was a lesson in humility – an example of how the grandiose plans of kings can be shattered by the overwhelming forces of nature. Yet it's easy to overlook this when we debate the controversy over the destination port. Those who argue that the 1601 armada should have sailed to the north of Ireland instead of to the south are forgetting that the *San Felipe* actually tried to do this and failed. Judging by Zubiaur's bruising encounter with the Atlantic storms, the Spanish couldn't have gone to the north even if they'd wanted to.

When Águila heard that his most important southern allies had been imprisoned in the Tower of London, he could not hide his shock. A Venetian spy reported that 'he seemed *molto turbato* – greatly upset and disturbed'.

The Sovereign explained the background. General George Carew, the President of the province of Munster, had carried out a pre-emptive strike and incarcerated the two men. Carew had earlier planted a spy at the chieftains' meeting where the destination was agreed. He had received a full, almost verbatim, account of the discussions. This intelligence was confirmed when he intercepted a letter from the Irish expatriate leader Dermot MacCarthy in

Spain, warning that the Spaniards intended to 'surprise' Cork.

Carew immediately (and illegally) seized the chieftain Florence MacCarthy, despite having promised him protection. In May, the fugitive Earl James FitzThomas FitzGerald was found hiding in a cave 'many fathoms underground'. Both men were safely quarantined in London. Their war was over.

Now, in Kinsale, the news threw Águila's plans into disarray. 'The man was much deceived,' wrote one English historian, 'for Sir George Carew ... had prevented all his designs.'

Dermot MacCarthy agreed: 'Since James FitzThomas and Florence MacCarthy had been apprehended, his hopes of assistance failed him,' he said. 'He thought his state desperate unless he were relieved.'

The well-informed Venetians, who seem to have had spies in Águila's ranks, also reckoned he was in big trouble: '[Águila] finds himself quite shut-in and deprived of all the assistance on which he reckoned – and is therefore in serious difficulty.'

All of Águila's worst fears had come true. He had been promised an enthusiastic reception from the Irish – with all the food, soldiers and horses that he needed. Instead, he was on his own. And to make things worse, his soldiers were already falling ill. 'Many of their soldiers were weak at their first landing,' said one English report, 'and many are still sick ... their provisions are scant.'

The English commander, Charles Blount, was grimly satisfied. The Spaniards were 'in their means scant and miserable; in their persons weak and sickly; and in their hopes dismayed and amazed', he wrote.

Alone in his quarters, Águila wrote a furious despatch to the King.

—I have been deceived by those who persuaded me to undertake this expedition. The facts are very different to the reports, he wrote angrily.

He urged that, in addition to sending reinforcements, the monarch should punish those in Spain who had promised a general rising in Ireland.

—Not a man has come to my support, he pointed out.

Águila's letter ended on a bleak note that reflected his sense of isolation and betrayal.

—I will never see my homeland again, he wrote. Although this does not grieve me on my own account … but for the sake of all the young men who are with me.

When Águila talked of being deceived by reports, he had one man to the forefront of his mind – Mateo de Oviedo. It was the Franciscan cleric who had persuaded Felipe to launch the invasion, who had told him exactly where to go, and who had reassured him his troops would receive such a warm welcome that they needn't even bring horses or fresh meat.

The fifty-four-year-old cleric seemed convinced that the religious nature of the invasion would overcome all its practical problems. The armada had embarked on 'a great service to God' and 'a holy enterprise'. An intense and emotional preacher, Oviedo would declaim that *La Inglesa*, the hated Englishwoman Elizabeth, was the enemy of the Faith. She was imposing 'a tyranny' on her 'miserable slaves'.

He had a uniquely bombastic style. 'O, immortal God!' he would thunder at the English in a typical outburst. 'Who is there that is not astounded at your bitter and indescribable cruelty? … Look upon your work and be ashamed.'

He could not understand why Spain was standing idly by while the Irish Catholics suffered. He demanded money and guns for the insurgents. For one gunrunning trip to Donegal, he demanded five chains of gold – one for each of the insurgent leaders. 'Money [lies at] the heart of all actions, especially war,' he once reminded Felipe III.

On the face of it, Oviedo seemed an unlikely candidate for Spain's Irish version of Lawrence of Arabia. Born in Segovia in 1547, he briefly studied law before joining the Franciscans. By his mid-twenties he was teaching theology in a convent. As he developed closer contacts with Spain's sizeable Irish community, his interest in the Irish Catholics developed into a burning passion. He vigorously advocated on their behalf to the Vatican and to the royal court, pushing for the despatch of armed forces to Ireland.

While in his early thirties, Oviedo was recruited to what might be described as His Holiness's Secret Service: he became an international agent for the Counter-Reformation movement. In 1579 and again in 1580 he sailed to Ireland on ill-fated 'Bay of Pigs' style invasions, tacitly supported by Spain but deniable. Both were ill-judged and both were disasters. The second, at Smerwick, had ended in a cold-blooded English massacre of the invading troops.

It was on this expedition that Oviedo had developed his distinctive approach, a challengingly combative style which did not endear him to the military men. When a commander made a decision, Oviedo would demand an alternative approach that was sometimes the exact opposite. Using his formidable powers of persuasion, he would stir dissent among the officers, undermining the commander's authority. It was a fatal pattern that was destined to repeat itself in Kinsale.

However, Oviedo was also a man of immense courage. He was well aware of the grisly torture and execution that would await any foreign priest who was caught assisting the insurgents in Ireland.

When full-scale rebellion erupted in Ireland in the 1590s, Oviedo made more trips to the war-torn north to offer Spanish aid to the insurgent leaders. However, he became more ambitious. He wanted a title. He had been appointed as head of a convent in Zamora, but introducing himself as the custodian of a Spanish sisterhood didn't really cut it in the war zones. 'I don't have much clout with them with only the title of friar,' he wrote to the King in 1599.

He asked to be made Spanish ambassador. Unsuccessful, Oviedo tried the

Church route instead. He wanted to be Papal Nuncio, but the Pope gave that job to an Italian. The post of Archbishop of Dublin lay vacant – it was just an empty title under Protestant rule, but if the Spanish won, it would become a position of real authority.

His Irish contacts lobbied ceaselessly on his behalf until finally, in early 1600, the Vatican gave him the position. There was only one problem – until he actually took possession of Christ Church Cathedral in Dublin, Oviedo would remain merely an 'Archbishop Elect'. In the ensuing years, he was stung by English descriptions of him as 'the Spaniard who called himself Archbishop of Dublin' but, technically, they were correct. The prize was almost in his grasp, but just out of reach, and this frustration may partly explain his impatience for a complete Spanish takeover of Ireland – not just the possession of a bridgehead in the south.

Emboldened by a new sense of power, Oviedo became arrogant and almost insulting in his dealings with the Spanish authorities. He griped that he wasn't given enough money to act as the envoy of a rich and important monarch. Addressing the Duke of Lerma, he complained that the Spanish had promised the Irish a fleet of ships but 'did not send so much as a miserable sailboat'. The delay was making Spain look ridiculous, he said. They were 'the laughing stock of our enemies'.

His sheer confidence convinced the authorities that he was an expert on the subject. So when this curious warship-and-worship expedition landed in Kinsale, it essentially had two land commanders – Juan del Águila representing the King, and Mateo de Oviedo representing God.

You might think that was a recipe for trouble. And you would be absolutely right.

CHAPTER EIGHT

Trust in God and Keep Your Powder Wet

Kinsale, late September, 1601
A few days after the invasion

S O this is Quinsale.

Juan del Águila paced around the steep, meandering streets of the ancient town, critically surveying its defences. He concluded that the walls, less than a metre wide, were not fit to withstand a concentrated attack from enemy artillery. The town itself was situated in a hollow beneath a hill. Águila dismissed it as 'a hole'. He was speaking geologically, but the Spanish term reflected his deep disquiet. He decided he would be safer fighting in the open, free from falling masonry and flying stone fragments. 'Kinsale is in a side of a river, environed with hills, and without any kind of defence,' he reported back to Spain. '[It is] open in so many parts, and so weak, that it is needful to have half the troops on guard at least.'

This meant that any attempt to launch an offensive against a besieging enemy must leave some part of the town walls unguarded.

The Irish writer Philip O'Sullivan agreed that the surrounding hills – and one hill in particular – posed a defensive problem. Whoever placed artillery there 'might easily either assail or defend the town', he pointed out.

An English military expert pointed out that Kinsale's harsh terrain made it difficult for the invaders to dig in. 'It is an old walled town, and standeth upon rocky ground, so that they cannot entrench or make any defence for themselves out of the earth,' he said.

Águila was also concerned about the shortage of fresh water and firewood for cooking. Although Kinsale was 'almost an island' he believed it wasn't self-sufficient in water, and he didn't have enough small craft to cross the estuary to fetch more.

For all these reasons, the Spanish commander was keen to quit *Quinsale* as soon as his fleet was reunited and reinforcements arrived. According to Philip O'Sullivan, Águila thought he 'would not be long here'. It was this sense of impermanence that caused Águila to make a series of crucial decisions which – with the benefit of hindsight – turned out to be terrible mistakes.

Admiral Diego de Brochero was even more keen to move on. And at least he had the perfect excuse. He reminded Águila that he had official orders to sail home after disembarkation. His own food supplies were running low, he complained, and the storms could mean a long journey back. Besides, his seamen were so fractious that he had to remain anchored more than a mile out from land. Águila pointed out that it would be extremely difficult for him to fight off an assault from landward without warships to guard his back against a naval attack. Brochero played his trump card – or, more correctly, a royal flush. He said disingenuously that he'd be prepared to stay if Águila compelled him – in other words, if Águila countermanded the King's clear order.

By this stage, the two commanders were barely speaking to each other. Brochero had been so slapdash in his haste to leave that he'd allowed his men to dump the vital food supplies onto a shore of wet sand, where they had quickly soaked up seawater. Most of the ship's biscuit remained on board ship. The admiral explained that he had no time to unload it.

—You will get them on my return, presently, he told Águila.

The army commander tried another approach.

—Conditions here are bad, he implored Brochero. At least assist me before you leave.

Águila explained he needed timber from the wooded area across the river, not just for firewood but to construct the vital willow-branch baskets that could make fortification barriers.

—If you provide the boats, three or four trips should be enough, Águila explained.

The admiral rejected that request as well.

However, the final insult came when Águila stalked down to the shore to find his Steward of Artillery engaged in fierce argument with Brochero's sailors.

—I can't be held accountable for this, the steward was shouting.

Águila followed his pointing finger. The precious gunpowder, wadding and matches for his field guns had been carelessly dumped at the very edge of the shoreline, where the tide lapped across the sodden sand. 'With great haste [Brochero's seamen] caused the munitions to be landed, which they left upon the shore without account or reason,' Águila later complained to Spain. 'Such was the haste, that on the dirt and ooze of the shore they were ill handled, and wet.' Clearly, Brochero's contribution to the campaign was almost at saboteur level.

Even before this incident, Águila had already faced a difficult decision about the guns themselves. The ships that had survived the stormy voyage to Kinsale contained some twenty pieces of artillery. Without drayhorses, the cannon would be extremely difficult to move around. They would commit him to staying in Kinsale even if the town proved indefensible. Even worse, they could end up in enemy hands.

The discovery of the ooze-soaked munitions settled the matter. Without enough gunpowder, the twenty guns would become a liability. He would take only a few guns – just enough for his meagre supply of powder. The remainder could be brought back in the next wave of the invasion.

By this stage Brochero had already unloaded four medium-sized guns. There were two field pieces – wheeled guns which could easily be moved around on a battlefield – and two *mediocanon*. These demi-cannon were smaller and more portable than regular cannon. Three-and-a-half metres in length and weighing 1,800kg, they featured longer barrels which could accurately propel a 15kg ball through a bore as wide as a man's splayed hand. Águila decided to make do with those four, 'leaving the rest of the artillery unlanded, not having munitions sufficient for so much artillery, for that the powder and match which remains is little, and the greater quantity came wet,' he explained.

He did not want to be 'encumbered with so much artillery without horses to draw it'. He trusted that 'in the next succours [reinforcements] may be sent munitions enough'.

His trust was misplaced. For the entire duration of the campaign, further succour would never arrive in Kinsale. He was on his own.

What happened after he announced his decision on the guns was quite bizarre. Águila was angrily challenged by his own Father Confessor, James Archer. Like Oviedo, Fr Archer considered himself an expert in military matters. He argued vehemently with Águila that all twenty guns should be taken ashore. The commander was in no mood to listen. To the astonishment of the watching soldiers and townspeople, the emotional and mercurial Fr Archer suddenly dropped to kneel before the army commander, his long black coat staining in the mud.

'On my knees,' the priest pleaded, 'on my knees I beg you to keep the twenty guns.'

Águila was not impressed. His attitude was that the clerics should do their job and leave him to do his.

—Your place is to pray, teach doctrine and hear confessions, he snapped with open disdain.

It was a snub that Fr Archer would never forgive. Águila had made a bitter and implacable enemy.

Brochero sailed off eight days after the landing, with around a thousand seamen and the remaining fourteen guns still intact in his hold. Only few of the merchant ships remained in the harbour.

Now, would Águila have made the same decision if he had known that he was about to spend three months in his beleaguered 'hole', deprived of help and pinned down by a relentless bombardment from the expert gunners of the English army? Probably not.

Still, the news wasn't all bad. From out at sea, several ships were looming out from the mists. The cheers from the troops guided the armada's scattered latecomers into Kinsale harbour.

Their arrival doubled Águila's force to around 3,400 (although some English sources estimated it at between 4,000 and 4,300) and brought him a few more guns. Two-thirds of his troops were Spanish regulars – the Venetian observers described these as 'a picked body of infantry' – and they were accompanied by some 1,000 Italian soldiers and around 200 Irish expatriates. Many were toughened veterans whose fighting ability was well respected by the English. As Charles Blount wrote: 'The captains ... are most ancient men, their bands – some from Italy, some from the Terceras ... specially well armed.'

Strangely enough, there were also a dozen or so English dissident fighters. 'The rest,' said John Meade scathingly, 'are poor slaves not worth the reckoning.'

Don Juan del Águila would not have disagreed with that assessment. When he carried out his first careful muster of his troops, he realised that a significant number were young and inexperienced. Another commander furiously described the original force as 'four thousand men, half of them boys'.

Others were '*besognies*' – rookies whose firearms training had to begin here, on the front line. 'Not knowing the use of their piece [firearms], nor how to discharge them, they are drawn out to exercise their arms daily,' Águila reported to Spain.

Two of his most experienced field marshals were missing – one had been too sick to leave Spain, and the other was with Zubiaur. There was a dire shortage of skilled workers like carpenters and smiths.

Sickness was an increasing problem. Soon, one man in every thirty-four would be an invalid, adding to the commander's problems. Oviedo was put in charge of a field hospital where – presumably aided by the nuns – he set to work tending the sick and injured. There were no medics. 'Send two doctors,' Águila implored, 'because there is none in the regiment of Spaniards.'

Águila's second major mistake was to underestimate the importance of a quirk in the Cork coastline. In a twisting, convoluted shoreline that can often frustrate the best of mariners, the Oysterhaven posed a special hazard to the invaders.

We've already seen how Kinsale sits to the north of the River Bandon which flows south-eastward in a routine, conventional manner until it almost reaches the sea. But just before the Bandon hits saltwater and loses its identity forever, it does a last hurrah, a sort of celebratory somersault, going up and around and down again in a shape rather like a horseshoe. Kinsale sits on the left bank, at the top of the upward curve. Opposite the town, on the south side of the river, embraced by the horseshoe, is the north-pointing promontory that contains Castle Park fortress. The river's final stretch (the downward bit of the horseshoe) forms the harbour entrance. Halfway down it, to the right, is Rincorran fort.

Águila had a good eye for terrain. He recognised the importance of fortifying the two forts that guarded the entrance. From his vantage point on the Desmond Castle his keen eye also noted the 60-metre high crest of Knockrobin, part of a ridge of hills to the north and west. He identified a second hill – Ardmartin – as another useful height.

Águila saw all this. What he failed to pay proper attention to was the Oysterhaven. This skinny saltwater estuary begins about a kilometre east of Kinsale harbour, and penetrates diagonally inland towards the northwest. From a military viewpoint it is crucial because the estuary sneaks up behind Kinsale on the landward side, to a point called Brownsmills where it directly faces the town's north gate. Here, the walls are almost within artillery range. So the English navy didn't need to assault the harbour entrance – they just needed to sail up the Oysterhaven to this perfect attack point.

This long, narrow, silvery estuary was a stiletto aimed at Águila's back. He just didn't realise it yet.

When the Spanish troops combed the nearby countryside for supplies, they reported back with more bad news. Carew's troops had smashed all the mills and burned any farmhouses. There were a few cattle, but the locals were in no mood to contribute to the cause – they wanted paid, and they wanted top dollar. '[The Spanish] had some beeves and muttons out of the country nearest the town,' one English report read, 'but paid treble the prices accustomed.' The clergyman John Rider wrote: 'A hen is worth five shillings, a little carrion cow six pounds, yet no man will scarce bring these to them.' He claimed some locals sold thirty cows to the Spanish, but stole them back the following night.

Disenchanted, Águila wrote: 'We receive neither flesh nor any other thing, except some few cows from the poor people, which they sell rather [than give] unto us. We pay them what they demand, yet within a few days there will be no flesh had.' He couldn't obtain local help for love nor money. 'I procure to draw from the country people, by love and rewards, all that I can,' he explained, 'yet withal this, find no assistance from them.'

Águila wrote home that he had found very little food in Kinsale itself. His men were particularly short of bread, wine, oil and vinegar. However, he had unloaded from the ships 4,800 bushels (around 130 tonnes) of wheat which he had safely stored in the town's granaries.

Bottom line?

—Those supplies that I have landed will last me, at most, fifty to sixty days, Águila wrote.

More than anything else, he needed horses. The local insurgent chiefs were supposed to provide him with mounts for his cavalry officers. 'The Irish priests promised them 1,000 Irish hobs to be delivered within ten days of their landing,' crowed John Rider, 'and so they brought 1,000 brave saddles.' Actually, the true figure was even higher – 1,600 saddles. A shadowy figure called Richard Owen – Hugh O'Neill's envoy to Spain – had convinced the Spaniards that no horses would be needed, only the riding gear.

Águila announced that he would pay six shillings a day – nine times a labourer's wage – to Irish soldiers with horses. Even this generous offer was largely ignored. 'It is a wonder unto us that … [the local Irish] fall not into flat defection,' wrote Blount's astonished secretary Fynes Moryson. According to John Rider, some Irish mercenaries signed up, took a month's pay in advance, and then scarpered.

Andrew Lynch, the Galway merchant, was in Oviedo's house when two minor Irish chieftains appeared offering seven hundred soldiers and a hundred cavalrymen to the Spanish ... at a high price. Oviedo cursed them.

—We are coming to defend you, he said. And you seek money before you'll do any service?

If one or two Irish horsemen did accept, Águila quickly realised that the word 'cavalry' meant a different thing to the Irish than it did to the Spanish. Irish warriors rode small, frisky horses which were ideal for hill trekking, but useless for withstanding a cavalry charge. Irish horsemen disdained the use of stirrups – those were for amateurs. It was indeed a great achievement to control a galloping horse while holding a spear aloft and allowing your feet to trail almost to ground level, but it left the Irish dismally vulnerable to the shocks and impacts of modern warfare. '[All] that they have are small horses,' Águila explained to his disbelieving masters in Spain, 'and their soldiers ... do only fight with half pikes and saddles without stirrups.'

The English were well aware of Águila's disadvantage and immediately exploited it. 'Two days after their arrival, the cavalry began to harass them,' spies reported. It set a pattern that would continue throughout the siege. A group of English horsemen would thunder out from cover and ride right up to the town walls, guns blazing in bravado. Without horses of their own, the defenders were powerless to fend off their tormentors. It was a source of intense frustration to the proud Spanish cavalry officers.

According to the Spaniard Alférez Bustamante, the English horsemen had the Spanish almost completely pinned down within the first nine days. 'The English cavalry had the run of the country, stealing cattle,' he wrote. 'It was impossible to leave the town or the forts without a large strike-force of troops.'

Later, Águila's critics were to claim that the commander had 'one whole month in which he was undisturbed by the enemy' but failed take advantage of this lull. In fact, the records show that the Spanish and English troops first clashed within twenty-four hours of the landing. When a Captain Francis Slingsby appeared with a company of infantry the day after the landing, 'a skirmish for a little space was entertained', says one English report. 'There were some hurt, but none slain.'

Águila soon had to face the harsh reality that his only friends were hundreds of kilometres away … across the stormy sea in Spain, or in the remote north of Ireland. They might as well have been on the far side of the moon.

He had already written to Spain seeking help. Now, as October ushered in chillier weather, he selected his speediest Irish messenger to convey an urgent plea to the insurgent leaders Hugh O'Neill and Hugh O'Donnell. Written by Oviedo, the Latin message said: 'We have arrived in Kinsale with the fleet and army of our King, Felipe. We look forward each hour to Your Excellencies' arrival. Come as quickly as you can, bringing with you a supply of horses, of which we are most in need … I will not say more. Farewell.' The first sentence was significant. This was no semi-official, deniable mission like Smerwick. This was an all-out hostile invasion by a foreign power.

Águila added his own understated, soldierly contribution, giving no hint of his desperate situation. 'We are here,' he said austerely, 'awaiting your most illustrious lordships.'

His wait would be a long one.

CHAPTER NINE

'IACTA EST ALEA –
THE DIE IS CAST'

Richmond Palace, Thursday, 4 October 1601

Thirteen days after the invasion

ELIZABETH heard the news as she was working on correspondence at Richmond Palace.

The Queen loved the tranquillity of Richmond. It was her 'warm winter
box to shelter my old age'. Every room, every corridor in the old palace
echoed with memories of family history. It had been built by her grandfather,
Henry VII. In the reign of Elizabeth's father, Henry VIII, it had become a
setting for the court's extravagant Christmas revelries. But in light of the
bad news that she had just received, there was a very real chance that, this
Christmas, the palace would instead resonate to the voices of Spanish monks
chanting the Catholic Mass.

Elizabeth had been composing a letter to her commander in Ireland,

Charles Blount, when the unwelcome intelligence of the Spanish landing came through.

Picture her as an ambassador described her at Richmond, dressed 'in taffety of silver and white, trimmed with gold; her dress was somewhat open in front and showed her throat encircled with pearls and rubies … her hair was of a light colour never made by nature.'

Up to that point in her letter to Blount, she had been referring to invasion as an 'if'. Her writing had been dull and businesslike. But confronted with yet another Spanish threat to her realm, the sixty-eight-year-old woman's eyes lit up with the same fire that had inspired her troops at Tilbury in the year of the Great Armada. On that legendary occasion, Elizabeth had thundered: 'I know I have the body but of a weak and feeble woman; but I have the heart and stomach of a king.'

This time she could not address her soldiers directly. But she instructed Blount to read out a brief message affirming her troops' ability to defeat the Spanish. 'Every hundred of them will beat a thousand,' she said, 'and every thousand, theirs doubled.'

Charles Blount wasn't so sure about that as he inspected his soldiers, many of them already weak and injured from battles in the north. But when he received the Queen's letter, what struck him most was that she had personally handwritten the final sentences and – unusually – signed it underneath. She had expressed her full confidence in him and addressed him as 'right truly and well beloved'.

That came as an enormous relief to a man who was still living under a shadow of suspicion after the abortive Essex coup. Not so long ago he had planned to flee to France to escape the executioner's axe. He knew that there were elements in London who would dearly love to see his innards torn out publicly, while he was still alive, in the traditional punishment for traitors.

Blount could breathe easier knowing that he still enjoyed the Queen's protection. But for how long? He was one mistake away from catastrophe. And what would happen when Elizabeth's death left him fully exposed to the cold revenge of his many enemies?

Blount had first met the Virgin Queen nearly two decades ago. She was aged fifty. He was barely out of his teens – 'brown haired, of a sweet face … tall in his person', as one contemporary witness wrote.

Blount had come from Dorset, where his family estate had been virtually run into the ground by an eccentric father who'd squandered a fortune on alchemy and an older brother who'd squandered another on alcohol. A noble family that could trace its origins back to a Prince of Denmark in the year 885 was now facing ruin.

Acutely conscious of his family's status as endangered species, young Charles was looking around for opportunities after achieving a law degree from Oxford. But in 1583, a casual visit to the royal court 'to see the fashion' changed his life forever.

—Who is that young man? the Queen asked in a stage whisper as Charles joined the royal party at dinner.

The whispers went around the table, loud enough for the embarrassed Blount to hear, until at last someone reported back that he was the second son of the late Lord Mountjoy. Throughout all of this, Elizabeth fixed a rigid, unnerving stare on Blount – something which, according to her amused courtiers, 'she was wont to do'.

The young graduate flushed bright scarlet, which was exactly the reaction the Queen had wanted: she may have been born in the same year as Blount's father, but she hadn't lost it – her mere gaze could still make a young man blush. Blount's involuntary reaction was the best career move he ever made. She called him to the head of the table and gave him the royal hand to kiss.

—I knew there was noble blood in him, she remarked loudly. The lords and ladies tittered, conscious that she was referring to Blount's rush of blood to the head.

She kept him trapped in her stare.

—What was your name again? she asked at length.

He told her. Noticing his extreme discomfiture, Elizabeth softened her tone. 'Fail you not to come to court,' she offered, 'and I will bethink myself, how to do you good.'

Soon the gossips were hinting at an intimate relationship between Blount and the fifty-something monarch. 'I hear she hath now entertained one Blount,' wrote one scandalmonger, 'a young gentleman whose grandmother she may be.'

Robert Devereux, the fiery young Earl of Essex, didn't take kindly to the new challenger at court – especially when Blount proved to be an expert jouster. After one celebrated jousting victory, Elizabeth presented Blount with a golden chesspiece Queen. The message could not have been clearer.

The gift left Essex seething with quiet fury. Matters came to a head next day when Blount walked through the court ostentatiously wearing the chess token on his cloak. 'Now I perceive,' Essex hissed to the entire room, 'that every fool must have a favour.' It was one of those pivotal moments. Blount could not hope to retain respect if he let the insult pass.

—I challenge you to a duel, he shot back.

—And I accept, Essex replied.

News of the drama raced around the court. Elizabeth could have stopped the duel with a single word, but the prospect of two young stags locking antlers over her favour probably came as something of a thrill.

The two men met in a tense standoff in Marylebone Park, then a rural area on the outskirts of London. The woods echoed with the sound of clashing steel and sliding blades, but soon it was all over. Blood flowed from Essex's thigh. Blount, the victor, took the Earl's sword and walked away. Honour had been satisfied.

The Queen was delighted that Essex had been humbled. 'By God's death,' she said, 'it was fit that someone or other should take him down and teach him better manners.'

Far from making an enemy of Essex, Blount had earned his admiration. The Queen insisted on a reconciliation, and from that point on, the two angry duellers became close friends. Essex's thirst for power, combined with Blount's burgeoning military skills, ensured that theirs would become a politically volatile partnership. But it was not the most troublesome relationship Blount would have with that family. Worse would come later when he first looked into the striking black eyes of Essex's sister, Penelope, and, like so many men before him, fell hopelessly under the spell of England's most beautiful and dangerous woman.

But more of that later.

By 4 October – the same day as the Queen was writing her letter from Richmond – Charles Blount had arrived in Cork city, just 27km from the Spanish-occupied town of Kinsale. The war was about to begin, and Blount was under no illusions about the real objective. If the Spanish had really intended to aid the Irish rebellion, he reckoned, they had chosen the worst location; but if they aimed 'to lay a sudden foundation for the war in England, the best'.

Blount had received confirmation of the landing on 24 September, when he was travelling through the heartland of Ireland with only his personal guards. He faced a dilemma. Should he return to Dublin to build up his army? Or travel southward to Kinsale immediately? His colleague, George Carew, the English President of Munster, was in no doubt.

—You must go to Kinsale, Carew told Blount, even if you bring only your pageboy with you.

When Carew told Blount that he had enough food to supply his army for up to three months, the delighted commander sprang to his feet and gave him a spontaneous hug.

Blount explained his decision to Secretary Robert Cecil. 'My resolution is this,' he wrote, 'to bend myself as suddenly as I can against these foreign forces. If we beat them … [they will] all return presently with halters about their necks.'

It was never difficult to find Charles Blount, but it was sometimes hard to see him. The eighth Lord Mountjoy was almost perpetually enshrouded in dense clouds of tobacco smoke. He was plagued by debilitating headaches, and believed that smoking helped to blunt the pain.

Now aged thirty-eight, he had matured into a refined and cultured figure. With his academic bearing, his large, expressive eyes, receding chin and cropped shock of curly hair, Blount looked more like a university lecturer than a warrior. The word generally used to describe his character was 'book-ish' – a critical term implying that he preferred academic study to the gritty reality of practical warfare.

In his lifestyle, Blount did little to dispel that notion. He kept a fine table, with 'the choicest meats with the best wines, which he drunk plentifully, but never in great excess'. This civilised lifestyle was a welcome perk for his secretary and constant shadow, a thirty-six-year-old Lincolnshire man named Fynes Moryson. In previous incarnations Moryson had been a civil lawyer and a university bursar. But he was also (long before the terms were invented) a backpacker, a thrillseeker and a war groupie. After four years of travelling throughout Europe and the Middle East, Moryson asked Blount if he could travel alongside him to write a journal of the Irish war. Blount agreed, making Moryson one of the country's first war correspondents.

The news that Moryson received immediately upon his arrival in Ireland might have deterred a lesser man.

—My chief secretary was killed in action today, Blount told him. Do you want the job?

Moryson soon found himself in the thick of conflict, which was exactly what he wanted. He narrowly escaped death when a bullet passed by close enough to graze his leg.

Blount didn't believe in regular hours. Night-time would often be broken by marches or inspections or briefings. He would nap in the afternoons 'and that long, and upon his bed', Moryson testified.

This combination of fastidiousness and eccentricity often led Blount's enemies towards a fatal error: they underestimated him. Hugh O'Neill, the Irish insurgent commander, was one example.

—By the time Blount gets dressed and has his breakfast, the war will be over, he jibed.

He couldn't have been more mistaken. Blount's velvet cloak concealed a backbone of steel. He slept in the afternoons only to catch up with the sleep he lost each night when he visited front-line troops to boost their morale. 'About 4am,' he wrote once, 'I nightly choose to visit our guards myself.'

In battle he enjoyed getting into the heat of action. According to one historian he was 'eminent in courage and learning'. Moryson praised Blount's 'extraordinary forwardness to put himself into danger', a policy that resulted in quite a few casualties to his immediate entourage, both human and animal. 'My Lord himself had his horse shot under him,' Moryson wrote. 'Yea, his Lordship's very greyhound, [who used to] wait at his stirrup, was shot through the body.'

One attendant soldier had his helmet grazed by a flying bullet; a chaplain and a secretary were killed; 'and I myself had my thigh bruised with a shot I received in my saddle'.

Clearly, it was a dangerous business to stand too close to Blount. But while his hands-on policy heartened his men, it was as a military tactician that Blount really shone. As a master of the theory of warfare, he rapidly identified the mistakes made by previous English commanders in Ireland. His predecessors had campaigned only in summer, allowing the part-timers among the Irish insurgents to return home in winter to tend their cattle and prepare next year's crop. Blount decided to campaign all year round, depriving the part-time farmers of this vital break and leaving the full-time insurgents exposed in the leafless deciduous forests. 'Their cattle [giving the farmers no milk in winter] were also wasted by driving to and fro,' Moryson explained.

According to his secretary, Blount survived the winter campaigns by wearing 'three waistcoats in cold weather' as well as a jerkin, a velvet-lined cloak, a white beaver hat, and a red scarf folded three times around his neck. Underneath he wore 'two, yea, sometimes three, pairs of silk stockings' under a pair of woollen socks, and 'a pair of high linen boot hose'. Moryson marvelled: 'I never observed any [man] of his age and strength to keep his body so warm.'

Blount eliminated the need for long, straggling marches by building a string of fortified garrisons. He also made secrecy a key policy, eliminating the leaks that forewarned the enemy of his intentions.

Blount had also identified his enemies' Achilles' heel – they always needed a safe route of retreat. Many of O'Neill's troops were better armed and disciplined than the English and quite capable of facing them in open battle. If they looked as though they were winning on the open field, O'Neill would ramp up the fighting and press home their advantage. But if it seemed they were losing, they would fade away into the woods. To the frustrated English, it must have felt like fighting a ghost. Even when the Irish lost, they still won.

Blount knew that O'Neill's tactics could not continue forever. Sooner or later, the Irish commander would be caught out in the open, with nowhere to run. O'Neill had spent much of his life avoiding this situation. Blount had spent most of the past nineteen months trying to make it happen.

The previous Tuesday, 29 September, Blount had ridden out to inspect the captured town. 'This town of Kinsale hath a good wall, and many strong castles in it,' he reported. The Spanish still controlled the sea entrance –

although only a dozen of the ships remained in harbour – but they had no cavalry. 'Our greatest strength and advantage consisted in our horses,' he reported. So it was imperative, he told London, to send large stores of fodder.

In order to attack Kinsale, Blount needed cannon. Frustratingly, there were already big guns in Munster and in Dublin, but the nearest ones lay 'unmounted on the ground' and the ones in Dublin could not be moved on shipboard without specialist equipment.

Towards mid-October, the weather turned nasty, with bitter cold and driving rain. Blount was stuck in Cork for three days. Together with Carew, he used the time to formulate a battle plan, and to establish a front-line hospital for future casualties. William Farmer, an army surgeon, recalled: '[To this] place should be sent all the sick and hurt soldiers that should happen in the time of siege … there was provided for them fire, lodging, meat and drink.'

Eventually the storms calmed enough for Blount to lead his troops out to the fringe of Kinsale. He camped overnight at Owenboy, around eight kilometres from the town, before moving to a closer camp under Knock-robin Hill, just eight hundred metres north of the fortress walls. Although he couldn't dig in yet – he had no entrenching tools – he felt it was important to register a presence. It was a risky move. He had no artillery, and 'scarce so much powder as would serve for a good day's fight'.

Conditions were grim. With no trenches to shelter them, many of the soldiers had to sleep out in the open and the officers lodged in hastily erected 'cabins' of sticks, mud and turf which provided only a little more protection. 'It rained upon us in our beds, and when we changed our shirts,' Fynes Moryson later recalled.

The camp sat astride the main road from Cork (now a minor road through Brownsmills) and consisted of thirteen large tents and around forty of the little cabins. It lay on the northern side of the Oysterhaven estuary, just before its only crossable point at a building then called the New Mill.

Sitting in his mud hut, amid dense clouds of smoke from his pipe, Charles

Blount surveyed Felipe III's latest possession through the drenching rain. He knew that this was to be the ultimate test of will: between two monarchs, between two nations, and between two seasoned campaigners whose skills were to be tested to the limits.

'*Iacta est alea*,' he wrote to Secretary Cecil, quoting Julius Caesar's famous phrase. 'The die is cast between England and Spain.'

CHAPTER TEN

Curses Like
Thunderbolts

There are only three ways in which fortified towns may be gained.
The first is by stratagem ... the second is by entrenchments and
batteries to prepare a breach and to make the assault ... the third is
by entrenching an Army about a fort, whereby all passages are
barricaded up; so that relief cannot possibly come to enter the town,
so that by mere hunger they are constrained to yield.
– *Robert Ward,* Animadversions of War, *1639*

AS CHARLES Blount cursed the rain and waited for his troops, Juan del Águila studied his favourite manual on fortifications and considered his next move. The veteran fighter had been in similar situations many times before, both as attacker and defender, and knew exactly what to expect.

Soon the full force of the English army would be hurled against these aged stone walls. The pleasant green countryside would be transformed into a blasted, muddy wilderness of dugouts and earthen ramps as his enemies relentlessly burrowed their way towards him in parallel and zig-zagging trenches. When they reached cannon range, they would mount their heaviest artillery behind barriers of compacted soil. They would establish new advance camps behind these lines, tightening their noose around the town. The great guns would roar. Dense iron cannonballs weighing eight kilograms or more would smash into the centuries-old walls. Their concentrated impact would weaken the tall, unstable edifices and, eventually, smash open a breach. No mediaeval stone wall could withstand modern cannon fire. It wasn't a question of tactics. It was pure physics.

Over the past century (and Águila had been a soldier for nearly 40 percent of that time) there had been a total revolution in the science of warfare. Once, defenders had felt safe behind high stone walls. But the development of powerful, mobile cannon had changed all that. Repeated impact would quickly destabilise the gangling, top-heavy structures. Heavy masonry would tumble down, burying the defenders. The same friendly stones that had once provided shelter would shatter into flesh-ripping shrapnel. 'Such is the shock of artillery,' wrote the Italian military expert Niccolò Machiavelli, 'that there is no wall, however strong, that cannon fire will not destroy in only a few days.'

Most modern European fortresses featured lower, wider walls constructed of hardened earth and faced by masonry. They were so bottom-heavy and stable that they rarely collapsed. Cannonballs fired at them would simply bury themselves deep into the earth, dissipating their energy. Viewed from above, modern forts resembled stars or magnified snowflakes, with angular, spear-like projections jutting out at strange angles from the wall. These 'bastions' ensured a clear view and a clean line of fire, however devious the enemy's approach.

If you added defensive trenches, moats and slopes, you had a fortress that was almost impregnable. Águila could testify to this: he had built a superb example of a star fort in Brittany which had prevailed for years without being taken. But that fortress had been built from scratch. In crowded, medi-aeval Kinsale, rebuilding was just not practicable. '[Kinsale] is well built and surrounded by walls,' Águila wrote home, '[but] it is not favourable for for-tification.'

He would have to opt for a more quick-and-dirty solution. Outside the walls, he would create a network of defensive trenches fronted by high earthen ramps. Some were oval. Others were 'ravelins' – outwardly jutting triangles, rather like bastions. Using these as refuges, his men could sally out and attack the English trench-diggers before they could approach within range.

All over northern Europe, war was being waged in this manner: by dig-ging down into the earth. 'We make war more like foxes than like lions,' one military expert, Roger Boyle, was to complain half a century later. (He was actually the son of Richard Boyle.)

So Águila would dig down too. He ordered his men to excavate a line of trenches 'upon a hill, [outside] the town'. Trenches and gun emplacements would also be thrown up around the two outlying fortresses, Castle Park and Rincorran. 'They set about fortifying their camp, and digging trenches, arranging and planting the ordnance [guns],' reported Hugh O'Donnell's seventeenth-century biographer Lughaidh O'Cleary.

According to the *Annals of the Four Masters*: 'They planted their great guns, and their other projectile and defensive engines, at every point on which they thought the enemy would approach them.'

Andrew Lynch, the Galway merchant who sailed with the Spanish fleet, witnessed some of these guns being set up. 'Three pieces were mounted on carriages and brought into the middle of the town,' he wrote. Lynch identi-fied them as 'sakers', medium-sized guns with three-metre barrels capable of propelling an iron ball of up to 2.7kg for over 2.5 kilometres. Rather than hit a specific target, the missiles were designed to bounce wildly and cause maximum damage.

Another witness, Scotsman John Clerk, said the town's churchyard was turned into a gun emplacement.

Later, Lynch saw Águila march his soldiers – reckoned at just over three thousand men – onto a hill outside the town for drill and mustering.

Set against the sombre green and dun backdrop of a damp Irish hillside, the muster would have made a colourful spectacle. Spanish army officers were encouraged to express their personality through their clothing, even in wartime. 'There has never been a regulation for dress and weapons in the Spanish infantry,' one commentator wrote in 1610, 'because that would remove the spirit and fire necessary in a soldier.'

Officers typically strove to outdo each other with their brightly plumed steel helmets, flamboyantly coloured topcoats, and padded doublets. In contrast, the ordinary troops wore doublets and stuffed knee-length breeches. But often they were shamefully under-clothed as well as under-equipped. 'I have 2,500 effectives,' Águila complained of his troops at Kinsale, 'so untrained and so naked that it is a piteous thing to see.'

Drills like this were essential. Throughout Europe, the Spanish were renowned for their disciplined troops and their tight, block-like battlefield formation. Known to the English as 'the Spanish Square', this was a rectangle made up of 1,000 to 3,000 pikemen, musketeers and arquebusiers. It was effectively a moveable human fortress for use in an open field. The pikemen's array of long, razor-sharp spikes would skewer any approaching cavalry as the mobile shooters at each corner unleashed murderous fire. Ideally, the overall force would form into three squares – hence the name 'tercio' or third.

Troops in a Spanish square could inflict almost unbelievable defeats upon a superior but less disciplined army. For instance, in two separate battles against the Dutch, the Spanish lost ten men and their enemies lost 5,000 and 7,000.

Meanwhile, back in Spain, Admiral Pedro de Zubiaur was having a tough time trying to get help for Águila's stranded invasion force. The bureaucrats agreed in principle, but things were moving painfully slowly. Zubiaur's main galleon, the *San Felipe*, had been seriously damaged in the Atlantic storms and would not be going anywhere before spring. Another of his missing ships had finally limped into El Ferrol in equally bad shape. By mid-October, Diego de Brochero – the admiral who had landed at Kinsale with Águila – had also returned to Spain. His ships, too, were in poor condition.

Zubiaur was anxious to rejoin his comrades in Ireland, but he was low on food supplies. In the meantime, his seven hundred troops were kicking their heels. He confessed he was so disenchanted that he was ready to quit after more than a quarter century of service.

Felipe III wrote to him personally, urging him to have another try. The ships should be re-fitted and ten infantry companies should be mustered as reinforcements.

—Speed is of the essence, he told Zubiaur.

But he added, contrarily, that Zubiaur should not spend too much because there wasn't enough money in the royal purse to pay the troops.

Noting the lack of enthusiasm, the ever-perceptive Venetian diplomats were even more convinced that the only aim of the invasion was to have troops on the ready for the Queen's death. 'They are content to keep Kinsale alone,' they wrote, 'as a card in their hands when they want it.'

By this stage Águila's position was difficult, but not a cause for despair. With the two harbour forts under his control and around a dozen ships remaining, he still commanded the sea entrance. His 3,000 to 3,500 men compared well to Blount's initial force. He had every reason to expect thousands of reinforcements from Spain, and if Hugh O'Neill honoured his promise to join him within fourteen days, he could soon have thousands more.

But there was no sign of help from O'Neill. From Águila's standpoint, the Irish chieftain's failure to promise a relief force was baffling. The two northern earls had been demanding Spanish help for years. They would have heard of the landing within a fortnight, and Águila had since sent several envoys to press home the point. '[The] Spaniards have lately sent three special messengers to [O'Neill] to labour his coming into Munster,' one English official reported.

At first O'Neill tried to persuade the Spaniards to come north, but the three messengers left him in no doubt that Águila wanted him to go to Kinsale.

—They are far away, the road is dangerous, and I have no horses, Águila mused aloud.

In Munster itself, the eerie silence from the Irish clans left the Spaniards worried. 'Nobody worth a garron [a cheap workhorse] has as yet adhered to them,' General Carew exulted. 'There is no appearance of war in the province, except at the walls of Kinsale.'

Another English official wrote: 'The Irish were never so mild … they hang their heads like hens who have been in the rain.'

No one on the Spanish side had expected a long wait and nobody had prepared for a shortage of food. They had brought large quantities of salt, expecting meat from the Irish. Águila boasted to locals that he had enough bread, rice, pulses and wine to last eighteen months, but he was probably putting on a brave face. 'What they have consists of bread and suet,' Carew wrote. 'Their greatest relief is the townsmen's provisions in Kinsale. They have no wine – except the officers. The soldier drinks only water.'

The captive Irish mariners testified that the Spanish had 'neither rice, oil, fish or flesh', only 'coarse bread, full of worms, and very little wine'.

Beef wasn't entirely absent from the menu. Before the English sealed off the surrounding countryside, Águila had built up a sizeable herd of cattle near Castle Park. However, these turned out to be easy prey for the English.

By day twenty, as Alférez Bustamante noted in his journal, it was 'hard work' to obtain any meat at all.

Inside the town, there was growing dissatisfaction among the wealthier townsfolk who wanted to take up Águila's early offer and leave with their possessions, but who also wanted to negotiate a pardon from the English. Eventually Águila lost patience and informed them they had to forfeit their goods and stay. However, he could not seal the town completely. 'Some English, Frenchmen and Scots have run from them,' read one report, 'and some Spaniards, Portuguese and other [deserters].'

The Cornish seaman John Edie had an especially good reason for wanting to escape. Even if the Spanish were to win, he could look forward only to a return to the galley oars. When an opportunity arose, he secretly slipped away on the road north to Cork, leaving Kinsale behind him forever.

As the two sides dug in like foxes, there was a bizarre twist to the conflict. The first serious battle of the campaign took place not on ground level, and not on the subterranean level … but on the heavenly plane.

In this strange war where power and empire-building were inextricably entangled with religion, it was not enough to win the hearts and minds of the public. It was also vital to win their souls. And the Spanish clerics had a super-weapon that was, in its way, far more powerful than anything in the English armoury. It was called excommunication.

Up until now, most priests in Ireland had instructed their Catholic flock to remain loyal to the Queen and to obey all her laws except those on religion. Philip O'Sullivan, a historian of Catholicism in Ireland, recorded that 'at this time there was no persecution of priests'. Most clerics preached that 'it was not only lawful to assist the Queen, but even to resist the Irish party and to draw the sword upon it'.

Blount's fear was that the newcomers would change all that by offering indulgences to the insurgents and damnation to those who opposed them. Anxious to pre-empt that, he issued a proclamation warning that Queen Elizabeth had been 'truly anointed' by God. Anyone who opposed her would defy the divine will.

Mateo de Oviedo hit back with his own proclamation, issued in the name of Águila but clearly written in his own distinctively bombastic style. 'We endeavour not to persuade anybody [to] deny due obedience … to his prince,' he said. However, he claimed, the heretic Elizabeth had been stripped of her crown by the Vatican – and therefore wasn't queen at all. In the words of one seventeenth-century writer, the proclamation announced that she had been 'deprived of her kingdoms, and her subjects absolved and freed from their oaths of allegiance'. The Spanish would 'deliver them out of the devil's claws and English tyranny'.

What he said next drew gasps of astonishment throughout Europe. 'The Pope, Christ's Vicar upon earth, doth command you to take up arms for the defence of the Faith,' Oviedo declared. '[Whoever] shall attempt to do otherwise, and remain in obedience to the English, we will persecute him as an heretic and a hateful enemy of the holy Church.' The Spanish cleric was unleashing the ultimate deterrent. And this was something he had no right to do.

Oviedo, desperate for Irish support, and impatient to reach his cathedral in Dublin, had unwittingly stumbled into a diplomatic minefield. There had been earlier Papal Bulls – official edicts – excommunicating Catholics who supported Elizabeth. But they had never applied in Ireland, and the backlash against the English Catholics had been so severe that the current Pope, Clement VIII, had quietly let them gather dust. Clement's main aim was stability in Europe. He had spent years enticing the Protestant King of France back into the Church and establishing peace between the great rivals France and Spain.

Oviedo's proclamation could be interpreted – and was interpreted – as meaning that the Vatican was upsetting this delicate balance of power by encouraging Spanish expansion against France's interests. In Venice, it was important breaking news. 'Don Juan del Águila ... has announced that His Holiness has renewed the Bull against the Queen of England, absolving her subjects from their allegiance,' ambassador Marin Cavalli reported from Paris.

When the French King Henry IV heard of the Kinsale proclamation, he was furious. He summoned the Vatican's representative and gave him an earful. 'The [invasion] has profoundly impressed the King of France and his Ministers,' Cavalli said. He warned that the news had put the French on a war footing. If the Spanish were to succeed in Ireland, France would be honour-bound to intervene.

The English were amused at the chaos the proclamation had caused. The Spanish were 'discharging curses like thunderbolts', one observer wrote.

Rome was highly embarrassed. For the ambitious Oviedo, it was not a good career move.

Oviedo could have lived with all these problems if his tactic had worked. But most Irish Catholics simply ignored his threat ... and for the titular Archbishop of Dublin, that was the greatest snub of all.

By late October, Águila's soldiers were falling ill with crippling abdominal cramps, fever and chills. When they began excreting blood, the hospital workers immediately recognised 'the bloody flux' – dysentery, the same illness that had killed Spain's arch enemy Sir Francis Drake a few years earlier.

In the crowded surroundings, the disease spread rapidly. Tiny microorganisms travelled from unwashed hands into mouths, and then burrowed deep into the intestines. The Spanish invaders were themselves being invaded – and the microscopic assailants were to kill more Spanish troops at Kinsale than the English could ever manage.

Then, just as his numbers were seriously declining, Águila received a message which many of his subordinates regarded as a chink of light in the darkness. An Irish clan leader on the western fringes of County Cork was offering to provide him with two thousand extra troops.

You can imagine how Águila reacted to this offer. After all, he was stranded in Kinsale with a rapidly depleting force; he didn't know if the northern earls were ever going to join him; and he could be waiting for weeks for any help from home. Two thousand extra troops?

No thanks, he replied.

CHAPTER ELEVEN

The Lord of Beara and Bantry

H E SAID *what?*

Donal Cam O'Sullivan Beare could hardly believe his own ears when his messenger conveyed Juan del Águila's polite rejection of his offer of two thousand troops. Sitting in his windswept stone castle some 120km from Kinsale, the fifty-year-old Gaelic chieftain had never felt so insulted and so bewildered at the same time.

Donal Cam controlled Beara and Bantry, a remote finger of County Cork pointing across the chilly Atlantic towards the Americas. And with thousands of warriors at his disposal, he had thought he was in a position to end the escalating Kinsale standoff with a game-changing intervention.

O'Sullivan Beare's sympathies were firmly with the invaders. He may have been born on this far-western salient of Ireland – but there was no doubt about his bloodline and ancestry. With his Don Quixote moustache and goatee, he looked more Spanish than the Spaniards themselves. According to one source: 'His face of dark olive complexion [was] lighted with large dazzling eyes … and wore a peculiar air of Spanish haughtiness.' He had been given the nickname 'Cam', or 'crooked', thought to be as a result of a disfiguring injury to his shoulder. He felt this disability had challenged him and made him stronger by tempering the 'inward conceit' he had shown in his youth.

Donal Cam claimed to hate the English oppressors, whom he regarded as 'these merciless, heretical enemies'. Now he had an opportunity to strike back. As his nephew Philip O'Sullivan later recorded: '[He] sent a messenger to Águila to say he and his friends had 1,000 armed men, and as many unarmed men unlisted, and if Águila would only supply arms for them, they would block [Blount's] road and prevent a siege until O'Neill and O'Donnell came to his assistance.' All Águila had to do was supply Donal Cam with guns and cash for a thousand men.

But after making a few inquiries among his Irish expatriate supporters in Kinsale, Águila discovered that things were not quite so straightforward. O'Sullivan Beare's credentials as a rebel were not impressive. He had acquired an English lordship by ferociously lobbying the very Queen he now claimed to despise. In a grovelling submission, he had emphasised how he had helped the English to defeat a previous Irish rising and how he had repudiated the system the Gaels used to elect their chieftains.

In response the English ousted his uncle, who was the foremost claimant under the Gaelic system, and appointed Donal Cam as 'The Queen's O'Sullivan'. At a stroke, he had gained full control over a small but lucrative fiefdom with a castle and several thousand inhabitants.

Now this same man was asking for a thousand guns. But was he a convert to the cause – or a double agent? It was a gamble that Águila was not willing to take. His reply to Donal Cam was diplomatic. His spare guns were with Zubiaur, he said, and he could not enlist any locals until they were vetted and approved by O'Neill and O'Donnell.

The rejection provided Mateo de Oviedo with yet another complaint to record in his little black book. '[Many Irish] would have come, as they did at the start, if we had trusted them and given armaments to them,' he wrote later, 'but we did nothing of the sort.'

By mid-October, English troops were being diverted to Kinsale from Leinster, Connaught and the north. One commander, Henry Danvers, had made particularly good time – his men marched the 200km from Dublin to Cork in just six days. (This shows that Águila was not being unrealistic in expecting O'Neill to travel from the north within two weeks.) Thousands more were on the way. Secretary Cecil had been busy conscripting troops all over England, and they were gathering at the West Country ports of Barnstaple and Bristol. A few of these were volunteers, but the vast majority had been dragged into the army by force.

The system worked like this. In each region, local authorities would be ordered to raise a quota. Naturally, they chose the misfits they wanted to get rid of: tramps, drifters and lawbreakers. (Sometimes even condemned criminals flatly refused to enlist, saying they preferred the gallows to dying like dogs in Ireland.)

An official known as a 'conductor' marched them to a mustering centre. Along the way, their bags were usually ransacked and their clothes stolen. By the time the conscripts reached port, only the dregs were left. Those who had any cash had bribed themselves free, and the fittest had escaped. The system was almost guaranteed to ensure that those who remained were least suited to be soldiers. One group bound for Cork was described as 'either old, lame, diseased, boys or common rogues. Few of them have any clothes: small, weak, starved bodies.'

The situation was further complicated by the curious system of 'dead pays'. A dead-pay was a non-existent soldier whose pay went into the captain's pocket. There could be six phantom soldiers in every company of a hundred, but no one ever knew for sure until they actually lined up for fighting. '[Ensure] they deceive you not with dead-pays and turn out to have no companies when the time comes for service,' one commander was advised.

Cecil's pitiful conscripts set sail from Bristol along with the big guns and the skilled workers Blount desperately needed. There was only one problem – the wind was blowing in precisely the wrong direction.

'God send us an easterly wind,' Blount prayed as he kicked his heels in his temporary camp.

His prayers were eventually answered. But when the wind did blow from England, it blew so hard that the thirteen ships were propelled right past Kinsale and several miles further to the west, leaving a frustrated Blount praying for a westerly wind instead.

There is a common misconception that Águila's Spaniards remained safely inside the town during the Siege of Kinsale, while the Irish did all the fighting. This not only flies in the face of all the evidence (in fact, many Spaniards died in fierce fighting outside the walls), but also misunderstands the nature of warfare in the early 1600s. The new technology of warfare had resulted in a shift away from dramatic, set-piece battles towards long, grinding sieges. The last thing a defender like Águila could do was to wait passively inside a fortress as the attackers burrowed their way closer to his walls. As soon as darkness fell each night, the defenders had to be out there, harassing the besiegers, delaying their trench diggers, and spiking their guns. It was more like a modern sabotage mission than a mediaeval battle, although dozens could die in the vicious hand-to-hand combat. Each attack was known as a 'sally'.

A military expert named John Muller described the process as it was in the early 1600s: 'The besieged had opportunities to sally out and fall upon the workmen and their guard on every side, drive them out of their works and destroy them … to nail up the guns and batteries, or to surprise a part of the guard in the trenches.'

A successful sally took place under cover of darkness. 'Sallies are never made in the daytime [except] by a presumptuous enemy, for then they are easily repulsed,' Muller wrote. The only way to prevent a sally was constant vigilance. The besiegers would post patrols in no-man's-land. '[They must] remain in profound silence till they hear or perceive some motion.'

The night of 19 October saw the first real clash between the two sides as Águila's Spaniards sallied out from their trenches and clashed with Blount's front-line guards. There were no injuries, but (at least according to the English) Águila was impressed with the courage of his enemy's troops.

—I never saw any [men] come more willingly to the sword, he said.

The following night, war erupted in earnest with the first casualties of the conflict. Águila despatched up to half of his entire force in a major offensive. Marching silently in the darkness, they wheeled around behind Knockrobin Hill and climbed the rise until they were directly overlooking the enemy camp. But a night patrol spotted them on the hill and beat them back into Kinsale. Four Spaniards died in that first engagement.

The English consolidated their first victory with a propaganda coup. They enlisted the aid of an Irish clan leader called Cormac McDermot, who had first offered his services to Águila but had now switched sides.

Earlier, McDermot had sent a gift of a hackney horse to the Spanish commander in Kinsale. Águila, who desperately needed warhorses, had looked at the delicate trotting-horse and responded in despair: 'Doth the country yield no greater horses than these?'

Blount ordered McDermot to march his Irish troops right up to the Spanish trenches in order to test his loyalty. As a precaution, he posted a larger force out of sight behind a hill.

But Blount need not have worried. McDermot launched an all-out attack on the Spanish, driving them out of their trenches before pulling back.

Blount threw in his reserve force under his friend Sir William Godolphin, a Cornishman who consolidated the Irishmen's victory and managed to pull off a spectacular rescue in the process. One English cavalry officer who had charged deep into the Spanish ranks had lost his horse and become stranded. Glancing around, he 'espied himself in great danger'. Ignoring the blistering fire from the Spanish muskets, Godolphin charged between the parallel lines of enemy trenches to rescue him. An eyewitness said Godolphin returned unhurt 'to the marvel of all the beholders, considering the multitude of shot made at them'.

Encouraged by the episode, the English decided to try to force an entry into the town itself. After dark on 25 October, a strike force of three hundred troops mounted a concentrated attack with pikes. The Spanish guards were surprised and retreated into Kinsale. The English 'fell into the gate with them', killing more than twenty Spanish before being beaten back again.

A pattern was being established, and it wasn't in the Spaniards' favour. Inside Kinsale, Águila was rapidly losing patience with his officers. And his officers were rapidly losing patience with him.

CHAPTER TWELVE

CONFESSIONS AND CONSPIRACIES

Kinsale is a famous sepulchre to [the Spaniards'] honour: that climate
perhaps having as natural an antipathy to intruders, as to noisome
and venomous beasts.
– *Paolo Sarpi,* A Discourse, *1628*

INSIDE the town, Águila was fighting another, more insidious, battle. Some half a dozen captains were secretly plotting against him – and it came as no surprise that the nucleus of all this dissent was Brother Mateo de Oviedo. 'Jealousies and disputes arose between [Águila] and his captains, and Matthew Oviedo,' Philip O'Sullivan recorded.

Oviedo was a prickly individual who fell out with most people, including, eventually, King Felipe. He even detested Fr Archer. (His rages were legendary. When one finance official queried Oviedo's accounts at Kinsale, Oviedo threatened to excommunicate him.)

Águila learned about the plots from a loyal officer who had spotted the captains creeping into Oviedo's house for confessions. In reality, they were voicing grievances against Águila and speculating that he was in league with the English. To these aggrieved officers, it all seemed to add up. If this were not true, why were they in such a weak fortress? Why hadn't Águila moved on? Since he'd stayed, why hadn't he built better fortifications? Why hadn't he installed more soldiers in the two forts? And why had he spurned O'Sullivan Beare's offer of two thousand troops?

Throughout it all, Brother Mateo nodded sympathetically. Oviedo seems to have been one of those people who crop up in every crisis – the carping critic who quickly identifies the spark of negativity in others, stokes it up into a roaring flame, and then uses the dissidents as a proxy for his own disaffection.

Oviedo was carefully keeping a log of all Águila's mistakes. This deflected attention from his own errors – for instance, his choice of destination and his misjudgement of local support. He would later plead to Lerma: 'Failure to succeed is commonly blamed on those least at fault.'

He maintained that more Irish would have supported the invaders if they had fortified Kinsale. '[The] entire country would have joined us if they had seen we were serious about defending our position,' he claimed confidently. Instead, 'like women, we let ourselves be surrounded and besieged by land and sea'.

Águila was furious about the meetings. He knew it was not the first time that Oviedo had undermined a commander in mid-campaign. It had happened before – in a place whose very name evoked dread among the Spanish troops. It was a place of horror called Smerwick.

It was a September day in 1580. A much younger and more idealistic Brother Mateo stepped ashore at the isolated port of Smerwick in County

Kerry, after a four-week voyage from Spain. He watched with pride as 300 crack Spanish and Italian troops marched ashore, carrying the crossed-keys banner of Pope Gregory XIII. Eyes afire with religious fervour, Oviedo was determined to free the Irish from 'that yoke imposed by the English heretics'.

It was the thirty-three-year-old theologian's second stab at the same task. The previous summer, in July 1579, he had sailed into Smerwick on a secret mission to Ireland 'to bring that isle back to Christ'. He hadn't achieved this ambitious goal, but he had returned to Spain with glowing reports. Oviedo was convinced that a quarter of the Irish population was in rebellion and that the other three-quarters would follow as soon as military aid arrived. These statistics were insanely optimistic, but he had managed to convince both Pope Gregory and King Felipe II that just a slight push would send Ireland tumbling into full-scale religious revolt.

Now, in 1580, Brother Mateo was back in Smerwick again, leading a second force. He was much more than just a chaplain. According to one authority on the invasion, Oviedo was 'the principal promoter of this undertaking'. The invasion was ostensibly a religious expedition sponsored by Pope Gregory. Its commander was an experienced Italian colonel named Sebastiano di San Giuseppe. As the expedition's 'apostolic commissary', Oviedo brandished a letter from the Pope and promised the bemused locals the same indulgences that were granted to the Crusaders.

San Giuseppe had more earthly considerations. Fearing an imminent English blockade, he dug in at Dún an Óir (the Fortress of Gold) a natural fastness surrounded by rocks. Immediately, Oviedo began to question his authority.

—This is not a good place to fortify, he told San Giuseppe.

—I am the military commander here, San Giuseppe replied. This is my decision and it stands.

Furious, Oviedo invoked the Pope's name. But San Giuseppe was not for turning.

What happened next was open to different interpretations. Brother Mateo's supporters claimed that Oviedo quit 'in disgust', left the expedition, and 'retired ... to the interior of the country'.

But in San Giuseppe's eyes, it was simple desertion – especially since Oviedo had persuaded most of the Irish insurgents and some key members of the invasion force to leave with him. Alone and abandoned on his exposed rock at the world's end, San Giuseppe didn't stand a chance without the mass Irish support that Oviedo had first promised and then snatched away. The insurgents had left a few hundred 'chosen troops' at the fort, but they were not nearly enough.

Oviedo stayed in Ireland a mere six weeks. In October, with the drama still escalating, he sailed back to the safety of Spain. The reason, or perhaps the pretext, was that he would plead for more troops. Despite San Giuseppe's protests, Oviedo took the best ships with him. The commander was left only with three smaller craft.

In November, the English battered the fort from land and sea. Although seriously outnumbered, the invaders repulsed one attack and left many English dead. But their position became hopeless – and with no sign of any relief from the Irish insurgent force, San Giuseppe was forced to plead for terms.

After a parlay with Lord Arthur Grey, the English commander, San Giuseppe believed that the invaders' lives would be spared if they surrendered. The English commander later claimed he made no such commitment, but told them that they would be treated as stateless adventurers who must yield to his will, for life or death. The distinction hardly matters: what followed was equally inexcusable.

As one English writer approvingly – and chillingly – recorded: '[Lord Grey] decided their quarrel by sheathing his sword in their bowels.'

Here's how Grey himself recalled it: 'Morning came ... [and they] presented [their ensigns] unto me with their lives and the fort ... then I put in certain bands, who straight fell to execution. There were 600 slain.'

San Giuseppe was spared to tell of the slaughter. He returned to a frosty welcome in a Spanish prison cell. Oviedo had already condemned him in his absence to anyone who would listen.

A year later, a friend wrote to San Giuseppe hoping that he would soon be freed 'to plead your cause ... against Father Matthew de Oviedo ... [who has] accused you of a thousand things'.

However, another source said that San Giuseppe obtained affidavits from officers testifying it was Oviedo's indiscipline that led to the force's destruction.

There was never any doubt about who would come off better in the dispute.

Oviedo retreated to the tranquillity of his rural convent. But he couldn't get Ireland out of his system. He had been bitten by the bug. He would continue to dream up plans for further Spanish missions to Ireland – probably never suspecting that, nearly two decades after Smerwick, he would be back in another indefensible coastal fortress, trying to explain away the lack of support from his beloved insurgent allies, and collecting evidence against yet another military commander who, infuriatingly, would not do what he was told.

In Kinsale, the dissident captains continued their secret meetings. But in attacking Águila, they may have had a hidden agenda which had nothing to do with this expedition. The underlying factors could have had more to do with social class, power and ambition. According to one source, these disaffected officers were annoyed because they were not receiving promotions.

If this is the case, it reflected the tensions that were tearing apart the Spanish army throughout Europe at this time. Old-style commanders like Juan del Águila had little in common with the new generation of young officers. They seemed to inhabit different worlds.

Although a nobleman, Águila had joined the army as a grunt soldier.

There was a reason for this. When he was a teenager, the Spanish *tercio* regiments had risen to unprecedented prestige under the brilliant but brutal general the Duke of Alba. Known as the Iron Duke, Alba had insisted that all aspiring officers work their way up through the ranks. They had to drill until they dropped. They had to become masters of the pike and musket. Only the best candidates would be selected. Alba fostered a sense of individualism as well as obedience, camaraderie and *esprit de corps*. His elite officers were given freedom to dress as they chose. One regiment was known as 'the dandies' because of their 'plumes, finery and bright colours'. Another, 'the sextons', wore fashionable black. What they rarely wore was a military uniform. As one veteran remarked disdainfully, they did not want to look like shopkeepers.

In the 1590s, a decade or so after Alba died, his methods were allowed to die with him. New officers no longer had to serve probation. The nobles, who comprised a tenth of Spain's population, were allowed to go straight into positions of army command. In one unintentionally hilarious exchange, some courtiers fretted that nobles should get at least *some* military training. Very well, said others, quite seriously: we'll teach them how to tilt with lances in jousting tournaments.

An unexpected side-effect was a logjam of young officers awaiting promotion. These pressures often exploded into mutiny.

Was this a factor behind the insubordination at Kinsale? It's interesting to speculate. Were the disaffected captains at Kinsale part of this widespread campaign against class bias, or part of the new influx of favoured courtiers who resented having to take orders from anyone?

Only one thing is clear: this was a clash of generations and of ideologies. Águila was from the old school of hard training and unquestioning obedience. These captains, with their constant criticism and resentment of authority, represented the new wave of Spanish officers – a generation who would live to see Alba's dreams turn to dust as the golden years of the *tercios* came to an end.

Meanwhile, tensions were rising between the townspeople and the invaders. Beef was running short. There were maggots in the bread. Águila reported home that his men could buy ingredients for tortillas locally 'but so expensively that it is an incredible thing. Now everything is gone.'

With no food to be purchased anywhere, the Spanish started to requisition what few supplies the townsfolk had. John Clerk, the Scots merchant, witnessed cows being commandeered. This was a shift from Águila's original position – 'we pay them what they demand' – and it created widespread resentment. 'The townspeople forsake [the Spanish],' Clerk said, 'because they kill up their cattle without payment.'

There were also disputes over living space. With a normal population of up to two thousand, and only two hundred houses within the walls, it had always been a bit crowded in Kinsale. With the arrival of 3,700 troops, the town became claustrophobic. The best and most spacious premises had gone to the officers, and other homes were requisitioned to cope with the overflow from the hospital.

The plague of dysentery exacerbated the problem. Águila summed up the increasingly horrific situation in a letter to the King. 'We have many sick and they are collapsing every day,' he wrote. 'They have too little food and too much work to do. The sentries can never leave their guns out of their hands. The winter alone is bad enough.'

Winter. It was the invisible enemy that devastated both sides in this conflict, and for those men used to warmth and sunshine, it must have been particularly hard. '[One] can readily picture the gloom and horror of the position of its defenders fresh from the sunny lands of Spain,' wrote Florence O'Sullivan, a local historian, in 1905. 'The almost incessant rain and fog of these months, the narrow ill-paved streets, dark as Erebus, the few hours of daylight, the deep depression of the position dominated by dark frowning cliffs … all combined to render the task of the Spaniards an heroic one.'

Meanwhile, another sound was drowning out the Spaniards' shouted orders and the locals' cries of protest. It came from outside. It was the rhythmic tramp of marching boots.

CHAPTER THIRTEEN

'Crested Plumes and Silken Sashes'

I N THE DISTANCE, they would have appeared a curious sight – a bit like rectangular hedgehogs, or shoeshine brushes with the bristles upraised.

Watching from the ramparts of Kinsale, Don Juan del Águila saw the grim column of English reinforcements march over the horizon and realised the seriousness of his predicament. With the arrival of every new English soldier, the odds against him were mounting. The Spanish had around 3,500 effective troops, and the number was dropping daily. By late October, Blount had 6,900 foot soldiers, increasing daily. Blount had 611 cavalry. Águila had none. You did not need to be a genius at mathematics to deduce the problem.

As Blount's thousands of Irish-based reinforcements approached the English camp, the details became clearer. The spines or bristles were actually hundreds of fighting pikes carried across the shoulders of specialist infantrymen. Each pikeman bore a strong ashwood pole two and a half times the height of a tall man. At the business end was a long, sharpened steel spearhead designed to skewer a charging horse. These pikemen formed the core of defence in battle and were highly esteemed for their unflinching courage. Even for a son of royalty, it was a noble profession to 'trail a pike' – although royal pikemen were a rarity and the weapons were often wielded by pitiable conscripts.

A full-scale Elizabethan army on the march was an awesome sight – enough to make a lesser commander than Águila throw open the gates in despair.

'All were exceedingly well furnished with all kinds of arms,' Philip O'Sullivan wrote of a similar English column. 'Foot and horse were sheathed in mail. The musketeers were equipped for the fight, some with heavy and some with light guns, girded with sword and dagger, and having their head protected with helmets. The whole army gleamed with crested plumes and silken sashes ... brass cannon mounted on wheels were drawn by horses.'

A contemporary illustration gives a sense of the dread that such a force could inspire. The column is led by mounted cavalry officers, each with a long 'partisan', or half-sized pike, held vertically. Full-bearded and grim-faced under their shining helmets, they are followed by two flanking units of musketeers, with guns shouldered and swords sheathed at the hip. A fighting dagger is strapped at waist level behind their backs. A drummer keeps marching time with steady taps.

Here in Kinsale, it was late October, so the troops would be wearing winter gear. Common soldiers were issued – in theory at least – with a cotton-lined cassock or long coat, a canvas doublet or jacket lined with linen, a coloured cap, a shirt, long socks and leather shoes, and Venetians (long trousers) of 'broad Kentish cloth' lined with linen. The tough linen was strong enough to stop a weak blade-thrust from breaking the skin. Officers wore much the same basic gear, but with silk buttons and lace trimmings.

Body armour was out of favour. It was mainly designed to withstand arrows, but it had been sixteen years since the longbow had been seriously used in battle. A skilled archer could still fire faster than a good musketeer, but any idiot could be trained to use a gun. Many soldiers had discarded their cumbersome armour, although those in the front lines still opted for steel breastplates, backplates, and shoulder- and thigh-padding.

Many foot soldiers wore red, and not just because it matched the St George flag – one contemporary said the colour was chosen for soldiers 'that they might not be discouraged by the sight of blood from their wounds'.

Depending upon the greed of their superiors, the troops could either be warmly equipped or shivering in rags. One Irish-bound unit mustered at Chester that year was so smartly dressed that the sight provoked a near-riot among others who had 'no apparel'. According to Fynes Moryson, many of the troops that arrived at Kinsale from other Irish bases late in October were 'very deficient in number, having been long worn out in skirmishes, journeys and sicknesses'.

Yet it seems that morale was high as they settled in. They were excited by reports that the Spanish had nine chests overflowing with gold. One official said: 'Our soldiers are very anxious to fight and make booty of their treasure.'

By 26 October, Blount's military experts had chosen a spot for a permanent siege camp. One location ticked all their boxes. It was Spital Hill, 'somewhat more than a musket shot from town'. Today that hill is known as Camphill – recalling Blount's encampment – although an adjacent townland called Spital keeps the old name alive. Lying almost directly north of Kinsale, it also sat astride what was then the main road from Cork. As part of the long and arcing Ardmartin Ridge, it also commanded the heights. It was less than a kilometre from the highest navigable point of the Oysterhaven. It was pretty much perfect.

Next night, the English scored an audacious coup. A cavalry officer named Captain William Taffe led a strike force fourteen kilometres through enemy territory to penetrate the Spanish-held promontory of Castle Park and steal hundreds of their cattle. There was 'a hot skirmish', according to Fynes Moryson, but Taffe managed to escape with all but twenty of the animals.

Soon ships from Dublin were regularly towing and warping to the head of the Oysterhaven. Their arrival was a godsend for Blount: at last, he could get his hands on heavy artillery and entrenching equipment.

It was time to begin the massive task of digging trenches and erecting fortifications. For that specialist job, they needed the best military engineer in the country. Fortunately for Blount, he had exactly the right man.

CHAPTER FOURTEEN

Digging for
Victory

NEXT morning, a military specialist named Josiah Bodley stepped
out at Spital Hill with a sense of purpose. His moment had come.
His half-century of life on this planet had been leading up to this point.

Bodley was the country's leading expert on the construction of siege
fortifications. Known as a 'trenchmaster' – an early military engineer – he
was entrusted with the task of transforming Spital camp into an impregnable fortress. It would be the greatest siege engineering construction built in
Ireland up until that point. It had to be big enough to hold thousands of
soldiers. Its walls had to be at least twice as high as a tall man. It had to be
built while bullets and cannonballs flew all around the workers. Then it had
to be rebuilt each morning as sallying Spaniards tore it down by night. It had
to be built by a deadline of yesterday. As for materials, he could utilise only
whatever grew on trees and whatever lay under his feet.

And no better man to do it than Josiah Bodley.

Josiah was the youngest of five sons, and was slightly less famous than the eldest brother, Thomas. Josiah admired what Thomas Bodley did with cataloguing old books, but that academic life wasn't for him. He preferred to be out in the open, in all weathers, pacing with his quadrant, keeping an eye on the enemy guns as he directed the trench diggers. Let Thomas stay in his dusty library at Oxford – the one that would one day bear his surname as the Bodleian Library. Whatever alchemy Thomas worked with books, Josiah would work with soil and clay.

Josiah was Devon-born and well travelled. He had learned his trade in the dirty wars of the Netherlands. Two years ago, at forty-nine, he had been transferred to Ireland, where a single incident earned him a legendary status.

The English couldn't shift Hugh O'Neill's insurgents from a remote island stronghold where they had stashed huge stores of gunpowder. Bodley prepared thirty arrows tipped with 'wild fire', an incendiary substance famous for its rapid spread. As musketeers pinned down the Irish, his skilled archers fired the blazing arrows into the island dwellings. They were soon raging infernos. The insurgents abandoned the island and swam to shore.

That incident faded into insignificance compared to his task in Kinsale, although, later, Fynes Moryson would nonchalantly dismiss Bodley's work in one sentence: 'The camp was round about entrenched, and all those works perfected.' To most people, a trench is just a linear dugout. But at the risk of sounding Tolkienish, this was much more than a hole in the ground. The trenches at Spital were a tribute to human ingenuity – a testimony to what people can achieve under pressure with nothing more than earth, clay, a few branches, and lots and lots of sweat. Josiah Bodley dug holes like Michelangelo painted ceilings.

Nothing remains of Bodley's creation but its new name, Camphill, and some sketches on a map. But those show it to be quite remarkable. The most striking thing is its sheer size. This was a small town, perhaps two-thirds the size of Kinsale itself. Angular bastions protruded from the rectangular walls (the 'curtain') and from each corner to give musketeers a clear line of fire in every direction. It was perfectly symmetrical, and from each corner fluttered the red cross of St George.

How did Bodley's men construct such a sophisticated structure from scratch?

It all began with a sap, or a preliminary trench, dug by specialist workers. These men were known as sappers or pioneers and had one of the dirtiest and most dangerous jobs in the army. They were well paid: one group of troops was given fourpence extra for every day they worked on the fortifications. (Bodley himself was paid ten shillings a day, more than a company captain.) The pay varied according to the danger they faced and the number of men left alive in their unit. 'If there are any killed,' explains an early trenchmaster named John Muller, 'the survivors of the Brigade receive their pay… [in some cases] one or two men have received the pay of twenty-four.'

The key to keeping them alive in the killing fields of no-man's-land was the gabion, an open-ended cylindrical basket woven from willow branches. The most basic version, about as tall as a man, was 'stuffed quite full with all kinds of small wood, or branches', says Muller. Laid flat and rolled, this stuffed gabion was enough to absorb most musket balls at a distance. The workers 'roll [the baskets] before them as they advance', Muller explains.

The pioneers also carried empty gabion baskets. As the first worker began digging, protected by the wood-filled gabion, he would shovel the displaced soil into the empty basket. 'He fills it with earth, giving it every now and again a blow with the spade or mallet to settle the earth,' Muller writes. 'And when this gabion is filled, he advances the stuffed gabion to make room for another … when this gabion is filled, he places another, and so on; then the second sapper fills the interval between the gabions with sandbags.'

These earth-filled baskets were given extra height using rolls of compressed sticks called fascines. (The word shares its origin with fascist, which derives from the fasces or rods carried by Roman magistrates. Personally, I find this connection fascine-ating.)

Fast workers could throw up a solid protective barrier within an hour. Then they could begin digging in earnest. They worked in units of eight, with four digging while the rest fetched tools. The first pioneer would dig a shallow trench about 45cm deep and wide. The man following him made it 15cm deeper and wider. The third and fourth did likewise until the four diggers had created a trench 90cm deep and wide. The four men could keep this up at high speed for two or three hours before swapping roles.

As they dug, they piled the soil into a solid earthbank on the surface, effectively doubling the height of their sanctuary. Other teams worked towards them until their trenches met and connected. 'Work [should] be continued with all possible speed, and without interruption,' dictates Muller.

The finished trench was impressive in its scale. Describing a typical siege-trench twenty-five years later, another military expert named Robert Ward writes that the surface earthwork was 'near ten foot high and fifteen foot thick at the bottom ... there were two footbanks for the musketeers to step upon, to give fire over the breastwork. This breastwork was ... five foot high ... This trench contained in circuit 16,000 paces.' In combination, the dugout and rampart could be two and a half times the height of a tall man, and the floor of the trench wide enough to take a tent.

With plenty of manpower, an ordinary field would be transformed into a labyrinthine earthen fortress in a couple of weeks. And during the three-month siege of Kinsale, several such networks were excavated.

'[The English] pitched their camp and entrenched themselves,' wrote the field surgeon William Farmer. 'They also builded a sconce [a detached out-post] and planted their great ordnance for battery.'

The result mightily impressed the Spanish and Irish in Kinsale. Spanish witnesses said that Bodley's trenches were as high as lances (presumably four metres plus) and ladders were needed to scramble out. When Hugh O'Neill saw the English camp, several weeks later, he was daunted by 'the great strength of the firm, impregnable walls'.

Bodley had done his bit. Now it was time for the gunners to take over.

CHAPTER FIFTEEN

THE TAKING OF
RINJORA CASTLE

A cannonball doth never range in a right line, except it be shot out
of a piece right up towards heaven, or right down towards the
centre of the world.
– *Niccolo Tartaglia*, **A Treatise of Shooting in Guns,** *1537*

IN ANY other circumstances, Ensign Bartholomew Paez Clavijo would
probably have enjoyed his posting in the little fortress the Spanish knew
as Rinjora. Rincorran's setting was idyllic, halfway along a wild headland
with an arrestingly beautiful view over the tide-ripped, wind-scudded waters
of the harbour entrance. To the left lay the open sea, and to the right, around
two kilometres away, the chaotic jumble of streets, rooftops and towers that
made up the town of Kinsale. Across the narrow water, Clavijo could see his
comrades guarding the twin fortress of Castle Park.

But this was no time to admire the scenery. Behind Clavijo, English supply ships were warping up the Oysterhaven with massive guns and crates of cannonballs. In front, along the main harbour entrance, an English pinnace called *The Moon* was preparing to bombard Clavijo's fortress from sea. On the peninsula itself, halfway between Rincorran and the Oysterhaven, two large English cannon were being awkwardly manoeuvred into position. The ensign immediately recognised them as culverins.

Just as the saker cannon was named after a hawk, the culverin was named after a snake – probably because of its ability to strike lethally from a distance. Its long barrel could propel an 18-pound ball accurately over 2,000 paces. The culverin's secret was that it could handle a pound weight of powder for every pound of ball. But this required thickly reinforced metal, which made it exceptionally heavy. Twelve yoked oxen would strain to drag it into position as its wheels sank into the winter mud. Once mounted, however, it was devastatingly effective. By repeatedly striking on a small area of wall, it could quickly open up a breach.

The Norman stronghold of Rincorran was a diamond-shaped stone structure with towers at each corner and three tower-houses inside. Both English and Spanish regarded its possession as vital. As one English official reported in the 1580s, its fate dictated the fate of the entire town. Águila ordered Clavijo to hold it against all attack. He could spare only 150 men, but he had promised to support them from the main town.

Fate had thrust Clavijo into the role of Rincorran's commanding officer when his captain, Pedro de Suazo, fractured his leg. Clavijo was a proud man as well as a brave man, and he intended to do his duty. He just wasn't sure whether everyone else in Rincorran felt quite the same way …

Don Pedro de Heredia, a sergeant in Clavijo's company, was also watching the developments with concern. As a veteran of the war in Flanders, he knew that the number of soldiers in Rincorran – the 150 Spanish augmented by perhaps thirty Irish – was not nearly enough to hold the fort. If Águila were to relieve them, he would have to do it by sea – and that meant running the gauntlet of the English ships.

Dermot MacCarthy, the Irish expatriate the Spanish knew as Don Dermutio, had even more reason to worry. He had spent the past fifteen years abroad working as an agent for the Irish insurgents. Whereas the Spanish defenders could ultimately negotiate terms with the English, the Irish would automatically face execution as traitors. He could not afford to allow himself to be captured.

Rincorran also contained 'a great multitude' of local women, children and menial labourers known as churls. The fate of these innocents could only be guessed.

Inside Kinsale, Águila also watched with mounting unease as the two mighty cannon were assembled. He couldn't afford to lose Rincorran. He resolved to send a seaborne relief force led by a battle-hardened sergeant-major named Juan Hortensio de Contreras. An almost legendary figure, Contreras had led his men to safety through many a tough engagement in Brittany.

As dusk fell, a hand-picked group of Spanish soldiers silently filed down to the quayside. The lashing rain provided cover as they pushed their boats out into the black River Bandon, aiming their prows across the harbour in an all-out bid to relieve their comrades in Rincorran.

On the deck of his pinnace *The Moon*, naval captain Thomas Button was peering into the Stygian blackness. His sailor's eyes could see in the dark better than most people's, and he was determined to thwart any attempt to relieve the castle by sea.

Perhaps it was a simple splash, or a whisper, or a shaft of moonlight that gave the Spanish away. Whatever the clue, Button spotted the relief force halfway across the estuary. His naval musketeers emerged on deck and fired into the night.

Caught in the murderous hail of fire, the Spaniards had no option but to retreat.

The English master gunner, who had the singularly inappropriate name of Mr Jolly, was having a bad day. It was Friday, 30 October, the morning after the failed attempt to relieve the fort. His two culverins had been ready to unleash shock and awe at Rincorran. The touch-holes were lit, the barrels belched fire … but almost immediately there was an embarrassing crunch of splintering wood as one of the carriages collapsed. Soon after, the second gun gave up. The red-faced gunners had to withdraw and call in the repair crews.

Now it was Águila's turn to fire. The Spanish gunners hauled their prize demi-cannon out from the gates and aimed for Blount's camp at Spital. With a barrel more than three metres long, a demi-cannon could miss its target dismally if the gunner didn't take account of the '*vivo*' – the difference in diameter between the breech and the muzzle. It would be ten years before technology solved the problem. But right now, the Spanish had perfected a painstaking technique they called 'killing the *vivo*'. It made their shots unnervingly accurate.

History doesn't record the name of the Spanish gunner. But he must have been a genius. He identified Blount's field headquarters, and hit it almost dead-on. 'All the shots that were made,' marvelled Blount's secretary, Fynes Moryson, 'fell still in the Lord Deputy's quarter, near his own tent.'

Moryson himself narrowly escaped death when a second perfectly aimed lead ball whistled clean through his tent and destroyed the cabin beside it, killing two soldiers. '[It] brake a barrel of the paymaster's money, with two barrels of the Lord Deputy's beer,' the secretary recorded.

By the morning of Saturday, 31 October the English had repaired the first culverin and mounted two other cannon. Soon all three great guns were blasting the brittle masonry of the old Norman castle. But as the gunners sweated over the powder and lead shot, they noticed a stocky figure marching out from the camp towards them.

It was General George Carew, coming to tell them that they were doing it all wrong.

George Carew, President of Munster and effectively Blount's second-in-command, was a brusque and belligerent figure. He hated Ireland, and he hated the Irish. He was convinced that the country was 'full of witches' and that Jesuit priests could conjure up bad weather. Carew longed for the day when he could return to civilisation. As his secretary Thomas Stafford put it, rather breathlessly: 'There was never ... a virgin bride after a lingering and desperate love, more longing for the celebration of her nuptial, than the Lord President was to go for England.'

The forty-six-year-old Devon man was unusual among the English officers in that he was a murderer in the civilian sense as well as a ruthless wartime killer. Eighteen years before, he had been walking the streets of Dublin when he lunged at another man and stabbed him to death. Carew explained that his elder brother, Peter, had been killed in a battle in County Wicklow and that he thought he had recognised his Dublin victim as the man responsible. In fact, the victim had been in the city under an official promise of safe conduct.

Carew was shrewd, determined and pitiless. If he felt an Irish leader posed a threat, he 'drew a draft' on them – his term for ordering their assassination. He had exhaustive files on every major player in Ireland, friend or foe. His military intelligence was fearsome. It wasn't for nothing that he acted as the eyes and ears of Secretary Robert Cecil – the two arch-schemers were moulded from the same material.

He was so prescient that many Irish were convinced George Carew possessed a witchlike 'familiar'. His enemies would whisper: 'They say [Carew] knows all things. Nothing can be hidden from him.' The truth was less glamorous – he had succeeded in compromising many key figures among the Irish insurgents. His double agents were everywhere.

Yes, Carew knew all things. But what he knew particularly well was guns.

—You are aiming too high.

Carew had been a master gunner for years, so he knew what he was talking about. He had been watching as Jolly's team blasted Rincorran, and he wasn't happy.

—Your shots are landing up on the spikes of the castle. And they never land in the same place twice, he told the surprised experts.

The master gunners must have been taken aback. Theirs was an arcane profession. For many years they had been a semi-secret guild, jealously guarding their mysteries. They were not used to being questioned.

—Stand aside, Carew told them. I am taking over.

He grabbed a gunner's quadrant, a specialist instrument that had been invented only a few decades beforehand. Deceptively simple, it consisted of two 60cm wooden rulers joined in an L-shape. It had a plumbline, with a brass gauge to measure its angle of fall. First, Carew checked that the gun was level by putting one arm of the quadrant into the cannon mouth and adjusting the gun's angle until the plumbline fell true.

The next thing (and, knowing Carew's personality, he was probably reciting all this aloud as he worked) was to find the distance to his target. The ingenious procedure involved a gunner's staff – a pole 240cm long, held vertically on the ground. Standing on a step, you set the quadrant on top and adjusted its angle until you could sight the base of the castle along one of its arms. Your assistant ran a thread along the other quadrant arm to the earth, creating a right-angled triangle with the pole, the thread and the small space of ground that separated them. Measure that space. Find its ratio to the length of the pole. Multiply pole length by that same ratio and you had the distance to your target.

The next question: was the target at point-blank, or beyond it? 'Point blank' was a technical term for the gun's effective range when held level. It was the furthest point at which a horizontal cannon, aimed directly at a mark of similar height, would hit it precisely. After that, the impetus faded and gravity took over. Point blank was usually not very far – just 200 paces in the culverin's case. But by tilting the barrel upwards in stages, you could extend its range 180 paces at a time. Eventually, at the maximum of 45 degrees, the range would increase tenfold to 2,000 paces. There were all sorts of mathematical tables to fix the appropriate elevation, but they were seldom accurate.

While concentrating on all this, it was easy to forget that you were in the front line of a war zone. Carew was literally under fire as he worked, and he had a narrow escape as two Spanish musket shots ricocheted off the gunmetal: 'One lighted upon the muzzle of the piece, the other upon the carriage.'

Finally the powder was ladled in and the cannonball rammed home. The gun snorted fire and the iron ball arced through the grey sky. But it rarely hit its mark the first time. 'Every shot will come shorter and shorter, as the gun grows hotter and hotter,' explained one contemporary expert.

When the shot began to land true on the same small area of wall, it was just a matter of pounding away until it yielded. The culverin could shoot eight rounds an hour, with sixty minutes' cooldown every three or four hours. When three guns fired in combination, the barrage never ceased.

Carew had calculated his aim so carefully that he could continue firing accurately, even in pitch-blackness.

For the defenders – and certainly for the helpless civilians and their children – it was a horrific experience. The constant roar of cannon, the crash of splintering masonry, the sprays of earth and the showers of jagged rocks must have been truly terrifying. The onslaught was continuous and relentless: 'without intermission', according to Moryson. Or, as the Irish annalist put it: '[The English] allowed the garrison there neither quiet, rest, sleep nor repose.'

While the cannon continued to bombard the hapless fort, Águila assembled five hundred of his best troops and ordered them to charge directly at the English lines. But this was a feint – the true purpose was to divert attention from the sea, where another force would again attempt to relieve the castle by boat.

The resulting battle of 31 October to 1 November was one of the greatest clashes of English and Spanish forces on Irish soil. In the first phase, two hundred charging Spanish pikemen and musketeers were held back by a hundred English cavalrymen. Thirty English musketeers returned the Spaniards' fire.

The Spanish pikemen charged the cavalry, who held firm and beat them back towards the town walls in the familiar pattern. But Águila had a surprise in store for them – he had dozens of marksmen hidden on the rooftops and turrets. They let loose with withering musket fire on the attackers below, and the encounter deteriorated into a long and bruising brawl. By the time the melee ended, ten Spanish and five English lay dead on the field. Seventy Spaniards were injured, some critically.

At the height of the fighting, the marshal of the English forces, Sir Richard Wingfield, spotted one Spanish officer who had fearlessly led his troops deep into the English lines. He was now surrounded and Wingfield's men were about to kill him.

—Stop! Wingfield shouted. This is a man of some account. We need to take him alive.

They captured the officer and brought him back to camp. He gave his name as Sergeant Major Juan de Contreras – the legendary veteran of Brittany.

Wingfield, who had also served there, kept Contreras as his personal prisoner and formed something of a bond with him.

—You look very sad, Wingfield told him at one stage. Be merry. It is but the fortune of war.

—I have served in the wars since my young days, the veteran replied. And I have never known the Spanish to take such falls at the hands of any nation.

Throughout the entire fray, Captain Thomas Button and his patrol ship *The Moon* had managed to hold back the entire seaborne force as well.

At nightfall on 1 November, Rincorran was still unrelieved.

The culverin 'snake' and the other big guns continued their relentless battering of Rincorran until six that evening. With massive breaches appearing in his walls and no relief in sight, Ensign Clavijo realised that defeat was inevitable.

Just after six, a drum thundered out from Rincorran requesting a parlay. Carew, who was overseeing the attack, ceased fire and waited impatiently as a lone figure walked out of the castle to negotiate. To his surprise, it was not the Spanish commander but an Irishman from nearby Cork.

—We will relinquish the fortress, the Irishman proposed. Simply let us withdraw into Kinsale town with all our arms and equipment.

Carew was contemptuous.

—Send out your commander if you want to talk, he snapped. And my only terms are these: that you yield to Her Majesty's mercy.'

Ever since Smerwick, everyone knew that 'yielding to Her Majesty's mercy' could mean massacre. When they heard Carew's response, a sizeable element of dissident Spanish soldiers – allegedly led by the sergeant Pedro de Heredia – began planning a secret getaway with the Irish volunteers of Don Dermutio MacCarthy.

Unaware of this, Ensign Clavijo sounded another drum for parlay. This time he sent Sergeant Heredia. But once again, Carew refused to talk.

By this time it was pitch black. Another drumbeat rolled across the heath, and as the guns fell silent, a figure emerged from the darkness. This time it was Ensign Clavijo. He made Carew exactly the same offer and was told, once again, to yield to the Queen's mercy.

The parlay ended abruptly and the English stepped up their bombardment. By midnight a serious breach was opening in the wall. This in itself was not a catastrophe: the usual response was to build a 'retirata', a ditch with a new barricade just inside the opening. Protected by this barrier, the defenders could pick off the attackers one by one as they entered the gap.

At 2am, the commander called for another parlay. An increasingly irritated Carew ignored the drum and continued firing.

Behind Clavijo's back, there was a fever of activity. The Irish volunteers had decided to make a run for it. Sergeant Heredia opted to join them, along with some fifty-three Spaniards. At a later inquiry, where he was accused of desertion, he would maintain that he had simply 'issued to make discovery' – presumably to seek out the enemy and engage. Heredia later pointed out that he could easily have scarpered while meeting Carew. '[If] I had any ill intention,' he protested, 'I might [have escaped] the day before.'

Águila didn't buy that argument.

Another Spanish officer, Alférez Bustamante, had no doubts about the motive. He said Rincorran fell purely because Heredia and Don Dermutio abandoned the fort, taking with them eighty Spanish and Irish soldiers.

Whatever their intention, the escapees stole out of the castle in the pre-dawn hours, accompanied by many of the Irish civilians. We can imagine the drama as they crept down towards the rocky shore. The Irish locals peering into the darkness to find landmarks. The terrified mothers, hushing their sobbing children. The Spanish soldiers, lost and bewildered in an alien land. Don Dermutio tense with the knowledge that he was only one step away from the torture-engine.

Few of them made it to safety. An English patrol spotted them and opened fire. They encountered little resistance. 'The enemy shot not a shot,' recalled one English source, 'but as men amazed, lay still.' Within minutes, thirty of the fugitives lay dead and twenty-three more were in captivity. One officer, Captain Roger Harvey, boasted that he personally 'had the killing of ten of them upon the rock'.

With local knowledge, several of the Irish escaped. But Don Dermutio – a most-wanted fugitive, the 'ace of clubs' in the English pack – was seized and marched back to the delighted Carew.

Amid the chaos, Sergeant Heredia managed to slip away and dash across the fields towards freedom. And for a time, it looked as though he might make it.

Back in the English camp, Blount was growing increasingly annoyed with Carew's bull-headed handling of the parlays. A skilled negotiator, the English commander knew it was better to leave some door open rather than back an opponent into a corner.

—It's important that we take this fort speedily, Blount told Carew. We need it to control the harbour before any Spanish reinforcements arrive.

Carew was adamant that the defenders must yield to unspecified 'mercy'.

—It's not just Rincorran, Blount argued back. We will soon be inflicting the same misery on Kinsale. If we are seen to humiliate the defenders of Rincorran, Águila will fight to the last man. No, we will offer to spare their lives and give them safe passage to Spain.

Carew nodded, and trudged back to his cannon. Meantime, Clavijo had independently decided to moderate his demands.

—We will surrender our arms, he told Carew. Just allow us to join our comrades in Kinsale.

Carew did not make the agreed counter-offer. He simply refused. The proud Spanish officer was left struggling for air.

—Then spare my men, he requested. I alone will keep my weapons and march into Kinsale.

Again, Carew refused.

Clavijo had been pushed over the edge.

—Very well, he snapped. I will bury myself in the ruins of Rinjora before I give it up.

He strode back into the castle and informed his few remaining men. But his troops had had enough.

—We want to submit to mercy, one of them retorted.

The others backed him up, but Clavijo would not budge.

—If you don't submit, they yelled, we will throw you out of that gap in the wall.

After hours of tense negotiations, the English and Spanish finally reached a compromise. The defenders would disarm within the castle, proving that they had not abandoned it. Clavijo would keep a symbolic sword by his side as he yielded the castle to Carew.

It was a nerve-racking moment for the Spaniards as Captain Roger Harvey entered Rincorran. Once they were disarmed, they would be vulnerable to another Smerwick-style massacre. However, in this case, the victors kept good faith.

The final haul from Rincorran was eighty-six Spanish prisoners and 'four women' who were distinguished from the 'Irish churls, women and children' who were also taken. Presumably the four were Spanish wives who had sailed to Ireland in the belief that they were founding a peaceful new colony.

After the prisoners had gone, Blount's men pillaged the castle for valuables.

As for Clavijo, Fynes Moryson reported that he wore his sword until the final moment of surrender. But Carew's memoir smugly added another detail: that Clavijo had yielded his sword to Carew 'upon his knees'.

Sergeant Heredia had almost got away. He had dashed across the field towards freedom, but in the pitch-black night had run straight into some English horsemen. He recalled: 'I fled, but the cavalry took me in the field, and brought me prisoner.'

He said Blount and Carew threatened to hang him because he had not been among those who had surrendered. But Blount 'using all clemency and mercy towards me, did me the favour to give me my life'.

Heredia was taken to Cork alongside Don Dermutio. There, their paths diverged. The Spaniard was deported. 'To me, with the rest of the prisoners there, passage was given to France.'

Dermutio, 'because he was a vassal of the Queen', was doomed to be executed. But first he faced the ordeal of interrogation.

After the castle fell, Blount sent a messenger to Águila in Kinsale.

—We have two prisoners you may want to ransom, he said. Ensign Bartholomew Paez de Clavijo, and your sergeant-major, Juan Hortensio de Contreras.

—I will pay a ransom for the sergeant, Águila declared. Because he was taken while fighting.

—And Ensign Clavijo? What shall we do with him?

Blount expected a larger ransom. But he didn't reckon on the 'cold commander'. It was then that Águila gave his notorious response.

—Do whatever you like with him, he replied. But if I had him here I would know what to do with him: hang him.

As for the runaway sergeant Heredia … Águila held him responsible for the loss of Rincorran Castle. Later, back in Spain, he would charge him with desertion. It was a vendetta that Águila would continue right up until his own death – and even beyond.

The Irish insurgent leader Don Dermutio was placed in the tender care of an inquisitor with the wonderfully Hogwartsian name of William Malefant. The English maintained that the resulting confession was 'voluntary', which was perhaps a euphemism for 'signed with no fingernails'. Or perhaps Dermutio thought he could avoid execution. Whatever the reason, he told all. He named all the Irish leaders in Kinsale, and their sympathisers nearby. He divulged the expedition's mission plan, and revealed that its force had been reduced 'by death and sickness'. He told how Hugh O'Neill was due to march south with 10,000 men, and disclosed that Águila hoped to receive 6,000 reinforcements from Spain by Christmas.

After he had been milked dry of information, he was instantly executed.

When George Carew pored over the resulting transcript, one name leaped out at him. It was the name of his great nemesis. If Dermutio was Carew's Ace of Clubs – then his Ace of Spades was the Jesuit priest and political activist Fr James Archer.

CHAPTER SIXTEEN

'THE MOST BLOODY AND TREACHEROUS TRAITOR'

I F THE JESUITS lived up to their description as the Vatican's shock troops, Fr James Archer was one of their top special-ops men. A tall, melancholy figure whose long, solemn face was further elongated by a salt-and-pepper beard, he looked an unlikely Pimpernel – which is probably how he managed to evade capture during his extended secret missions.

One description read: 'Archer the traitor is black of complexion, his hair spotted grey, his apparel commonly a white doublet.' Another said he was 'tall, black, and in visage long and thin'. He was dubbed 'the poison of Ireland' and officials were told: 'To have him taken would be a great service.'

Aged in his early fifties at the time of the invasion, Archer was much more than a humble priest. As an envoy for the Irish insurgent leader Hugh O'Neill, he had ready access to King Felipe of Spain and the Archduke of Austria as well as the Vatican's top diplomats. The English regarded him as 'a principal plotter to draw [the Spanish] into Ireland' – and he would have taken that as a compliment.

What made him particularly dangerous was that he posed a threat to the life of *La Inglesa*, the English Queen. Nine years beforehand, Archer had allegedly asked a sympathiser to find him an assassin – a 'tall soldier, an Irishman' – who would be willing to kill Queen Elizabeth. Archer explained that it would be 'a most godly act'. He offered 2,000 crowns, a pension, and eternal salvation.

A Tipperary man named Hugh Cahill volunteered for the contract.

—Go to London and buy a horse, Cahill was instructed. When *La Inglesa* rides out to take the air, set spurs to your horse and strike your sword at her head.

Failing that, Cahill should wait at a palace door and 'thrust a dagger or a strong knife into her body'. Cahill went to London all right, but instead went straight to the authorities and confessed everything.

Whatever truth lay behind this story, it was enough to elevate Archer to the 'most wanted' list. Every English reference to Archer burns with genuine loathing. 'Detestable' is a typical description. 'The most bloody and treacherous traitor,' says another. His power was said to be 'absolute'. The greatest Lords held him in awe. 'None dare gainsay him.'

Archer would sail into Ireland incognito and live undercover for months at a time. His religious role was to promote the faith, but he affected a military air and sometimes crossed the line between pastor and soldier.

He could slip into any identity with ease. He sometimes posed as 'a courtier, and other times like a farmer', wrote his exasperated pursuers. Often he would sleep in ditches and cattle sheds, at other times in grand castles. He was present for the Irish insurgents' victory at the Yellow Ford, where he wrote: 'The English Government hates me very much … [and has] set a price on my head. This forces me to live in the woods and in hiding places … there are spies in every port on the lookout for me.'

His narrow escapes were so incredible – once he even escaped from under lock and key in a London jail – that his hunters felt he must have used witchcraft. 'They believed him able to walk dry-footed over the sea; to fly through the air; and to possess other superhuman power,' wrote the Irish historian Philip O'Sullivan.

All nonsense, obviously. What Archer did possess was a sharp intelligence, limitless energy, and access to the Jesuits' network of highly placed secret sympathisers. He was also – like his great rival Juan del Águila – a man born without fear.

Let's picture Archer in Kinsale on Sunday, 15 November – a tall, soldierly man in black, striding quickly and purposefully through the rubble-strewn mediaeval streets. Perhaps he is dressed as an English sketch artist depicted him. If so, he cuts a dashing figure in a long black cloak which swirls around his hurrying frame. His collar is a ring of fur, and his unruly hair is half-hidden by a tall white hat which he clutches against the wind and rain. His eyes are large, dark and watchful, his face grim.

He is rushing to Águila's house to put forward another plan. Fr James Archer is never short of plans – but, since they usually involve the transfer of military power to Fr James Archer, the Spanish commander usually gives him short shrift.

Today, the town is abuzz with news. Six Irish clan leaders have ridden into town, offering to support the rebellion. Archer is convinced his moment has come. He confronts Águila in his new quarters, a private house formerly occupied by a Kinsale man named Philip Roche.

—If I join these men and travel throughout the countryside, Archer says eagerly, I can convince the entire nation to join our cause.

He might even meet Hugh O'Neill and persuade him to hurry to Kinsale.

Águila must have sighed inwardly. He remembered the last time a disenchanted cleric left a beleaguered fort to travel up-country to enlist help from a nearby insurgent army. Instead, the cleric convinced the insurgents that the commander was incompetent and that they should stay well away. The outcome was massacre. The cleric in that case was Mateo de Oviedo. The fort was Smerwick.

So once again, Águila refused permission. And once again, Fr Archer fumed silently and scribbled in his journal, waiting for his day of retribution.

If truth be told, Águila was rapidly losing patience with Hugh O'Neill after fifty days. He had sent several messengers to the northern insurgent chieftain, but to no avail.

Águila still didn't know whom he could trust. A few days earlier there had been a stir in Kinsale when a man crept to the town walls on his hands and knees. He claimed to be a priest with a letter from O'Neill. He was escorted to Águila, who read O'Neill's prevarications and lost patience. His reply to the northern leader took a tough line.

—You must come immediately with all the forces you can gather, he told O'Neill. If you delay any longer, I will withdraw my forces.

The priest nodded and conveyed the reply … not to O'Neill, but to Charles Blount. He was a genuine messenger from O'Neill, but he had been turned and was now Blount's double agent.

The English officers took some black humour out of the Spaniards' threat to withdraw.

—I believe them, one officer laughed. They would withdraw in a heartbeat … if they only could.

Dealing with Águila always left Fr Archer furious. But then, anger was not a feeling that was unfamiliar to him. As an evangelist, he had always worked at the rough end of muscular Christianity. He deliberately chose the tough-est targets to convert – Protestant sea-merchants at the Galician docks, or stubborn Scotsmen in the north of Ireland. Once he had tried to convince a soldier to stop his 'evil-doing'. When words weren't enough, Archer flew into a rage and used blows – unfortunately in this case the priestly attacker came off worst and was badly beaten up.

This was a strange vocation for a man who had been born into a staid establishment family of Kilkenny lawyers. According to one source he was 'altogether Englished'. He once wrote that the Irish were 'an uncultivated and barbarous people'.

After attending a Continental seminary, he became a Jesuit novice. The Jesuits were extremely good at reading character. They observed that at times Archer would be 'melancholic' and at other times 'choleric' – hot tempered and irascible. Today, these opposing traits might prompt a psychologist to think of two other words: bipolar disorder.

The low cycle of this disorder is marked by a debilitating depression – the Jesuits' 'melancholia'. But far from enjoying untroubled good cheer in the high cycle, sufferers often become impatient, irritable and irascible. They can develop what leading psychiatrist and author Kay Jamison describes as 'an inflated self-esteem, as well as a certainty of conviction about the correctness and importance of their ideas'. Sufferers sometimes believe they are mes-siah figures. Tellingly, Archer compared himself to a Biblical patriarch who would lead his people out of bondage. During his sermons, he was 'calling the Queen King Pharaoh, the rebels the afflicted Israelites, and to himself arrogates the name of Moses'.

But, of course, in relation to Fr Archer the bipolar theory is pure specula-tion. As a military chaplain, Fr Archer was undeniably a brave and resource-ful man who chose to work undercover in Ireland knowing full well the horrific torture he would face if captured.

However, his zeal sometimes put his own flock in danger. Officially, Jesu-its were not supposed to become involved in politics. When radical priests

like Fr Archer worked to overturn the regime, it stoked up Protestant paranoia and resulted in an increase in persecution. Ordinary worshippers asked
Archer to stay away from their areas – even his suspected presence gave them
a hard time. Less radical Jesuit priests complained: '[He has] made us all be
called seditious men.'

The manhunt for Archer was intensive, but somehow the English could
never manage to run this 'detestable enemy' to ground.

Until now. Now they had him pinned down within the besieged town
of Kinsale.

It was only a matter of time before James Archer fell into their hands. And
George Carew, for one, just could not wait.

CHAPTER SEVENTEEN

There Will Be No Retreat

ARLY in November Águila posted a notice on every gate in Kinsale: No soldier shall leave his allotted position unless he is ordered to do so by an officer. Even if that soldier's firearm is broken and he is left with only his sword, he will remain in place and defend his position.

The proud Spanish troops muttered bitterly at the new hardline policy, with its implicit accusation of weakness. However, there had been a series of damaging routs. The latest had left twenty-one Spaniards dead.

The English army had been weakened by the temporary departure north of some two thousand troops. Seizing his opportunity, Águila had mustered hundreds of his best men for an attack. A decoy unit of sixty troops marched to Spital Hill to draw out the English troops. If that ruse succeeded, seven hundred hidden Spaniards would emerge from the trenches to crush them. However, Blount had anticipated the stratagem. He sent a small force to fight the decoys, but posted his main force to the side, towards Rincorran, where they could fire directly into the Spanish trenches.

Caught in withering flanking fire, the main force scrambled out of the trenches and retreated into the town. The decoys were left isolated. They retreated towards the expected safety of the trenches, only to find them occupied by English troops. Fierce fighting left a score of Spanish dead before the decoy unit made it back into Kinsale, pursued right to the walls by the English. 'We beat them from one trench to another,' Blount later recalled, ''til I had much ado to make our soldiers come off.'

Águila was incensed. He singled out the trench commanding officer and threatened to behead him. Then he delivered a blistering address to his men.

—Shame upon your cowardice! he shouted. The only valour I saw today was displayed by the English. In my time, the Spanish army was the terror of all nations. You have tossed that reputation away.

He turned on his heel and stalked off. The next day, the 'no retreat' order was posted.

Every single one of these encounters was reducing Águila's force. He had lost 108 men in the battle for Rincorran. Now he had lost another twenty-one, including one of his most popular captains. He could not sustain that haemorrhage for much longer. Morale, too, was suffering. The death of the captain had sent his men into despair. From the English camp, Fynes Moryson could hear the 'very great moan' of the grieving Spanish.

A couple of days later, Águila scored some revenge when his master gunner came close to killing Blount … a second time.

The English commander was in chipper form. He was suddenly awash with reinforcements. At the harbour mouth, a fleet of warships had appeared. They were led by *The Warspite*, under Admiral Sir Richard Leveson, and *The Garland*, under his deputy, Sir Amias Preston. The ships were carrying two thousand fresh troops from Rochester, together with guns, ammunition and skilled workers.

The Spanish were in big trouble, and Blount wanted to rub their noses in it. Amid 'thundering peals' of cannon, he mounted his charger and led his reinforcements close to Kinsale 'for the greater terror of the Spaniards'.

The terror, however, was all Blount's. Águila's expert gunner lined him up in his sights as he rode past. Rapidly calculating the *vivo* to ensure a precise aim, he let fly. It was an almost perfect shot. Blount's charger reared as the ball landed right beside him, scattering him with dirt. '[The shot] grazed so near him,' reported Fynes Moryson, 'that it did beat the earth in his face.'

Águila's minor triumph was short-lived. The 2,000 fresh English troops were soon joined by another 1,000 foot soldiers and 140 cavalry. Then, on 16 November, another 1,100 troops arrived under the command of a pro-queen Irish general named Donough O'Brien.

Donough O'Brien, the Earl of Thomond, was living testimony to the fact that this was not simply a war of English against Irish. The cliché that a civil war sets brother against brother was literally true in O'Brien's case. His own brother had joined the insurgents. Another brother had been held prisoner by Hugh O'Donnell. But while O'Brien detested Hugh O'Donnell, he bore a particular grudge against Fr James Archer. He still carried a scar on his back – the legacy of a deep pike wound for which he held the priest directly responsible.

O'Brien and Carew had met a supposedly neutral Irish clan leader for a parlay when Archer had appeared without warning, shrouded in a long, black cloak. An argument erupted and Archer raised his stick. Taking this as a signal, the Irish troops moved in to attack. The two English generals managed to escape, but a pike gouged five centimetres of flesh out of O'Brien's back. 'This treachery,' he maintained, 'was contrived by that villain Archer.'

O'Brien should have arrived in Kinsale weeks ago, but he had been held back by contrary winds. Then, when the wind shifted, it blew him right past

Kinsale and further west. By that stage, his troops were in terrible shape. Blount took one look at the emaciated and wraithlike figures, and realised that they wouldn't last for an hour on the wind-blasted hillside of Spital. 'Most of them would have died before they could have made cabins,' he reported.

Blount sent most of them away to recuperate. Even so, 'they began to die in great numbers that night'.

Overall, though, Blount was in much better shape with around 9,700 infantry and 575 cavalry at his disposal. He immediately organised a 1000-strong flying column under an officer named Sir Henry Power. His men were excused all guard duty and kept on the alert for emergencies.

Now, Blount's next challenge was to capture the second fortress at Castle Park. 'God be thanked, we had plucked 150 Spaniards by the ears out of Rincorran,' he wrote with satisfaction.

And when he found out how small a force Águila had left to guard Castle Park, he almost laughed aloud. Compared to Rincorran, this job should be, almost literally, a walk in the park.

CHAPTER EIGHTEEN

COLD AS STONE, DARK AS PITCH

THIRTY-three men and a boy. That was the total force charged with the defence of Castle Park. It seemed a pushover for Blount with his new guns and his thousands of fresh troops; so much so that he decided to postpone the attack until 17 November, Coronation Day, and present his victory, neatly wrapped, as a gift to Her Majesty on her anniversary.

It was a rare misjudgement for a man who had served on the Continent, and who already knew how doggedly the Spanish could fight when their backs were to the wall. But then, no one could have foreseen the determination and sheer heroism that spurred less than three dozen defenders to keep Blount's 10,000-strong army at bay for four full days, against near-impossible odds.

Despite its grand title, 'Castle' Park was quite a compact building: Carew called it 'a small fort, well ramped with a stone wall of sixteen foot high'. Roughly square in shape, it had two tall towers with battlements from which defenders could 'shower the fort' with gunfire. The outer corners of the fortress had the usual arrow-shaped bastions. Beyond the main fort was an external defensive ring with a gate lodge providing the only entrance.

The English decided to soften up the defenders with a barrage from sea, but a howling storm blew the cannonballs off course. All the gunners managed to do was clip the tops of the high turrets.

Blount was determined to have the fort in English hands by nightfall on Coronation Day, so when the storm finally eased he despatched Josiah Bodley with four hundred infantry to hack a breach though the wall with pickaxes. To protect them he employed a curious mediaeval device known as a siege engine. Nicknamed 'the sow', this was a portable house designed to protect workmen from attack from above as they slowly chipped their way through a castle wall.

Picture a sort of hefty caravan, a wooden hut on wheels. Its roof is made of stout beams protected against fire – the main risk – by metal and calfskin. It is ridiculously heavy. It needs to be hauled by oxen, or by men inside using crowbars to crank the wheels around. Once at the wall, a 'penthouse roof' jutting forward from the main structure protects the pickaxe men as they undermine the stonework. Combined with the leather cladding, this snout-like projection gives the engine the appearance of a pig – hence the nickname. (It wasn't the only nickname. Some maintain that 'humpty dumpty' was slang for a siege engine, inspiring the famous nursery rhyme.)

The sergeant commanding Castle Park didn't panic as the sow lumbered towards the wall. It was an unsophisticated device, and the defence was equally crude – you bombed it with heavy objects. Recently, in Sligo, a clever defender had rigged up a device rather like a modern pile-driver, using a heavy timber pole.

The Castle Park defenders had already assembled 'a store of very great stones'. Heaving the giant boulders over the battlements, they heard the satisfying sound of splintering timber and the muffled yells and curses of their enemies. Inside the sow, there was consternation. Slowly and steadily, their defensive roof was being smashed to matchwood. This was not supposed to happen – not on the Queen's Coronation Day. More boulders fell. More timber splintered. And then, as the roof gave way completely, the rocks were crashing down on human skulls. Two men lay dead before the attackers decided enough was enough.

They scrambled out of the sow and ran for their lives. To the watching garrison, the exodus resembled a real mother-pig giving birth to piglets. When exactly the same thing happened at a siege in Scotland, the defenders yelled triumphantly: 'The English sow has farrowed.'

The attackers had outnumbered the defenders by around twelve to one – and yet the victory on Coronation Day had gone to the thirty-three men and a boy.

The defenders of Castle Park did not have time to rest on their laurels after their victory. On 19 November, they watched with trepidation as a new demi-cannon was hauled into position on the opposite shoreline. All that day, the sergeant had his work cut out as the cannon hurled fire and iron, smashing its way through the stonework. As soon as the defenders threw up emergency *retirata* barricades at one gap, the cannon would shift aim and open up another breach. And even as they toiled to repair one wall, the same masonry would explode in a shower of spearlike splinters. Before the long day was over, several of the defenders lay dead.

After night fell, Águila made a desperate bid to relieve Castle Park by sea. But it was just Rincorran all over again – the English navy was waiting and the Spanish were easy targets in their open boats.

The grey, wet dawn of 20 November revealed an even more dispiriting sight for the sergeant and his weary band. During the night, the English had mounted a second cannon. In combination, the two guns unleashed a remorseless assault. The ships in the harbour joined in. From the main gate of Kinsale, the Spanish responded with a hail of fire. The ships wisely withdrew behind a hill.

The hellish bombardment continued. A breach opened in the wall. But when a hundred English infantry stormed forward to enter the gap (outnumbering the defenders by at least five to one) they found that the sergeant's men had already sealed it up.

However, the attack was the final straw for the sergeant. Half his tiny force lay dead, and the survivors were wounded and exhausted after four days without sleep. The fort would inevitably fall that day, and he felt it pointless to sacrifice sixteen brave men to a lost cause. He hung out a sign for parlay. Unlike the haughty Bartholomew de Clavijo at Rincorran, his terms were realistic.

—We will yield ourselves and the castle, he offered, on the promise of our lives only.

Blount agreed.

History does not reveal whether there was applause, or even a respectful silence, from the English forces as the sixteen pale and bloodied defenders filed out of the castle to join the other prisoners of war in Cork. Only the commanding sergeant was kept aside. He joined Ensign Clavijo of Rincorran and Wingfield's valiant captive, the legendary sergeant major Juan de Contreras, as the English officers' guests of honour.

The seventeen Spaniards who died at Castle Park were interred in alien earth – in soil that was granite-hard with frost. Buried beside them, in their unmarked grave, was the boy.

Winter had set in with a vengeance, and it dealt out death to both sides without fear or favour. The lashing rains and ice-cold winds were joined by a bitter frost that clamped down over the countryside at nightfall and chilled the soldiers to the bone. Each evening the frost stole silently in, and each morning, more stiff corpses were taken out. The ground itself became yet another hazard – hills were turned into treacherous ice-slopes, and even the churned-up mud froze into ridges as sharp as steel blades. Sentries died at their posts, and those who survived became more wraithlike each day, their eyes hollow from lack of sleep and their beards white with hoarfrost.

Just a few days beforehand, Blount's war council had decided to use the Irish weather as a weapon against the Spanish. By blowing the roofs off their houses with artillery, they believed they would 'expose them to the same extremities of cold and rain as we were exposed to in the camp'.

Yet it was the besiegers who were suffering most from the weather. Their hillside camp could not have been more exposed to the elements. Hypothermia was killing more English soldiers than Águila could ever manage – one observer calculated that they were dying from exposure at the rate of forty a day. 'The difficulties of a winter's siege … will soon waste a greater army than ours,' Blount wrote to Cecil in mid-November. 'For the weather is so extreme, that many times we bring our sentinels dead from the stations.'

His men were fading away to the point where they looked like ghosts: 'I protest, even our chief commanders … do many of them look like spirits with toil and watching.'

The Irish soldiers in Blount's army were expert at improvising shelters from earth-sods and branches. At the most basic level, their heavy cloaks could be transformed into makeshift tents. They were natural survivalists. Blount's conscripts, on the other hand, were usually townsfolk who had never camped in woodland or trekked across mountains after cattle herds. Blount complained that they would rather die than build huts for themselves.

Sometimes the Irish built shelters for their English comrades, but often they would be left to sleep in the open, or to huddle in the flooded trenches. 'Our approaches this winter were so difficult, that the very trenches we made were continually filled with water,' Blount wrote, 'and the decay of our men was so great, by continual labour, sickness, sword and bullet.'

The weather also took its toll on Blount, who was getting as little sleep as his men. 'It groweth now about four o'clock in the morning,' he wrote to

Secretary Cecil, 'at which time I nightly choose to visit our guards myself ... in a morning as cold as stone, and as dark as pitch. I pray, Sir, think whether this is a life that I take much delight in.'

He confessed that he missed his life in England and missed being in the company of the Queen. However, Robert Cecil knew better. He knew that when Blount finally fell asleep in his 'house of turf' he would not be dreaming about a sixty-eight-year-old monarch with dyed hair and ghoulishly white skin. More likely, he would be dreaming of a younger woman with golden hair and eyes as black as the night. He would dream that he was back in the warm, scented arms of Lady Penelope Rich.

CHAPTER NINETEEN

Stella and the Centaur

T HERE had been another reason why Blount wanted to capture
Castle Park fortress on Coronation Day – a reason he could never
have admitted to the Queen.

The victory, had it happened, would have been his secret anniversary gift
to Penelope. All couples have their special days, and 17 November belonged
to Charles Blount and Penelope Rich. It was the date when he had first
publicly declared his love for her. He had done it in chivalrous style, like
some Lancelot pledging his troth to the married Guinevere. Neither of
them would ever forget the moment eleven years ago when he had galloped
out into the jousting arena, visor lowered, lance levelled, boldly carrying the
colours of a lady who belonged to another man.

The date: 17 November 1590. The royal court had been in full festival
mood to celebrate the anniversary of Queen Elizabeth's accession. Charles
Blount was now aged twenty-seven. He had overcome his early gauche-
ness and had matured into a self-assured courtier. Coronation Day featured

a mediaeval jousting competition, a colourful Arthurian extravaganza in which courtly knights championed a lady and carried her colours as they tilted lances against an opponent. Everyone watched eagerly to see whose colours would be carried by the single and highly eligible Sir Charles Blount.

Blount was an adept jouster. 'As centaurs were … so he seemed on the horse,' remarked one observer. As he donned the armour bearing his family crest – a sun containing a watchful eye – he scanned the ranks of ladies in the arena and viewing-rooms, looking for one particular face. Her golden hair and jet-black eyes would be unmistakeable.

When his charger thundered into the daylight to the jousting beam, a collective frisson swept through the ladies in the crowd: He is carrying the colours of my Lady Rich, they whispered in scandalised delight.

It was true. Blount's colours of blue and gold proclaimed his love for Lady Penelope Rich, the twenty-seven-year-old trophy wife of one of the wealthiest barons in England.

One fashionable poet was beside himself with excitement. He punned that Blount was 'Rich in his colours, richer in his thoughts/ Rich in his fortune, honour, arms and art.' It was not the first time that a poet had used the same wordplay on Penelope's married surname. The chivalrous soldier-poet Sir Philip Sidney, who was once equally besotted with Lady Rich, had penned a sonnet praising a nymph who was 'rich in all beauties' but who 'hath no misfortune but that Rich she is'.

This remarkable woman, who had enthralled so many men, was born as Penelope Devereux, eldest daughter of Walter, Earl of Essex, sometime around 1563. She is better known to history by her married name, but in the world of literature she had already been immortalised as 'Stella'.

As the great muse of Philip Sidney's life, she inspired his long sonnet cycle 'Astrophil and Stella', a thinly disguised account of his doomed and painful passion for her. No one knows whether their relationship was ever consummated, but to the heartbroken Sidney it seems to have taken a disturbingly masochistic twist. He wrote the poem, he says, in order 'that the dear She might take some pleasure from my pain'. Penelope was 'most fair' but also 'most cold'. Trying to win her heart was like storming a citadel, 'so fortified with wit, stored with disdain, that to win it is all the skill and pain'.

(Curiously, another poet was later to use much the same words about Penelope Rich. Dedicating a poem to her in 1594, the eccentric poet Richard Barnfield described her as a woman 'whose speech is able to enchant the wise, converting joy to pain, and pain to pleasure', which, it must be said, are extremely odd words to use in a dedication.)

Penelope had first met Philip Sidney when she was in her early teens and he was twenty-two. They were engaged to be married. Sidney was lukewarm at first, but as Penelope grew into adulthood he fell hopelessly in love with the stunning beauty whose coal-black eyes were set in a skin white as 'alabaster pure'.

It was too late. Her father had died, and her guardian nominated the wealthy landlord Robert Rich instead.

Rich appears to have been a dour and antisocial individual, and the gregarious Penelope objected strenuously. Blount was later to claim that she interrupted the actual wedding ceremony with a loud declaration of protest.

There is no evidence that she retained Sidney as a lover, but if his poem reflects real life, she definitely kept him hanging on. Resisting his advances, the married Stella assures her suitor that only 'tyrant honour' stops her from succumbing. Eventually the poet gave up. He later married Frances Walsingham, daughter of the famous spymaster, Francis.

Sidney had been wasting his time with Lady Rich (at least romantically, if not poetically). Penelope had already found the true love of her life in Charles Blount. As a close friend of Penelope's brother Robert (the new Earl of Essex), Blount was a regular visitor to her family home.

Sir Charles Blount would have cut a dashing figure at this stage. As an army captain, he had been wounded in the Low Countries. He had been present when Sidney died from an infected wound near Zutphen. When the Great Armada threatened England, Blount had been in the centre of action aboard the fighting ship *Rainbow* at Gravelines. Well-read, well-travelled, well-dressed and well-connected, Blount was in every way the opposite of Penelope's boorish husband, Robert Rich.

No one knows how early their love affair began. If it pre-dated her marriage, they must both have been very young at the time. One seventeenth-century writer recorded that the 'gallant' Blount fell headlong for Penelope's 'graces of beauty, wit and sweetness of behaviour, which might render her the absolute mistress of all eyes and hearts'. The source claimed the couple became secretly betrothed before the forced marriage wrecked their plans. Or at least delayed them for a while.

As the same writer reported: 'Long had she not lived in the bed of Rich, than the old flames of her affection unto Blount again began to kindle in her.' He said that their secret meetings soon became dishonourably 'familiar'. The dalliance became a full-scale love affair by, at the latest, 1591, when their first daughter, Penelope, was conceived. Five other children – four of whom survived infancy – were to follow in this 'parallel family'. Meanwhile, in her other maternal role, the busy Penelope had borne five children with her husband, Robert Rich. One died as an infant. In total she was to give birth to eleven babies, raising five surviving children by Blount and four by Rich.

Shortly after her first child with Blount, Penelope had a crisis of conscience. She secretly met an undercover Jesuit priest and announced she wished to end her 'life of frivolity' by converting to Catholicism. The priest was preparing her for her first Confession when Blount 'rushed down to see her and began to talk her out of her resolve'. Blount was an expert in theology and a convert from Catholicism, but of course he had another agenda. As the priest said: '[He] loved her with a deep and enduring love.'

Love won, and the priest lost his convert.

Blount became the new Lord Mountjoy after the death of his elder brother. The Queen lavished him with lucrative positions, partly because she wanted to keep him close to her at court. However, Blount was born to be a soldier. He quietly disobeyed, slipping away from London to fight in Brittany, where Juan del Águila and his Spaniards were causing such a head-ache to the English. Elizabeth testily summoned him back home, saying she didn't want him to end up dead like Sidney. 'You shall go where I send you,' she commanded. 'Lodge in court where you may follow your books, read, and discourse of war.'

That had been the Queen's plan for Blount. But as Penelope and Charles knew all too well, life does not always work out the way you plan it.

CHAPTER TWENTY

THAT WONDROUS
WINTER MARCH

NO, life doesn't always go as you planned, as George Carew was discovering. Marching on tortuous mud tracks through impenetrable forests as he tried to track an elusive and unseen enemy, the English general must have felt he was truly entering the heart of darkness.

At every hamlet, suspicious and hostile eyes stared out at him from behind long flops of hair – the traditional Gaelic fashion that hid the face in a discomfitingly similar way to a mask. Each sight of a hooded figure in some dank, dripping woodland track could make a man clutch his sword for fear of an ambush. Those old women grinding corn and muttering to each other – were they villagers conversing in Irish, or hags casting some witch-like spell?

Carew did not enjoy this sort of war – the long, wearying march through ambiguous territories, trying to pin down an enemy who was as hard to capture as a will-o'-the-wisp. He would have been quite happy to have stayed in the camp, supervising artillery by day and dictating his memoirs by night over a cordial glass of claret. He was most at home in the murky world of espionage and dirty tricks. He had left his comfort zone a long way behind as he trekked north into the deep, unfathomable heartland of middle Ireland.

Maybe that was why Blount had sent him on this mission.

In early November, a council of war at Kinsale camp had decided to despatch Carew with around 2,500 men to intercept the Irish insurgent army. Blount believed that Hugh O'Neill was already on the march south and that he would reach Kinsale within a few days. (In reality, when Carew set off on 7 November, O'Neill was still at home.)

Carew was joined on the way by a contingent of Irish troops from the Dublin area. They were commanded by Sir Christopher St Lawrence, a Howth nobleman from an ancient Norman-Irish family. St Lawrence had been kidnapped as a child by the legendary pirate queen Grace O'Malley. He later served under Essex in Ireland, and was notorious for hot-headedly offering to kill Lord Grey – the butcher of Smerwick – after he offended Essex by riding past him without saluting.

With these reinforcements, Carew's intercepting army totalled an impressive 4,500 infantry and 500 cavalry, easily outnumbering any force O'Neill could assemble at the time.

As he continued his march into the dark core of the heavily forested countryside, Carew became increasingly uneasy. He was spooked by the silent hostility, and convinced that his retreat route could be cut off. He believed – wrongly as it turned out – that he was about to meet an insurgent force of 6,000. Blount constantly had to talk him down. 'In good faith, my Lord,' he wrote to Carew on 15 November, '… they are not yet above 1,300 fighting men … their whole number will not exceed 3,000.' He advised Carew that the insurgent force would not meet him in battle, but instead would try 'to steal by you'.

In one letter, Carew hinted that he should return to Kinsale, let the insurgents follow, and do the fighting there. Blount refused – Carew's very presence showed the Irish that they meant business. 'Therefore, although … I desire your presence, I fear I shall not enjoy it as soon as I covet,' he wrote. Reading between the lines, you get a feeling that Blount was actually relishing his rival's discomfiture.

After a 'long and weary march', Carew's force reached Ardmayle, near Cashel in Tipperary. It was at this point that real life made one of its frustrating departures from the script. Carew discovered that he would not be encountering O'Neill after all. The chieftain he would be meeting – or, more accurately, not meeting – was Red Hugh O'Donnell.

When he had heard of the Spanish landing, Red Hugh had been 'full of satisfaction and joy'. According to his seventeenth-century biographer, Lughaidh O'Cleary, he was so confident of the success of the invasion that he had no hesitation in leaving his Donegal homeland to march south. He was certain he could reclaim it later.

He and his allies assembled their three thousand troops in Ballymote, County Sligo, on 22 October. Marching south, he crossed the Shannon near Athlone, where he was joined by the mercenary forces of Richard Tyrrell, an insurgent captain paid by the Spanish. Tyrrell had been promised that, after victory, he would rule large swathes of the midlands.

O'Donnell's march south has become the stuff of legend. In the popular imagination, he storms south from the outset at a cracking pace, crossing 'many a river bridged with ice' and 'past quaking fen and precipice' to reach his allies. It's hard to know how this perception arose, since his biographer, O'Cleary, makes it clear that he proceeded 'by very slow marches', taking time to plunder Irish-owned territories on the way. One region was 'plundered and spoiled entirely' and left under 'a heavy cloud of fire'. He paused for quite some time in north Tipperary, 'searching and seeking, plundering and exploring' throughout mid-November before arriving at Holycross, south of Thurles. It was easy plunder at the time – but his men were later to pay a high price for it on their way home.

O'Donnell wasn't fazed when he heard that Carew's army was blocking his way. 'Neither fear nor dread nor death-shiver seized him,' Lughaidh O'Cleary recorded colourfully.

Red Hugh had encamped only eight kilometres away from the English. He had scattered his troops over a wide range of woodland – some of his camps were seven kilometres apart – and had burrowed deep into the densest thickets. According to Carew, they were camped 'in a strong fastness of bog and wood' with all approaches plashed – sealed with interwoven branches. But fortunately for Carew, he did not have to ferret O'Donnell out of his forest bolthole. His job was merely to stop him joining the Spaniards … and Carew's armies were blocking the only routes southward. 'He blocked up the passes and narrow roads,' wrote Philip O'Sullivan. True, there was another route which led west across the boggy Slievefelim mountains to Limerick. However, the torrential rains had turned the mountain pass into a quagmire. Some light-footed troops might be able to flounder through the muck, but the main army with its heavy equipment would become bogged down within minutes. It wasn't even an option.

Yet again – as so often in this saga – the gods of weather had other ideas. The same Siberian frost that had gripped Kinsale hit Slievefelim with a vengeance, freezing the quagmires into concrete and transforming the squelching goat-tracks into serviceable pathways.

Red Hugh saw his chance and didn't waste a moment. Assembling his troops in the dead of night, he silently stole out of the woods and into the mountains. It was in these circumstances that the tough Irish rural guerrillas showed their superiority over the English. They slogged uphill without a pause, jettisoning heavy baggage if it threatened to slow them down. Eager hands coaxed and pushed the beasts of burden up impossible slopes, through the freezing peaks and down the other side to safety. 'He marched on due west … [and then] south-eastwards, day and night, without stop or halt,' reported O'Cleary.

By 11am on 22 November, Red Hugh's force was nearly seventy kilometres away, at Croom in Limerick – an astonishing march for infantry alone, but an almost unbelievable achievement for a column burdened down with equipment.

Carew was dismayed. For once, his intelligence had let him down. He force-marched his men forty kilometres to intercept the Irish at a likely point, only to find that Red Hugh had already passed and was more than twenty kilometres further on. Highly embarrassed, he had no choice but to praise his enemy's achievement. It was 'the greatest march with carriage … that hath been heard of', he said in grudging admiration. 'This long march is incredible, but upon my reputation … it is true.'

Red Hugh allowed his men just one night's sleep before resuming his march. As he waited for O'Neill to join him, he headed southwest to friendly territory to recuperate and gather support. Meanwhile, Carew's weary troops began their sad footslog back to Kinsale. On the way, however, they met a man whose irrepressible energy and enthusiasm could only boost their spirits. He was a remarkable soldier-poet who was destined to play a decisive role in the battle to come.

His name was Richard de Burgh.

'Gaillimh abú!'

The rolling Irish warcry greeted Carew's despondent troops as they trudged back across the border into County Cork. Carew's men must have gripped their pikes and firearms, convinced that they were about to be attacked by O'Neill's insurgents.

Every fighting clan in Ireland had its warcry – it usually consisted of the name or area followed by the word '*abú*' or 'victory'. It was howled not in unison but in a rolling, shuddering Mexican wave of sound. This unearthly human baying would always spook the English troops – and '*abú*' was turned into a new English word for clamour: 'hubbub'.

But for now, Carew's men could relax. The Galwaymen who faced them on the road to Kinsale were pro-Queen Irish, led by the twenty-eight-year-old Richard de Burgh, the new Earl of Clanrickard.

De Burgh thundered up on his stallion and saluted Carew. He explained that he was en route from Galway to Kinsale with fifty cavalry and 150 infantry in response to Blount's summons.

The clichéd description 'dashing young cavalry officer' could have been coined especially for Richard de Burgh. Fearless and impulsive, he was one of the rising stars of the Queen's forces in Ireland. He was good-looking, personally charming, and a popular figure at the London court, where he had already become a firm favourite of Elizabeth. In both looks and attitude, he reminded the ageing monarch of a younger – but more biddable – version of her beloved Earl of Essex.

The resemblance had also been noticed by another woman – Frances Walsingham, the beautiful daughter of Elizabeth's spymaster Francis Walsingham. As the widow of poet Philip Sidney, she had married the roving Earl of Essex but had recently taken Richard de Burgh as her secret lover. Now that Essex had been executed, they could finally marry.

The new Earl was a true renaissance man in the spirit of the age. He had matriculated at Oxford at the age of twelve, and had become a talented poet. His writing, tense and spare, resembles the works of John Donne. 'My love doth fly with wings of fear,' went one verse, 'And doth a flame of fire resemble / Which mounting high and burning clear / Yet ever more doth move and tremble.'

But what made Richard de Burgh's success truly remarkable – even astonishing – was his national and religious identity. He was not some English colonist, but an Irishman from County Galway whose true-green credentials were impeccable. More than that, he was a proud Catholic recusant who continued to practise his preferred religion with a daring defiance. That was a dangerous attitude with people like George Carew around – and even more so when you consider Richard's volatile family background. The de Burghs – or Bourkes, or Burkes – had been hard-core rebels for many years.

They were an old and venerable family – according to *Debrett's Peerage*, the de Burghs 'rank amongst the most ancient in the united kingdoms' – who came over with the Normans and later adopted the Irish language, customs and dress. Another thing the de Burghs enthusiastically adopted was the Irish hostility towards English authority. In 1576, the de Burghs torched the pro-English town of Athenry and put everyone to the sword 'out of a barbarous hatred against the inhabitants'. The rebel family went on the run, to be hunted across the countryside 'from bush to bush and from hill to hill' by the exasperated authorities.

However, young Richard went to England at an early age and fell under the spell of Essex and his entourage. Among his mentors were Essex and his wife Frances, the bewitching Penelope Rich, and of course, Charles Blount.

During the 1590s, Richard de Burgh supported the English against Hugh O'Neill. Blount relied upon him to hold Connaught against the insurgents. According to Fynes Moryson, he 'served the Queen ... nobly, valiantly and faithfully'. But many true-blue English officers fiercely resented the Irishman's rise to power.

Like Blount, Richard de Burgh was now in bad odour for his association with the Essex circle. Protesting his own 'innocency', de Burgh wrote to Secretary Cecil swearing that just 'as I unfainedly loved him [Essex] whom I esteemed her Majesty's most dutiful and worthy servant', he was now offering the same devotion to Cecil.

Fortunately for de Burgh, he shared another advantage with Blount – the favour of the Queen. She refused to believe the 'many scandalous rumours' that surrounded him, and she ordered the reluctant Carew to advance his career. Carew had no option but to obey. But as the enlarged convoy marched back to Kinsale, de Burgh must have wondered which enemy he needed to fear most – the Spaniards ahead of him, or George Carew at his back.

When Juan del Águila heard how an overnight frost had facilitated O'Donnell's miraculous escape, he must have experienced a sense of *déjà vu*. Because sixteen years before, in the Low Countries, he and his men had been saved from slaughter by exactly the same phenomenon.

It was in the winter of 1585 – a dreadful, pitiless winter just like this one. Juan del Águila had been leading a Spanish *tercio* regiment against the Dutch Protestant insurgents in an area of reclaimed marshland near Empel, south of Amsterdam. The Dutch had pinned down his force. They threw open the river dams, flooding the entire region and leaving Águila's men stranded on an island of high ground. The Dutch sent a naval fleet into the flooded zone. It surrounded the island. There was no escape.

The rain poured down relentlessly, raising the water level even higher. Stuck for five days on a bare islet, drenched and chilled, with no food supplies, Águila and his troops seemed doomed to annihilation. Yet Águila never gave up. He kept the Dutch ships at bay, buying time.

But buying time for what? Everyone agreed his situation was hopeless.

Meanwhile, in the nearby town of Empel, there was an eerie coincidence. A Spanish sapper unearthed a buried image of the Virgin of the Immaculate Conception. It was the eve of the same feast-day, 8 December. The Spaniards were in no doubt – this was a sign from God. They installed the image in a church.

December 8 dawned to reveal a dramatic change in the weather. The rains had ceased and the region had been blast-frozen by an arctic wind. The flood surface turned to solid ice. The encircling ships were forced to retreat before they were crushed. Astonishingly, unbelievably, Águila's troops simply strolled off their island prison to freedom.

'God turned into a Spaniard,' a Dutch leader declared with stunned incredulity.

The freak incident marked a turning point in Águila's career. He went on to capture a string of townships and to establish his reputation as the man born without fear.

Ever since 1585, the feast of 8 December has been a special day for Spain's military forces. Parades and celebrations are held to mark the escape of Águila and his fellow officers in the 'Miracle at Empel'.

CHAPTER TWENTY-ONE

A DIRECT HIT ON DON JUAN

WHEN Juan del Águila summoned a Friday-night council of war on 20 November, he knew it was going to be an explosive session. He just didn't realise *how* explosive.

Castle Park fortress had just surrendered, and the clerics were baying for his blood. Their criticisms were later reflected in a report to the Pope, which could be paraphrased like this:

—You could have gone to Cork, where we would have had plenty of space behind strong walls. But since you did choose to stay here, you should have fortified the two castles to keep the harbour entrance open for reinforcements. Instead, what did you put in Castle Park? Sixteen soldiers! And even *they* were badly equipped!

The furious Fr James Archer let fly with personal insults: Águila was afraid to fight. He was a quaking coward.

But Águila had more on his mind than raking over the ashes of past decisions. He needed to counter Blount's latest challenge. Earlier that day, the

English commander had moved forward to establish a new gun emplacement, closer to town but further to the west, at a prehistoric ringfort. From
here he could rain gunfire into the very heart of Kinsale. Despite the frost,
the sappers had already dug deeply enough to accommodate a demi-cannon.
By dawn, that gun could be spitting fire into the very area where Águila sat.

Night was falling. But Blount was still smarting with humiliation from
that day, earlier in November, when a Spanish cannonball struck the earth
near his horse, spattering him with muck in front of his newly arrived
troops. He needed an artillery spectacular. He aimed the cannon *before* the
light faded. And thanks to the information from Spanish deserters, his gunners knew exactly where to aim.

At Águila's new headquarters in Philip Roche's house.

Águila's war council didn't know what hit it. With the very first shot, the
English cannon scored a direct strike on the roof of Roche's house. Broken
tiles, chunks of masonry and splinters of wood showered down on the star-
tled officers.

'[We delivered] Don Juan the good night,' crowed one English eyewitness,
Patrick Strange. '[In] the night, when Don Juan expected no such matter,
the cannon lighted upon the house where … his council [were] in consul-
tation.' A Spanish sentry confirmed the direct hit. 'The first piece shot off
went through the house where Don Juan lay, and otherwise did great hurt.'

(I like to think that Águila would have stayed calm, and perhaps even
remained seated, amid the chaos that ensued. Coolness under pressure was a
prized quality of a *tercio* commander. Águila would have been familiar with
the story of the Duke of Parma, who was once enjoying an al fresco lunch
with his officers when a lucky shot from the enemy hit one diner on the
head. A splinter of his skull took a second officer's eye out. With the table
covered in blood and brain, the Duke remained seated, coolly ordered a

clean tablecloth, and resumed the meal.)

This was just the beginning of a concentrated barrage of fire. Blount's selection of the ringfort had proved to be inspired. 'The second [shot] lighted at that instant on one of their storehouses of munition,' recalled Patrick Strange. 'The third battered through the parapet of the wall … [the Spanish] lost many men, and are now enforced to stand in their cellars, for they cannot go well in the streets.'

Throughout all this mayhem, what was life like for the Irish in Kinsale? There were two groups of Irish in the besieged town. The first comprised the expatriate insurgents from Spain, who had been organised into a military company under their charismatic leader 'Don Carlos' – Cormac Mac-Carthy. Secondly, there were the indigenous townsfolk. Some had left, some had died, some had escaped, but the remnants included a significant number of women and children who were still living through the hellish bombardment. One of them, a James Grace, kept a scanty journal. His log is brief and incomplete, but it is the nearest thing we have to a diary kept by an Irish source inside Kinsale.

Grace had watched and carefully taken note as the Spaniards placed their four big guns. He noted that one resident – a Mr James Meaghe – had his garden requisitioned as a gun emplacement for two cannon. A third gun had been mounted in the churchyard, but 'the other, biggest of all, is at the Water Gate to play upon the shipping'.

Grace had kept his eyes and ears open as he wandered around the town. 'They have nothing but rusk and water,' he noted as he passed the food kitchens. And as he lingered near Oviedo's sick-bay: 'There are two hundred sick and hurt in the hospitals.'

He was worried about the gunpowder, which the Spanish had kept at the Castle but were now moving to a cellar for safety. And he was fascinated by the fabled hoard of treasure which John Edie had described and which the English troops lusted after: 'It lies at the house where Captain Bostock lay.' Grace saw how the once-hallowed Friary to the west of the town walls had been filled with compacted earth and turned into a Spanish gun emplacement. He'd been nearby when the English scored their direct strike on Águila's house, and he saw how that event affected the locals. 'The townsmen will stay no longer there, for fear of the shot,' he wrote.

Grace also recorded a rare admission from the proud Spanish commander that the mission was now in big trouble. 'Don Juan says privately that the Lord Deputy [Blount] was born in a happy hour,' Grace recorded, 'for he will have the town, unless they be relieved from the North.'

The morning after the direct hit, Águila saw the English mount a second cannon at the ringfort and decided that the Irish women and children could no longer remain in the town. With Blount's agreement, they were allowed to evacuate, rest briefly in the English camp, and then leave to seek out friends or relatives in the countryside.

It was fortunate timing. Soon afterwards, the English set up four more cannons at the ringfort, fired directly into the busy marketplace, and killed four people.

Meanwhile, Blount was setting up another camp at Ardmartin Ridge, the belt of high ground that girdles the town to the north. Donough O'Brien, the Earl of Thomond, was given command of this second major camp. He took command of the forces of George Carew – who had just returned from his unsuccessful trek north – together with those of Richard de Burgh and Christopher St Lawrence. In an effort to save face, Carew volunteered to lead a death-or-glory charge into Kinsale. Blount demurred.

The English weren't having things all their own way. The Spanish blasted back at the naval ships in the harbour and scored three direct hits. Admiral

Leveson returned fire. The Spaniards' chief gunner – the man who had twice come within an ace of killing Blount – was badly injured and his fearsome cannon was silenced.

As November drew to a close, the English began to feel complacent. They believed Águila could not hold out much longer against such concentrated bombardment. An illogical end-of-war fever swept through the English force. Patrick Strange was so confident that he told his hometown 'to prepare for a celebration of a victory'. Admiral Richard Leveson wrote snidely to Secretary Cecil that Blount was 'a very fortunate man' facing such 'a weak and distressed enemy'.

Blount was more circumspect, but his intelligence reports convinced him that Águila was willing to make a deal. He himself was weary of the siege. '[It] may please God to bring it to pass sooner than we think of,' he wrote.

As 28 November dawned with high winds and torrential rain, Blount decided to give Águila an opportunity to leave with honour. He despatched a trumpeter to approach the town gate with an offer: surrender Kinsale, and we will allow you to return home.

Águila must have been tempted to accept. He was outnumbered, outgunned and surrounded. Could anyone blame him for taking the sensible option?

But Blount had made a serious misjudgement in his timing. He could not have picked a worse day to ask his enemy to compromise. For the English, it may have been 28 November. But in the Spanish calendar it was 8 December – the anniversary of Águila's escape across the ice in the 'Miracle at Empel'. It was the day that symbolised the no-surrender spirit of the elite Spanish regiments to which he had devoted his life.

The Spanish commander didn't even let the trumpeter darken his door. He answered him at the gate, clearly and defiantly. 'We hold this town first for Christ, and next for the King of Spain,' he said. 'We will defend it *contra tutti inimici*.' Against all enemies.

That caught the English by surprise. The intoxication of victory was replaced by the hangover of the realisation that this could be a long and bloody campaign which only a minority of them would survive. 'I had hoped to be able to send you news of the happy conclusion of this business,' Blount wrote despondently to Cecil, admitting that his expectations would now have to be deferred.

The younger English officers were bemused: we have greater numbers, they must have thought, why can't we storm the town and get this over with? However, the veterans of the French war knew better. They had fought through the hell that was Brittany. They knew that the Spanish commander meant what he said. And the unspoken message was even clearer.

I am a proud general of the Spanish *tercio*, Águila was saying. I will make you battle every inch of the way. You will have to fight us street by street and house by house. You will pay dearly in lives for every brick and every cobblestone. Eventually, you will win a heap of rubble that was once a town, and you will fly a victor's flag over a mountain of your own dead.

These officers looked at Águila, and they thought 'Tomaso Praxède'.

They looked at Kinsale, and they thought 'El Leon'.

CHAPTER TWENTY-TWO

HELL AT
SPANIARDS' POINT

E L LEON was a vivid example of the bloodbath that Kinsale could become. Águila had built the Fort of the Lion on the shores of a rocky promontory in Brittany seven years beforehand. Nearly four hundred Spaniards had died in a heroic attempt to defend it. But when the triumphant English and French attackers examined their 'victory' they found it had cost them even more lives – half as many again. And after all the bloodletting, the fort had been demolished, leaving a windblown sea-crag occupied only by cormorants and seagulls.

The carnage had broken Queen Elizabeth's heart. Shocked at the thousand lives that had been squandered over a desolate chunk of Atlantic rock, she admonished her commander: 'The blood of man is not to be used prodigally.'

Blount knew all about El Leon – and he wasn't about to go down the same gory road if he could help it.

It is worth telling the story of El Leon, because it gives valuable insight into Águila's character, corrects some misinformation about him, and explains why both the English and Spanish commanders acted the way they did in Kinsale.

Eleven years earlier, in 1590, Juan del Águila had been sent to Brittany with five thousand Spanish troops, ostensibly to aid the Breton Catholic League in its revolt against the French King. However, the Spaniards had their own agenda. They wanted to build a string of impregnable naval bases on France's Atlantic coast, just a short hop from England. The Breton insurgents, under the ambitious Duke of Mercoeur, realised King Felipe II's true goal and from the start, the Spanish-rebel alliance was blighted by suspicion and mistrust.

When Águila set up his first base at Blavet – modern-day Port Louis, near Lorient – the English didn't rate him highly. One official referred to 'this new come-hither Águila'. But they had to think again when he created a superb fortress. With its four spear-shaped bastions, it jutted out into the sea in a symbol of its commander's stony resolve. Even today, the remains of this fort still bear his name – Fort de l'Aigle, a French translation of Fuerte del Águila. Troops were ferried into the new base by an up-and-coming young admiral named Diego de Brochero.

Soon the region was engulfed in flames as French troops, supported by their English allies, rushed to oust the dangerous new arrivals. Throughout the conflict, no one could predict how the 'cold commander' Águila would behave. For instance, when he seized the city of Hennebont after a gruelling forty-day siege in December 1590, he 'gave the garrison twenty crowns apiece and let them go'. However, after taking Craon he showed no quarter to the English defenders in retaliation for the slaughter of the Armada survivors in Ireland.

The simmering feud between the Breton insurgents and the Spanish reached boiling point at Morlaix, in the summer of 1594. The rebel leader Mercoeur wanted Águila's Spaniards to rush the well-fortified city and take it in one glorious charge. Águila, who mistrusted him, said he would prefer to entrench for a longer siege. He asked Mercoeur if he had a proper battle plan.

'We go in on foot with three hundred good men, pikes in hand,' Mercoeur said dismissively. 'We charge headlong in. You can follow.'

The reply was classic Águila. 'My men never go in anywhere headlong,' he said. 'We keep our heads screwed on, we take our time and we do it right.' And with that, he wheeled away and led his troops back to camp.

Mercoeur never forgave the Spaniard – and he later savoured his cold revenge at the siege of El Leon.

Águila had wider ambitions. Earlier, in March 1594, he had set up a second, more northerly base near Brest, at an isolated promontory of the Crozon Peninsula which is still known as Spaniards' Point. This was a far more dangerous threat to Elizabeth than Blavet.

The fort of El Leon at Crozon was a masterpiece of military engineering. Perched on a natural rock, it seemed virtually impregnable. Águila installed four hundred seasoned fighters under a trusted veteran commander, Tomaso Praxède, and issued an unambiguous order: they must defend it to the death.

The English and French royalist armies moved in to besiege the fort. Outnumbering the defenders by around fourteen to one, they battered the fort with intensive fire. But Praxède's Spaniards fought back like cornered wildcats. In one courageous sally, they killed more than two hundred of the besiegers.

As the crippling siege continued, Praxède begged the Duke of Mercoeur for assistance. But the Duke also had his own agenda. As the seventeenth-century writer Henrico Davila explains: '[Mercoeur] was not displeased that the fort should be taken, knowing that the Spanish aimed to possess themselves of all that coast ... [and so] he deferred the relief.'

Back in Blavet, more than 150km away from El Leon, Águila faced a terrible choice. He had already staked his own reputation on his second fort holding out for at least four months. But Praxède was vastly outnumbered. Should he, Águila, leave Blavet and try to relieve El Leon? If he stayed, he could hold Blavet. If he left, his enemies would rush to attack it. And there was no guarantee he could save the second base at El Leon, either.

Stay: risk losing one fort. Leave: risk losing two.

Yet, says Davila, 'it seemed to him a very great fault to let his own countrymen be destroyed without assistance.'

Águila made his decision. Ignoring the warning voice of his internal 'cold commander', he opted to head north. He left Blavet with four thousand foot soldiers and two cannon. His was a naval mission with no warhorses, so he had to march 'warily [and] very slowly', taking a circuitous route to avoid enemy cavalry. He made it all the way to Plomodiern, at the neck of the Crozon Peninsula, before being blocked by royalist forces. He was just 37km from Spaniards' Point, but he had arrived exactly one day too late.

Learning of his approach, the attackers at El Leon had launched a massive push to end the standoff. They managed to create a breach, and had poured wave after wave of fresh troops into the gap. At the end of that day, Praxède and nearly all his four hundred defenders lay dead or dying on the blood-stained rock of El Leon.

'Being overcome more by their own weariness than the valour of their enemies,' reported Davila, '[they] were all cut in pieces without stirring one foot from the defence of the rampart.'

News of the defeat rapidly reached Águila, who had been close enough to hear the last of the fighting. Yet for the attackers, it was not a victory to celebrate. The assault cost six hundred of their best men – including the famous English explorer Sir Martin Frobisher.

It was recognised by writers of that era that Águila's relief force had arrived just too late to save the Spanish garrison. Davila's near-contemporary account, which is quite sympathetic, makes it clear that he had moved heaven and earth in a bid to reach El Leon. However, endless trouble was caused by Davila's next remark. He speculated that if Águila had marched on to El Leon, 'perchance' he might have inflicted a great defeat and won back his fort. But Davila did *not* suggest that he could have saved the Spanish defenders – they were already dead.

Later generations of Irish historians were to use this throwaway comment as a basis for their claim that Águila was a coward who had deliberately abandoned El Leon's defenders while he was close enough to have helped them – and who was quite capable of similarly betraying the Irish at Kinsale. The truth, according to another contemporary source, was that the besiegers had 'layed the fort [of El Leon] level with the ground, the same day Águila was ready to bring them aid'.

Not all the Spanish at El Leon had been killed. Thirteen survivors were later found shivering in the rocks nearby. The French royalist commander, impressed by the tenacity of the Spanish, released them to rejoin Águila.

But as we know by now, Águila was not the sort of person to welcome them home with a hug. He watched the thirteen bedraggled refugees as they lined up in front of him.

'Where have you come from, *misérables*?' he asked.

'We have come from among the dead,' they replied.

'That was the reason I put you there,' Águila replied. 'To die.'

A cold commander, indeed.

Within a few months, Águila had avenged Praxède and his heroic defenders by launching an audacious commando raid on England. We'll return to this dramatic episode later because, as we'll see, it was highly personal to one of the English officers who would be instrumental in ending the Kinsale siege.

Águila hung grimly on to his base at Blavet for the duration of the war, but funds dried up and his men went hungry. In his letters home, he complained that they were 'all naked … and six payments behind in their pay'.

In 1597 the force at Blavet had had enough. They mutinied and took over the base. Águila and his officers were locked up by their own men. Some later commentators have assumed from this evidence that Águila was an especially harsh and unpopular commander. But contemporary records make it clear that 'the reason is want of pay'. And in fairness, it would be hard to find a Spanish commander in 1590s Northern Europe who *didn't* face some sort of a mutiny. A wave of troop revolts was fuelled by sheer poverty as niggardly paymasters held back the troops' pay to stop them deserting. One historian has counted forty-five mutinies between 1573 and 1607 in Spanish armies in Flanders alone. So it was nothing personal or specific to Águila.

Eventually, Spain made peace with France, and the fort at Blavet was peacefully relinquished under treaty. Águila was able to sail home, proud and undefeated, to a homeland that did not appreciate his achievement.

Back in Kinsale, Charles Blount was merciless when he heard that Águila had spurned his offer of terms. He cranked up his cannon and made them thunder out with a ferocity that the Spaniards had never known before. The naval guns were ordered to batter Kinsale until 'no man shall dare to look over the walls'.

The cannonballs ploughed up so much soil that Águila's front-line soldiers were literally buried in churned-up earth. By nightfall on Saturday, 28 November, the town's east gate had been practically demolished. The terrified townsfolk crouched in cellars and under tables. Some Spanish defenders tried to escape the onslaught by sheltering in the western trenches, but they found Christopher St Lawrence's Dublin troops waiting for them.

The battering continued all weekend until 'a great part' of the eastern wall collapsed. By night, the Spaniards worked like demons to repair the damage, but each morning the English brutally tore open the stitched wound. At long last, the English had opened up their breach.

Elated, Blount ordered a full-scale assault. Later, the English would try to downplay this attack, claiming they had merely put on a '*bravado*' or show of strength. In fact, it was one of the greatest English offensives of the campaign. Two thousand men were hurled into the gap, but they encountered an unexpected level of resistance from the defenders.

The English grudgingly admitted that the Spaniards fought heroically. Guarding the gap in the wall, a captain named Pedro Morejón restored his men's morale with a display of contemptuous courage that evoked the classic spirit of the Spanish *tercios*. He stood upright in full view amid a blistering gale of English gunfire. He 'walked across the breach, animating his men', recalled Fynes Moryson.

The English army marshal Richard Wingfield ordered all his musketeers to aim directly for the Spanish captain.

—I will personally give £20 to anyone who hits that man, he shouted in frustration.

But as Fynes Moryson reported, with obvious pleasure, his namesake walked through the fire unharmed. 'Brave soldiers … are by some secret influence preserved,' he marvelled. 'Many great shot did beat the dirt in his face, and stones about his ears, yet … he continued walking in this brave manner.'

After an hour of heavy fighting, the English gave up. Later, Carew – sounding like some sort of building inspector – reported that they had studied the breach and 'found it not to be assaultable'. It was a neat euphemism for having been firmly beaten and repelled.

Captain Morejón's example had given an injection of confidence to the beleaguered Spanish. They were no longer the underdogs. They'd heard of Hugh O'Donnell's nifty side-step and of Carew's embarrassment. They knew that Red Hugh was marching towards Bandon, just twenty kilometres to the west. And they were aware that the main Irish insurgent force under Hugh O'Neill was heading southward at last.

However, the most heartening development of all was still unknown to them. On 27 November, Admiral Pedro de Zubiaur had sailed out of La Coruña with nine ships, their prows pointed north towards Kinsale. He was carrying guns and munitions and food. And he had eight hundred of the men who were supposed to have landed in Kinsale back in September. They were not so much reinforcements as latecomers, but, together with the other developments, their arrival would change the game beyond recognition.

CHAPTER TWENTY-THREE

'LET US SETTLE THIS IN SINGLE COMBAT'

ON 27 November, Admiral Pedro de Zubiaur had left La Coruña on the midnight tide. He had nine ships carrying between eight hundred and a thousand troops. His fleet was like an early version of the United Nations: his own ship was Dutch, with forty Dutchmen aboard; his vice-admiral's ship was Flemish; and the other seven included French merchantmen and Scottish luggers.

One of the most courageous and remarkable Irishmen on board was a Jesuit brother named Dominic Collins (since beatified as The Blessed Dominic Collins). Born in Youghal, Collins had enjoyed a chequered career as an innkeeper's servant and an army captain in Brittany, before joining the Jesuits and becoming a military chaplain.

Also in the fleet was a press-ganged Scottish skipper named David High, whose vessel, *The Unicorn*, had been forced into La Coruña with a leaking hull. The ship was instantly requisitioned. Where was he going? Bordeaux. No. You *were* going to Bordeaux. Now you're taking us to Kinsale.

Eighty armed Spanish soldiers had piled on board, accompanied for some reason by half a dozen women. High's cargo was replaced with twenty-five tons of bread and six barrels of wine. While in port, High had overheard the Spanish talking about the Irish campaign. They were remarkably upbeat.

—Ireland is already won, a soldier said. After Ireland, we take England. Then Scotland.

However, Admiral Zubiaur must have been full of misgivings as he stood on the forecastle of the flagship and set his prow northward. He had wanted warships, but he had been given crocks. Even his admiral's and vice-admiral's ships were little better than 'hulks' and the other craft were 'small barks' or basic merchantmen. He had asked for fighting men, but he had been given untrained convicts who were 'very poor' and 'naked'. To save money, King Felipe had emptied the prisons. A sixth of his force was made up of sullen jailbirds. It made no sense to Zubiaur to mount a key expedition and then to ruin it all by 'raising companies of lowlifes from the jails ... and sending them to a strange kingdom, naked and lacking swords or shirts or shoes. I've seen this with my own eyes.'

But there was a more immediate problem. As they passed the coast of northern France, a tempest slammed into his fleet. One ship was smashed against the pitiless rocks of the Brittany coast. Another was hurled directly back to Galicia, and a third went missing. Meanwhile, the same fierce wind sent Zubiaur and the remaining vessels scudding northwards at an astonishing speed. As November drew to a close, they were already within sight of Ireland. Relief was imminent for Águila and his beleaguered defenders at Kinsale.

There are conflicting reports of what happened next. One account says the storms prevented Zubiaur from reaching Kinsale. This was a blessing in disguise, because he would have sailed straight into the hands of the English navy. 'It was the mercy of God,' concluded one Spanish report. However, a later Spanish account says the ships sailed into the mouth of Kinsale thinking it was full of Spanish warships. When they discovered they were actually English ships, they turned tail and sought out another port.

Either way, Zubiaur was lucky to escape capture. But not so lucky as the Scotsman David High, who managed to win his freedom amid the confusion. According to one report, High and his Scottish crew had earlier persuaded the Spanish soldiers to huddle below decks as the gale raged.

—We can ply our tackle better if you stay out of the way, they shouted above the storm.

Then they quietly fastened the hatches, trapping the Spaniards below as they sailed into Kinsale.

Whatever the circumstances, as soon as his ship entered port, David High slipped overboard, seized a small boat, and rowed hell for leather towards an English naval vessel.

—That ship is filled with Spanish soldiers, he shouted breathlessly to Vice-Admiral Amias Preston.

Preston armed his men and approached the Scottish vessel warily. But the eighty Spaniards, who were probably reluctant warriors in the first place, surrendered peacefully.

Meanwhile, Zubiaur was sailing westward with his six remaining ships. By 1 December, he had reached the next available port – the harbour of Castlehaven.

—A warm welcome to you! My port and castle are yours!

Sitting in his rowboat at the entrance to Castlehaven harbour, Dermot O'Driscoll beamed genially up at the new arrivals in their tall ships.

—But if you continue on this course, O'Driscoll went on, you will founder on the hidden rocks. Follow me. I will guide you safely in.

Zubiaur's first encounter with the native Irish could not have been more different to Águila's. The leader of the Castlehaven O'Driscolls was 'a Catholic and an adherent of His Majesty', as the Spanish recorded later.

Admiral Zubiaur looked around him, impressed. Tucked into a pleasant cove to the east of Baltimore, Castlehaven was indeed a serviceable port. 'Ships may come to anchor in twelve fathoms,' read one contemporary report. '[The haven is] of reasonable bigness, and very clear and clean.' Zubiaur warily accepted the O'Driscolls' offer and disembarked his sea-weary army. His commander of land forces, Captain Alonso de Ocampo – who was later to play a major role in the Battle of Kinsale – mustered the men and gave him the bad news. Ocampo was scathing about the quality of the troops, whom he dismissed as 'naked *bisonos*' or rookies.

—We left La Coruña with a thousand men, he told Zubiaur. Now we have only 750.

Zubiaur had lost a quarter of his force before a single shot had been fired.

Back in Kinsale, tempers were becoming frayed. The two overstressed commanders – who had previously communicated with a formal, almost mediaeval courtesy – were now snarling at each other like fishwives. Relations between Blount and Águila had soured a few weeks earlier, while the English were setting up their heavy artillery. Just before the first bombardments, Blount had sent a message asking if Águila wanted to send the 'ladies and women' of Kinsale out to safety. But according to Blount, Águila interpreted the request for women in the worst possible light.

—I'm not here to be your pimp, he shot back.

Did Águila really say that? Or was it just English black propaganda? Perhaps his true reply was lost in translation. Whatever the truth of the matter, relations deteriorated rapidly. On 4 December Blount despatched another messenger to ask Águila if he wanted to bury his fallen soldiers. Águila responded with characteristic politeness.

—I pray you to bury them, he replied, and I promise to do the same for any of your men who fall in my territory.

But this was just a pretext for an English complaint.

—We treat all your injured prisoners with respect, Blount protested, but you killed one of ours.

—I have no knowledge of that, Águila replied indignantly. If it is true, I will punish it severely.

Blount was far from happy with that response. After that, the messengers trekked back and forth, conveying allegations and perceived insults like weary lawyers for a divorcing couple. It was a bad case of martial break-up.

Blount claimed that when his envoy recently called for negotiations, some of Águila's Italian soldiers had called the English *meschini* or lowlifes. Águila blamed it on poor translation. Blount fired back that, in his day, honourable enemies showed each other an honourable respect.

—I will be ever true to my own honour, he sniffed, whatever others may be to theirs.

Águila supposedly reacted 'with a Spanish shrug of the shoulder'. The surreal squabble – remember, this was amid a battlefield littered with corpses – reached its climax in an episode reminiscent of *Don Quixote*. Astonishingly, Águila offered to settle the entire siege standoff in the traditional mediaeval manner.

—Let us settle this in single combat, he told the stunned English commander. Whoever wins this trial by combat wins not just the town of Kinsale, but the entire war.

Was he serious? Nobody doubted it. Not for a minute.

In Castlehaven, Zubiaur unloaded his cargo without any interruption. His war materials included 200 arquebuses with powder, wicks and bullets,

1,000 pikes ... and 4,000 horse-shoes. The Spanish authorities, who had earlier sent 1,600 saddles with Águila, still didn't seem to have grasped that it was the horses themselves that were in short supply. He also had shiploads of the food supplies – biscuit, wheat, rye, wine and oil – that Águila so desperately needed.

Zubiaur's original orders had been simple. He was to land at Kinsale and hand over his ships to Águila. He was not to take them away, as Brochero had done in September. Then Águila was to 'make such arrangements as he thinks desirable'. (It's worth noting that the Spanish warlords still had full confidence in Águila, and apparently realised they had made a mistake over Brochero's orders.)

What was Zubiaur to do now? Luckily, two new opportunities opened up to him.

His arrival at Castlehaven, combined with Hugh O'Donnell's entrance into West Cork, had proved a tipping point in the campaign. For the first time, it seemed possible that the Irish-Spanish axis could actually succeed. Many Irish chieftains in Cork looked at the way things were shaping up and decided they wanted to be part of it after all. They were probably swayed by the disinformation deliberately put out by Zubiaur that he had a relief force of 3,000. In nearby Baltimore, the steadfastly pro-Queen chieftain Fineen O'Driscoll shifted his allegiance to the Spanish, under the influence of his headstrong son Conor. Others followed. The lord of Bearhaven, Donal Cam O'Sullivan Beare, openly declared for King Felipe. 'Of my own free unrestrained will,' he wrote, 'I place [my castle] in the keeping of General Zubiaur.'

Zubiaur had failed to gain Kinsale, but three other key fortresses – Castlehaven, Baltimore and Bearhaven – had been handed to him on a plate. 'The lords of [these] places submitted to His Majesty,' the Spanish recorded. 'Spanish garrisons were put in all of them by the consent of their owners.'

All three ports had their advantages. Bearhaven's appeal was its sheer remoteness. Castlehaven, although nearer to Kinsale, was assaultable only from sea. From land, it was 'inaccessible either for horse or for great artillery'. But it was Baltimore that most appealed to Zubiaur. It had the best harbour in Ireland, he reckoned. He earmarked two castles – Dún na Séad and Dún na Long – as forts suitable for modernisation. Conor O'Driscoll, the chieftain's son, was happy to give them over in exchange for weapons that would allow his men to fight the hated *Sasanach*.

—Single combat?

—Yes, your Lordship. He says that 'the question between England and Spain should be tried by combat' between you two.

We're not privy to Blount's reaction when the messenger conveyed Águila's challenge to a duel. Blount himself was no wuss – he'd defeated the Earl of Essex in single combat in his younger days – but he wasn't stupid enough to wager England's crown on a two-man scrap.

As a veteran of the Brittany campaign, Blount probably remembered an occasion when the positions were exactly reversed. Águila, as Spanish commander in France, had surrounded an English general named John Norreys. The Englishman – displaying a blue scarf he had been given as a champion of some lady – stalked up and challenged Águila to settle the battle by single combat. The Spaniard briefly considered the offer and said he would pass.

So Blount didn't feel too embarrassed about declining.

—Your message is more quarrelsome than honourable, he replied. Otherwise I would be most willing to accept. But thank you for the noble offer.

Zubiaur's landing caught the English completely on the hop. The Spanish had been safely ensconced in Castlehaven for more than twenty-four hours before the first report reached Blount. He immediately summoned Admiral Leveson.

—Seek out the Spanish fleet at Castlehaven, Blount ordered. Capture them if you can. If not, cause them trouble.

It was easier said than done. With a ferocious wind blowing in exactly the wrong direction, it would take Leveson several days just to clear the harbour mouth. However, the news that a relief force had landed provided a huge psychological boost to Kinsale's defenders. Moryson wrote that the Spanish 'took heart again, when they were otherwise ready to yield'.

And so, on 2 December, two thousand of Águila's troops burst out of Kinsale in a furious and determined effort to prise Blount's fingers from their throats once and for all. The epic clash has virtually been forgotten by history – but it was much more of a 'battle' than the later, anti-climactic Battle of Kinsale which has eclipsed it in fame. With thousands of troops engaged and hundreds killed, the battle of 2 December was probably the largest single military engagement of Spanish troops on Irish or British soil. Although it did not achieve Águila's objective of severing the tightening garrotte of English siegeworks, it was at least a partial victory. It silenced the English guns for a while; it made Blount abandon any attempt to storm through a breach; and it may have helped to persuade some local Irish lords to join the insurgents.

It all began an hour after sunset on a dark and rain-lashed night. Peering through the sinister black mist that enshrouded the town, Águila discerned human silhouettes swinging pickaxes. He realised that the English were using the fog and the late moonrise as cover to dig a circle of trenches all around his walls. 'Seeing the great destruction that the enemy's guns were causing,' reported the Spanish officer Alférez Bustamante, 'Don Juan instructed us to sally out.'

The Spanish commander mustered two thousand men – virtually his entire force – and by eight o'clock they burst out 'with exceeding fury' carrying tools to tear down the wicker gabions, spikes to destroy the cannon touchholes, and stones to block the barrels. They seized the new trenches to the west before swinging around to attack the eastern gun emplacements. Their sheer rage and energy took the English by surprise, and as fierce hand-to-hand fighting erupted in the trenches, it looked as though the Spanish would force their tormentors to retreat.

Richard Boyle, the man who would later make the marathon ride to London, witnessed it all. 'The Spaniards made a sortie last night in great number,' he wrote. 'They divided themselves into three parts, intending to force our quarters, and came up very gallantly for a time, beating out men from the [western trenches] which they possessed for nearly two hours.'

With a rare candour, one captain named Peter Bowlton reported that the English companies guarding the trenches had fled 'very shamefully'.

Blount's marshal Richard Wingfield threw hundreds more men into the battle zone, and the bloody fighting continued until the muddy wasteland was littered with bodies. Wave after wave of assaults by the English failed to shift the Spanish from the trenches until Richard de Burgh and thirty of his Galwaymen arrived to save the day. They bulldozed into the main body of Águila's army, 'broke them, and did execution upon them towards the town'. Wheeling westward, de Burgh then charged the new trenchworks and forced the occupiers out 'at the push of a pike'. His small band doggedly held the trench until daybreak before relief arrived.

De Burgh's courage that night 'got him much honour' according to one contemporary. And it was a turning point in the battle, if not the siege itself. '[The Spanish], having slain great numbers … would have slain more, were it not for the Earl of Clanrickard [de Burgh],' wrote the Irish annalist, 'for it was he … who compelled the Spaniards to return to Kinsale.'

Cormac (Don Carlos) MacCarthy, the captain of the Irish company in Kinsale, was right in the thick of the fighting. By dawn's light, his body was found lying in the mud alongside scores of others. According to Philip O'Sullivan, he 'fell fighting bravely … having first slain two English captains and spiked a cannon'. So it was a significant quirk of history that in this epic clash of Spanish against English, the greatest heroism was displayed by two Irish officers – Richard de Burgh on the English side, and Carlos MacCarthy on the Spanish.

Next day's bleak dawn revealed a grisly sight. Many of the dead Spanish were found draped across the barrels of the cannon, their hands still clutching spikes and hammers. 'There was a very lusty Spaniard … [who] drave a spike into a culverin,' reported the surgeon William Farmer. 'He was slain sitting astride upon the piece.' English troops had killed another Spaniard by hammering his own spike into his back.

Fynes Moryson recorded: 'The trenches in some places were filled with their dead bodies.' The English troops took morbid interest in the fact that many Spanish carried 'spells, characters and hallowed medals' and that many others had signs of sexually transmitted diseases. There were horrific scenes in the English trenches, too: corpses were found frozen in positions of defence, as though awaiting another attack.

Richard Boyle claimed that the Spaniards had 'at least two hundred men killed, and almost as many dangerously wounded' while the English escaped with twenty-seven deaths. However, another English witness maintained Blount lost forty men, and a third estimated it at a hundred. The Spanish officer Alférez Bustamante reckoned English losses at five hundred, and Philip O'Sullivan claimed that 'more English than Spanish were killed'. It's also difficult to believe English claims that all their damaged guns were back in action by next morning.

The revival in the Spaniards' fortunes forced Blount into a radical rethink. Until now, his focus had been on storming the town. Now he had to think defensively, blockading the approach routes while ensuring that Kinsale itself was encircled in case 'they both at one time should give upon us'. He held a council of war, which decided to 'leave off battering' Kinsale and to save their ammunition for use against the Spanish-Irish relief force.

Blount shifted the big guns to Spital to defend his main camp from attack from the north. He dug deeper trenches to protect his rear. To the west, the new camp commanded by Donough O'Brien, the Earl of Thomond, was shifted forward to the old ringfort at Rathbeg, much closer to the town. Two minor forts were thrown up between that camp and the river to the southwest.

Josiah Bodley's 'foxes' excavated a complex network of new trenchworks connecting Blount's camp, O'Brien's camp, and the two new forts. Their zig-zag design ensured that no trench could be exposed to flanking fire. By the time Bodley had finished, Kinsale had been completely sealed off.

In Castlehaven, Zubiaur was rapidly succumbing to the charm of West Cork. He said the land, although mountainous and treeless, was excellent for farming cattle and grain, and free of petty crime – at least until his own jailbird troops arrived. 'I have forged a great friendship with these chieftains,' he wrote warmly. 'They are very fond of me.' His enthusiasm shines through the pages of his letters home. He compares the Irish to young stags, prancing impatiently, eager to fight. 'They are courageous and ready for action in the war of faith … this kingdom has many good people, fearless people.' If only his own troops were as pure, he mused. 'From Lisbon they sent us robbers and brigands – useless among these impoverished people who are so Catholic, so welcoming and who love Your Majesty.' His sailors were no better: they took their pay and then scarpered. 'They're afraid of neither God nor Your Majesty,' Zubiaur complained.

Over dinner in their Great Hall, the Castlehaven O'Driscolls emphasised Águila's plight. Speaking in Latin, Dermot warned Zubiaur that Kinsale was besieged by 11,000 to 12,000 troops, about half of them pro-Queen Irish. It was only a matter of time before Blount would despatch warships to attack Castlehaven.

—My advice, said Dermot, is to ask for help from Donal Cam O'Sullivan Beare.

This was the western chieftain whose early offer of aid had been rejected by a sceptical Águila. Zubiaur had no such qualms. He sent a messenger to Donal Cam that very night. Then he ordered five of his ships' cannon to be hauled ashore in preparation for the battle to come. His lookouts began scanning the horizon, preparing for the inevitable naval onslaught.

CHAPTER TWENTY-FOUR

THE BATTLE OF CASTLEHAVEN

TRANQUIL and untroubled, the little cove of Castlehaven seems a highly unlikely backdrop for one of the greatest naval contests ever to take place between Queen Elizabeth's fleet and a hostile Spanish armada intent on invading England.

It is one of those impossibly serene havens that seem to have remained at peace since the beginning of time. It is difficult to imagine that on the morning of 6 December, its silence was shattered by the roar of guns, the scream of red-hot cannonballs, the splinter of ships' timbers, and the cries of the hundreds of men who died.

The Battle of Castlehaven was one of those ambiguous clashes that both sides claimed as a victory. Here's one contemporary English account:

'Sir Richard Leveson valiantly entered the harbour, drew near their fortifications, and fought the enemy for the space of one whole day, his ship being an hundred times shot through, and yet but eight men slain. God so blessed him, that he prevailed in his enterprise, destroyed their whole shipping, and made [Zubiaur] fly by land to another harbour.'

But here's the Spanish take on the same battle:

'Thanks to the support of the castle and the artillery they landed, [the Spaniards] drove the enemy away from the port.' The Spanish added that they 'sank the Queen's flagship and greatly damaged the others. Two of our ships were sunk, but the men on board saved as well as their cargoes. We lost twenty men killed, and some wounded. The English then departed.'

Meanwhile, here's how the Irish perceived it:

'In this battle, 575 English fell ... One Spaniard, a kinsman of Zubiaur's, was killed, and two were wounded.'

And Zubiaur himself? He marked it down as 'a victory' for the Spanish ... even as the English were toasting their great win.

So what are the facts?

Leveson arrived in Castlehaven at 10am on 6 December, determined to drive the Spaniards out. In his fleet were the fighting ships *Warspite*, *Defiance*, *Swiftsure* and *Merlin*. He entered the habour mouth with all guns blazing. However, Zubiaur's Spaniards had been expecting him. '[Leveson] found eight pieces of artillery planted upon the shore attending his coming,' wrote Vice-Admiral Preston. The hidden cannon blasted back at the English ships, reinforced by small-arms fire from six hundred musketeers 'very near and thick on the shore'.

The roar of gunfire was so loud that its thunder could easily be heard in Kinsale. In Castlehaven itself, the noise must have been deafening. One English witness, Thomas Gainsford, claimed some Spanish thought the end of the world had come. Leveson 'battered the walls so forcibly from his ships ... that the enemy thought their Lady of Heaven was willing to affect us on earth'.

For the first few hours, Leveson rolled all over the Spaniards. Zubiaur's flagship was driven onto the rocks with its rudder smashed and nearly three metres of water in its hold. The Spaniards' second biggest ship was driven ashore where it 'lies bulged and half sunk – never able to rise again', according to Preston. Two other Spanish vessels, including the vice-admiral's ship, also went aground. The *Maria Francesca* was sunk with its precious cargo of wheat, and the *Cisne Camello* was reduced to matchwood.

Eager to capitalise on his success, Leveson launched several landing craft and headed for shore to complete his takeover. But the tide of the battle was about to turn. Donal Cam O'Sullivan Beare had been waiting 24 kilometres away and had received Zubiaur's call just in time. He force-marched five hundred veterans to Castlehaven. Together with the Baltimore O'Driscolls, they arrived just as the English were closing in for the kill. Leveson saw the Irish relief force and had second thoughts. He stayed on board his ships.

Donal Cam's nephew, Philip O'Sullivan, described what happened next. 'Zubiaur, elated and emboldened, took his cannon from the vessels and for two days right vigorously bombarded the English fleet,' he wrote. 'Finally, the balls, rendered red-hot by the rapid firing, pierced the English ships which they struck from stem to stern, hurling men and planks into the sea.'

Leveson's flagship, the *Warspite,* was riddled with cannonball holes. 'Zubiaur's first shot into this ship killed sixty men who were seated at table,' claimed O'Sullivan. As the bombardment continued, 'soldiers and sailors fell right and left'.

Leveson tried to retreat, but a pitiless wind kept blowing the *Warspite* back into range of the Spanish gunners. '[I was] forced to ride four and twenty hours within the play of those five pieces of ordnance,' Leveson later recalled, 'and received in that time about three hundred shot, through hulk, mast and tackle.'

He fought free only by cutting his cables, abandoning all his anchors and towing out his ships – a hideously dangerous task under fire – in order to find a usable wind. 'He pulled out of Castlehaven on the 9th,' wrote Preston, 'but did not put out till he saw all his ships out before him.' Leveson later explained that he left Castlehaven only because he had done 'as much as might be done by sea'.

Miraculously, the *Warspite* did not sink but survived the journey back to Kinsale, where everyone was amazed by the hundreds of holes in its hull.

With a precision worthy of John Lennon, the surgeon William Farmer had to count them all – a total of 209, he finally calculated.

English reports claimed that all Zubiaur's Spanish ships were sunk 'save one' and that Zubiaur was forced to flee the port. The English lost just eight men. Spanish reports tell a dramatically different story. Zubiaur's ship was badly damaged, but was already so high and dry that it could be repaired. Two of the Scottish merchantmen were also salvageable. Two ships were write-offs but the final ship, a French vessel, was almost unharmed. It was fitted with cannon and sent to Baltimore. The Spanish claimed that they lost forty men in the encounter.

Viewed realistically, the battle must have claimed many English lives: probably well into three figures, if not the 575 that some Spanish claimed. They didn't win back Castlehaven and they didn't wipe out the Spanish fleet. What they did do was place Zubiaur into much the same position as Águila in Kinsale: with his transport crippled, the Admiral could no longer simply sail home if things went wrong. His Spaniards were fighting with their backs to the sea, facing either victory or death.

CHAPTER TWENTY-FIVE

'Send Us Home Some Greyhounds'

MEANWHILE, back in Spain, there was almost total ignorance of the desperate situation in Kinsale. A letter written around this time to Águila's secretary, Jeronimo de la Torre, reveals the staggering lack of awareness. Jeronimo's brother Nicholas believed that the Spanish had created a prosperous new colony in Ireland and that anyone with insider knowledge could make a fast buck out of the business opportunities.

—Which goods should I bring to turn a profit? Nicholas asked. Oh, and by the way, he added: can you send me back some greyhounds and horses?

Nicholas obviously had no inkling of his brother's plight. If Jeronimo had possessed a greyhound during those dark and hungry days, it would probably have gone into the cooking pot.

But then, nobody else had any idea, either. There had been silence from Kinsale since 21 October, when the authorities had received Águila's letters asking for more men and provisions. An order issued from Spain in early December also reveals how out of touch they were. 'Don Juan del Águila has been instructed to raise in Ireland two companies of [cavalry],' it said.

King Felipe also demanded that a swift ship should 'go and come with news' from Kinsale. That was on 25 November. The news the King obviously hadn't received was that Águila was in a totally blockaded harbour.

Now, in December, Águila anxiously scanned the grey-green horizon every day for the reinforcements he'd requested. But they never came. Instead, a letter from the all-powerful Duke of Lerma was winging across the ocean. Perhaps it was just as well that Águila did not receive it until much later. Its message was enough to drive the stoutest heart to despair.

Answering Águila's plea for thousands of soldiers, Lerma waffled like a true politician. 'There is a good quantity of everything, and more is being provided,' he wrote. 'His Majesty is keeping this matter before his eyes.'

But what was actually being done?

'There are now on the march 150 lances, and they will embark shortly,' Lerma pledged. Then in a triumphant postscript: 'Since writing this … there is to be added another company of horse with the 150 lances, so there are to be sent 200.'

Two hundred soldiers. To fight Blount's seven thousand.

Another letter from War Secretary Esteban de Ibarra raised the figure to 220 soldiers, 'well armed and well horsed'. The relief ships would also carry corn, oil and honeycombs.

But if compliments were cannonballs, Águila would have had no shortage. 'His Majesty has confidence in your care and worth,' Lerma assured him. Ibarra was more personal with his praise. 'When I remember who Don Juan del Águila is, my heart is lightened,' he wrote, 'and I begin to hope for great things, as I hope God will grant them to your valour.'

The reality was that Ireland was far from the top of the Spaniards' agenda. They had other problems on their minds – the war in Flanders, the threat from the Ottomans in the Mediterranean, and the possibility of English reprisal raids. The commander of military forces in Castile, Don Martin de Padilla, seemed to have the best grasp of the Irish situation. 'We shall not be able to finish our task with so small a force,' he told Felipe on 30 November. 'The reinforcement needed is one that will end the business once and for all.'

He added pointedly: 'From motives of economy, expeditions are undertaken with such small forces that they principally serve to irritate our enemies, rather than to punish them.' While they might still hope for 'a good result' if O'Neill linked up with Águila, the only solution was to send a huge armed force. Yet the pragmatic Padilla accepted that this would not happen. 'I consider it difficult, if not impossible, for us in so short a time, at whatever cost, to fit out the [necessary] fleet and forces,' he wrote.

Zubiaur was equally exasperated. In one letter home, he colourfully compared the Spanish authorities to swarms of flies, always frantically in motion but getting nowhere. 'They take a full year to assemble 4,000 men, and then half of them are youngsters. Thousands who are sent here will die. It is shameful.'

The Spanish Council of State suggested to the King that troop levels in Ireland should be brought up to six thousand. And by 7 December – unaware that Zubiaur's fleet had been severely crippled in Castlehaven the previous day – the Spanish officials unveiled a plan for what could be called the Fourth Wave of the Armada to Ireland.

'Five ships are ready in Lisbon, only awaiting a fair wind to sail,' they assured Felipe.

However, the troop levels were mostly aspirational. Only 190 infantry were actually waiting at port, together with 'some' soldiers levied from the nearby forts. Another three cavalry companies might be requisitioned from the local guards. They would join the two imaginary cavalry companies that Águila was supposed to conjure up in Ireland. As for infantry, 'orders have been sent' for the raising of another 2,000 Portuguese – but they admitted there had been difficulties in turning these orders into reality. 'Men are being levied in all Castile and Portugal,' Ibarra declared confidently. There were other grandiose plans to divert 14,000 infantry and 1,200 cavalry from Flanders.

The King's advisors did their best to create the impression of genuine action. But to modern readers, it is all too reminiscent of the ghost regiments of non-existent troops that Adolf Hitler moved around his eastern front in 1945.

By mid-December, the Council of State was ready to announce a decision. 'As the Irish affair has been undertaken, every possible effort should be made to continue,' it ruled. '... but we cannot hope to fit out a great fleet.' The council recommended: 'The force in Lisbon should therefore sail immediately the weather permits.' (This was the 220 lancers.)

Once that Third Wave had departed, preparations for the Fourth Wave should begin. Local officials were supposed to raise the proposed guards' cavalry and the notional two thousand Portuguese infantry 'with all speed' for despatch in the New Year. 'The most important thing in this business is that the Earls [O'Neill and O'Donnell] should join Don Juan del Águila,' Lerma wrote to Oviedo. 'His Majesty charges you to make your utmost efforts to this end.'

The Council of State ruled: 'If they have not already effected a junction [between Irish and Spanish] they should be urged to do so.'

And if that was not possible? 'Try to hold out,' ordered the Council of State.

So as the Spanish prepared to celebrate Christmas, the only message of good cheer that the folks back home had for Águila's beleaguered Spaniards was essentially: Hang in there.

No, wait. The Spanish authorities did have a Plan B. 'Since Your Majesty's treasury ... cannot meet all the demands upon it,' the council wrote to Felipe, '... it will be necessary that God with his Almighty hand should come to our aid.'

But how, specifically?

'The first and most important of all preparations will be to appease His anger, provoked by the vices and sins so prevalent in this country,' the council explained. 'We must therefore earnestly seek a remedy by mending our ways of life, and by constant prayer.'

As the Spanish wrote their plea for a joining together of Irish and Spanish, Hugh O'Neill was still somewhere in the heartland of Ireland, making his slow and tortuous journey south.

He claimed to have first heard of the invasion in early October, which sounds about right, since the news reached the English in northern Carrickfergus at the same time. Yet nearly fifty days elapsed between the landing and the date his trek south began in earnest – he left his hometown of Dungannon on 9 November.

He had spent most of those fifty days burning, looting and pillaging the areas around Louth and Meath which were part of 'the English Pale', a small region in the east of Ireland that was usually solidly under English control. A report on 7 October said he was 'burning and spoiling in Louth' and 'took a great prey [of cattle]'.

Bizarrely, these raids became a spectator sport for O'Neill's family and entourage. On one major raid in Meath, he 'spoiled 22 villages, burning both horses and corn ... [and stole] 2,000 cows, 1,000 garrauds [work-horses] 4,000 sheep and swine'. He razed another seven villages, forcing the impoverished Irish inhabitants out of their blazing homes and onto the roads as beggars. All of this was watched with interest, even enjoyment, by O'Neill's wife and sixteen society women, whom he had brought along purely for the ride.

The English wondered if this would be the extent of O'Neill's war. They theorised that he was afraid that the winter march and the inevitable battle would make it 'dangerous for him to advance so far from home'.

Modern writers are deeply divided on O'Neill's mindset. Some believe he was vacillating, over-cautious, even cowardly. Others state that he was prudently building up his forces; that he was trying to open up an eastern front; that he was laying false trails; or that he was implementing some brilliant strategy that transcended the obvious. Of all the controversies that surround Kinsale, this is the most likely to send sparks flying. The truth is that nobody knows what was going on in O'Neill's head.

Ludhaigh O'Cleary says he 'waited till everything was ready' before leaving, and 'spent some time' preying on the Pale. Philip O'Sullivan keeps it simple: 'O'Neill, finding an opportunity, invaded Meath, where he ravaged the English and Anglo-Irish far and wide, and returned home laden with booty.'

O'Sullivan's take is uncomplicated and honest. There is no reference to any far-seeing strategy, just the basic pleasure of pillaging and returning with loads of spoil. O'Sullivan doesn't even have to explain to his 1600s readership why that made sense.

In Gaelic society, cattle raids and burnings were a traditional way of asserting dominance over neighbours. Chieftainship was based on bloodline, yet no one could inherit power: you had to be elected by your kin. Once in power, you could be deposed or killed in a heartbeat, often by a close relative, so it was important that you kept up a tough reputation. And the best way to do that was to terrorise adjacent territories.

As historian Cyril Falls wrote in 1950: 'The first adventure of a young [Gaelic] lord … was to raid his neighbour's cattle in order to bring on a fight.' In one Ulster castle, a poet wrote approvingly how the menfolk went to sleep knowing they would be up at daybreak to burn the next town, to rustle its cattle, and 'to leave many a wife husbandless'.

Today a social scientist might describe this as typical of 'a culture of honour', a technical term referring to a general readiness to use violence to defend one's status and assert one's will on others. It was particularly prevalent in the cattle-based societies of north Ireland and the Scottish borders. Herding communities are different to crop-growing communities because a person's property – the herd – can be stolen within minutes. Where there is no effective central power to inhibit or to punish theft, an individual must develop a reputation for strength and toughness. He can't leave it until after the theft – he must get his retaliation in first.

Cyril Falls's insight meshes perfectly with the observation by modern social scientist J. K. Campbell that, in similar societies in rural Greece, 'the critical moment in the development of a young shepherd's reputation is his first quarrel'. The dispute must demonstrate in public that he will react violently to any insult.

In this interpretation, O'Neill was taking advantage of the absence of English troops to enhance his reputation as a man of power, to settle a few old scores, and to enrich his cattle stocks. This was how the Gaels had always done things. O'Neill was going back to his roots.

Águila simply did not understand this mindset. In his view, it was parochial and failed to see the bigger picture. 'I am sent to conquer the country,' he admonished O'Neill in exasperation, 'not to burn the people's corn.' According to a spy in Kinsale, that frustration was widely felt among the invading troops. 'The Spanish mislike [O'Neill's] burnings,' he reported, 'and say they came to win or lose the country.' In this author's opinion O'Neill's tragedy was that he could never escape his 'culture of honour' roots to share that grand vision.

Eventually his army of around three thousand men trudged down through the midlands to Tipperary and into County Cork, where they joined forces with O'Donnell at Bandon a few days after Zubiaur's arrival at Castlehaven.

The combined might of the insurgent army was now a mere fifteen kilometres from Kinsale.

O'Neill's sluggishness had been steadily lowering morale among Águila's troops.

According to the surgeon William Farmer: 'The Spaniards in the town, being daily beaten with shot from the camp ... began to repine at [O'Neill] and his adherents for breaking their promises with them.'

It was all reflecting badly on the clerics Oviedo and Archer, who had staked their reputations on rapid support from the insurgents. 'The Spaniard curseth the priests, the priests curseth the Irish, [and] the Irish curseth them both,' wrote the Dublin clergyman John Rider.

Fr Archer demanded the right to travel to the Irish camp and argue his case. He claimed to be the only one they would deal with. Águila refused – the last thing he wanted was to let his greatest critic spread his disaffection around the countryside, Smerwick style.

For the same reasons, Águila also did his best to keep Oviedo out of the loop. But then, Oviedo was doing much the same with Águila. The insurgent chieftains were writing confidential letters directly addressed to Oviedo. Águila intercepted them and tore them up.

Bearing all this in mind, Águila's next letter to O'Neill in mid-December was a masterpiece of self-control. 'I was confident that Your Excellencies would have come [after the Spanish arrived at Castlehaven],' he wrote. 'I beseech you to do so with as much celerity and as well furnished as you possibly may.' He assured O'Neill that the English forces were so weary and depleted that they could not guard more than a third of their trenches. 'Their first fury resisted, all is ended,' he predicted.

When O'Neill still failed to appear, he took a tougher line.

—You have promised to attack the enemy in all parts, he wrote bluntly. If you will not do so, I will make my own composition and return home.

To complicate things further, Oviedo began his own negotiations. Without telling Águila, he held meetings with the disaffected Spanish captains and selected one officer to slip out of the town and trek to the Irish camp at Bandon. His message was simple.

—We are in desperate straits, Oviedo told the Irish chieftain. If you cannot join us within six days, everything is lost.

English spies were intercepting nearly all the written communications. Blount could have destroyed the letters, but instead he read them and put them back into the system. It would play into Blount's hands if O'Neill attacked Kinsale. That would mean an open battle – a clash Blount believed he could win.

Both commanders had narrow escapes at around this time. Blount was standing in the open with Carew, inspecting a new earthwork, when a sharp-eyed Spanish musketeer spotted them and took aim. The ball passed right between them, shattering the backbone of an English soldier. Elsewhere, Águila was 'slightly wounded in the face by the splinter of stone broken by a great shot'.

In Castlehaven, Zubiaur was still licking his wounds after the sea battle. Any sense of celebration at their 'victory' over the English navy soon disappeared amid the screams and moans of the casualties.

'These poor people who've had arms and legs amputated are suffering and dying because they have no beds, and no sheets to cover them,' Zubiaur complained to the King. 'I have given all my shirts and sheets for coverings and bandages – if I had more, I would give more.' He pleaded for more resources, 'for the love of God'. Even the able-bodied were suffering from the brutal Irish weather. Zubiaur's plea for five hundred long cloaks to protect his sentries from the driving rain demonstrated just how ill-equipped they were. His men were literally shivering in the cold, he said. 'It is pitiful to see these poor soldiers, naked and exposed to the rain and the bad conditions.'

He had already written to Águila regretting that he had not the ships or firepower to join him in Kinsale. Still, he had good news about the naval battle at Castlehaven.

—The English cannot brag of victory, he wrote to Águila. Their flagship was shot through.

Alonso Ocampo, the veteran leader of Zubiaur's ground troops, reported to Águila that, while one Spanish ship was undoubtedly lost, the others could be refloated. Even their ammunition had been safely beached on the sand. Ocampo was not impressed with the 'castle' that gave the port its name.

—Five thousand men could not defend this place, he wrote. And all we have is five hundred naked conscripts and 150 sick.

Zubiaur had brought with him an expert quartermaster-general, Pedro Lopez de Soto, who confirmed that Castlehaven was 'not defensible'. He recommended that they concentrate their forces on Baltimore and Bearhaven.

Admiral Zubiaur agreed. In fact, he seemed to become obsessed with transforming Baltimore into an impregnable modern fortress. Its harbour was *maravillosisimo*, he raved – not just wonderful, but superb. Zubiaur's dangerous preoccupation with Baltimore was diverting him from his main task: breaking the English stranglehold on Kinsale. He despatched only 120 of his five hundred troops to join O'Neill and O'Donnell. Later, he sent another eighty. Even now, it seems inexplicable that he should send a mere two hundred of his men to the front. Águila had ordered him to send as many as he could spare. Alfonso Ocampo, who was placed in command of the two hundred, wrote to Águila explaining that others were needed to guard the guns and ammunition: 'The cause I sent no more [troops] to O'Donnell was to guard the munition.'

Zubiaur also armed around seven hundred Irish troops from West Cork and sent them to O'Neill along with his two hundred Spaniards, issuing them with six standards or flags to give the impression of a larger Spanish army. The locals were trained and disciplined in *tercio* style and fitted out with corselets (upper body armour) and knee-length metal waistbands known as taces. In one of his oddest decisions, the admiral sent a hundred Spanish fighters to guard remote Bearhaven, far away from the war zone, while its chieftain, Donal Cam O'Sullivan Beare, took his less experienced Irish troops to fight alongside O'Neill. No one seems to have thought that it would make much more sense to do things the other way around.

By 13 December, O'Neill was still ten kilometres away from Kinsale, but closing in fast. He encamped at Coolcarron Hill, just north of the English camp, closing off his enemy's landward supply route. It was Blount's turn to feel the tightening garrotte of besiegement.

For the next week he remained invisible to the English. They could sense the presence of the 'arch-traitor' and feel his icy grip, but they could never catch sight of him. Then, on 21 December, he suddenly appeared about 1.5km from Spital. 'Towards night,' Carew wrote, '[O'Neill] showed himself with the most part of his horse and foot upon a hill.'

Even in the half-light, it would have made a daunting sight. By this stage O'Neill commanded an army of around six thousand, so even a section of infantry and cavalry would have been an impressive force. The variety of soldiers was remarkable. There were traditional Irish light horsemen, armed with javelins, their fighting techniques virtually unchanged since the days of Cúchulainn. There were the ferocious Scottish 'redshanks' – the gallow-glass warriors with their giant battleaxes. At the other extreme, there were O'Neill's and Tyrrell's modern troops with their smart red uniforms and modern firearms, and Ocampo's Spaniards with their fluttering banners and shining steel helmets.

When he saw the force he was about to face, Blount reputedly burst out: 'The Kingdom is lost today.'

Riding at the head of this mighty, multi-coloured army was his arch-enemy – Hugh O'Neill, the Earl of Tyrone, who now preferred to be known by his Gaelic title of The Great O'Neill.

CHAPTER TWENTY-SIX

THE GREAT PERSUADER

I T is strange to think that the man who held the title of *The* O'Neill – the chieftain who represented the essence of this ancient family – may not even have been *an* O'Neill.

Hugh's supposed grandfather, Con, had kept a mistress, who in the free spirit of the age also had a relationship with a blacksmith named O'Kelly. Her child, Matthew, was widely acknowledged to be the blacksmith's son. But much later, she presented him to Con as his own son, and he accepted him as such. Legally, under the Gaelic system, a love-child had equal rights to any other child, so Hugh O'Neill, as Matthew's second son, was fully entitled to join the family queue to become chieftain. But genetically, Hugh may not have had a single drop of O'Neill blood in him.

The Great O'Neill was not a tall man – in fact, Fynes Moryson, who met him, says he was 'of mean stature'. But he was robust and 'able to endure labours, watching and hard fare'. The familiar portrait of O'Neill as a powerfully stocky figure with cropped hair, bushy black beard and full armour is almost certainly a Victorian fantasy. Drawings from the 1620s are probably nearer to the reality: they show a small, thin, wiry man with mid-length hair, pointed beard and dark, intelligent eyes.

Young Hugh had one huge advantage over his relatives: he had the support of the English colonisers. Even as a child, he had been earmarked as their puppet leader. They had no idea that they were dealing with an expert puppetmaster who would soon be pulling their strings instead.

Hugh was raised in the English manner by a foster family near Dublin, and was soon moving between the two worlds of Saxon and Gael with consummate ease. By his thirties Hugh was enthusiastically fighting Irish rebels in Munster and Ulster. 'A creature of our own' was how Queen Elizabeth described him.

Meanwhile, the complex mess that was the O'Neill succession race had been simplified when both Hugh's father, Matthew, and Hugh's elder brother, Brian, had been liquidated by rival relatives. The clan leadership went to Hugh's elderly cousin.

Then, in 1587 the English made Hugh the Earl of Tyrone and granted him huge parcels of land. However, they covered their risks by playing him off against the elderly cousin. The territory was divided, with Hugh controlling only the southern part. He seethed with a silent resentment. And behind the scenes, he was hedging his bets too. He was building up family ties with other clans, including the powerful O'Donnells of Donegal. Hugh O'Neill was declared next in line for the chieftaincy, but one man had other ideas – a relative named Hugh Gaveloch O'Neill. Hugh had Gaveloch executed; some say he strangled him himself.

For seven years, Hugh O'Neill remained superficially loyal to England. He helped to quell a local rebellion, but felt cheated when the English commander Henry Bagenal deprived him of the credit. Yet all the time his loyalties were shifting. The Great Armada shipwreck symbolised the widening split in his personality – he slaughtered many of the Spanish survivors, yet sheltered another group that included several prominent noblemen.

Above: 'Meet the man born without fear': Spanish commander Don Juan del Águila challenged English commander Charles Blount to single combat to decide the standoff at Kinsale. He is pictured here in his younger days, several years before the invasion.

By kind permission of the Casa-Museo de Los Colarte (Antequera), Málaga.

Top left: The English commander Charles Blount – 'the die is cast between England and Spain'. But for Blount personally – as for Don Juan del Águila – the confrontation at Kinsale was the last throw of the dice in his military career.

Top right: 'A fair woman with a black soul': Penelope Rich, Blount's married mistress, was a revolutionary who challenged Queen Elizabeth and survived. This early portrait may not do her legendary beauty full justice.

Bottom left: George Carew – the intelligence expert who spent much of his time spying on his own commander, Charles Blount.

Bottom right: Robert Cecil – the Queen's secretive and all-powerful Secretary was quite prepared to throw Blount to the wolves after he negotiated a peace deal with Águila.

Left: The proud Irish chieftain Donal Cam O'Sullivan Beare – 'The spirit of our people will be broken.'

Right: Fr James Archer – the master of disguise who was always one step ahead of his English pursuers. He was furious when Águila refused his military advice and told him that his function was to pray and hear confessions.

Right: Richard Boyle – he galloped across England to bring news of victory to the Queen.

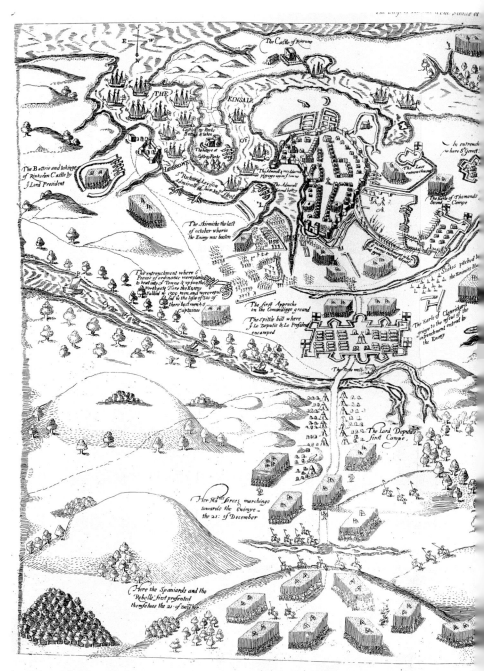

This remarkable map from *Pacata Hibernia* depicts the Kinsale siege with all events taking place simultaneously. Top, pointing south, it shows Kinsale town and harbour, Rincorran and Castle Park (top left); the English main camp and the Oysterhaven (to left of centre); the battle itself on the banks of the stream (right of centre) and the rout of the Irish troops and the last stand of Ocampo's 200 Spanish (bottom right).

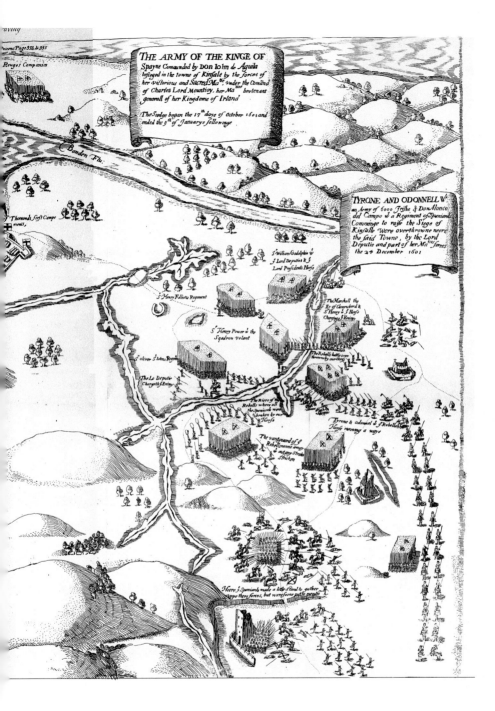

Left: Irish insurgent leader Hugh O'Neill submits to Charles Blount at Mellifont – yet right up to his death in 1616 he will continue to dream of revolution.

Left: These signatures give an insight into the personalities of the four commanders: Hugh O'Neill, Hugh 'Aodh' O'Donnell, Charles Blount (Mountjoy) and Don Juan del Águila. O'Neill defiantly uses his Irish title of 'The O'Neill' rather than the English title of Earl of Tyrone.

Above: 'The execution continued a mile and a half, until the horses were out of breath and the horsemen wearied with killing': a contemporary painting shows the English and pro-Queen Irish cavalrymen pursuing O'Neill's red-coated troops after the rout at Kinsale. From 'The Battle of Kinsale' (detail), 1601, oil on canvas, artist unknown.

The Trinity College Dublin Art Collections.

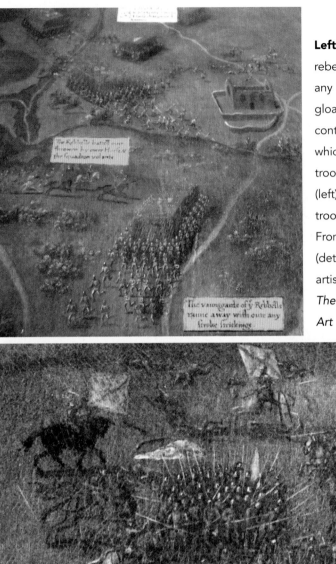

Left: 'The vanguard of the rebels ran away without any stroke stricken' gloats the caption on this contemporary painting, which shows the English troops fording the stream (left) and O'Neill's Irish troops falling into disarray. From 'The Battle of Kinsale' (detail), 1601, oil on canvas, artist unknown. *The Trinity College Dublin Art Collections.*

Above: The final moments: Alfonso Ocampo's 200 defiant Spaniards make a last desperate stand on the Kinsale battlefield as English horsemen surround them, hack them down and trample their flags into the earth. From 'The Battle of Kinsale' (detail), 1601, oil on canvas, artist unknown. *The Trinity College Dublin Art Collections.*

O'Neill feared for his future when he saw how the English illegally jailed young Red Hugh O'Donnell and framed an Irish leader in nearby Monaghan in a shameless land grab. A claimant to some territories of the McMahon clan had petitioned the English for approval only to be arrested on a trumped-up charge, convicted by a rigged jury dominated by soldiers, and executed within two days. His lands were seized and divided out among Henry Bagenal and his colonist cronies. O'Neill sympathised with young turks like Red Hugh, who wanted the English out and the Spanish in. Soon he was giving them covert support. His rift with the English became highly personal when he eloped with Mabel Bagenal, the twenty-year-old sister of General Henry Bagenal. Immature and gullible, Mabel was captivated by O'Neill's charm but quickly came down to earth when she realised she was just one of many women in his life. Henry never forgave Hugh and worked constantly to destroy him.

The English began to suspect O'Neill's loyalty and summoned him to answer complaints. But his remarkable powers of persuasion convinced them he was still their man. O'Neill was clearly a man of immense charm: Fynes Moryson describes him as 'affable' with a 'dissembling, subtle and profound wit'. It seemed he could fake sincerity like nobody else. His eyes overflowed with tears of passion as he told opposing sides, in turn, how his heart was truly committed to their cause.

One English judge interrogated the suspect. '[O'Neill], much lamenting with tears, said, I pray you let me not lose you, that hath been my dear friend,' he recalled. Overwhelmed, the judge held his hand – unaware that O'Neill was currently plotting to replace all English judges with Spanish inquisitors.

O'Neill vowed emotionally to an English friend that if he ever discovered that O'Donnell was involved with Spain he would be 'a mortal enemy to him'. As one modern author comments, he had 'an apparently infinite capacity for duplicity'.

Some claim that he was always fully committed to the Irish cause. His double-dealing was a necessary exercise in an asymmetrical conflict. He was buying time. But that doesn't explain why he sometimes acted, needlessly, against his own revolutionary interests during his pro-English phases. It is more likely, in my opinion, that he was genuinely torn. He was like a married man in the grip of an affair, pledging his future to his new love and then to his old, and, each time, genuinely meaning it. But who knows? O'Neill was, to quote Winston Churchill when referring to the Soviet Union, a riddle wrapped in a mystery inside an enigma.

All this time O'Neill was quietly raising a powerful private army. He was allowed a militia of six hundred men, but nobody said they had to be the same men. By training successive batches, he soon assembled a force of 2,500 in County Tyrone alone, with another 5,500 throughout Ulster. He reputedly rode from village to village, showing locals how to use a musket. If any man showed particular skill, he was given the gun to train others. He modernised his farms to make more money to buy guns. He imported lead, supposedly to roof his forts. It was melted down to make bullets.

The first big test of arms came when O'Neill attacked and defeated Bagenal at Clontibret, County Monaghan. Bagenal was amazed to see that the insurgent army wore neat red uniforms and shot their muskets with professional skill.

O'Neill was declared a traitor in 1595. The following year he offered a grovelling submission, 'craving the Queen's mercy on the knees of [my] heart'.

But this was just the beginning. In 1598 O'Neill crushed an English force at the Yellow Ford in Armagh. Between 800 and 1,000 English died in this, O'Neill's greatest victory. Among the fatalities was Henry Bagenal.

The following year, the Earl of Essex arrived with a 17,300-strong army and smugly swore he'd crush O'Neill. Instead, O'Neill made a fool out of him. After Essex had lost 75 percent of his army in pointless marches, O'Neill met him for a secret parlay where he talked him into a truce. One insider claimed that O'Neill promised to help Essex become king of England and to control Ireland if O'Neill were given the title of Irish

Governor – but no one knows for sure.

If the story were true, it would come as no surprise. Over the years, Hugh O'Neill had offered to give Ireland over to an Austrian (the Archduke Albert VII), two Spaniards (Felipes II and III) and a Scot (James VI), so it would not have been a huge leap to offer it to an Englishman as well. One of the greatest misapprehensions about O'Neill was that he wanted only a free and independent Ireland.

O'Neill had another motive for seeking a truce with Essex: he was now playing in a much bigger ballpark. He was in regular contact with Spain and expected aid soon. It suited him to stall for a while.

Meanwhile, in a bid to force Felipe's hand, he had reinvented himself as a campaigner for religious freedom. Although a traditional Catholic, O'Neill was not particularly devout. He had happily attended Protestant services. Essex once snorted at O'Neill: 'Thou carest as much for religion as my horse.' However, when O'Neill saw Spain's eagerness to aid the Catholic League rebels in Brittany, he declared a crusade. He compared Protestantism to an infection which had to be eradicated. He lobbied Águila in France, Felipe in Spain, and the Pope in Rome. 'Chiefly and principally I fight for the Catholic faith to be planted throughout our poor country,' he announced. He had always felt that way, he maintained, but hadn't shown his hand. 'I refrained myself from giving others to understand my intentions.'

This was an important moment, because O'Neill had created a terrifying template: that armed insurrection and the cause of Catholic freedom were one and the same thing. The inference drawn by extremists on the other side was that every Catholic was an insurgent by definition. Although this was obviously a specious argument, it created a spiral of mistrust that still plagues us today.

Many devout Catholics were cynical about O'Neill's change of emphasis.

—We were Catholics when you weren't, one Dubliner snapped back at him.

O'Neill's only hope was to persuade the Pope to force all his co-religionists into his crusade. However, the neutral-minded Catholics also had powerful voices in Rome.

It was during this propaganda war that O'Neill's nastier side emerged. He had plenty of good points – he was an inspirational figure, a born leader and a brilliant general – and because of this, history tends to whitewash his darker deeds.

In O'Neill's heartland, Catholic priests often had common-law wives. Missionaries like Fr James Archer stridently demanded they return to celibacy. O'Neill decided to curry favour with the Pope by taking direct action. His representative at the Vatican explained that O'Neill did not punish the priests themselves, out of respect for Rome. Instead, he punished the wives. When they repeatedly ignored his recriminations, he would mutilate them by slashing their faces wide open. Others were flogged or branded with irons. Even in a brutal age, these punishments were particularly cruel and permanent, much harsher than the penalties recorded for similar 'offences' elsewhere. And remember, this was not an accusation by his enemies. It was something O'Neill actually took pride in.

(Águila's great-grandfather, a canon of the Church, kept a female partner. It is strange to think that, had O'Neill been in power, the lady would have been mutilated and disgraced instead of founding St Teresa's convent.)

All in all, O'Neill's record with women was not great. He treated his wives badly, and not just poor Mabel. His fourth wife, Catherine, claimed that he used to get drunk and beat her up.

By early 1600, O'Neill's rebellion had flared up far and wide. He took a lap of honour around Ireland, dispensing favours and punishing opponents. He was at the height of his power. A Spanish invasion at this point might actually have succeeded.

The arrival of Charles Blount, with his ruthless scorched-earth policy and his 24/7/365 campaigning, forced O'Neill to concentrate on his northern base, where he was rapidly squeezed between two enemy fronts. Águila's arrival left him with no option but to bet everything on the journey south. As Carew put it, he had 'to win the horse or lose the saddle'.

Now, three months after the landing, he had finally reached Kinsale. And the dice were ready to roll.

CHAPTER TWENTY-SEVEN

'THEY DIED BY DOZENS ON A HEAP'

The siege continued, with great miseries to both the armies, and not without cause, considering the season of the year, and the condition of the country, that afforded little relief to either.

– William Monson, seventeenth-century English historian

B Y EARLY December, both sides were losing soldiers at a truly terrifying rate. Blount was losing forty men every single day to sickness, exposure and exhaustion. Fynes Moryson also reported that the newest arrivals were 'dying by the dozens each night'.

Meanwhile, inside the town, the bloody flux continued to ravage the Spanish. 'Dysentery is daily carrying off [considerable] numbers,' one priest reported.

Let's take a virtual-reality tour through Kinsale's two opposing army bases to see what life is like for the pitiable soldiers – few of them volunteers –

who are condemned to suffer the rigours of a siege through the worst winter in anyone's memory. Our tour may be virtual, but the sights we will see are all based on witness records, and the words we hear will all be authentic.

Before we set out, make sure you are well wrapped up – we are in the chilly core of Europe's Little Ice Age, and the temperature by night is well below freezing. Even in daylight, chilling fogs often enshroud the blighted landscape, locking out any cheering rays from the sun. On a bad day, the lashing rain will soak you to the skin within seconds. On a good day, the insidious misty mizzle will have the same effect within minutes. The moaning winds, often carrying flurries of jagged hail, create a wind-chill that leaves you shivering with cold.

In order to fade into the background, we will wear the clothes of a common English soldier – a cassock, a doublet, leather shoes, and the trousers of Kentish cloth known as 'Venetians'. This is basic gear, but we are among the lucky few who have kept it intact. According to Fynes Moryson, many of the impoverished soldiers swap their coats for extra money. 'In a hard winter siege, as at Kinsale … they died for cold in great numbers … upon a small cold taken, or a prick of the finger.'

First, let's walk through Blount's main camp. To enter it from any direction, you will have to slip and slither through a muck-filled trench. These are twice as deep as a standing man, so you must negotiate a rickety wooden ladder. When you reach the bottom, you exclaim in disgust as you splash into cold, stinking floodwater right up to your knees – at least, let's hope it is nothing but water. The relentless rain makes it impossible to drain the dugouts, so they are 'continually filled'.

You flounder to the next inward-facing ladder, nodding a greeting to the sentries who stand on elevated mounts, their heads protruding over earthen banks. Each man's face glows eerily from the dull light of his gun's match, a coiled cord of fuse whose end will smoulder slowly until the musketeer is ready to touch it to the powder. One sentry does not reply. You touch him and discover that he is a corpse – frozen in position, still standing at his post.

The surgeon William Farmer will later recall: 'The winter now began to grow cold and stormy with winds and bitter frosts, and snows, so that some of the soldiers were starved to death with cold standing upon their sentinels, and many had their feet and toes mortified and rot off with standing and lying on the cold ground.' Blount confirms this: 'Some are found dead, standing sentinel [who] when they went hither were very well and lusty,' he writes.

You climb the slippery ladder to the surface, and after negotiating your way past cannon emplacements and gabion baskets, you find yourself in the main camp. Originally it was laid out with military symmetry, with thirty-six tents in four squares of nine, one in each corner, with room for overflow in the fields to the north. Now, however, it is a scene of unimaginable squalor. Ever since O'Neill arrived, everything has been moved into the central camp – even the cattle, the warhorses and the dray mares, which are sickening and dying for lack of fodder. 'The Irish reduced the English to great straits,' writes the Irish annalist, 'for they did not permit hay, corn, or water, straw or fuel, to be taken into [the] camp.'

'Our horses and the new men fall sick and perish rapidly,' says George Carew, with an interesting choice of priority. So bad is the fodder shortage that the War Council is considering sending the horses away altogether. It is becoming a choice between 'sent away or starved'.

Ludhaigh O'Cleary vividly sums up the filth and stench of the place. 'The fear they had of the Irish did not allow them to send their mares or horses to the pastures,' he writes, '... so that many of these and numbers of the soldiers also died owing to cold and hunger ... They were not able to bury outside the walls the corpses of the soldiers who died ... the entrails of the horses and the corpses of the dead men lay among the living ... there arose an intolerable stench in consequence of the great blasts of air ... from the filth and dirt.'

The smell turns your stomach. But at least you are fortunate enough to be still breathing.

As you squelch miserably up the slope, you pass the exhausted off-duty soldiers who are trying to sleep in rows on the wet hillside. 'Our force grows weak rapidly,' writes one English official, 'being forced to lie in the field and watch these long tempestuous nights.'

Many are moaning and feverish. 'A great part of our companies [are] extreme sick, through the exceeding misery of this winter's siege,' writes Blount. He reckons that only a third of the remaining 7,000-strong force is able for duty.

According to George Carew, there are only 1,500 able-bodied men left out of one batch of 6,000 new recruits. Overall, he estimates each company of around a hundred men has thirty or forty men sick and unfit for duty. 'Of these, few recover,' he says grimly. 'A more miserable siege has not been seen, or so great a mortality without a plague.'

Another witness, Peter Bowlton, reverses the ratio, with forty men healthy and sixty sick in each company. The recent recruits, especially, 'do die and drop away through cold and extreme foul weather'.

You notice an imposing figure, exhausted by overwork, walking through the rows of men, stooping and singling out the worst cases for treatment. This is Dr Hippocrates D'Otthen, the most eminent physician in England and a field surgeon *extraordinaire*. He is supposed to be Blount's personal doctor, but he has been freed to supervise the military hospital. Born into a distinguished family from Lower Saxony, D'Otthen comes from an impeccable medical background – he is the son of the Holy Roman Emperor's personal physician. After a long service in war zones, he had hoped to retire to peaceful private practice when Blount 'commanded' him to come to Ireland.

The Kinsale field surgeon William Farmer is warm in his praise of the physician – 'an excellent man'. As he puts it: 'A soldier was no sooner fallen sick or hurt in the camp, but [D'Otthen] did very carefully look into all sick persons, sending some of them to the hospital at Cork, and keeping some of them in the camp ... that there was not any one hurt or sick man that was left unprovided of relief.' A whip-round among the officers paid for the medication and treatment.

You see some of the infirm queuing for a soup kitchen. Blount's concern for his men is quite advanced for his time. According to William Farmer, he 'ordained a common kitchen where hot meats and broths were dressed from day to day and given to the hurt and weak soldiers'. In his opinion this has saved a large number 'which otherwise would have perished'.

However, Fynes Moryson has a different story. 'They died by dozens on a heap,' he recalls, 'for want of a little cherishing with hot meat and warm lodging.'

You walk on. In a corner you see the latest batch of rookies doing firearms training. Their incompetence is embarrassing. 'Not ten [of them] can shoot a gun,' complains George Carew, who is worried because they are using up his precious gunpowder.

Higher up the hillside you spot a 'house of turf' guarded by sentries. Dense clouds of tobacco smoke issuing from the doorway testify to the fact that Charles Blount, eighth Lord of Mountjoy, is at home.

As always, Blount is happiest when surrounded by his close friends, many of them members of the former 'Essex Circle'. There is Essex's protégé, Richard de Burgh, the Earl of Clanrickard. There is the twenty-eight-year-old Sir Henry Danvers – he is the brother of Charles Danvers, a close friend of Blount, who was executed for his part in the coup and whose testimony implicated Blount so damningly. Like Carew, Henry Danvers is a murderer in a civilian sense – he was outlawed for several years for shooting dead a neighbour in a family feud. There is Sir William Godolphin, a Cornishman and another Essex protégé, who has already played a major role in the Kinsale skirmishes. And, of course, there is George Carew, who styles himself as Blount's friend while quietly and consistently undermining him to Secretary Cecil.

You sidle close to the house and eavesdrop on their conversation. If their talk echoes their written reports, it might go something like this.

'The weather has been such that we have had difficulty keeping our men alive,' Blount complains.

'It seems to me remarkable that any of them are living,' responds Carew, complaining that it is the veterans who most 'decay by sword and sickness'. He adds with feeling: 'There has never been a more miserable siege than this, in which many die, many more are too sick to serve, and others run away from faintness of heart.'

Carew has touched on a sensitive problem, for deserters have been fleeing the English camp for weeks now. Pathetic runaways are daily sneaking off to ports like Waterford, desperately hoping for a safe passage home. As they whisper their negotiations with sailors in the taverns, the Government's spies are listening. Usually, the only journey they will make is a short one to the end of a rope.

Both Carew and Blount are agreed that deserters need to be 'severely punished'. However Blount is understanding, if not sympathetic: 'The misery they endure is such as justly deserveth some compassion.'

The Irish writer Philip O'Sullivan claims – contentiously – that Blount's pro-Queen Irish forces have already promised Hugh O'Donnell they will switch sides to join him. 'They had commenced to fulfil their promise, deserting the English in twos, threes and tens. Now, if the desertion of all had been waited for, it would have been all up with the English.' Equally contentiously, O'Sullivan maintains that Blount is about to abandon his siege and retreat to Cork city. Ludhaigh O'Cleary, too, sees the English as being 'in intolerable straits and difficulties'.

Whatever about the finer detail, the general outlook seems bleak for Blount's army. 'So here was the case,' the English philosopher Francis Bacon wrote soon afterwards, 'an army of English, of some 6,000, wasted and tired with a long winter's siege, engaged in the middle between an army of greater numbers than themselves, fresh and in vigour, on the one side; and a town strong in fortification, and strong in men, on the other.'

You have seen enough of this circle of hell. Let us switch sides, discreetly change uniforms, and cross no-man's-land to see what life is like within the blasted battleground that was once the prosperous port of Kinsale.

To our modern eyes, the centre of Kinsale resembles a World War II blitz zone, its streets and buildings almost levelled by heavy munitions. To Elizabethan eyes, its destruction is almost unprecedented. George Carew describes 'houses so torn with our artillery, as I think the like hath been seldom seen'. But luckily for the Spanish, this is a wine-importing town. Carew confesses that it is 'hard to make any great slaughter of men by reason of the vaulted cellars in which they lodge securely'.

The Spaniards risk their lives every time they scurry across a road. The town walls no longer offer any protection – they are so flattened that even the feet of any man in the street are clearly visible to the English gunners. As Águila will later testify: 'The enemy have battered [my] defences so they could walk straight in, but they dare not.' The surgeon William Farmer observes that the Spaniards are so 'cooped in, that they durst not well peep out of the gates of the town, but to their loss'.

One Spanish officer reckons that Águila has lost 1,000 of his 3,400 men from injuries and sickness, since the siege began. Of the remaining 2,400, more than a third is ill. '[Águila] has now with him 1,800 men capable of bearing arms [and] 900 sick,' says a Spanish report.

Those still ambulant walk around in a daze, shell-shocked, bruised and half-deafened by the bombardment. The dandies of the officer class have had their finery reduced to tatters; the ordinary troops are shoeless and virtually unclad. A depleted force means fewer people to share guard duty. According to another Spanish report, more and more sentries are dying daily from sheer exhaustion. 'The soldiers laboured all through the day and night,' says the Spaniard Alférez Bustamante, 'working on defences ... digging earthworks and binding *fascines*.'

Like their enemies, they are thin and haggard from malnourishment. As Carew puts it, the Spanish 'endure infinite miseries, grown weak and faint with their spare diet, being no other than water and rusk. Dogs, cats and garrons [small workhorses] is a feast when they can get it.' Admiral Leveson agrees: 'Their best victuals … is horses, dogs and cats.' However, Bustamante says they have long since trapped and eaten all the domestic animals. 'The troops have been suffering very badly,' he wrote. '[They were] unshod, unclad, and unfed except for bread and some horses we took from the enemy at great peril. All the cats and dogs in the village had been used up.'

Oviedo's hospital, already overflowing, can't cope with the numbers of sick. 'We did not have doctors or surgeons,' says Bustamante, 'and because of this many suffered.' An official Spanish report says Águila was 'in want of fish, medicines and delicacies for the sick'.

There are conflicting reports about food reserves. According to Zubiaur, Kinsale has enough provisions to last until mid-March. However, Águila will later report that his staple diet of biscuit could last only until the English New Year. 'The Spaniards were in great straits and helplessness,' writes Ludhaigh O'Cleary, adding that Águila's men would rather die on the battlefield than slowly from starvation: 'They preferred to be killed immediately.'

Desertion is a serious problem here, too. 'About a hundred men left and went over to the enemy,' Bustamante estimates. Blount doesn't need spies, he says bitterly, because these runaways provide a constant stream of intelligence.

Mateo de Oviedo confirms the desertions, but ascribes it to low self-esteem and blames it on Águila. However, many of the absconders are driven by nothing more than hunger. 'Don Juan's miseries [are] incredible,' George Carew writes, pointing out that the latest runaways 'deserted for want of food'.

The Spaniards' only hope is that the authorities back home will sympathise with their plight and send relief – troops by the thousand, food by the shipload, gunpowder by the barrelful.

They may dream. But it's not going to happen.

CHAPTER TWENTY-EIGHT

A Meeting in the Fastness of Wood and Water

O N MONDAY, 21 December, Águila lost patience with O'Neill and O'Donnell. His letters were either being intercepted by the English or ignored by the Irish. And sometimes, he suspected, both.

He had drawn up a new strategy which he felt the chieftains could accept. But it was so sensitive that he couldn't put it in writing. He needed a trusted messenger – someone who, in the words of another Spanish report, would be 'so trustworthy that he will allow himself to be cut to pieces before he divulges his mission to the enemy'. He knew just the man for the job.

We know little about Alférez Bustamante except that he was an army ensign – something like a second lieutenant – and that he was clearly an educated man with an analytical mind and a keen sense of observation. He was obviously experienced in covert operations. And he must have been a man of remarkable courage, stamina and resourcefulness.

Bustamante was based inside Kinsale. O'Neill and O'Donnell were about six kilometres north on Coolcarron Hill, far beyond the English cordon. In order to avoid their sentries, the ensign would have had to sneak out far to the west, and then double back through the valley beyond Ardmartin Ridge before finally climbing the hillside to Coolcarron. There was a spectacular storm that night, with 'continual flashings of lightning' and 'terrible thunder', so Bustamante's journey was all the more dramatic for the deafening thunderclaps and the blinding electrical flashes that would have exposed him vividly to the enemy's view. His trek took a gruelling three hours, but eventually he found himself in what Carew colourfully described as O'Neill's 'fastness of wood and water'.

The genius of the Irish rural guerrilla tactic was that there was no single central camp. Instead, the men spread out over large areas of forest. Once in place, each unit would seal all entrance pathways with 'plashings' of tightly interlaced branches. When Bustamante arrived at the camp, he would have been greeted by scenes that were every bit as alien to Spanish eyes as any Inca settlement in Peru. There were thousands of fighters of every description, from aristocratic lords in their English-style finery to barefoot woodkern wearing little but long linen shirts and woollen mantle cloaks. There were the fearsome Scottish gallowglasses, giant close-contact bruisers with their razor-sharp battleaxes. There were the elite cavalrymen and their humble horseboys, all settling down for the night. Many used their thick cloaks as tents, for according to Moryson, 'mantles are as a cabin for an outlaw in the woods, [and] a bed for a rebel'.

—My lords, all Christendom is watching you, Bustamante told the Irish chieftains as he devoured some badly needed sustenance. They all have a stake in this war. You are serving Our Lord and His Majesty the King, who has been generous in funding you from his own pocket. But think about this: it is you who will receive the glory and the rewards after the Conquest.

Was that a promise or a threat? O'Neill listened silently, waiting for Bustamante to come to the point.

—Don Juan del Águila wants you to do one thing, and one thing only, the messenger continued.

The two chieftains tensed. Everything hinged on a credible battle plan.

Bustamante asked them if they were familiar with a particular hill that overlooked the English encampments. They nodded. They had already identified Ardmartin Hill as a strategic point on the terrain.

—Your only task is to hold that height, Bustamante instructed. There is a wood just behind the hill: bring up all your baggage and store it there. Then take trenching tools and create a new base on the hilltop. Create a strong redoubt. And hold it. That's all.

Bustamante went on to spell out Águila's orders in unmistakeable terms.

—We must be clear, he said. Whatever happens, you should not attack the English trenches yourselves. If you are attacked, then defend. Just do enough to hold that hill.

It was not an ideal strategy, but it was probably the best battle plan in the circumstances. Águila was acutely conscious of the Irish chieftains' weakness in the open field. His tactic was to feign an imminent Irish attack. With his enemy distracted, Águila's men would emerge in force and smash the English up against this unyielding defensive phalanx.

—Once you are established, Bustamante summarised, Don Juan del Águila will storm out from Kinsale and assault the enemy squadrons. If you carry out these orders exactly, within the next eight days, Our Lord will grant us not only Kinsale … but all of Ireland.

This was Bustamante's recollection of events, backed up by Spanish witnesses at the camp. It was later to be hotly contested by others. But Águila himself confirmed his orders in a letter after the event. He said it was 'impossible' that the Irish chieftains could have been confused or deceived: 'All that I sent him to say to them … was to bid them to post themselves on a mountain opposite to the enemy, who were strong, and to get themselves entrenched there, and that I would make a sortie with 2,000 men, more or less, and break through the trenches of the enemy and join them, and that once this was done, all would be well.'

It was also confirmed by an unlikely source: the Papal Nuncio to Ireland, Fr Ludovico Mansoni, who was later to become one of Águila's most vociferous critics. Mansoni said Águila had instructed O'Neill to a come to a designated hill in view of Kinsale, and to stop there until Águila saw him and sallied out. The Spanish Council of State, in its later investigation, concluded that Águila had asked them to 'concentrate, and take up a strong position, so as to present a bold front to the enemy.'

So whether or not it was a sound plan, at least it was simple – and crystal clear.

O'Neill and O'Donnell told Bustamante they would consider the matter overnight. Fires were settled and mantles wrapped around tired bodies. Next morning – Tuesday, 22 December – Bustamante claims they agreed 'in good spirit' to participate in Águila's battle plan.

As Bustamante recalled it: 'They replied to me … that with the grace of God, they would obey Don Juan. They would go to that place, and fortify it, and bring up all the baggage and fighting eqiuipment.' Águila later confirmed that the Irish had agreed to his plan: 'The Earls themselves replied that they would do it.'

The chieftains volunteered a precise time and date: first light on Thursday, which for the English was Christmas Eve.

As he prepared to trudge his tortuous route through the bogs and goat-tracks back to Kinsale, Alférez Bustamante felt uneasy. Something wasn't right. In his view, the Irish seemed strangely half-hearted.

He had good reason to be worried. Although he would not find out for sure until much later, the Irish had no intention of moving their base forward. And while they had shown enthusiasm and unity in front of their Spanish visitor, in reality they were deeply divided.

The most credible record of this split comes from the writer Philip O'Sullivan, whose uncle Donal Cam was a witness. Philip confirmed that Águila had proposed a junction between the Irish and Spanish, but 'O'Neill, O'Sullivan, and others thought this risk ought not to be run'.

Why not? The conventional explanation is that the patient, prudent O'Neill wanted to continue the siege and to starve out the English. Instead, he was persuaded to fight by the impetuous O'Donnell – with tragic consequences for Gaelic Ireland.

But that is not what Philip O'Sullivan – the original source – says. He states that O'Neill was counting on a mass desertion by the Queen's Irish troops in Blount's army. Supported by Donal Cam O'Sullivan Beare, O'Neill merely wanted to 'await the coming over of the Irish'.

According to Philip, O'Neill's plan was not to starve out his enemies, but to absorb the deserters and then to allow Blount to limp away to Cork city with his few remaining men. 'In this manner,' writes Philip, 'the Catholics might have obtained a victory without a struggle or any loss.'

However, Philip says O'Donnell was 'of a different opinion'. After a heated debate, Red Hugh had his way.

Philip claims the Irish troops in Blount's camp had promised to defect in three days – presumably from the meeting of the chieftains' council that Monday. So the most likely explanation is that O'Donnell won the dispute but, as a concession to O'Neill, agreed to wait for three days until Thursday to give Blount's Irish troops a chance to keep their promise.

So where do we get the idea that O'Neill wanted to let starvation win the war? Mainly from Lughaidh O'Cleary, O'Donnell's biographer and cheer-leader.

In his version, O'Cleary claims O'Neill said 'it was better to continue the siege carefully … till they [the English] should die of hunger'. He says that

O'Donnell, on the other hand, 'felt it a shame and disgrace' to stand idly by while the Spaniards suffered. Red Hugh thundered that the Irish would be 'condemned by the King of Spain if they suffered his soldiers to be in hardships and straits … without being aided'.

However, O'Cleary had hidden agenda. Writing in the 1620s, after O'Neill's death, he needed to convince the Spaniards to support the O'Donnells in Ireland. To this end, he depicted Red Hugh as Spain's gallant ally in the face of O'Neill's inactivity. The message was that Spain could always depend upon the O'Donnells.

O'Cleary's version was copied by the Irish annalists known as The Four Masters and has been accepted as gospel for centuries.

The difference between the conventional explanation (that O'Neill wanted to dig in for a siege) and Philip's version (that he simply wanted to await the mass desertion) is quite important. In the first case, it could be argued that O'Neill was right: that if he had had his way, he could have won at Kinsale. But if we accept Philip's version, O'Neill could not have been more wrong. The mass desertions never took place and would never have taken place, because, as we now know, most of the Irish in Blount's army were not only loyal but gung-ho almost to excess.

In any case, it is far from certain that an Irish siege would have succeeded in starving out the English. It's true that Blount was just twenty-four hours away from sending his horses out of camp for lack of fodder. On the other hand, the Irish army wasn't equipped for long sieges and the English still controlled the sea approaches.

A third possibility is that there never was any split – that it was all just a later invention to excuse the humiliating defeat at Kinsale.

Of course, O'Cleary's version has more appeal. It is a wonderfully classic and mythic tale – an archetype of age and caution overruled by impetuous youth, or of pragmatism versus doomed romantic idealism. It is a saga that has resonated down the ages. But that doesn't necessarily make it true.

For the Irish army, Christmas had literally come early. O'Neill's Catholic troops were adhering to the Vatican's new Gregorian calendar and had celebrated the Feast of the Nativity on the date the English regarded as 15 December. According to O'Cleary, their chieftains passed Christmas 'feasting and rejoicing together in delight and gladness of mind and soul'. But a few days later, the good cheer had run out and so, presumably, had the whiskey. This hit one Irish chieftain particularly hard.

Brian McHugh Óg McMahon was a 'principal commander in the Irish army' and a member of the chieftains' council that had agreed the battle plan. He was also a man 'with a tooth for the cratur', as the Irish saying goes. He loved his drop of whiskey.

Using the sort of logic that can appeal only to an alcoholic, he decided to plead for a bottle from his enemies. But what could he exchange for the firewater? That was easy. He could trade information.

Like O'Neill himself, McMahon had hopped easily back and forth across the fence of loyalties. Queen Elizabeth, frustrated at his duplicity, had once described him as 'a bad limb'.

That Tuesday, 22 December (English style), he sent a message through an English captain named William Taffe. He reminded George Carew that his son Brian had once acted as his page-boy and begged him for some whiskey. Sensing an opportunity, the crafty Carew sent the bottle 'for old acquaintance'. The following day, Wednesday, McMahon surpassed all Carew's expectations in his gratitude.

—Thank you for the aquavitae, McMahon wrote (according to Carew). Tonight, you should stand well on your guard. At daybreak on Thursday, O'Neill's army will attack you from the rear. Hearing battle, the Spanish will attack from the town. They will spare no man's life except yours and Blount's.

Carew informed his commander, who put his troops in arms, ready for the onslaught. And so the classic Irish weaknesses of drink, division and deception had betrayed the Gaels to their enemies. Or so we are led to believe.

However, many experts on Kinsale have since cast doubt on the story – or at least, Carew's embellished version of it. One modern historian, Hiram Morgan, says Carew's elaborated version 'must be discounted' as the key evidence is missing – the crucial McMahon letter which Carew, a scrupulous archivist, would certainly have retained. Another historian, John J Silke, dismisses the entire tale as 'a fabrication' invoking all the most obvious anti-Irish clichés.

Others aren't so sure. In fact, the experts seem pretty much split down the middle on the issue. F. M. Jones says it's difficult not to believe it. Standish O'Grady points out that McMahon had other strong motives which weren't alcohol-related. He didn't trust O'Neill. By secretly helping the enemy, he could ensure he would remain lord of his native Monaghan in the event of an English win. In short, he was playing both ends against the middle.

I believe that the whiskey did indeed change hands, but that the warning of the attack was so vague as to be useless. The risk of attack was obvious, and Blount had 'many sources of intelligence' warning him of an imminent assault. After the battle, Carew could not resist the temptation to 'spin' the episode, giving himself the credit for an English victory in which he actually played only a minor role. Unfortunately, his version gives the wrong battle plan. As we now know from Bustamante, the real plan which Águila had formulated, and which the Irish had accepted, was for O'Neill to remain static on the hilltop. Had McMahon given this crucial information, it could have altered Blount's entire strategy.

By being wise after the event, Carew managed to fool his contemporaries. But he couldn't fool history.

The sober reality was that Blount had been expecting an attack ever since O'Neill's arrival. 'We kept very strong guards, and every man was ready to be in arms,' says Fynes Moryson. In fact, Blount was worried that he would 'weary our men by keeping them continually in arms, the weather being extreme tempestuous, cold and wet'.

During all this, Águila kept the English busy with sallies from Kinsale, and O'Neill probed to test the English reaction. On Monday night, O'Neill ventured within two kilometres of the English lines. Blount despatched two regiments and the Irish melted back into the woods.

On Tuesday – the day after Bustamante's first meeting with the chieftains – O'Neill sent out a substantial body of troops – five hundred infantry, backed by cavalry – in a bid to break through into Kinsale. Meanwhile, the Spaniards sallied out in force, almost as though they intended to meet them halfway.

This activity does not fit with the image of the cautious commander reluctant to attack. And it seems to fly in the face of the agreement made with Bustamante only hours beforehand. But that would be no surprise with a man like O'Neill, who, after all, had spent the past decade telling people one thing and then doing exactly the opposite.

When Bustamante finally made it back into the crumbling town, he found Águila pensive rather than overjoyed at the good news he brought. A promise was one thing. Whether the Irish chieftains would keep their word was quite another.

—Did they seem frightened? he asked his agent.

—I felt they were half-hearted, Bustamante replied. They were tepid and timorous. If I were you I should be careful.

Águila thought for a while.

—You must go back again, he told Bustamante. Bring their fears out into the open, and then reassure them. Emphasise that they are not required to fight the English except as I instructed. Assure them that if they follow the plan, this war will end well for them.

The following day – Wednesday, 23 December – Bustamante set out from Kinsale at nightfall. After three hours of dodging English patrols, he finally hacked through the vicious interwoven briars and saplings and stumbled into the Irish camp at around nine o'clock. It was just around ten hours before the crucial dawn. Bustamante repeated Águila's assurances and urged the two chiefs to trust his commander.

O'Neill and O'Donnell listened quietly, then gave their solemn under-taking.

—We will be at that hill at daybreak, they pledged.

There was to be no sleep for Bustamante that night. This time he was not to return to Kinsale, but to accompany the Castlehaven Spaniards as they marched alongside the Irish to Ardmartin Hill. Like those interlaced willows that had guarded the camp, Bustamante's fate was now inextricably entangled with that of O'Neill and O'Donnell.

The Irish forces fell into ranks at midnight. The usual practice in modern European warfare was to use the classic three-division formation with the vanguard in the lead; the principal force ('main battle') in the middle; and the rearguard following. These units, often referred to as the van, battle and rear, would keep their names even when lined up alongside each other on the battlefield.

Some Irish and English sources claim that O'Neill adhered to that practice, with the Irish mercenary Richard Tyrrell leading the vanguard, O'Neill heading up the main battle, and O'Donnell leading the rear. However, Bustamante reports that they had only two divisions – the vanguard led by O'Neill and including Tyrrell; and the rearguard led by O'Donnell.

Wearing their breastplates and polished helmets, two hundred Span-iards under Captain Alonso de Ocampo also marched with O'Neill. They proudly carried the flags of King Felipe – white flags with the red cross of Burgundy. One English source says they also carried Papal banners: 'These black bands come from Spain, with Antichrist their master's banners spread,' he writes. 'Stoutly advanced, spreading in the air, richly set out with Christ's five bleeding wounds, and quartered with supposed Peter's keys.'

Backing them up were the Munster Irish – the Bearhaven men under Donal Cam O'Sullivan Beare, and the O'Driscolls from Baltimore and Castlehaven.

The main body of the force comprised O'Neill's men from Tyrone, some in their modern uniforms and some in traditional Gaelic garb. Peppering the mix were the Scots gallowglasses, and bringing up the rear were O'Donnell's northwesterners from Connaght and Donegal. 'They took ... their weapons of battle and their implements of war silently,' says O'Cleary, 'and they went in order and array as their chiefs and nobles, their lords and counsellors directed them.'

The final act in this great drama was soon to be played out. The Battle of Kinsale – the most decisive conflict in their nation's history – was about to begin.

CHAPTER TWENTY-NINE

'My Lord, It Is Time to Arm'

The kingdom of Ireland lay bleeding, and put almost to
the hazard of the last cast.
– John Speed, 1612

I
T WAS the English scout who spotted it first. Initially, it was just a spark in the night, a brief pinpoint of red flame glimmering like a glow-worm in the pre-dawn darkness.

But soon it was joined by another. And then more. Soon there were dozens – hundreds, maybe, all dancing a grotesque galliard as they moved across his vision.

It could be an illusion. Staring into the pitch darkness every night could do strange things to a man's senses, particularly those of a patrol soldier in no-man's-land, one who hadn't had a proper night's sleep for a while. The dancing lights could be will-o'-the-wisps, those ghostlike flames that sometimes flared over this ancient bogland. Or they could be quirks of the thunderous atmosphere that had lately played strange tricks on them. Just before the scouts had left on patrol, their comrades in the cavalry ranks had noticed with awe how the metal points of their lances seemed to burn with an eerie flame, as though they were carrying long lamps. Spirit candles, the Welsh called them, although the sailors knew it as St Elmo's fire.

No, it was none of those things. The experienced scout knew exactly what they were. Those lights dancing just above the ground betrayed the movements of musketeers as they marched across the uneven terrain carrying their matchlock guns. The powder had to be ignited by hand using a long cord of fuse known as a match. The fuse had to be lit in advance of any battle, and it smouldered continuously in its serpent-shaped holder. The advantage was that you were always ready for action. The disadvantage was that the light gave away your movements.

As the scout counted them, his heart must have skipped a beat. This was no low-key night patrol. There were hundreds, maybe thousands, of men out there. No doubt about it. The insurgent army was on the march towards Kinsale, and towards the English besiegers who stood in their way. The attack that would decide the fate of this siege, the fate of the three commanders, and perhaps even the fate of a kingdom, was about to begin.

The scout turned and spurred his horse back towards the English camp. There wasn't a moment to lose – with every wasted second, the odds were stacking up against them.

Inside the rubble-strewn town of Kinsale, the Old Eagle was waiting rest-lessly – a caged bird of prey, chained to the crumbling walls of this hellish town. He longed to lead his troops into an open battlefield, to organise them into solid *tercio* formation and to fight like his Spanish heroes of the old days.

It was an hour before dawn, and the Spanish commander hadn't slept.

He had honoured the promise given to the Irish chieftains that he and his men would remain in arms all night, waiting for their allies to appear on the hilltop at dawn. He hoped against hope that this would be the moment of destiny, the day when it would all be decided. Hugh O'Neill had postponed it for as long as he could. But a master strategist like Águila knew that all this delaying, all this hit and run, all this ducking and diving, could only last for so long. Eventually, *inevitably*, there would come a day when O'Neill would have to stand still and deliver. Águila prayed that this would be that day.

But sometimes praying wasn't quite enough.

Hugh O'Neill was growing concerned. His force had left Coolcarron Hill at midnight, with less than 5km to go to their objective on Ardmartin Ridge. Yet as the grey steel of dawn was edging the horizon, he had still to reach his destination – and the various units had become separated. O'Donnell's rearguard was nowhere to be seen.

That bothered O'Neill. His greatest victory, at the Yellow Ford in Armagh, had been possible only because the English had allowed their divisions to drift apart. It would be ironic if he were to be defeated for the same reason. What on earth had gone wrong?

According to George Carew, O'Neill had become hopelessly lost, 'by the darkness of the night and the ignorance of his guides, having but two miles to march at the most, missing his way'. The Irish annalist said the troops 'mistook their road and lost their way'.

That hardly rings true. The route from Coolcarron to Ardmartin – from one hill to the next – was straightforward, and O'Neill had local guides. If Bustamante could repeatedly find his way to the camp in the dark, it would have been astonishing if those guides could get lost in their own backyard.

This was a distance that most people could walk in an hour. Yet O'Donnell – the fleet-footed rural guerrilla who had left Carew dumbfounded with his 70km march over icebound mountains – somehow couldn't manage it in seven hours.

Another explanation, from the same annalist, is that the various chieftains wasted time arguing over who took precedence, before compromising on walking 'shoulder to shoulder, and elbow to elbow'. Although modern historians tend to dismiss this alleged dispute as a lame excuse for the ensuing defeat, anyone who has ever attended an Irish political meeting will find this sort of self-defeating squabble quite believable.

The Castlehaven Spanish later twisted the knife by claiming that the Irish forces deliberately dragged their feet on the journey. And there was confirmation of this from the Irish side, of all places. Ludhaigh O'Cleary says: 'There was not the desire for battle nor anxiety to attack … they were timid, languid, slow, cowardly …'

Only two things are clear: O'Neill made it to the hilltop by dawn, and O'Donnell didn't. 'O'Donnell with his column wandered about all night, owing to his guides' ignorance of the route, and was far off,' recalls Philip O'Sullivan. Bustamante even claims – and this is contentious – that the stealthy approach of the attackers was thwarted when O'Donnell shattered the silence by calling his troops into action prematurely. 'He uttered a false alarm,' says the Spaniard, 'when he should have been coming up quietly.' But if the Spaniard thought that O'Donnell's alleged clanger had awakened the dozing English, he was completely mistaken.

Blount, like Águila, had never been asleep.

The English commander, fully dressed in his multiple layers of clothing and no doubt smoking his pipe, heard the news as he sat conferring with Carew and marshal Richard Wingfield in his 'house of turf' just half an hour before dawn. For several nights now, he had given up any attempt to sleep. Now, exhausted, he was about to call off the alert for the night. He had been warned of an impending attack, but had concluded that 'some accident' had postponed it. If O'Neill had been delayed for another half-hour, Blount might have been sound asleep.

There was a thunder of hooves outside the hut as a cavalryman galloped up, dismounted and burst through the door. 'My Lord,' he said breathlessly, 'it is time to arm, for the enemy is near unto the camp.'

At around the same time as the English scout noticed those dancing pinpoints of light, the thousand troops in Henry Power's emergency flying column were patiently waiting below Ardmartin Ridge, on the Kinsale side. Captain Power had known since 11pm that an attack was imminent, and believed he could anticipate the route O'Neill would choose.

Ardmartin Hill is part of a long ridge that arcs around Kinsale town to the north and west. To the east of this ridge (to the right if you look at a modern map) is Camphill or Spital Hill, the site of Blount's camp. Ardmartin Hill, where Donough O'Brien had his first camp at Liscahane Mór, is further to the west and left. Beyond this ridge, much further north, is Coolcarron Hill. Between the two heights is a long valley sweeping from right to left, from east to west, down to low, boggy ground near the River Bandon. (Think of it, schematically, as something like a modern Wi-Fi symbol of two arcs and a dot. The dot is Kinsale town. The inner arc is Ardmartin Ridge, with Blount's camp to the right and Ardmartin Hill a bit left of centre. The outer arc is the high ground around Coolcarron, and between the two arcs is the valley.)

Captain Power reckoned that O'Neill would either approach directly over Ardmartin Hill, or bypass the ridge by going along the valley, circling around, and approaching the town from the west. From the seaward base of Ardmartin, Power could cover both routes.

And sure enough, just as dawn broke, Power spotted O'Neill 'very nigh the place where I was'.

Blount jumped to his feet and called for his horse. While Marshal Wing-field dashed off to double-check the scout's report, Blount rapidly implemented a plan he had prepared days beforehand. Since Águila was the main threat, he needed to keep the bulk of his troops in place to guard the town.

He turned to Carew.

—You will be responsible for defending us against attack from Kinsale, he instructed. Five regiments under Carew and O'Brien were lining up to guard the two main English camps.

Blount was taking a huge gamble. This left him with only around 1,200 infantrymen to face O'Neill, compared to the 5,000 or so that he left behind. But the canny commander was taking nearly all his cavalry – around 300 to 400 men. They would be more useful in the open field.

Wingfield galloped back to confirm that O'Neill's troops were indeed 'making towards the town in good order of battle' by way of the hilltop. Power, his flying column dwarfed by the might of the insurgent army, was holding the line against them, barely 365 metres downhill.

Blount mounted his horse and rode off towards the flashpoint, pausing to identify a spot in front of the town where he felt the Irish advance should be halted. It was not needed – they would never get that far.

Hugh O'Neill was standing on the bleak hilltop, watching the light of dawn reveal the full strength of his opposition. From the 88-metre height of Liscahane Mór he could clearly see the main English camp to his left – bastioned, forbidding, virtually impregnable. Ahead of him, Josiah Bodley's formidable trenchworks zig-zagged across the devastated terrain to Don-ough O'Brien's second camp, itself a masterwork of earthen ramparts and trenches hollowed twice as deep as a grave. Beyond it, almost invisible in the mist and drizzle, lay his prize – the town of Kinsale.

Another black tempest was moving in from the Atlantic. Recent storms had featured the sort of crashing thunder that seemed to explode right inside a man's head. One English officer memorably compared it to having a stake driven into your skull while rocks fell on you from the skies: 'It lightened and thundered accordingly, as if the stones from heaven should fall on Sisera's head,' wrote Thomas Gainsford, invoking the Biblical figure who was killed when a tent-peg was hammered through his cranium.

Across the entire murky panorama, O'Neill could discern thousands of shadows forming into battle order. The five regiments under Carew and O'Brien were lining up to guard the two main English camps. Their massed pikes bristled from the ranks like poisonous spines from some aggressive creature disturbed in its lair. Directly in front of O'Neill stood the thin line of Henry Power's flying column. And more enemy cavalry was already thundering across towards it in the half-light. Directing and orchestrating the army was his old nemesis, Charles Blount.

It was a daunting sight, according to Philip O'Sullivan: '[The route to town] was very strongly fortified with a trench, ditch, towers and cannon,' he writes. 'The soldiers were under arms, and the horses were bridled. Moreover, they were superior in numbers to the Irish.' Clearly, the only surprise in this 'surprise attack' was experienced by Hugh O'Neill.

Meanwhile, around half of O'Neill's 6,000-strong force was still out there somewhere in the misty bogland behind him. According to Philip O'Sullivan, O'Donnell's division 'had not arrived'.

And yet ... O'Neill still had the upper hand. He had reached the designated spot on time. He had around 2,600 men by his side – his own 2,000 troops, Tyrrell's 400 Leinstermen, and Ocampo's 200 Spaniards. Crucially, he had the advantage of the high ground. If he stayed put, the English would have to exhaust their weary, malnourished horses in an uphill charge against his massed pikes.

O'Neill waited for a while, watching and analysing. In the bogland below,

Blount did the same thing. But it was O'Neill who blinked first.

To the astonishment of the English and the fury of Ocampo's Spaniards, he gave up his only advantageous position and ordered his troops to retire, back down the hill, away from the English, and away from his Spanish allies in Kinsale.

Why did he do it? What on earth possessed him? It is one of the most hotly debated controversies in the entire saga, and unless any of us meets O'Neill in the afterlife, we will never know for certain. In abandoning a defendable position for the open countryside, he was pushing his luck to the uttermost. An army caught in an open field could defend itself only by mimicking the structure of a fort, with pikes for walls and rigid bastions of musketeers at each corner. It required iron discipline. Were his men up to it?

The most obvious reason for his retreat was that he had been overawed by the opposition and decided to withdraw to fight another day. In his detailed journal of the battle, an unidentified English soldier known only as 'IE' reported this as fact: 'Discovering [us] stopped at the foot of the hill and, anon, thinking it to be no day for him, [he] retired the troops.' Another English officer agreed, but added that O'Neill had felt himself 'cozened' or betrayed by the Spanish. 'Seeing himself both out of his way and cozened … [he] began to make his retreat.'

Philip O'Sullivan says that 'in the state of things … [he] put off the enterprise to another time'. But he adds, preposterously, that Ocampo and the other Spanish officers persuaded him to do so. In reality, these officers were furious at his retreat. According to Bustamante, they warned him it was a bad decision, 'but although they told him so emphatically, there was no stopping him'. Ocampo later confirmed this to the English. He said he had pleaded with O'Neill to 'embattle his men' and join with Águila.

Another theory is that O'Neill retreated to prevent Blount driving a wedge between his hilltop force and his latecomers. One Spanish captain later quoted O'Neill as giving that reason. An alternative explanation is that O'Neill left because Águila had not sallied out to meet him as promised. But this might be more convincing if he had stayed around a little longer than thirty minutes or so.

Perhaps the most incredible explanation was given by the Irish annalist. O'Neill's advance had been *too* swift and efficient. When dawn revealed his position, he found himself at the front line before he was ready to fight. According to Ludhaigh O'Cleary, it was not so much a retreat, more a temporary withdrawal to reorganise. 'They tried to go a short distance that they might regain their ranks and good order.' Blount agreed that it gave that appearance, but he believed it was a feint. '[O'Neill] retired beyond a ford at the foot of that hill, with purpose (as he feigned) till his whole army were drawn more close.'

The main reason may have been much simpler. All this time, the English were already moving up the hill towards him. Carew maintains that Blount's entire attack force had 'advanced towards them' and Henry Power says he began to 'draw towards them with my regiment'. Blount was already going on the offensive, and O'Neill had to react.

Whatever his reasons, O'Neill took the fateful choice that was to cost him a battle, a campaign, a war and a kingdom. He led his men off the peak, down the far side, and across a stream. Presumably he thought that the advancing English would see him off, but not actually pursue him.

He thought wrong.

Blount sniffed the air and smelled vulnerability. It is an axiom of war that an enemy retreat means nothing unless you take advantage of it. Throughout the late 1500s, battle after battle had shown how an infantry body in retreat could be overtaken and defeated by a pursuing cavalry. A retreating commander sought the safety of distance. The speed and adaptability of the pursuers' horses cancelled out that security. As an expert military theorist, Blount knew this. He spurred his horse up to the abandoned hilltop. According to IE, he wanted 'to see what profit could be made of an enemy thus troubledly retiring'.

He wasn't expecting a battle. He was just looking for an opportunity.

Just then, as though in proof of Carew's theory that the Jesuits could conjure up bad weather, a thunderstorm slammed into the side of the hill, blinding the pursuers for a full fifteen minutes and covering the retreat. The weather cleared to reveal that the Irish had crossed the stream at the landward foot of the hill and had formed themselves into units with their cavalry at the rear.

The Irish veterans were uneasy. 'They were in fear,' wrote IE, '[because] there was not before them any place of so good advantage … as those they had passed and quitted.'

Blount decided to edge forward with caution. The Irish still outnumbered his force by at least four to one. He ordered his infantry to descend the hilltop to the stream the Irish had just crossed. It was a move to test the Irish resolve, and it paid off. There was only a limited amount of skirmishing, but the bulk of the Irish force kept retreating westward along the valley to another ford.

Henry Power's flying squadron was in the thick of this action. 'The rebels, finding my Lord prepared to fight, drew back both horse and foot,' he wrote. 'Notwithstanding, we went on, and upon a ford they made a stand and skirmished with us, from whence they were beaten back to another ford not far distant.'

Still, Blount was reluctant to attack. He didn't want to be suckered into one of O'Neill's notorious tiger traps, in which a pursuing army could be lured into a hidden valley filled with deadly pitfalls or concealed reinforcements. Pausing, he called for a scout who knew the area intimately.

—Think carefully, he said. Is there any feature of this landscape the enemy could use to their advantage?

The scout shook his head.

—None, my Lord, he replied. There is only a fair champaign.

'A fair champaign' – those poetic words, signifying an open plain, were music to Blount's ears. At long last, he had O'Neill where he wanted him. There was no escape – if not quite as far as the eye could see, certainly for as far as a man could run. This open plain was an agoraphobic's hell. It was O'Neill's worst nightmare. It was Blount's dream come true.

This moment, rather than any other, was the decisive point in the Battle of Kinsale. The serious fighting had yet to begin, but Blount had looked at the future exchanges in the game and realised, like a chess master ten moves from the end, that victory was almost certainly in his grasp.

—Follow them and attack, he ordered.

From the Irish ranks, Alférez Bustamante watched grimly as the English closed in. He counted a thousand infantry and three hundred cavalry in the pursuing force, but despite O'Neill's numerical superiority, the Irish were already on the back foot. After a minor skirmish at the first ford, they had called a further retreat – much to the disgust of the Spanish officers – and had forded another stream. 'We went across another river to a wide-open field where our squadrons re-formed and waited for the enemy's next move,' Bustamante recalled.

Now on solid ground, with the river between them and the English, O'Neill's insurgents finally made a serious stand. Ocampo and his colleagues, experts in *tercio* formation, arranged the Irish infantry into the classic Spanish square, a complex exercise even among the most experienced troops. For many of O'Neill's Ulstermen, it was already second nature. For the Cork volunteers and the wilder woodkern, it must have been awkward and claustrophobic. Their joy lay in the flying attack, an athletic manoeuvre in which Irish light cavalry would burst from cover and swoop down upon the unsuspecting enemy with their own foot soldiers hanging onto their saddles like skateboarders gaining speed from the tailgate of a truck. They would detach at the point of contact: the foot soldiers would cut a swathe through the surprised enemy, while the horsemen would hurl their short spears. With no stirrups, the horsemen constantly fell off, but would simply vault back on again like circus performers. 'In swiftness, they equal and sometimes surpass the horses,' marvelled one witness. 'They mount their horses seizing them by the left ear.'

Rider and foot soldiers would reunite for the equally swift retreat into the concealing woods. The idea of staying in one place and weathering the shock of a charge must have seemed to them an illogical, and probably quite terrifying, idea.

Shane Sheale, O'Neill's trumpeter, was an eyewitness on the Irish side. He watched carefully as O'Neill's 6,000-strong force fell into position. He counted twenty ensigns with 300 men under each flag. But there was one force missing. Contentiously, Sheale maintained that the deputy leader of the insurgents was still out there in the wild, wandering somewhere in the drizzly miasma, 'severed from them by reason of a mist in the morning'.

The most significant battle of the entire rebellion was about to begin … and Red Hugh O'Donnell was not going to be part of it.

Both sides took time to organise, but by mid-morning the situation was clear. At the western end of the valley behind Ardmartin Ridge, Blount's 1,200 infantry and 400 horsemen were lining up on the east side of a stream that seemed fordable only at one point. Some insurgent musketeers were stationed at the same side, guarding the passage. Beyond the river, on firm ground, the insurgents were lined up in two units – O'Neill's main battle force and a detachable flying column comprising Tyrrell's Irish and

Ocampo's Spanish. Most of the Irish cavalry was behind them, held in reserve. O'Donnell was either nowhere in sight or commanding a rear-guard far off to the east, according to which source you believe.

The retreat had been abandoned. O'Neill now had 'a resolution to fight'.

Even then, at that late stage, the odds were still in O'Neill's favour. He outnumbered the immediate enemy force by at least four to one, and he occupied what Blount described as 'a ground of very good advantage for them, having a bog behind us and a deep ford to pass'.

For a while there was a tense standoff as the Irish taunted and jeered their enemies in the traditional way. The heavy English warhorses snorted and squelched uncomfortably in the peaty muck. No one moved.

Then Richard Wingfield and Richard de Burgh sent Blount a message that changed everything.

CHAPTER THIRTY

'The Day of Trial': The Battle of Kinsale

This was the day of trial ... for if the enemy had prevailed in battle

... Ireland would hardly ever have been recovered.

– William Monson, seventeenth-century English historian

I T IS around 10am on Christmas Eve when the Battle of Kinsale begins. At around the same time, in the streets of faraway London, citizens are dressing meat and fowl to celebrate the feast-day when there is a low subterranean rumble and the ground shifts terrifyingly beneath their feet.

The earthquake that hits England's east coast on 24 December 1601 is relatively minor. But it is such a rare event that it is immediately taken as a portent for the wars in Ireland. 'Many times such signs prove [an] omen,' a seventeenth-century historian will later declare. 'This proved fortunate to us [at Kinsale].'

At the standoff beside the ford near Kinsale, the earth does not shudder. But thunder rolls ominously and the air is tense, charged, electric. Lightning flashes in the distance. Mist swirls and hovers over the bogs. Everything smells of wetness – wet air, wet grass, waterlogged bogland, damp wool, damp horsehair, damp leather – but it finds a sharp counterpoint in the acrid fume of smouldering musket cord.

For a time it looks as though O'Neill's musketeers have succeeded in holding the deep ford, the only passage across the stream, and that they have blocked Blount's advance. But the position changes when Marshal Richard Wingfield's messenger gallops up to Blount.

—Your Lordship, he gasps breathlessly. Sir Richard has found another passage across the river, a musket shot further along. There are no enemy musketeers there, only their cavalry. If you give him leave to charge, he hopes to do some good service.

Blount assimilates the new information.

—Tell him I approve, he replies. He is to attack at his discretion.

Richard de Burgh, the young Galwayman, adds his voice to the plea. Thundering up in a spray of mud, steam rising from the flanks of his galloping horse, he urges Blount to take advantage of the new passage.

—We must attack now, Your Lordship, he pleads. We cannot lose this moment.

Blount nods his assent and redeploys his troops. De Burgh's cavalrymen and the English scouts under their captain, Sir Richard Graeme, rejoin Wingfield at the second crossing.

Meanwhile, a hundred English musketeers and a hundred cavalrymen from Henry Power's flying squadron move in to seize the first passage from O'Neill's musketeers. The English veterans are expert in the art of skirmishing. They are co-ordinated by a specialist – a Lieutenant Cowell – who wears a distinctive red cap that makes him always visible to his men. The two sides slam together in a fury of musket powder and clashing steel. In this phase of the battle, O'Neill's men prove better at the art of skirmishing than Blount's. 'They poured on them a strong shower of globular balls … from their straight-firing, costly muskets,' reports Ludhaigh O'Cleary. 'The armies on both sides were pell-mell in consequence, maiming and wounding each other, so that many were slain on both sides.'

Before long, Cowell and his veterans are forced to retreat until they find their backs up against their own cavalry. But as the English pile on reinforcements, the tide turns and O'Neill's men are forced back to the river-bank. Still, nothing has changed: the English remain blocked on their own side of the stream.

Not for long. A couple of hundred metres downstream, Wingfield, Graeme and the loudly enthusiastic Richard de Burgh are charging the second passage. The light Irish cavalry who guard the ford are taken completely by surprise. The three English cavalry officers 'forced the enemy horsemen that kept the passage and passed over', records the surgeon William Farmer.

De Burgh is so closely engaged that his clothes are pierced in several places by swords and spears. Later he will discover that musket balls have gone right through the fabric, narrowly missing his skin. He has 'many fair escapes', as Fynes Moryson later marvels.

Now Wingfield's cavalry have established a toehold on the enemy's side. Blount orders more troops to wade across to join them. 'The enemy called off the pursuit from the side of the river and took another route across, further down,' says Bustamante.

But in the meantime, Wingfield's tiny force of 250 horsemen is in a precarious position. Because they detoured down the river, they have ended up side-by-side with the rear end of O'Neill's main battle force. It is impossible to go back – they will be cut off. '[Since] they could not get back without much loss,' says one cavalry officer, '[they opted] to try a fortune.'

Wingfield and de Burgh launch an all-out charge against O'Neill's flank, even though their opponents outnumber them by at least four to one. It is not as foolhardy as it seems. In theory, the inexperienced Irish should abandon their *tercio* formation and scatter in the face of the threat. But if they don't, the English cavalry are well trained in charging right up to an enemy's front line and wheeling off at the last minute.

A contemporary painting (reproduced in this book's picture section) captures the drama as they charge in: horsemen clad in black leather or shining armour, half-pikes raised to strike, their black and grey chargers at full gallop. But to everyone's surprise, the Irish ranks 'stand firm' and take the psychological shock as the 250 tank-like warhorses thunder down upon them. Unflinching, they hold the line. The monstrous horses close in, their nostrils flared, their massive bulk blocking out the sky. The pikemen dig their lances into the earth and prepare to take the impact. But the attackers wheel around, clearing the bristling pikes at the very last second, and gallop off to the side. It is a sophisticated game of 'chicken', and O'Neill has won.

The Irish ranks explode in a mighty roar of triumph. '[It] cause the rebels to give a great shout,' says Henry Power.

However, the insurgents are misreading the situation. Just one charge, they think, and the English are already retreating! They don't realise that this is just the first move in a repeated contest of nerves.

O'Neill calls up his main cavalry, which is being kept in reserve to the rear of the main force. '[The insurgents] taking courage, drew on their horse with a cry to charge,' recalls the English soldier known as IE.

Five or six hundred Irish horsemen canter up to cries of encouragement. These are not just ordinary ranking soldiers. They comprise the elite of Gaelic society, 'being all chiefs of septs and gentlemen'. At first they advance confidently on their small mounts. '[They] came on bravely to within fifty or sixty paces of our horse,' says IE, 'and there, after their country fashion, stopped, shaking their staves and railingly vaunting.'

Probably they hope to goad the English into abandoning formation and descending into the sort of free-for-all which the Irish could win. If that is their tactic, it doesn't work. Wingfield's cavalry stays put and the Irish stay put too, unsure of their next move. Their bluff has been called. A direct charge against the much heavier English warhorses would be suicide.

'They durst charge no further,' says IE.

No one is sure what happens to trigger off the cataclysm that follows.

Perhaps Bustamante is right when he says that the English musketeers fire a volley into the Irish cavalry at a mere fifty metres' range, taking down several riders and a horse. Carew may confirm this when he says the rout follows 'a few volleys of small shot'. Or perhaps it is just the sight of the English reinforcements that spooks the Irish cavalry. Throughout all this, Blount has been steadily moving more troops across the unguarded stream. Philip O'Sullivan leaves his options wide open, saying that it happens 'either by accident, or somebody's cunning or treachery'.

We may never know the true reason. But what happens next is quite astonishing. And it happens 'in an instant'.

The Irish horsemen abruptly turn around and gallop back towards their own *tercio* formation – not around it towards the rear, in the direction they've come, but heading straight smack into the front line of the tightly massed ranks. They are not fleeing from an English charge at that point. No one is pursuing them. But, inexplicably, they are turning tail and heading on a course which will guarantee disaster. If the Irish infantrymen hold their ranks, the horsemen will be skewered on their own pikes. If they break ranks, there will be chaos.

Bemused and baffled, the Irish pikemen raise their lances and the musketeers lower their guns as they see their own horsemen gallop towards them, eye to eye and obviously not about to alter direction. At the last minute, the men in the ranks open to let their betters through. After all, these are their superiors, the elite who lord it over them every day. Nobody is about to tell them to go around the back.

The horsemen blunder right through the ranks, not slowing down, until they emerge at the other end. Fynes Moryson cannot believe what has just happened. '[Out of] fear, they broke first through their own bodies of foot,' he marvels, 'and after withdrawing themselves to a hill distant from the foot, [they behaved] as if they intended rather to behold the battle rather than to fight themselves ... [it was] the chief cause of their overthrow.'

Even from the insurgent viewpoint, Philip O'Sullivan has to concede that the Irish cavalry 'forced the [Irish] foot to open their ranks. The disordered foot took to flight.' From the English viewpoint, Carew agrees that 'their horse fled and their foot ... brake'.

Shane Sheale, O'Neill's trumpeter, assumes that the cavalry are fleeing from a charge.

—Our horsemen ran away when the English cavalry charged them, he recalls later. They broke into our main battle force and disordered our infantry. That was the cause of our defeat.

Alférez Bustamante is equally dumbfounded. 'We'd suffered only a few casualties [by then],' he says, '[but] our forces fell back in such a way that our own cavalry shattered our own squadron.'

There is total mayhem as some soldiers try to close the ranks while others move back. The cheek-by-jowl formation of the *tercio* has become a serious handicap. Watching incredulously, Marshal Wingfield sees his chance and grabs it. With his cavalry now unopposed, he swings around the enemy's rear and charges. Meanwhile the English infantry joins the attack.

Henry Power takes up the story: '[Our] horse and foot together charged through them [and] brake that gross, which consisted of 1,500 men.' Blount adds: 'Both horse and foot fell into disorder and brake.'

O'Neill's force is now in disarray at both ends. According to Power, this is a huge psychological blow to the insurgents, since the worst chaos reigns among the veterans from O'Neill's own heartland of County Tyrone. 'This being such a fearful thing to the rest,' says Power, 'that they all brake and shifted for themselves.'

The contemporary painting shows the Irish fleeing, not headlong, but in an uncertain, desultory and very human fashion. Some of the red-uniformed soldiers are running flat-out down the road, ahead of the pack. Others are slowly detaching themselves from the ranks, hesitantly walking away, unsure what to do next, before joining their fleeing comrades. The whole scene is summed up from an English viewpoint: 'The vanguard of the rebels fled,' it says, 'without any stroke stricken.'

Within minutes, the carefully constructed *tercio* is reduced first into disorder, and next into headlong retreat. 'Thus all were panic-stricken,' says Philip O'Sullivan, 'or rather, scattered by divine vengeance.'

That may be, but right now it is the English who are wreaking the vengeance. They tear through the fleeing Irish ranks like foxes in a poultry-run, murderous and unopposed. 'They fell upon O'Neill's people,' says the Irish annalist, 'and proceeded to kill, slaughter, subdue and thin them.'

A grotesque turkey-chase ensues, with the English riders galloping after the fugitives, hacking and chopping them down at will. In this carnage, a human being can survive only if he can run faster than a galloping horse.

—If we had not been swifter of foot than the English horses, not one of us would have escaped, one of O'Neill's soldiers will later admit.

More than three thousand discarded weapons are scattered on the ground.

The same contemporary painting captures the horror. The field is a pastoral dreamscape, a sweet rolling hill of green grass and brown heather, broken only by dry-stone walls and an ancient ruined church. Across this serene backdrop the English riders thunder like figures from a nightmare. They are apocalyptic horsemen, dark avenging angels who charge up to each of the fleeing Irish redcoats, their half-pikes raised, about to plunge sharp blades into unprotected backs. Some horsemen leap across the stone walls in pursuit of the terrified fugitives. The dead and wounded are strewn across the verdant hillside.

'The execution ... continued a mile and a half ... until the horses were out of breath in running and the horsemen wearied with killing,' one English source exults. 'The dead bodies of the rebels on every side were like the weeds of the field.' Another writer describes the carnage: '[In] each dike and gap they gruelling lay, besprinkled all with blood. One legless lay, another wants his arm; some all too cut and mangled, back and face, that streams of blood were shed in every place … wounded sore, and hurt in grievous ways … howling with loud cries … there you might see them languish and make moan.'

'Make no Irish rebels prisoners! Put them to the sword!'

The yell rises above the shouts and screams of the rout. It is Richard de Burgh, the Galway-born Earl of Clanrickard. All his pent-up resentment at his neighbour O'Donnell is exploding in a bloody lust for revenge.

Yet the trumpeter Shane Sheale records a pathetic scene at the height of the rout. He claims that many of de Burgh's Irish troops take pity on their fleeing countrymen. While pretending to attack them with their spears, they actually use 'the butt end of their staves'. Without that small act of mercy amid the cruelty and carnage, says Sheale, the death toll would have been much higher.

'The main battle [force] was almost all slain,' says surgeon William Farmer. 'Twelve hundred bodies were there found presently dead, and about eight hundred hurt, whereof many died that night. The chase, continuing the space of two miles, was left off by reason the Englishmen were tired of killing.'

Bustamante, who reckons eight hundred died in the chase alone, says no one would have survived but for the English reluctance to spread their small force too thinly. However, Blount has a slightly different story. 'Had not the weather been extreme foul, and our horses weak and not of heart that we could no longer follow the execution … we might have done what we wished, for they never made any resistance nor looked back.'

More than a thousand men lie dead, but still the battle is not over. O'Neill's main battle force is just one of three units lined up across the valley and plain. To the centre is Tyrrell's 400-strong force with the 200 Spaniards under Ocampo. Further out to the left (facing forward from the Irish ranks) is O'Donnell with his 1,500 northwestern Irish.

O'Donnell plays very little part in the battle, if any. Later, Philip O'Sullivan will claim that it was his troops who defended the river against Wingfield, but this seems impossible since Red Hugh's rearguard is far away from that scene. Even the O'Donnell-centric Lughaidh O'Cleary states that the vanquished unit is O'Neill's. It is only after the defeat that it reunites with O'Donnell, 'who happened to be to the east of them, and had not yet come to the field of battle'. Shane Sheale says simply that O'Donnell was 'not in the fight'. It may well be true, however, that O'Donnell shouts after the fugitives, calling on them to stand firm.

—Stand your ground! he calls out to O'Neill's soldiers, according to the Irish annalist. You nobles, stand by me and fight your enemies! It is a disgrace to turn your backs on the enemy. Never before has our race done such a shameful thing!

But before long, he is shouting to his own men as well. They, too, are heading for the horizon. Red Hugh keeps shouting until his voice cracks with 'vehemence and loudness'. As we'll see, his frustration, hopelessness and despair are about to send him into a tailspin of mental anguish which he cannot correct.

Effectively, there is now just one insurgent unit left in play. In the centre, stuck between O'Donnell on their far left and O'Neill's fleeing troops on their right, are Tyrrell's four hundred Irish troops and Ocampo's two hundred Castlehaven Spaniards. Tyrrell, who is in overall command, watches as the English move in pursuit of O'Neill's shattered main force. He decides to move to his right and interpose his flying squadron between them – a heroic gesture since he is now outnumbered by two or three to one. Unfortunately for him, there is another enemy unit moving in to his left – the English rearguard, now commanded by Charles Blount.

In his concentration, Tyrrell leaves his left flank exposed. It is a rookie mistake and he pays dearly for it. Blount charges in and wreaks so much damage that the Irish-Spanish unit abandons its plan and seeks sanctuary on a nearby hillock.

Blount closes in for the kill. Tyrrell's mercenaries watch their comrades fleeing for their lives and decide – understandably enough – that their contract is null and void. They, too, begin to melt away. 'They made a stand a little while,' says William Farmer, 'but at the last, Tyrrell and his Irish soldiers quitted the Spaniards and left them alone.'

Now completely abandoned, Alonso Ocampo and his brave two hundred are the only ones left on the field. They make a valiant stand on that hill, courageously defending the honour of Spain and protecting the royal flags. The painting shows them grouped together in a desperate huddle, their steel helmets gleaming, their pikes thrusting out at every angle. But they are surrounded, and the outcome is inevitable. One by one, the Burgundy flags are torn away from the grip of the fallen defenders. 'The Spaniards, like amazed men (cursing the day they ever they came to Ireland) made a stand,' says one English witness. 'Many of them were killed.' Farmer agrees: 'The most part of them were slain.'

According to Bustamante, 'three of His Majesty's colours were lost in fighting, and up to seventy Spanish were taken prisoner.' Quartermaster Lopez de Soto reckons that 140 were either killed or captured.

One English officer, a Captain John Pikeman, spots Ocampo in the midst of the fray and hacks his way across to take the honour of capturing him. On the way he sustains three wounds, but he makes it across to the Spanish field commander and takes him prisoner. At the precise moment when Ocampo yields up his sword, the Battle of Kinsale is over. It has lasted only two to three hours.

Amid the chaos, Bustamante and some sixty other Spaniards manage to escape. Although stunned by the rout, and exhausted after several nights without sleep, Bustamante suddenly has a moment of blinding insight.

Águila had clearly instructed the two insurgent chieftains to bring digging tools to entrench Ardmartin Hill. They didn't bring so much as a shovel. He also ordered them to bring all their baggage forward and south to their new front line at the ridge. They didn't. Instead, they sent their baggage even further *back* – a full 15km to the northwest of the camp at Coolcarron.

At that point, the Spaniard finds himself wondering if O'Neill and O'Donnell were ever really serious about doing battle with the English at Kinsale. As Bustamante put it: 'Did they really want to fight – or what?'

Inside the rubble-strewn town of Kinsale, Águila's Spanish soldiers still wait for O'Neill to keep his appointment on the hilltop. (Unbeknownst to them, O'Neill has already appeared there briefly, shrouded by the dawn gloom, before retreating back into the mists of the valley.) Águila himself is standing in full armour at the gate. Watchmen are posted at the highest points. All ears are craned for the sound of an army approach, or for some sort of signal, but amid the relentlessly driving rain and the rolling thunder it is impossible to tell which noises are real and which are illusions induced by sleeplessness and wishful thinking.

At one stage, Fr Archer thinks he has heard the sound of 'artillery' – impossible, since cannon will never feature on the battlefield – and demands that Águila open his gates and sally out to the attack.

—All we need to do is make a show of our troops, he insists, and we will certainly triumph!

But Águila is too old and shrewd a fox to rush into a fight without knowing the facts. He orders his scouts to slip out to the front line to confirm. They report back that there is still no sign of the Irish army on the ridge. If there was gunfire, it was probably a subterfuge by the English.

By this stage the troops are restless, jumpy and anxious for action. Águila makes a proclamation to calm everyone down.

—There will be no attack at this point, he instructs firmly. The gunfire was a trick to lure us out into a trap.

The two clerics are livid at the decision. But Águila is adamant. If the Spanish were to sally out prematurely with O'Neill still on his way, then all would be lost. Waiting is all they can do.

The minutes drag by, agonisingly slowly, until the weak midwinter sun reaches its pathetic apex. Then: a furious explosion of noise. Hundreds of muskets and arquebuses are blasting out. There are shouts, yells, a deafening commotion ... all the sounds of a full-blown battle.

The Spanish glance at each other and then at Águila. He nods and orders the sally-ports flung open. Yelling warcries, the veteran troops pour out into the open ...

... only to be confronted by the sight of flags fluttering on the English side of the trenches. The red crosses of Burgundy. The beloved colours of King Felipe of Spain. Seven of them.

For an instant, it must seem like a dream come true – as though their Spanish reinforcements have burst through and taken the English positions. But those flags are all in the hands of their enemies. Enemies who are mocking them as they flaunt the flags, drag them in the dirt, and point to their captive comrades, the Castlehaven Spaniards. It is a dreadful moment, a stomach-twisting and sick realisation.

Those noises were not the sounds of battle. They were the sounds of a victory celebration.

Águila's Spanish are not the only ones taken in. George Carew too hears the noise and advances from the main camp ready for a full-scale fight. When he hears that it is just Donough O'Brien's men firing in celebration, he does the same. His men 'spared no powder and did make their pieces [guns] pronounce their joy'.

One English officer is delighted to have fooled Águila: 'The Spaniards, hearing of the terrible noise and hot skirmish (to their thinking) did assure themselves that Tyrone and our forces were in fight,' he crows.

For honour's sake, Águila's Spaniards press ahead with their attack. But they are 'quickly beaten back' and the gates of Kinsale are firmly closed once more.

Before he leaves the corpse-strewn battlefield, Blount has one more duty to do. He calls over the young Richard de Burgh, who has personally killed twenty insurgents in the fray, and signals him to kneel on the turf.

—You carried yourself worthily on the battlefield, Blount tells the Galwayman. Not only in your words, which encouraged others to fight, but also in your deeds and actions. No man did bloody his sword more than you. Here on this plain, even among the dead bodies, I dub you a knight. From this moment on, you will have the honourary name of the battlefield. Arise, Sir Richard Kinsale.

This honour, the only one to be granted that day, makes an enormous impact on the officers. Thomas Gainsford will later tell de Burgh: 'When I saw you knighted on the field (and none but yourself), yea, in the dirty fields before Kinsale, my heart leaped for joy ... When death has undertaken to obliterate our memories, yet shall after-ages demand, who this Earl of Clanrickard was.'

His words seem ironic in hindsight, since Richard de Burgh, Earl of Clanrickard, has been almost totally forgotten by history. But at that moment, he is the acknowledged hero of the English. In fact, two seventeenth-century histories will later credit de Burgh with the entire victory. One says the Irish were 'disordered and routed by the Earl of Clanrickard'. Hugh O'Donnell will later tell Felipe III that de Burgh's actions at Kinsale did 'great harm' to Spain.

The dramatic bestowal of the knighthood is a shrewd move by Blount, since de Burgh is also an insider in the Essex circle. To rehabilitate de Burgh is to rehabilitate himself.

We know from other sources that many members of the English military establishment are jealous of de Burgh's success. It will not be lost on them that the man who turned the tide of the battle against the Catholic Irish forces of Hugh O'Neill is not only a native Irishman, but also a proud and uncompromising Catholic.

Now all that remains is the grisly count of the bodies which lie, not just on the plain beside the ford, but spread out over three kilometres northwards.

On the Irish side, the death toll is either 500, 800, 1,000 or 1,200, depending on which source you accept. O'Neill reported 500 deaths to King Felipe. Henry Power says 800 lay dead at the scene. Blount first assesses the total at 1,000 dead and 700–800 injured, but Carew claims 1,200 dead with 800 injuries. Later Blount's official report refers to 1,200 bodies, and Fynes Moryson and IE concur with that higher figure.

However, the Irish themselves downplay the figures. The Irish annalist dismisses the deaths as 'trifling' and 'not so great'. Philip O'Sullivan claims O'Neill lost two hundred infantry. Only O'Cleary concedes that 'many' were slaughtered.

The figures reported by individual Irish combatants are more realistic. One chieftain named O'Hagan has died alongside 480 of his 500-strong company. Of the remaining twenty, seven die later of injures. Another company of 100 has been obliterated. Yet another company of 300 is reduced by nine-tenths to thirty-one. Among the worst affected are the MacDonnells – the Scots and Antrim mercenaries known as 'redshanks'. Two companies of 100 are wiped out and another originally numbering 300 is now down to a mere thirty.

Total: 'Captains slain, fourteen. Soldiers slain, 1995.'

That final figure probably includes further losses on the long journey home. As a rough figure, we can put the Irish deaths on the battlefield at around a thousand.

In contrast, the English have lost a mere handful of men – one, two, three or seven, depending upon your source. William Farmer says: 'There was but one of the Queen's soldiers slain that day … John Taylor, that was cornet to Captain Richard Graeme.' However, Philip O'Sullivan claims they lost 'three nobles' and the English physician Dr Hippocrates D'Otthen agrees with that number. An English officer named Captain Dutton says they lost 'only two men' but the seventeenth-century historian Richard Cox makes it seven: 'one cornet and five or six soldiers.'

These low figures are doubted, even in England. The contemporary courtier Francis Bacon will say that the loss of only one man was 'scarce credible'.

It hardly matters. The fact remains that during the battle itself, the English have inflicted wholesale carnage on the Irish at little loss to themselves. The bloodletting is so great that the river will be renamed 'the Ford of the Slaughter' because for a time it literally runs red.

And now, Blount must deal with the captives. He follows his usual policy of treating the Spanish as prisoners of war. However, some are pushed into Kinsale town to tell their full horrific story.

The Irish insurgents he views differently – he sees them as traitorous subjects of the Queen. Some of the richer Irish prisoners 'offer great ransoms', but there are very few exceptions – only 160 of them are spared. The rest are strung up on the spot. And to ensure maximum propaganda effect, the gallows are erected close to the town, so that the sight of their allies twisting and kicking in their prolonged death-throes will forever haunt the nightmares of Águila's defenders on the ramparts of Kinsale.

Afterwards Blount, 'with sound of trumpet, called the whole army together and concluded this, his glorious victory, with prayers, praise and thanksgiving to God who is the giver of all victory'.

CHAPTER THIRTY-ONE

WONDERING WHY

THE LORD giveth, and the Lord taketh away. And as the Irish survivors limped miserably back to their first base camp at Innishannon, thirteen kilometres away, they must truly have felt as though they had been punished by God. There could be no other reason for such an unexpected and humiliating defeat. 'God did not will it [a victory] and he chastised us for our sin, for there is no other reason,' Oviedo wrote. 'Our sins snatched victory from our hands.'

There was plenty more in the same vein. 'Divine vengeance' says Philip O'Sullivan. 'Manifest was the displeasure of God,' says the Irish annalist. 'For our sins, the enemy broke up the weakest squadron,' writes Zubiaur. 'It was not the will of God to give victory,' says O'Cleary.

However, modern analysts don't have things quite so easy. There are many complex factors to be untangled. Why did it all go so horribly wrong for the Irish? For centuries, the debate has raged even more fiercely than the battle itself. Before resuming the narrative, let's hold a brief post-mortem. Having combed through most of the accounts and analyses, I have compiled the principal theories:

THE 'COWARDLY IRISH' THEORY

The standard English explanation for the victory. As Carew put it: 'God cast in their hearts a needless fear' as they faced a charge. The terrified Irish abandoned all discipline and bolted. This explanation suited the English because it reinforced the image of a superior race subduing barbarians. The contemporary writer Francis Bacon even joked about it: 'There appeared no difference between the valour of the Irish rebels and the Spaniards, but that the one ran away before they were charged, and the other straight after.'

But that wasn't true. Before the rout, O'Neill's musketeers had fought fiercely in a bid to hold the second river crossing, and their *tercio* had withstood the shock of an all-out charge by Wingfield's cavalry with steely discipline before they made the fatal error of parting ranks to admit their own retreating horsemen.

In disarray, they broke up under an English charge and ran. But, remember, a tactical runaway was standard practice for the Irish in this asymmetric war. It had served them well in the past. 'They think it no shame to fly or run off from fighting, as they advantage,' wrote Fynes Moryson.

The difference at Kinsale was that they had been suckered into fighting in open countryside. Blount showed his military genius in ensuring that it was 'a fair champaign' before committing himself. Moryson again: 'At Kinsale, when they were drawn by the Spaniards to stand in firm body on the plain, they were easily defeated.'

The tragedy for the Irish was not that they ran. It was that they had nowhere *to* run … and nowhere to hide.

THE 'COWARDLY SPANISH' THEORY (1)

In the 1800s, a new wave of nationalist Irish writers revived Kinsale as a touchstone of doomed heroism. In this revisionist version, the gallant Irish chieftains stormed southwards across icebound rivers to help the incompetent, timorous and geographically challenged Juan del Águila, who cowered safely in town while the Irish did all the fighting. Spanish inaction was the main reason for the defeat, helped along by treachery (the whiskey), by incompetent guides and by O'Donnell's brave impetuosity.

But as we have seen, Águila was far from inactive, the chieftains took their time about joining him, the whiskey betrayal didn't make any real difference, and the final two reasons are open to doubt.

THE 'COWARDLY SPANISH' THEORY (2)

The idea that a spineless Juan del Águila caused the Irish defeat was given fresh impetus in the mid-1900s when researchers unearthed some little-known letters of his fiercest critics, Archer and Oviedo. Archer's view that Águila was 'cowardly and timorous' seemed to be supported by his claim that Águila had heard the noise of the battle but ignored it as an English ruse. The officers were keen to fight but he overruled them.

However, the commander's reputation was rescued by another historian, Henry Mangan, who pointed out that Águila was relying on front-line information from scouts. Oviedo and Archer had no better information. The historian said this was just one of the many instances where the opinionated clerics had undermined the military campaign. Later, military-history expert Gerard Hayes-McCoy supported this verdict. The churchmen's enthusiasm was far beyond their military knowledge, he wrote, adding that nobody in Kinsale knew anything about the battle until the English returned victorious.

Which poses the question: Why didn't Águila hear anything?

In my opinion, there are several reasons. The battle was fought on a low plain several kilometres beyond an eighty-metre high hill. No big guns were used. The weather remained 'extreme foul' with an initial thunderstorm followed by rain that could easily have drowned out the muffled pops of muskets. Meanwhile, at Kinsale, the English troops were noisily manoeuvring.

Interestingly, Águila was vindicated on this count by unlikely champions – his enemies. I have found an obscure passage in a near contemporary English history (1620s) which says Blount was lucky because 'the wind blew from such a quarter that the discharging of the small shot [at the bat-tlefield] … was not heard in the town'.

THE MULTIPLE ERROR THEORY

As every air crash investigator knows, disasters are usually caused not by one huge error but by a build-up of minor ones.

Admiral Zubiaur was highly critical of the organisation on the battlefield. He complained that, instead of creating a formidable fighting unit using the best captains and soldiers, O'Neill scattered the troops all over the place, 'divided into different parts, where they fought and lost spirit'.

Military history expert Gerard Hayes-McCoy has identified several tactical errors on the Irish side. Their divisions were too far apart and made little attempt to support each other. O'Neill had no secure line of retreat, and the mostly inactive Irish horsemen allowed the English cavalry to dominate the field. Tyrrell bared his flank to a potential English attack and suffered the consequences. O'Neill had shown a fatal caution when decisive action was needed.

The reason for the defeat, the writer concluded, was that the Irish had affected to be a disciplined *tercio*-style fighting unit when they had not the experience nor the iron will to hold ranks under pressure.

It is difficult to dispute any of Hayes-McCoy's points, except to restate that the Irish *tercio* did successfully resist the shock of the first English charge. In fact, it was their own cavalry that broke their infantry ranks, not the enemy's.

THE STIRRUPS THEORY

Recently, historians have also highlighted the archaic nature of the Irish cavalry. Hiram Morgan points out that the local horses were much smaller than the English warhorses, and because O'Neill's horsemen disdained the use of stirrups they could not withstand the sort of collision that was inevitable between cavalry. The Irish cavalry did not lack courage, just the right horses and equipment.

Fynes Moryson would have agreed. 'They use no saddles,' he said of the Irish cavalry, '[and] may easily be cast off from their horses, yet being very nimble, do as easily mount them again, leaping up without any help of stirrups, which they neither use nor have.' In contrast, the heavily armed English used 'deep war saddles'. Moryson believed the inactivity of the Irish cavalry left the infantry exposed and was 'the chief cause of their overthrow'.

In a recent RTÉ documentary, *The Story of Ireland*, the lack of stirrups was given as the main reason for the defeat.

Yet this was a general disadvantage which proved fatal only at Kinsale, when O'Neill fought in the open. As Hiram Morgan observes, he must have wished he had stuck to Águila's plan and remained on the ridge. Instead, by retreating, 'O'Neill had pulled defeat from the jaws of victory.'

THE TREACHERY THEORY

Philip O'Sullivan suggested that the defeat was due 'to somebody's cunning or treachery' and Papal Nuncio Mansoni claimed Águila's familiarity with Blount created 'grave suspicions'. Oviedo maintained that there was an enormous betrayal. In the 1880s it was being stated by at least one historian that 'English gold ... corrupted the integrity of the Spanish commander'.

Historian Enrique García Hernán has recently re-examined this idea. He says there was much talk in Spain at the time that either O'Neill or Águila – or both – had reached an understanding with the English before the battle. This could explain O'Neill's retreat and Águila's inactivity that day. He says it is impossible to remove this suspicion, but adds that, in fairness, many other factors could have accounted for their behaviour.

On the other hand, Hayes-McCoy says he can find no evidence of treachery. The theory is intriguing, but until someone finds the 'smoking gun' of firm evidence, we can only speculate.

ANOTHER POSSIBILITY

The word 'panic' has often been applied to the rout of the Irish troops at Kinsale. Drawing upon the popular notion that human beings degenerate to a primitive and bestial level when threatened, this viewpoint implies that O'Neill's men stampeded like terrified cattle. An English account vividly fosters this image, saying that the Irish 'ran confusedly', discarding their weapons 'for fear ... to carry away their cursed carcasses'.

Philip O'Sullivan appears to agree. 'All were panic-stricken,' he writes.

However, recent research has shown that blind panic in crowds is largely a myth. Under threat, massed groups actually tend to co-operate and help each other. In my view, a more likely explanation for the infantry's sudden disintegration was the creation of a compression wave or 'crowd turbulence'. When crowds are tightly compressed, as at a sports match or rock concert, the slightest movement can rapidly gather powerful energy, amassing enough force to bend steel railings five centimetres thick.

When the Irish cavalry punched into their own tightly packed foot soldiers, those in the front few ranks had to step back. The process gained momentum, creating an irresistible force wave. In his classic 1993 study of crowd disasters, Dr John J. Fruin says that when a critical density is reached, a crowd 'becomes almost a fluid mass. Shock waves can be propagated through the mass, sufficient to lift people off their feet and propel them ... three metres or more. People may be literally lifted out of their shoes and have clothing torn off.' Once this compression wave surged through the ranks, it would have been impossible for even the most determined fighters to stay in place. It is one of the many ironies of Kinsale that O'Neill's tightly packed *tercio* could resist a charge by enemy horsemen ... but was forced under by friendly ones.

THE CULTURE OF HONOUR

We've already seen how O'Neill's burning and looting of his neighbours' territory – to him, the most natural way to behave – left his Spanish allies exasperated. I believe the 'culture of honour' also manifested itself to the disadvantage of the Irish on the day of the battle. The squabble over precedence on the night march is sometimes dismissed as a myth – but I suspect it was true, and that, seen in this context, it was pivotal. A chieftain could not afford to lose face. To accept a place behind one's neighbour showed a dangerous weakness that could be exploited for decades. The inevitable delays may have proved fatal.

Secondly, there was no true sense of solidarity between the Irish confederates: they simply didn't trust each other. They saw no point in rushing to the aid of a neighbouring chieftain who had stolen their cattle before and would happily do so again. Seen from this perspective, the defeat and slaughter of a neighbour's forces might not have been entirely unwelcome. They were confederates, but they were not allies.

WHERE WAS THE BATTLE FOUGHT?

So much for the 'why'. Another unresolved question is 'where'?

Soon after the battle George Carew and Donough O'Brien 'rode out to see the dead bodies'. O'Brien was particularly interested, because he had read an ancient prophesy forecasting the precise ford and hill near Kinsale where the Irish would be overthrown. Carew asked some locals to name the area. They supposedly responded with the names from the prediction.

Infuriatingly, Carew doesn't mention the names. It wouldn't have proved the power of prophecy – but it would have saved decades of wrangling over the true site of the Battle of Kinsale.

Today, a sign stands at Millwater, some 5km northwest of the town. It says: 'Kinsale lies about three miles south, hidden behind the high ridge of hills on which the English Army stood. This ridge is called Ardmartin, and the battle was fought at its western end.' There is little else to see apart from a pleasant patchwork of green and golden fields.

Many historians agree that this was the battle site. One, Nora Hickey, says that as you approach the sign from the east, you are in the middle of the action: 'The English troops controlled the hillside on the left, and the Irish armies stood on the lower ground to the right.'

Of course, the battle covered a wide area, and the nearby locations of Whitecastle, Ardcloyne and Ballinamona bog have been suggested as possible settings for O'Neill's last stand. In 1916, a local historian named Florence O'Sullivan drew from oral tradition to precisely pinpoint the location. It surrounded 'the crossroads near the farmhouse of Mr Coleman of Milewater [aka Millwater] about half a mile inland from the near extremity of White Castle Creek'. Interestingly, he says the stream running into White Castle Creek was known locally as 'the Ford of the Slaughter'.

This is extremely valuable, since O'Sullivan was writing only four human lifetimes from 1601 – and it seems inconceivable that the location of such a cataclysmic event should not have been passed on from generation to generation.

Recently, however, Damian Shiels, an expert in battlefield archaeology, has painstakingly overlaid a copy of the old picture map from Trinity College, Dublin (see picture section) on the modern ordnance survey map. He wrote that if the hilltop O'Neill reached at dawn was Liscahane Mór, and if the retreat was as depicted on the map, then the battle could not have been fought at Millwater but much further west, near what is now Dunderrow.

With modern technology, it is probably only a matter of time before archaeologists establish the site for certain. In the meantime, if only someone could just find Donough O'Brien's prophesy …

CHAPTER THIRTY-TWO

HONOURABLE TERMS, OR A THOUSAND DEATHS

DON'T think it's over. It's far from over.

That was the clear message from Águila as Christmas Day dawned to reveal a new Kinsale – a warscape in which the balance of power had dramatically shifted in favour of the English besiegers.

Far from acknowledging defeat, the Spanish commander turned up the heat on Blount with a series of vigorous attacks. In a two-hour sortie that night, he drove Blount's troops out of their trench and managed to sabotage six of the big guns. They broke through the trenchworks and stormed forward as far as O'Brien's lower fort, where they were forced to retreat only after getting 'a volley of shot in their teeth'. Zubiaur reported that Águila's men 'attacked the enemy's trenches, which are so deep that ladders were needed to scale them', and killed five hundred infantry – a figure that seems to be wildly exaggerated.

Blount wasn't resting on his laurels, either. After giving his men a brief break on the afternoon of 24 December, he instructed Josiah Bodley to push on with the trenchworks.

Despite the deaths of around a thousand men, the battle had not yet proved decisive. Águila still held the town. Storming it would still cost the English dearly. Zubiaur still held two ports and had a garrison in Bearhaven. Most encouragingly of all for the invaders, Hugh O'Neill was still out there with an army of up to four or five thousand men and still had the power to keep the English pinned down until either side sent reinforcements.

Águila was down, but far from out. As soon as the battle was over, he sent a messenger to Hugh O'Neill.

—Return to your siege camp, he ordered. We will reunite our forces, and attack the English afresh.

He probably suspected that he was wasting his breath. What he didn't realise was that, with the bodies of his fallen warriors yet to be buried, the mercurial, unpredictable Hugh O'Neill was already making secret plans to switch sides and offer his services to the English.

It was a wretched, humiliated and deeply divided Irish army that gathered for a council meeting in Innishannon. Ludhaigh O'Cleary summed up the mood of self-loathing dejection: 'Ill luck was evidently with [O'Neill and O'Donnell] … when they did not resolve to fight bravely, courageously, zealously, mercilessly in defence of their faith, fatherland and lives … their princes were left lying on the earth, their champions wounded, their chiefs pierced through …'

Zubiaur concurred. 'Many very brave people were scattered over the field,' he wrote home. 'The poor Irish who had declared against the Queen were stricken by grief.' Their misery was compounded by the knowledge that 'the heretic army and their allies were very happy'.

The fragile web that had bound a disparate force together was rapidly disintegrating. Alliances were dissolved in accusations, inter-reliance was replaced by incrimination, faith was supplanted by finger-pointing.

'There prevailed much reproach upon reproach, moaning and dejection, melancholy and anguish, throughout the camp,' says the Irish annalist.

One group, led by Donal Cam O'Sullivan Beare, argued for renewing the siege. They claimed that by carrying on the fight they would honour the sacrifice of those who had fallen.

Others believed they should return to their individual homes and guard their territories against the inevitable English retaliation or against challenges from within their own clans.

—My brother is planning to snatch the chieftaincy from me, one leader complained. I have to return to defend myself.

Everyone sympathised. Few of the chieftains were so secure that they could not be supplanted by eager relatives in their absence.

Hugh O'Neill's position was, as usual, ambiguous. Bustamante clearly suggests that O'Neill was reluctant to return to Kinsale. But Philip O'Sullivan claims he wished to continue the battle. It is possible that O'Neill, the ultimate chameleon, was able to convey both impressions simultaneously.

All eyes were on Hugh O'Donnell. But the 'fighting prince of Donegal' had become a tragic figure. His life's dream had been the Spanish liberation of Ireland. Within hours, all had been lost. Shell-shocked and stunned, he had lapsed into a traumatic state in which unbearable angst alternated with a blind, uncontrollable rage: Red Hugh was experiencing the 'red mist'.

'O'Donnell was seized with great fury, rage and anxiety of mind,' says the Irish annalist, 'so that he did not sleep or rest soundly for the space of three days and three nights.' O'Cleary says his followers even feared for his life. He adds, very perceptively: 'Rage and anger had seized upon his soul, and he would have been pleased if he was the first who was slain ...'

To a modern therapist this could be a warning signal for the psychological phenomenon known as 'survivor guilt'. Now recognised as an aspect of Post

Traumatic Stress Disorder (PTSD), Survivor Guilt occurs when survivors of combat, crash or natural disaster feel remorse at having come through the ordeal when others have perished. Sufferers often state, like O'Donnell, that 'I should have died instead.' Sometimes they feel guilt at having failed to do more to help. This self-blame is nearly always unjustified. O'Donnell's intolerable grief may have been intensified by embarrassment at having arrived too late and done too little in the battle. In any event, the classic symptoms include anxiety and 'hyperarousal' with sleeplessness and outbursts of anger, and they match almost exactly O'Donnell's symptoms as described by O'Sullivan and O'Cleary.

We will never know which particular ailment, if any, made O'Donnell react to defeat in this way. However, we can be certain that he was in mental crisis. He was in no condition to make any major decision – let alone a fateful choice that would shape the destiny of an entire nation for four centuries.

Which is exactly what he proceeded to do.

When O'Donnell finally spoke, it was from the bitter depths of his rage. He wouldn't go back home. Nor would he stay, either.

—I will never fight with the Irish again, he thundered. And especially not in company with those who ran away at the very first blow.

There was a stunned silence among the chieftains. Everyone knew he was talking about O'Neill and his Tyrone warriors.

At that moment, it must have been clear that the rebellion was essentially over. The O'Neill-O'Donnell alliance had been severed, with the younger man questioning his leader's courage and command. Without that cohesion, the confederation would never hold together.

—I am leaving for Spain, O'Donnell said. I will petition the King personally and plead for more soldiers.

The decision caused 'violent lamentations and loud wailing cries' among his followers. Because, although O'Donnell promised to return in March with twenty thousand Spaniards, his troops suspected that they would never see him again. It was, says O'Cleary, a plan formulated 'in great grief'. That is a reasonable psychological explanation for an insane scheme. For any commander to abandon his troops, to quit the battlefield and to flee the country at such a crucial juncture is otherwise inexplicable, even inexcusable. The war was not lost on the battlefield of Kinsale – it was lost at a council meeting in a camp in Innishannon.

O'Neill agreed to the plan 'with reluctance' and it was approved by the chieftains. Both leaders then wrote to inform Águila. The remaining Spanish captains argued vehemently with them, but they were talking to the chieftains' backs. 'In under an hour, everything was dismantled,' says Bustamante.

O'Donnell and his entourage arrived in Castlehaven on Saturday afternoon and broke the bad news to Zubiaur, who urged them not to give up. 'I encouraged them, saying that God and Your Majesty would help them, starting from the beginning,' he reported later to the King. He was taken aback when O'Donnell announced that he planned to sail for Spain the following day. He and quartermaster general Pedro Lopez de Soto used all their efforts to try to persuade him to remain in Ireland. They pointed out that his people would be helpless without him. 'I urged him to stay and give courage to everyone,' Zubiaur wrote. But he could see that Red Hugh's spirit was broken. The admiral wrote sympathetically: 'The poor lord was completely *acabado*' – finished, worn-out, up against the ropes.

On Sunday, 27 December, just three days after the battle, Hugh O'Donnell set sail on a Scottish merchant ship, never to return to Ireland.

It was left to Donal Cam O'Sullivan Beare to gather up the remnants of the insurgency. He headed west to make a last stand at his faraway redoubt at Dunboy Castle in the western Beara Peninsula.

—Do not lose courage, he wrote to Águila.

However, unknown to any of the insurgents, Hugh O'Neill was secretly negotiating with the English. On the morning after the battle, he sent an emissary to Blount.

—I am willing and desirous to become a subject of the Queen, he said, if she will deal justly with me. To redeem all my errors I will do all possible service to Her Majesty.

The last sentence was quite remarkable. The man who had led the insurgency was offering not only to surrender – but to join Blount in fighting his own Spanish and Irish allies.

While Blount sent the envoy back with a cool response, he left the door open for negotiations. The English commander didn't trust O'Neill, but it suited his purpose to have time-out. With the northern Irish threat sidelined for the next couple of months, he could devote his full attention to the task of ousting Águila from Kinsale.

Meanwhile, George Carew was busy plotting. He had taken no part in the battle at Kinsale and, throughout the entire siege, he was most noteworthy for having let O'Donnell slip past him in Tipperary. It irked him to think that the English heroes of the hour – Blount, Richard de Burgh, Christopher St Lawrence, and to a lesser extent Richard Wingfield – were all Essex's associates. Carew, of course, was in the opposing faction at court. When Carew heard that the wounded Sir Henry Danvers was planning to travel to London with Blount's account of the victory, he seethed with indignation. Rehabilitation of the former Essex group would lessen the power of his own cabal, the rival grouping led by Secretary Robert Cecil.

No, he concluded. It couldn't be allowed to happen.

He prepared his own version of events, emphasising how he had acquired the battle plan for a bottle of whiskey. Blount had simply acted on his tip-off. History was rewritten. It was he, George Carew, who was handing the Queen her great and glorious victory. Now all he needed was a messenger who was tough enough, and ambitious enough, to push himself beyond the point of human endurance in order to get Carew's version to London first.

—Fetch me Richard Boyle, he ordered.

For the northern insurgents, the march home was an excruciating ordeal – a seemingly endless hell in which every freezing river held lethal flash-floods, every castle held a hostile army and every village was full of enemies bent on revenge. Except in this case, the enemies weren't the English. They were the Irish whose lands had been burned by the chieftains on their way south. They swooped on the weary insurgents at every turn, driving them into rivers where hundreds were drowned.

'Many more were drowned on their retreat than were killed [at Kinsale],' said O'Neill's trumpeter Shane Sheale. 'As a herd of swine would take to the water for fear, so they did, and were drowned in great numbers.' Soldiers who fell down exhausted in the swamps were trampled into the slime for the sake of their firearms. 'They that would kiss them in their going forward did both strip them and shoot bullets at them in their return,' Sheale recalled.

Carew claimed: 'A troop of women would have beaten his army.'

Those lucky enough to make it back were determined to stay there even if the Spanish sent a new armada.

—O'Neill can go if he pleases, Sheale said. But he won't find a man to go with him.

Five days after the battle, an exhausted and bedraggled figure stumbled through a side gate of Kinsale.

It was Alférez Bustamante, who had endured an epic trek by night across hostile countryside in a bid to rejoin his unit in the town. After the battle, he had retreated with the other Spanish survivors to Castlehaven. Instead of remaining there in comparative safety, he footslogged the seventy kilometres back to Kinsale. 'I could keep out of danger only by travelling by night, and with extreme care,' he wrote.

Bustamante found his comrades still traumatised by the defeat. No one knew what had happened to the Irish chieftains. Águila had asked them for support. They had replied that they were unable to help him. Meanwhile, the town's hospital was packed with nine hundred groaning sick and wounded, and the meagre food supplies were almost exhausted. 'Within eight days,' wrote Bustamante, 'the dearth of food would force us out.'

The Spanish survivors felt no loyalty towards O'Neill. 'They rail much against Tyrone,' Carew says, '… [and] task him with cowardice.' The Spanish and the English agreed that Felipe III had been duped. '[The] poor Spaniards have an Irish trick played on them,' crowed another English writer, 'in a triple turn betwixt their heads and their shoulders.'

Águila asked Bustamante if Castlehaven could hold out. Bustamante told him it couldn't. It had no bastions or earthworks, only a mediaeval wall.

The commander took Bustamante aside. He told him he was going to seek a peace deal before Blount realised their true predicament.

—If we can leave with honour, undefeated, we will come to terms, he said. If not, then we will all die here in the fields of *Quinsale*.

Bustamante knew that his commander meant every word.

—It is what we are expected to do, Águila said.

As dawn broke on the last day of 1601, Águila sent out a trumpeter for parlay.

'[I] pray Your Lordship to send hither a person of weight and trust,' he wrote.

Blount had many good candidates for the job of negotiator. He selected Sir William Godolphin, another Essex protégé. Godolphin had excelled in the fiercest fighting during the siege, and currently bore a fresh thigh-wound inflicted by a halberd at Millwater Ford. In fact, one early historian credited Godolphin with the entire victory, claiming he 'broke through the whole body of the Spaniards and rebels, entirely routing them'. But that wasn't the only reason why the Cornishman was chosen to beard Águila in his lair. The main reason has rarely, if ever, been mentioned by historians.

William Godolphin had an account to settle with Águila. And it was intensely personal. To find out what it was, we must briefly fly back in time, to another place and another war.

Brittany in July 1595. Águila, the Spanish commander at Blavet, was still smarting from the loss of his fort at El Leon and was planning a punitive strike on his enemy's home turf. His target: Cornwall in the southwest of England. This expedition, now virtually forgotten, was spectacularly successful. History would record it as the last Spanish invasion of England.

In mid-July, Águila despatched four hundred musketeers under a Carlos de Amezola. The fleet that transported them was commanded by none other than Pedro de Zubiaur. At daybreak on 23 July, four ships dropped anchor at Mount's Bay and landed two hundred troops. The two villages of Mouse-hole and Paul were 'burn'd and spoil'd'. The Spaniards boasted: 'We burned more than four hundred houses, some outlying hamlets and three ships.'

They moved on to Newlyn and Penzance, where they celebrated Mass at a local church and left a poem warning that they would return to make it into a friary. As they proceeded to sack Penzance, the Deputy Lieutenant of Cornwall, sixty-year-old Sir Francis Godolphin, tried desperately to mount a defence. But the local militia deserted him in terror. He could persuade only a dozen of his own servants to join him. They had two guns. In Penzance marketplace, his pathetic Dad's Army formed a thin line against four hundred heavily armed Spaniards. When the Spanish burned the town around them, Godolphin's defenders were forced to withdraw. A subsequent English investigation found that Penzance would have been saved 'had the people stood with Sir Francis Godolphin ... but the common sort utterly forsook him'. It was the sort of heroic stand that Águila would have admired and respected.

And now, in Kinsale, one man was chosen to negotiate an end to Águila's second great strike against the Queen. He was thirty-four-year-old William Godolphin – Sir Francis's son.

A circle of history was about to be closed.

Godolphin didn't know what to expect as he picked his way through the scarred and potholed streets of Kinsale. The wreckage was a testimony to the effectiveness of the English barrage – and yet the besiegers could not take the town without inflicting carnage upon themselves.

After the usual military courtesies, he found himself face-to-face with a bearded man who exuded an air of authority and determination.

—I have found your commander to be a sharp and powerful opponent, yet an honourable enemy, Águila said.

Godolphin remained silent. His role at this stage was only to listen.

—In contrast, Águila continued, I have found my Irish allies weak, barbarous and perfidious.

The English officer nodded. He wondered where all this was leading.

—Because of my admiration for the one and my distaste for the other, said Águila, I propose to hand over Kinsale and the other ports. Then we will depart on honourable terms that are fitting to men of war.

Having put forward the idea, Águila's attitude suddenly hardened.

—But do not mistake our attitude for weakness, he warned. If your commander insists on dishonourable terms, he will find us ready to bury ourselves alive, and endure a thousand deaths, rather than yield.

Blount must have felt like cheering, but he couldn't accept without some bluff and bluster. The negotiations continued through Godolphin.

—We have just defeated your allies and cut off your only source of aid, Blount reminded Águila. We could take Kinsale in a very short time. Yet we know that Her Majesty would not want her victory to be blemished by needless bloodshed. We will entertain your offer on two conditions. Firstly that you surrender all your arms, artillery and treasure. And secondly, that you yield up all Her Majesty's subjects.

He meant, of course, the Irish insurgents.

Águila was incandescent with fury at the very suggestion.

—I speak on behalf of every last one of my men, he said. We would rather endure the greatest of misery rather than be guilty of so foul a treason.

And that was not all.

—If you so much as mention such disgraceful terms again, Águila warned, my previous offer is withdrawn and your commander should return to his sword. When we meet in the breach, I will lay five hundred of your best men in the earth.

Águila finished by justifying his decision to make a deal. Was he trying to convince Blount, or himself?

His mission had been to join the chieftains. Now that they had fled, he felt relieved of his duty. 'I expected long in vain … [they were] every hour promising to relieve us,' he pointed out. '[But I] saw them at last broken with a handful of men, blown asunder into divers parts of the world – O'Donnell into Spain, O'Neill to the furthest of the north.'

Behind all this bombast lay a desperate need for peace on both sides.

What Águila was really thinking was this: He was down to 1,800 effective fighters. He was almost out of food. He had been deserted by his allies. He was running out of time. 'If the enemy knew what was going on in the matter of food and men,' he said later, 'they would never have [entered negotiations].'

Meanwhile, what Blount was really thinking was this: It was important to get the Spaniards out before their reinforcements arrived. His own army had been so seriously reduced that it was almost as weak as it had been at the beginning. 'The sufferings of a winter's siege [fell] more upon us in the field than upon them in the town,' he said.

Interestingly, the two sides privately held opposing views on the value of the other three ports. While Águila considered them weak and indefensible, Blount and Carew saw them as almost unassailable. Carew compared them to Águila's Breton strongholds at Blavet and El Leon.

Despite all the bravado, negotiations continued. Eventually, on 2 January, a deal was struck. Águila's forces would yield up Kinsale, Castlehaven, Baltimore and Bearhaven in return for safe passage back to Spain – not only for the Spaniards but also for 'other nations whatsoever', a crucial clause that included the Irish insurgents. In the event, 'a great company' of Irish was protected by this provision. In a major coup, Águila also retained all his treasure, guns, ammunition and flags. Honour was upheld. He would leave Kinsale undefeated.

However, there was one stipulation that was destined to damage Águila personally – although he did not know it yet. He was to remain in Ireland until the last ships left. This gave O'Donnell plenty of time to trash his reputation in Spain.

After the agreement was signed, the two commanders dined together in the Spital Hill camp. Next day, Carew dined with Águila in Kinsale and saw at close quarters the damage his guns had inflicted on the now 'miserable' town.

One week later, on 9 January, Blount formally lifted his siege. The gates of Kinsale swung open and remained open as Águila and his principal captains rode off to Cork city to stay as hostages. Afterwards, the councillors of Kinsale approached Carew and asked for their seal and mace back. Carew, still annoyed by the warm welcome given to the Spanish, told them they would get their town back if they rebuilt it stone by stone ... at their own expense.

The peace deal was controversial and unpopular. Sceptics on both sides began studying the fine print to find loopholes. Secretary Cecil noticed that the agreement covered this Spanish expedition, but not any future one. Many in London felt the deal 'too weak', he complained. If Spain sent another five thousand troops, they could coldly sacrifice Águila. 'Who doth know that they might not be commanded to abandon Don Juan?' he asked.

Cecil was equally prepared to throw Blount to the wolves. In a guarded letter to Carew, he insinuated that Carew should prepare to move suddenly against Águila's Spaniards by orchestrating 'a breach of some formal article'.

In Kinsale, Oviedo was working hard behind Águila's back to undo the deal. He wrote to the Duke of Lerma urging him to tear up the treaty. 'We can easily get out of the agreement,' he said, claiming that the English would technically break the treaty if they couldn't get everyone home within one month. He must have been confused, to say the least, because there is no month's deadline mentioned in the treaty.

With a blatant disregard for the facts, Oviedo claimed that the chieftains had come south with 8,800 troops and that they could reorganise 'very easily' to join the Spanish in Kinsale.

—We have 3,400 soldiers and a good supply of munitions and money, he claimed.

In reality, Águila had only 1,800 effective fighters, and the insurgents' army of around 5,000 was irreparably scattered.

Fr Archer was equally indignant.

—Águila claimed he was forced to come to terms through a shortage of soldiers, the cleric fumed. In fact, we have 3,300 troops who are fit to fight.

Papal Nuncio Mansoni claimed that the Spanish could renege on handing over the other ports using the technicality that it was Zubiaur, not Águila, who was in command there. Unfortunately for his case, Zubiaur had already set sail for home.

It was Donal Cam O'Sullivan Beare who lodged the most convincing, and most heartbreaking, objection. His castle was his ancestral home, and Águila had no right to give it away. 'All of us who took the part of the King are on the verge of ruin,' he said, adding that his family and dependants would be 'driven to run to the mountains, there to live like wolves'. Presciently, Donal Cam forecast that the outlook would be bleak for the Gaelic race.

He predicted: 'The spirit of our people [will be] broken.'

CHAPTER THIRTY-THREE

'A Barbarous Nation for Which Christ Never Died'

AN OFFICER named Martin de Oleaga was the first to bring the bad news of the defeat back to Spain. He said that the Irish chieftains, with six to seven thousand infantry and six hundred horse, had been 'surprised' by the English near Kinsale. 'They fell upon the weakest of the Irish squadrons, and beat them, whereupon the rest fled without fighting,' his report read.

The Spanish Council of State told the King it regretted the defeat of O'Neill and O'Donnell, whose support had been crucial. 'The few troops we have there can hardly hold out,' it predicted, adding: 'The worst of it is that Your Majesty's prestige is at stake.'

The Council said there was no prospect of sending aid to Águila due to lack of resources. 'If the time were further advanced,' it mused, '… galleys might be sent to rescue Don Juan or take him to a safer place; but that is not to be thought of, at least until the end of April … The great difficulty is the troops which must be raised, for there are none.'

In the meantime, it would be great if Águila could just hang on. 'It will be most advantageous,' wrote the Council, 'to keep that thorn in their flesh.'

Young King Felipe took the news surprisingly well. He certainly didn't blame Águila for the defeat – on the contrary, he promised to richly reward him. 'I recognise that our only hope now rests upon your bravery and prudence, which I prize highly,' he wrote to his besieged commander on 20 January. Felipe praised his commander's 'spirit and experience', and in a final footnote, promised: 'You, and the army that is with you, shall experience my liberality and thanks.'

They were words that Juan del Águila would later recall with bitterness … as he was hauled before a Spanish court martial.

After Carew despatched Richard Boyle on his epic trip to London, news of the surprise defeat flashed across Europe. The Venetian ambassador in Paris reported that the Irish and Spanish had marched to the relief of Kinsale when '*nel quale essendi fuggiti li Irlandes li Spagnoli furono rotti*' – the Irish ran away and the Spanish were routed. He added: 'The Spanish were left to the mercy of the English, who with only 1,000 foot and 300 horse routed the whole army … 1,200 were left dead on the field, 800 wounded.'

The Venetians predicted: 'Don Juan del Águila will not be able to hold out for long.'

There were sighs of relief in Paris for, as the Venetian diplomats had warned, a Spanish success would have necessitated a French invasion of Ireland to restore the balance of power.

As O'Donnell sailed south with Zubiaur, the unwitting Don Martin de la Cerda was sailing north toward Kinsale with the two hundred soldiers and a cargo of food and ammunition. However, most of his fleet was forced back to Spain by a howling gale. Only two ships made it to Kinsale. They arrived on 4 January, when the ink was scarcely dry on the two-day-old agreement.

Blount sent a boatful of eleven men to greet him.

—You can approach safely, they said. Peace has been made. Don Juan del Águila and Charles Blount are now good friends.

But Cerda was taking no chances. He snatched the eleven men and headed home 'with all speed'. In Spain, the news of the deal was greeted with scepticism. 'There is, up to the present, no confirmation of this,' cautioned the Council of State.

The Spanish diarist Luis Cordóba was bemused. 'Although it is said that Águila made a deal with the English, which lets him leave Ireland and gives him passage back to Spain with his people, it is doubtful,' he wrote in late February.

But when questioned separately, the eleven men stuck to their story.

—We personally saw Don Juan dine with Charles Blount, they said.

The Council decided to send two fast ships to Ireland to verify the news. In the meantime, they continued to plan a Fourth Wave of eight ships which would carry supplies and munitions to Ireland. More should follow and 'every possible effort [be] made to relieve Don Juan'.

'Don Juan and I are good friends.'

The wording of Blount's message to Cerda was warmer than it needed to be in order to describe a temporary accommodation between enemies. The truth was that he had forged a friendship with the crusty Spanish commander. They were enjoying their conversations over dinner in the bishop's house in Cork city. The two military buffs probably re-fought many a classic battle late into the night. At one stage Águila talked of 'the kind friendship which your Lordship has shown to me'.

The Spanish commander said he would be glad to leave Ireland. 'Truly,' he told Blount, 'I think that when the Devil took our Saviour Jesus Christ to the pinnacle of the Temple and showed him all the kingdoms of the world, he kept Ireland hidden … to keep it for himself. For I believe that it is the Inferno itself, or some worse place.'

(It recalls the reaction of British Home Secretary Reginald Maudling as he flew home from his first visit to Northern Ireland in the 1970s: 'For God's sake, bring me a large Scotch. What a bloody awful country.')

The conversation took a serious turn, with Águila suggesting that they both lobby for a general peace between their nations. Blount remained noncommittal.

However, this air of camaraderie didn't stop the English playing dirty. Carew heard that a Spanish ship had secretly arrived with despatches for Águila. They were to be carried by hand across the county and delivered to him.

—Would you like to know the contents before he does? Carew asked Blount.

Blount didn't hesitate. They could be orders countermanding the peace deal.

—Intercept them, he said, if you can handsomely do it.

Carew knew exactly what 'handsomely' meant. He called in a dirty-tricks specialist named Captain William Nuce. Nuce enlisted a few soldiers who dressed like road brigands. As the messenger came close to Cork, the 'robbers' swooped and snatched his letters. Leaving him tied up, Nuce headed straight back to his boss. It was mealtime and the unsuspecting Águila was being hosted to dinner at George Carew's home in Cork. Carew excused himself and brought the letters to Blount at his temporary lodgings in the bishop's house.

Eventually the messenger managed to free himself. He made his way to Águila, who immediately smelled a rat. He stormed across to Blount's quarters.

—My messenger was robbed by your soldiers, the furious Águila complained.

—They were probably just country thieves, Blount told him. If they were soldiers, they were renegades.

Águila was far from satisfied.

—I suspect that this was President Carew's doing, he stormed.

Blount was earnest in his reply.

—I can swear upon my faith that he does not have your letters, he said truthfully.

The letters, which Águila received only while leaving Ireland, were from King Felipe, Lerma and War Secretary Ibarra. They ordered him to hang on, but gave no solid assurances that any sizeable reinforcements would arrive any time soon. Perhaps Águila was later secretly relieved that he hadn't seen them.

Meanwhile, other relationships were being formed between the English officers and the temporary guests they labelled 'Don Diegos'. They found they had much in common, and this curious meeting of minds among influential officers on the far fringes of Europe was a key element in creating the future peace.

Fynes Moryson became fascinated with the family roots of his namesake, the Spanish hero Pedro Morejón, and quizzed him about his English background. Ocampo gave his captor John Pikeman a jewelled gold chain. In Baltimore, Captain Roger Harvey had a long chat with the expedition's quartermaster general, Pedro Lopez de Soto. Lopez de Soto confided that the expedition was not about religious freedom. It was revenge for Elizabeth's aid to the Dutch rebels. 'Did you ever think otherwise?' Lopez de Soto asked.

The quartermaster expressed contempt for Ireland, 'a barbarous nation for which, I think, Christ never died'.

Were the Spanish sincere in these racist rantings? Secretary Robert Cecil doubted it. He believed it was all a red herring – 'howsoever Don Juan did flatter you all at his departure with seeming to detest the country'.

As he said farewell, Águila presented George Carew with a gift – a military handbook on how to erect and destroy fortifications.

When the Spanish garrison finally quit Kinsale, they marched out with colours flying. The musketeers shouldered their firearms and almost certainly carried their bullets in their mouths – an important symbol, since that was how soldiers carried them in battle. It showed they had not surrendered.

It was 20 February before the first batch was shipped home. There were nearly 1,400 of them – twenty captains and 1,374 soldiers. Águila joined the second batch on 8 March, but the wind shifted and he spent eight days at anchor before finally setting sail on 16 March. He had with him '1,200 able men', but there were also 'boys and women', testifying to the fact that many of the Spanish settler families had survived the entire ordeal.

A separate tally puts the first consignment at 1,880 soldiers, including 400 prisoners and deserters, and the second batch at 1,000 soldiers and 300 civilians.

Águila was returning with 60-70 percent of his original force, which was quite an achievement considering the energy of his sallies and the losses suffered by Blount and O'Neill. O'Neill lost 1,000 to 1,200 in the battle. Águila must have lost at least 1,000 in the mission. More were dying daily of sickness. In the entire siege, the English came off worst. Philip O'Sullivan reckons they lost 8,000 overall, although one eminent historian later estimated it at 10,000. Carew was more conservative. 'I do verily believe,' he wrote, 'that at that siege and after the sickness we got, we lost about 6,000 men that died.'

He concluded: 'Kinsale was bought at so dear a rate, that while I live, I will protest against a winter siege.'

CHAPTER THIRTY-FOUR

DOSSIER OF TREASON

BLOUNT may have scored a major victory on the battlefield of Kinsale – but he still did not feel secure.

For months, he had been under suspicion after having been implicated in the Earl of Essex's plot. Only the Queen's irrational favour had kept him from being arrested and interrogated. Now he felt that his controversial peace agreement with Águila, not to mention their cosy dinner chats, would give his enemies enough rope to hang him. The peace deal could unravel, for any number of reasons. Only two years before, Essex had organised an unauthorised truce with Hugh O'Neill. It had destroyed his military career.

Throughout December, Blount had come under increasing pressure for failing to capture Kinsale. It was Admiral Richard Leveson who was hero-worshipped in London. 'Sir Richard Leveson played the man when all men's hearts failed,' the influential courtier Dudley Carleton wrote pointedly in a letter of late December, before hearing of the Christmas Eve victory. '[Blount] is blamed for delay in this desperate state of our affairs. He was expected long ere this to assault the town.' Carleton dismissed Blount's reasons for holding back as 'his excuse'.

On 24 December, the Lords of the Privy Council in England wrote coldly and critically to Blount complaining of his 'long and unexpected silence'. The only positive thing the lords could say was that 'you have done as much as you could'.

The new peace agreement added fuel to their paranoia. Even Secretary Robert Cecil was suggesting that Águila had played Blount for a fool – or worse – and that the Spanish would rip up the agreement in a heartbeat.

There was also controversy over Blount's decision to enter into peace talks with O'Neill after the Ulsterman's request to be 'received into Her Majesty's mercy'. On 4 February, Blount sent a trusted negotiator to O'Neill with a list of conditions for pardon. (The resultant exchanges were to drag on for weeks, with O'Neill professing himself to be 'heartily sorry' and 'grieved' for his actions in the war. But the talks were doomed to failure. Negotiations would rapidly collapse and the two sides would be back at war by summer.)

By 15 February, Blount was deeply depressed and ready to quit. He bared his soul in a bitter *cri de coeur* to Secretary Cecil: 'I protest I was never more accompanied with more unquiet thoughts [than now],' he confessed, '...seeing no end of my labours ... [and] fearing that they are valued of so little merit.'

Referring to his enemies at court, he said: 'I never deserved any ill of them by deed ... nor by word ... so I do as much scorn their malice, as the barking of so many whelps ... but when I think that their false evidence doth sway the opinion of my supreme judge [ie the Queen] ... I cannot but fear.' He said he now hated 'this unhappy profession' and longed to retire 'in quietness'. There was no mistaking it – Charles Blount had reached the end of his tether.

But only a few months beforehand, he had been very, very lucky not to have found himself at the end of a gallows rope.

It all began in the summer of 1599, when all England was racked with fears for the future. The childless Queen Elizabeth was in her final years but refused to hear any talk of a successor. The Essex circle favoured the Protestant King James VI of Scotland and believed that Secretary Robert Cecil controlled a powerful secret cabal in support of the rival Spanish Catholic candidate, Felipe's half-sister the Infanta Isabella. They felt Cecil's motives were purely selfish, because he had every reason to fear that James would exact revenge on the Cecil family over their involvement in the execution of his mother, Mary Queen of Scots. Essex and his followers were utterly convinced that Cecil was selling England out to the Spanish in order to ensure his own survival. They decided that Elizabeth must be forced, in the national interest, to nominate James as successor and clear up the uncertainty once and for all.

The highly politicised Penelope Rich, Essex's sister and Blount's lover, was at the centre of this movement. She had been secretly corresponding with King James for more than a decade, declaring that her brother Essex was living 'in thrall' and longed for a change of regime. Some of her letters were so 'dark' that they left even James baffled.

Blount was deeply imbedded in the Essex group, but respected Cecil's elite status and was trying to keep friendly with him as well. However, his equivocation had isolated him from the centre of power and he was kept firmly outside the influential Privy Council.

He, too, was deeply worried about his nation's future. '[We] that are not of the Council do see no hope to keep long together this State from assured ruin,' he wrote to Essex at one point. 'I pray God, the Queen may with all prosperity outlive their negligence.'

Halfway through 1599, Blount was spurred into action. He secretly wrote to James assuring him that Essex and other like-minded nobles would back him as successor if the Scottish King gave the signal.

Fast forward to late autumn, 1599. Essex had been commanding the Queen's troops in Ireland, but had deserted his post after making his unauthorised truce with O'Neill. On his return to London, he stormed into the Queen's bedchamber while she was still undressed. During the resulting row Essex and Blount vanished in a 'discontented' state to Portsmouth, where the pair ignored several royal orders to come back to London. On his return, Essex was disgraced and put under house arrest.

Blount – who was preparing to take command of the troops in Ireland – intervened to help his friend by planning what amounted to a treasonous military uprising. He held a secret meeting where, to salve his conscience, he first insisted that his fellow plotters pledged loyalty to the Queen. (Contrarily, he felt he was acting in her best interests, whether she appreciated that or not.) Then he revealed that he planned to take four to five thousand English troops from Ireland to Scotland, where their threatening presence across the border would force Elizabeth to nominate King James as her successor. Whether Blount intended to put on a mere show of strength or launch a full-scale invasion of England was never made clear, because the Scottish King replied that he was 'not ready to enter into that attempt … and so that business ended'.

The next scene in the drama came in December 1599. Lady Penelope Rich, in her late-thirties and mother to Blount's five children, descended on Elizabeth's court like an avenging angel, dressed in dramatic black. Head held high, she swept into the Queen's presence and demanded better treatment for her brother. Did Her Majesty not realise that Essex was ill and at the point of death?

There was no love lost between the two women. The Queen disliked her 'for violating her husband's bed'. They were rivals for Blount's affections, although Elizabeth had to be content with fanciful love letters while Penelope shared his embraces. Lady Rich stated her case, left gifts of expensive jewellery, and sashayed out. The Queen noted with irritation that her entranced courtiers were all fawning over her.

A month passed. It was January 1600, and Elizabeth had still not released Essex. Penelope, seething with indignation, decided like any modern whistle-blower to unleash the power of the press. She wrote a sarcastic letter to the Queen and watched with satisfaction as printed copies were circulated. 'Early did I hope this morning to have mine eyes blessed with Your Majesty's beauty,' she wrote tongue in cheek. But the 'divine oracle' had given her 'a doubtful answer'. She claimed Essex's enemies were motivated by revenge: '[If] your fair hands do not check the courses of their unbridled hate, [it] will be his last breath.'

This stuff was dynamite, and circulating it was effectively a clarion call to London's citizens to support their hero Essex against the Queen. As anxious courtiers snapped up all available copies, Elizabeth ordered Penelope's arrest over this 'impertinent letter', claiming that she was showing 'a plain contempt'. The Attorney General denounced her as 'insolent' and 'saucy'.

However, Lady Rich pleaded her case to the sixty-four-year-old Lord Treasurer, who was persuaded to let her go – much to the Queen's annoyance. She believed Penelope had wrapped him around her little finger.

The quiet-natured Blount was undoubtedly embarrassed by his feisty lover. He sailed for Ireland, still quite prepared to use his troops for dissident political ends. But as he immersed himself in the war, his priorities shifted.

Campaigning in Ulster in the spring of 1600, Blount received a visit from another Essex conspirator, the Earl of Southampton. Henry Wriothesley cut an unusual figure – he was a colourfully foppish bisexual who was also renowned as a courageous and effective soldier. Wriothesley – often identified as the 'fair youth' of Shakespeare's sonnets – told Blount it was time for action. He must lead the five thousand troops to England to challenge Elizabeth. This time Blount drew the line. He 'utterly rejected' the plan, according to Wriothesley's later testimony.

On to February 1601. In London, Essex had been released but impoverished – Elizabeth had removed his source of income. His creditors were at the door, and he was banned from court. One courtier suspected he was going insane.

On Sunday, 8 February, he organised a revolution. He led three hundred men along the Strand to the City, shouting: 'The Crown has been sold to the Spanish Infanta!'

Silence. No one joined him. His great rebellion fizzled out in a fiasco.

Bizarrely, Essex took a break for lunch, then 'stood for a while with his halberd in his hand, and a napkin about his neck'. Breaking into a visible sweat, he fought his way home past a military patrol. He fortified his house, which was soon under heavy siege. Both sides agreed to release the women inside, who included Penelope and Essex's wife, Frances.

After a standoff, Essex capitulated and was hauled off to the Tower. It was all over within twelve hours.

The interrogations of the prime suspects revealed some damning information about Blount and Penelope Rich. Penelope was clearly one of the prime movers in the revolt. She had dined with the ringleaders on Saturday night as they finalised the plan, and on Sunday morning had driven out to persuade a vacillating nobleman to join the rising. Under questioning, Essex blamed his sister for humiliating him into action: '[She told] me how all my friends and followers thought me a coward.' Penelope responded humbly that she was 'more like a slave than a sister'.

Before his execution – it took three strokes of the axe – Essex also implicated his close friend Charles Blount as an 'accessory to his design'. Blount's name was mentioned again and again when the conspirators were interrogated. The most damning parts were suppressed, but Cecil and Carew knew all about his scheming.

On 22 February 1601 Blount's friends on the Irish campaign noticed he had become suddenly silent and anxious. It all began when he received a letter informing him of Essex's failed coup. Blount demanded his private papers from Moryson and destroyed all the evidence. '[He] had good cause to be wary,' wrote Moryson, '… since by some confessions in England, himself was tainted with privity to the Earl's practices.'

By coincidence, just a few days before the revolt Blount had written home asking permission to take a break in London. In hindsight, this looked bad.

Blount waited daily for the summons to London. Had it arrived, he was determined to flee to France in a ship that was already waiting at port.

—I will not put my neck under the blade, he admitted privately.

But amazingly, the summons never came. The Queen, who wouldn't hear a word against her favourite, had 'dissembled and concealed' the scandal. Blount was considered to be too valuable an asset in Ireland. And one of the conspirators had pleaded on the gallows that 'Lord Mountjoy [Blount] be cleared as ignorant of the matter', an assertion which was certainly true in relation to the actual rising.

Blount wrote to Cecil in a bid to clear the air. 'I am confident in my own conscience,' he declared, assuring the Secretary that 'the army was free from the infection of this conspiracy'.

And Penelope? Astonishingly, she was able to talk her way out of this crisis, too. In 'custody' she had her own private cook and insisted that her long-suffering husband, Lord Rich, supplied her with beddings and wall hangings suitable to her station in life. Fortunately, her interrogator was Lord Nottingham, who was Blount's commander in the battle against the Great Armada of 1588 and who was very well disposed to him. He reassured Blount: 'She used herself with modesty and wisdom ... [and was] set at liberty.'

In response to Blount's request to return to London, Lord Nottingham wrote playfully that the Queen would be glad 'to look upon your black eyes [if] she were sure you would not look [on] other black eyes'.

By March, Blount had received a positive letter from the Queen saying she was pleased to pardon those who had been 'seduced and blindly led' by Essex. He began mending fences with Cecil, but although the Secretary made all the right noises, deep down he was still uncertain about Blount's good faith. Throughout the Spanish invasion and beyond, Cecil continued to conspire and collude with his friend George Carew as though Blount were the enemy. Using coded language, Cecil made what one historian describes as 'dark allusions' about Blount's links with 'unworthy friends'. Amid the scare of the initial invasion, Carew made his sinister assertion to Cecil that Blount 'is [either] a noble gentleman, and all yours, or else he is a devil.'

It was an extraordinary situation, as a nineteenth-century historian would later comment: 'It is sad to think … that it was possible, in such a crisis, for [the Queen's] second in command to cast suspicion on the loyalty of her first officer in a letter to her chief adviser at home.'

The Queen did nothing to stop this relentless sabotage. When Blount complained that he was treated like a house servant, Elizabeth thought it was hilarious. She labelled Blount as 'Mistress Kitchenmaid' and teased him with this nickname until her death.

The most serious bid to undermine Blount's authority came in February 1602, when Cecil effectively ordered Carew to wreck the Blount-Águila peace deal on a pretext if he had the chance. But all through 1602, Carew continued sniping. In April he sent Cecil new information about Blount's disappearance to Portsmouth with Essex in 1599 – 'an ill tale' – and added: 'How to deal with these slanderous causes I know not.'

However, during his entire time as Ireland commander, Blount never gave them the satisfaction of the slightest lapse in loyalty. Eventually, Carew admitted grudgingly to Cecil that 'the emulation [presumably of Essex] you feared, and myself was doubtful of, is, I think, wholly removed'.

In fact, during Blount's command, the only 'disloyalty' shown by anyone in the army top brass was the blatant disloyalty shown by Carew to his commanding officer.

CHAPTER THIRTY-FIVE

A Dead Juan Walking

[Children], you will be glad to hear that when [Águila] reached home, King Philip, in great anger, degraded him, and kept him in prison, and there he died of a broken heart. – Irish schoolbook, 1904

Á GUILA HAD a pleasant passage home, arriving at La Coruña on 21 March – Palm Sunday for the Spanish. He knew better than to expect flags and bunting, but he probably didn't expect the chilliness he encountered at the Galician port. His vessel was about as welcome as a plague ship.

The old warrior was arguably in more danger in Spain than he had ever been in Kinsale. O'Donnell had spent the previous two months thoroughly poisoning the air against him. His story of Águila's supposed incompetence, cowardice and traitorous agreement was about to be given further credence by the furiously indignant Mateo de Oviedo.

Águila stepped ashore to find the thunder-faced O'Donnell standing on the quay, flanked by Pedro de Zubiaur and some twenty Irish exiles. Both commanders had just returned from pleading their case before the King.

Águila assumed a buoyant, positive tone.

—Be of good comfort, he told O'Donnell. We will have one more turn at Ireland.

O'Donnell's reply was not recorded.

All Spain was buzzing with the Águila scandal. In Valladolid, the diarist Luis Córdoba recorded in his journal for 20 April that the expedition had returned 'helpless' with six hundred fewer men than it had taken. 'Most of them died from disease, others are sick, others suffering from mistreatment from the work they have endured without having achieved anything worthy of consideration,' he wrote.

Some observers believed Águila was already a dead man walking. One merchant claimed: '[The] general report given out [is] that so soon as he comes, he shall be executed.' The Venetian ambassadors agreed that he was doomed. '[The Spanish authorities] now insist that Águila made a mistake in coming to terms with the English and surrendering to them three places which he held,' they said. 'Some prophesy ill for him, declaring that he has escaped an honourable death in Ireland to meet with a shameful one in Spain.'

The Irish, in particular, were 'calling out loudly' against Águila. And one English informant wrote: 'Don Juan is mightily railed at for deceiving the King.' He had turned Felipe's investment 'into dross'. O'Donnell, on the other hand, was 'in great credit'.

Carew was picking up the same intelligence. O'Donnell's reputation was 'great in Spain' and there was widespread 'dislike held of Don Juan'.

Águila had more immediate concerns. His men were still dying in large numbers. He set up an emergency hospital, but the men continued to sicken. It was soon reported that they were 'almost all' dead. One tally estimated 1,500 able men and seven hundred sick. When the authorities eventually transferred Águila's force to other duties, they found that only eight hundred of the 2,600 to 2,800 men who'd left Ireland were alive and fit for duty.

The Spanish authorities held an emergency council meeting to discuss the terms of Águila's peace agreement. Meanwhile, they called off the relief expedition they'd planned. 'Some few ships that lay ready to have come for Ireland were straight unfurnished,' reported one witness.

And, although there would be much posturing over the next few months, that's where this particular naval campaign came to an end. The Spaniards would never send an armada to Ireland again.

Two months beforehand, in January, O'Donnell had made a dramatic entrance to the royal court. Kneeling before the King, he had sworn not to rise until his three requests were granted.

—The first is that you send a Spanish army with me to Ireland, he said. The second is that, once you rule Ireland, I will be the most powerful Irish noble there. The third is that you protect the rights of the O'Donnells forever.

King Felipe agreed and told him to rise.

O'Donnell remained at court for two weeks, during which he detailed his case to anyone who would listen. It seems that the royal court rapidly tired of hearing the chieftain's grievances. Felipe genuinely wanted to help him, but at the same time he didn't want him anywhere near him. He granted O'Donnell a generous pension, but ordered him to go to La Coruña, 450 kilometres away, to supervise the naval preparations.

During his time at court, O'Donnell also worked with Oviedo to assemble a damning case against Águila. In order to persuade Felipe to mount another Irish expedition, he had to establish that it was Águila, and not the Irish, who had caused the Kinsale debacle.

The Council of State took four hours to pore over O'Donnell's submissions. 'His zeal and loyalty should be highly praised,' they wrote. '… He should be assured that His Majesty regards the Irish Catholics as his subjects.'

(Note, once again, that the Irish insurgents were not regarded as equal allies from a potentially independent nation. It was clear that Felipe planned to rule Ireland as a Spanish colony.)

Reading the rumours that flew around Spain during this period, it appears that Felipe's officials were telling O'Donnell anything he wanted to hear. There were wild claims that 5,000, 10,000, even 13,000 troops were being assembled for Ireland. But the action was always supposedly happening at some other port. English Secretary Robert Cecil knew better. 'Of all the great army whereof they speak, no man ever saw 4,000 together,' he scoffed. The well-informed Secretary kept a cool head as nearly everyone else predicted an imminent Spanish invasion. There would be no armada that year, he stated with certainty.

Cecil was right. O'Donnell did not know it, but an event in France that summer had just put paid to any chance of another Spanish invasion. A French general, the Duc de Biron, was executed for plotting with the Spanish to overthrow his own King. The delicate peace between the two giants of Europe was hanging by a thread. The risk of a provocative Spanish invasion had been reduced by 'Biron's conspiracy, in which Spain has given the French King occasion of offence,' Cecil wrote.

Back in Spain, O'Donnell was being fobbed off with bureaucratic waffle. His advisor later summed up the frustration of the Irish exiles: 'Another report had to be submitted to Your Majesty, and another the following week, and still another a month after that … seven months have passed … [we are] utterly tired out and desperate.'

O'Donnell's mental turmoil intensified, with 'anguish of heart and sickness of mind'. According to O'Cleary, 'He was in this condition until he prepared to go into the King's presence again to learn the cause of the delay.'

Although effectively barred from the court, O'Donnell set out for Valladolid. He got as close as Simancas, just thirteen kilometres away, before falling ill with an unidentified malaise. After sixteen days of suffering, he died. It was 10 September on the Spanish calendar. He had yet to reach his thirtieth birthday.

There were rumours that he had been poisoned by a turncoat insurgent, James Blake from Galway. Blake had extracted himself from a sticky situation with the English by promising to kill O'Donnell in Spain. Although there is no evidence that Blake was even sincere, never mind successful, in his plan, Carew still claimed credit for the supposed contract killing. It is arguable that the youthful O'Donnell actually died from a cancerous tumour. Just one month later, English agents were reporting from Spain that 'a kind of snake or serpent was found within him', which may have been a crude description of a malignant growth.

After O'Donnell's death, and perhaps to assuage their guilt, the Spanish authorities decided to send 10,000 ducats a month to O'Neill, who was now back at war and facing a renewed onslaught from Blount in Ulster. Possibly they had not heard of his offer to defect to the English, because they said it was O'Neill who had 'kept the spark glowing'. They made further promises of troops, but nothing materialised.

The Duke of Lerma was in no hurry. He was still playing the long game. He aimed for peace with England, and Kinsale had achieved his aim of strengthening Spain's hand. True, Queen Elizabeth had inconsiderately refused to die while Águila clung on to his bridgehead: that was too bad. But still, for the price of a thousand Spanish deaths in Ireland, his Irish expedition had cost the Queen 6,000 to 10,000 of her best soldiers, diverted her from the Low Countries, and almost bankrupted her. It had worked out okay. Now it was time to move on.

Soon the Council of State would recommend a new policy towards the Irish: 'These people should be undeceived, so that they may be enabled to make the best terms [with the English] they can, bad as the consequences may be.'

As one prominent count advised the King: '[I] would take no heed of Ireland, which is a noisy business and more trouble than advantage to Your Majesty.'

Slowly the pendulum of opinion began to swing back towards Águila: if not actually in his favour, at least into a neutral position. His returning troops were able to refute some of the more ridiculous claims of his critics – for instance, the allegation of Papal Nuncio Mansoni that the Spanish had fired their guns only on one single day during the entire siege.

The Spanish had decided in March that, in all fairness, no action should be taken against Águila until he had a chance to defend himself. A full inquiry was ordered and officials from the War Council began taking depositions.

In April, Águila wrote from La Coruña: 'To say the truth, I am very glad that I am in Spain.' It was hardly the remark of a man who had been flung into prison in disgrace, as some histories assert. In reality, he was allowed to go home to prepare his defence, although this was effectively house arrest on remand. 'Don Juan del Águila is restrained in his lodgings,' one Waterford man was to report the following March.

Águila was not out of the woods yet – far from it. He was still 'in the King's disfavour' and he suffered a major setback when Fr James Archer made a dramatic arrival in La Coruña in July. Archer had not trusted Blount's good faith and had fled from Kinsale into the west, where he continued to stoke up the insurgency. Eventually he had quit the country, trusting himself 'to the fortune of the sea in a small French ship with one mariner, without compass card, or glass' and somehow finding the right port. '[Archer] spared not to speak liberally in disgrace of Don Juan del Águila,' wrote the English naval officer Sir William Monson. 'He went to the court to inveigh against him to the King.'

The War Council took note of Archer's numerous criticisms. It continued its painstaking inquiry, which was to last the best part of a year.

Meanwhile, Águila had taken an enormous risk by renewing contact with Charles Blount and George Carew. And so began the saga of Lemon Diplomacy – one of the strangest and most bizarre exchanges between former enemies in recorded history. It began with the lemons, it ended with a horse, and in between it involved an English spy on a delicate and hazardous mission to Spain.

Águila had pledged that, on his return to Spain, he would advocate for peace with England and keep Blount informed. Blount was wary, yet felt destiny's hand on his shoulder. 'God many times doth work by unlikely, yea, by contrary means,' he pondered. 'Out of [our] commission to make war … [we] might prove commissioners for making a peace.'

Within a few days of arriving home on 21 March, Águila sent a selection of gifts to Blount and Carew. His accompanying letter, addressed to Carew but sent to Blount, was warm with gratitude:

> 'Muy illustre Señor.
>
> '… I am so much obliged for the honourable and good terms which the Lord Deputy [Blount] and your Lordship used … that I desire some apt occasion to manifest myself to be a good paymaster … And for that, in this country, there is no fruit of more estimation than the wines of Ribadavia, lemons and oranges. These few are sent to make a proof thereof.
>
> 'Don Juan del Águila'

He had sent lemons, oranges and at least five barrels of wine.

Blount didn't receive the packages until May. In the meantime, he had suffered a high fever – 'a likely effect of his watchings and cold taken during a hard winter siege', wrote Moryson – and had to be conveyed to Dublin in a horse-litter.

In early June, Carew heard of the gift and wrote asking for his share. Blount sent him a decidedly odd response that suggests it was written after a few glasses of Águila's fine Ribadavia. 'The bearer told me they were all sent to me, and although I knew the contrary, yet in plain fraud I was content that they be brought unto me,' he joked. However, he claimed the fruit had gone off and the wine wasn't worth sending.

Carew was not impressed. In a viciously backstabbing letter to Robert Cecil, he informed the Secretary of the gift 'not wishing to conceal any kindness which may have come from an enemy'. He said Blount was refusing to share the goodies and added waspishly: 'Much good may the present do him … for I [take no] joy in an enemy's kindness.'

However, the two arch-plotters obviously saw potential to groom Águila as a secret ally in Spain, because Carew's reply to Águila that July took a completely different tone. '[I] render your Lordship humble thanks for your favours,' he wrote to the Spaniard. 'The wine and fruits came not into my hands … [but I] am as well satisfied with it as if it had come into my own hands, for the love I bear to his Lordship [Blount] is no less than to myself.'

Meanwhile, Blount was still waiting to learn more from Águila about the peace proposals, but he heard nothing further. 'By Don Juan's silence from Spain,' writes Fynes Moryson, 'this overture passed as a dream.'

Carew and Cecil were not giving up so easily. They concocted a scheme whereby an English military agent – one Lieutenant Walter Edney – could gain safe passage to Spain to talk directly to Águila under cover of delivering Carew's reciprocal gift of a hackney horse. Carew confided to Cecil that the visit was a front 'that they may not think that he is purposely sent to negotiate the business intended, or to come as a spy'. He promised the Secretary that once Edney returned, 'your Lordship shall have certain intelligence of Spanish affairs'.

The plan swung into action on 17 September, when Carew again wrote warmly to Águila, introducing Edney as the bearer of the letter. 'I have received profit by the book of fortification which Your Lordship left me,' he wrote, 'and hold it as a relic in memory of you.' He said he lacked only a teacher of Águila's quality, because he considered the Spaniard pre-eminent in the military profession. However, he joked that Águila would find out how much Carew had improved in the subject if he ever returned to Ireland, 'which I hope in God will be never'.

Carew's last words to Águila were: 'I beseech God to preserve you with many happy years.'

Edney landed safely, but found La Coruña seething with suspicious Irish exiles. When he asked for Águila, he was told that he 'was in disgrace, confined to his house'. This was 'by the accusation of the Irish fugitives'. Edney himself was accused of spying and detained indefinitely in La Coruña. His goods were sold off, his ship sent home, and even the horse seized. He was to remain there until July 1603, when diplomatic relations began to thaw.

The agent used the opportunity to file secret reports to Carew. He pointed out perceptively that the credibility of the Irish exiles hinged on the outcome of Águila's trial. But meanwhile, it was Águila's life that was on the line. 'Don Juan the 24th of [March 1603] comes to a public trial for his Irish voyage,' Edney reported back. 'All captains who were with him are sent for and commanded to attend, on pain of death.'

CHAPTER THIRTY-SIX

THE TRIAL

I T WAS the trial that all Spain was talking about – the hearing that would dictate whether the famous Don Juan del Águila would be hailed as a hero ... or hanged as a traitor.

On one side stood Águila himself, backed up by some loyal officers. On the side of the accusers stood a heavyweight line-up of Irish expatriates, supported by the disaffected Spanish captains, driven by the cold, cheated fury of Mateo Oviedo, and all backed up by the formidable persuasive skills of the Jesuit priest Fr Archer. In the centre, sitting in judgement, was King Felipe's powerful Council of War.

Hearings of this nature were unusual in Spain, and this one had left the citizens of Valladolid and the former capital, Madrid, split down the middle. Everyone waited in anticipation of the verdict.

First, the accusations were put forward. There were twelve specific charges, grouped into five topics:

ONE: The Choice of Destination. That out at sea, eight days after the departure of the fleet, Águila had changed the target from Cork or Limerick (as originally listed in O'Neill's 'numbers formula') and replaced it with Kinsale or Castlehaven.

TWO: The Disembarkation Debacle. Even though Brochero had been under a royal command to return home quickly, in view of the circumstances Águila should have instructed him to wait in Kinsale *'por algún tiempo'* – for a little time longer – until they received fresh orders from the King.

THREE: The Failure to Relocate. Given Kinsale's poor situation and the impossibility of defending both town and harbour entrance, Águila should have marched on to Cork, or demanded that Brochero ferry his troops to Castlehaven.

FOUR: The Failure to Fortify. Águila had not fortified Kinsale properly and had not ensured that the harbour entrance remained under Spanish control for the expected reinforcements. He had also failed to stock up enough food for the siege.

And most gravely of all, with its implications of cowardice and dereliction of duty …

FIVE: The Betrayal of the Irish. That, on the morning of the battle, Águila failed to sally out from Kinsale to offer any help to the insurgent chieftains who had obeyed his orders via Bustamante, and who had occupied the position he had stipulated. This was particularly serious 'if he heard them fighting, as some say'.

The twelve precise charges were more detailed. Many gave specific examples of the claim that Águila had failed to fortify or to stock up on supplies. One of the most outrageous allegations was that Águila had deliberately refused to acquire mounts for his cavalrymen even though 'there were many horses available for practically nothing'. Another charge alleged that Águila left most of his big guns on board ship, and that the few he actually took were unloaded only 'at the great insistence of the Archbishop of Dublin [Oviedo] and many captains'. Yet another charge alleged he had wasted twenty-five days before informing the chieftains of his arrival.

The most damning were the charges numbered ten, eleven and twelve, which expanded on the general accusation that he had betrayed the Irish insurgent leaders. These claimed that Águila had negligently failed to secure O'Neill's initial approach route into Kinsale; that he had dithered indecisively for more than fifteen days after the Irish troops had arrived in the area; and, of course, that he had abandoned them on battle day. 'This resulted in their destruction, and that of His Majesty's infantry,' the charge sheet concluded.

The Council listened carefully to the evidence of both sides. Oviedo, Archer and the Irish expatriates had drawn up an impressive array of witness statements, but Águila had done his homework too. Submitting a lengthy defence, he pleaded with King Felipe to read the document with his own eyes. He assured him that everything in it was true and comprehensive: 'You are not going to find another thing.'

He submitted this to the Council with the brief soldierly comment: 'I conducted everything with *mucho valor*.' With great bravery.

On the question of destination, there was a flurry of bewildering accusation and counter-accusation. Zubiaur, for instance, declared that Águila had gone to 'the worst place in Ireland, where the Queen enjoyed all the advantages, and our allies the complete opposite'. But Águila could produce the paper trail to show that he had been given little choice in the matter. Among his limited options he had taken the best decisions he could.

It was impossible to answer the charge of failing to relocate to Cork city, because his critics' case was based on what *might* have happened. Here's the Count of Caracena, one of his most vociferous accusers:

—If Águila had marched straight to Cork, Caracena said, the town would have been his. He is to blame for not having taken that city.

In fact, with its mediaeval walls and hills, Cork had much the same disadvantages as Kinsale.

As to the charge of failing to fortify, Águila had declared at a very early stage that he hadn't enough men to defend both Kinsale and the forts. Besides, he had enough trouble trying to rescue the wet gunpowder and food from the shoreline.

Águila's accusers made themselves easy targets with their allegation that he had deliberately refused to buy Irish horses. Águila was not only able to prove the contrary, but to turn the charge around to his own benefit. 'The Irish deceived the King in promising him horses, for the which [I] brought saddles,' he said. This could be easily verified. The Spanish officials had specifically been assured before the invasion, by O'Neill's agent Richard Owen, that horses weren't necessary. 'Harnesses and all accessories should be sent,' Owen had instructed, 'but not horses.'

The most dramatic moment came as the Council investigated what actually happened inside Kinsale while the battle was raging. Here, there was a direct conflict of evidence. Archer and Oviedo both claimed to have heard the noise of fighting. They had wanted to emerge with guns blazing, but Águila had overruled them. 'Whether it was from treachery or accident,' raged Oviedo, '… we listened to the loud musket and arquebus gunshots, but we did not sally out, as we had agreed.'

Archer accused Águila of outright cowardice. He testified that he'd heard artillery as the Irish kept their promise and began fighting, but the Spanish commander 'refused to go out of Kinsale'.

Águila told the hearing that he had instructed O'Neill and O'Donnell ('the Counts') to take up position on the mountain opposite the camp, to do nothing except to hold it, and to advise him on their arrival. 'I was perpetually on the alert,' he said, 'but for most of the day, I heard nothing. [Then] the enemy made a great salvo of gunshot in their quarters after having routed the Irish. I understood this to be the Counts [fighting], so I started hurling my people out.' He had been dismayed to find the enemy positions better occupied than ever. Finally: 'We spotted [Spanish] flags which some [English] cavalrymen were showing off to the whole camp, and sometimes dragging on the ground … we found absolutely no trace of the Counts' troops.'

Separately, the inquiry also had to decide whether Águila was guilty of dereliction of duty with his peace treaty and surrender of the ports. Donal Cam O'Sullivan Beare complained that Águila had 'ignominiously surrendered to the English heretics, our deadly foes, greatly to the dishonour of His Majesty'. The Spanish quartermaster Pedro Lopez de Soto was convinced that Águila had made a grave error of timing.

—If Don Juan had not come to terms so soon, he claimed, six thousand men would have been sent to second him.

Águila responded that he had held out as long as he could. He had to start negotiating before Blount realised just how badly off he was. 'I waited six days until I had no more biscuit … nor any kind of man who could fight,' he said. 'I was already ruined … I had no other way to escape.' The other ports were not defensible. And most importantly, O'Neill and O'Donnell had fled from the front line. 'One tempestuous puff of war had blown one of them into Spain,' Águila said, 'and the other into the North.' O'Neill's logic, expressed in a letter to Felipe III, was that he wouldn't have had to leave to go north if the King had sent his armada north in the first place.

The hearings continued for several months until at last, on 12 July 1603, the Council was ready to pronounce its verdict.

On the first four of the five general accusations, Águila stood acquitted.

Águila was relieved. But despite his reputation as a cold commander, his heart must have been thumping under his military tunic as he awaited the verdict on the fifth and most serious accusation relating to his alleged betrayal of the Irish 'Counts' on battle day.

'On the fifth charge that the Counts came to the place agreed with Alférez Bustamante, but that [Águila] did not go to help,' intoned the Council, 'we find that the Counts did *not* come to the position that he conveyed.'

Águila must have breathed a little easier.

'As he was under the impression that they were going to be there,' the Council continued, 'Águila issued orders to go out and help them. By doing this, he risked losing the place [Kinsale] but had calculated that he would not need it any more if things went well, and that in any event he could not sustain it for much longer.

'He had everyone in position, with the sentries in elevated positions watching and listening. He himself was at the gate, waiting for the moment when he could prudently sally out. But no one saw or heard anything as the Counts fought.'

The Council said that when Águila finally sallied out with a hundred men, he found the English troops still firmly in position and unengaged.

Commenting on the battle itself, the Council said that the Irish had been defeated by a much smaller force of English. This had happened not only because of their poor organisation on the battlefield, but also because they'd never had any real intention of advancing – as evidenced by the fact that they'd earlier shifted their camp baggage backwards rather than forwards.

But what of the accusation that Águila had abandoned Kinsale to the English in a traitorous deal?

On this point, the Council gave a clear endorsement of Águila's tactics. 'He defended the place with a valour that claimed the lives of many enemy troops,' it ruled. Águila had not been defeated by force: 'He had been given too few supplies, and had been left with neither advice, nor hope of aid, from Spain … his people were either dead, or injured, or exhausted by the defence. He negotiated with the enemy a treaty and conditions that were more honourable than many other deals that were made in less troublesome circumstances.'

Despite a dissenting opinion by one member, the War Council summed up with a ringing vote of confidence in Don Juan. 'The Council concludes,' read the verdict, 'that Don Juan del Águila satisfied his obligations to Your Majesty. He did everything that he should have done as a very prudent and valiant captain. No blame attaches to him. More than that: he deserves a position of even greater responsibility in future.'

It was all over. The man from El Barraco had been completely exonerated and could stand tall again.

The Council's work continued for many more months. There were still serious charges against Admiral Zubiaur and the quartermaster general, Lopez de Soto. Zubiaur was accused of returning to Spain in the original expedition instead of joining Brochero in Kinsale. Both he and Lopez de Soto had to explain why they had sent only a niggardly two hundred troops to aid O'Neill. (When Zubiaur sailed back to Spain with O'Donnell, he still had 400-500 troops available.) Zubiaur replied that he had actually sent 900 men – the 200 Spaniards and 700 Irishmen whom he had trained. The case against the two men was to drag on for years.

In a side-issue, Águila had made a formal complaint against Sergeant de Heredia for abandoning Rincorran Castle before its official surrender. Heredia was arrested in Ostend, in Flanders, and thrown into prison. He was to remain there for another fourteen years, long after the death of his accuser.

The news of Águila's acquittal was well received in England. 'Don Juan del Águila hath endured all that could be said against him by the Irish, and hath well acquitted himself … to the good liking of the King,' read one report from Spain in 1603. It was suggested that he was 'again received to the King's favour' and there was talk of him leading another mission.

But Águila never did get to lead his beloved *tercio* into battle again. The ordeal at Kinsale had blighted his health, as it had Blount's. The repeated slurs on his character and professionalism had left him deeply scarred. The effort of mounting an effective defence against intelligent and resourceful opponents like Oviedo and Archer was every bit as exhausting as defending Kinsale.

He returned to his birthplace of El Barraco to spend his remaining days there. 'Wounded by all the vengefulness, he retired to the serenity of his homeland,' wrote the contemporary historian Gil Gonzáles Dávila.

Águila had hoped that he would be given a substantial pension, wrote Gonzáles Dávila, but 'death came before rewards' and he never had the opportunity to enjoy 'the glory that was his just entitlement'.

According to another source, Águila died 'of grief'. He was in or around sixty. The precise date of his death is contentious. It's commonly given as August 1602, but English records show he survived well into 1603, and Spanish archives prove that he was still writing letters from Avila that year. His tombstone in a chapel built after his death is dated 'May 1605'.

His funeral and burial were lavish affairs and certainly refute any suggestion that he had become a social pariah. He was laid to rest in a side-chapel of his local church, underneath an elaborate altarpiece. Águila bequeathed a trust fund to help the daughters of the local poor to make good marriages. He gave twice as much to any who were named 'Juana', thus ensuring that his name would live on. His bequest also paid doctors to treat the elderly. And every Friday, grain was distributed to the poorest townsfolk in his name.

'He made El Barraco famous,' wrote Gonzáles Dávila, 'with the memory of his ashes and triumphs.'

In his will, Águila said he looked forward to his actions being judged in the divine court. He would certainly get a fairer hearing than he has received from some historians over the centuries. Let us say farewell to Don Juan del Águila by listing some quotes about his life and character. We will start with the vitriolic assessments of some Victorian writers whose views dictated public opinion for decades. We will end with the opinions of his admirers, who included his most bitter military enemies. Read them, and judge the man for yourself.

Matthew O'Conor, military historian, 1845: 'The least competent of all the generals whom Philip could have chosen ... had signalled himself by defeats and miscarriages.'

John Mitchel, Irish writer, 1845: '[He] exposed a brave garrison to destruction through his cowardice and incompetence.'

Charles Gibson, historian, 1861: '[He] was desperate, but this did not justify the black treachery with which he acted towards his Irish friends … he could use his tongue and pen better than the sword.'

Edward d'Alton, historian, 1906: 'He was impetuous and self-willed … defeats and disasters were all that could be placed to his account … there was nothing heroic in the character of Águila … he had been in fact the main cause of [the Irish] defeat … By the Irish his memory was execrated, and not without some justice.'

Fr James Archer, Jesuit priest, 1602: '[He] has the reputation in other parts of being a brave soldier, but [in Ireland he was] cowardly and timorous.'

Robert Cecil, English Secretary, 1563–1612: 'One of the bravest commanders in Spain.'

Francis Bacon, English statesman, 1561–1626: 'A man of good valour.'

George Carew, English general, 1602: '[A] man of quality, honour and merit … a master [of military arts] in which I give [him] the pre-eminence.'

Charles Blount, English commander, 1601: 'One of the greatest soldiers the King of Spain hath.'

Richard Leveson, English admiral, 1570–1605: 'A great captain and a gallant fellow.'

Philip O'Sullivan, Irish historian, 1621: 'A Spanish gentleman, of military skill … [and of] great valour.'

Fernando de Toledo, Spanish nobleman 1580s: 'The man born without fear.'

Spanish War Secretary Esteban de Ibarra, 1601: '[A man of] valour ... When I remember who Don Juan del Águila is, my heart is lightened.'

King Felipe III, 1602: '[His] bravery and prudence ... I prize highly.'

Gil Gonzáles Dávila, historian, 1578–1658: 'One of the greatest luminaries that war has produced.'

Martin Hume, specialist in Spanish history, 1901: 'A chivalrous soldier of the old school, brave as a lion.'

Standish O'Grady, historian, 1896: 'Heroic ... I hardly know of a better soldier and more honourable or loyal gentleman operating in Ireland ... the country is the richer because Don Juan was here.'

CHAPTER THIRTY-SEVEN

THE AFTERMATH

THE WAR in Ireland continued for another year after the Spanish left Munster – and the intervening months were among the blackest periods in Irish history.

In the north, full-scale hostilities resumed in the summer of 1602. O'Neill made renewed attempts to obtain a royal pardon, but Queen Elizabeth refused. She ordered Blount to strike 'while the iron is hot'. Blount obeyed, ravaging O'Neill's territories in a relentless scorched-earth campaign. Some of his commanders took this to extremes. 'We have killed above 100 people,' reported one general, Arthur Chichester. '… We spare none of what quality or sex soever.' There was widespread famine. Fynes Moryson recalled seeing 'multitudes of these poor people dead with their mouths all coloured green by eating nettles'. Other victims were forced into cannibalism.

(It does not mitigate the horror in any way to point out, for the sake of balance, that such pitiless scorched-earth tactics were used by both sides. O'Neill's ravages in Munster and Leinster had left whole regions destitute. Similarly, O'Donnell had passed through the west 'plundering, devastating, ravaging and destroying'.)

O'Neill held out, hoping for better terms after Elizabeth's death. Negotiations were re-opened, and were still continuing when the Queen died in 1603 – but the English withheld that news from O'Neill until after he had submitted to Blount.

O'Neill negotiated excellent terms. Since he retained nearly all his lands and kept his English title of Earl of Tyrone, it was almost as though he had hit an 'undo' button and wiped out his recent past. This left his former foes embittered. '[I] went near to starving, ate horseflesh in Munster, and all to quell that man, who now smileth in peace!' stormed one. It was Blount who held these enemies back, reckoning that it was better to keep O'Neill inside the tent spitting out, than outside spitting in. In an odd twist of history, he became O'Neill's protector – and when Blount died in 1606, the Ulsterman lost his only shield against attack. O'Neill, who had spent much of his life cheerfully hopping back and forth between sides, was running out of room to manoeuvre. He was dogged by spies and kept under surveillance. But exactly why he chose to leave Ireland, suddenly and secretly, in 1607 is a fiercely disputed question.

One explanation is that he had been due to go to London but had been warned that he would be arrested and executed. Another explanation is that he'd been caught in the act of plotting a new insurgency.

In any event, on 14 September, he and around ninety-nine followers boarded a Breton ship in Donegal and set sail towards Spain in the renowned 'Flight of the Earls'. That phrase is itself contentious. Some say it wasn't a 'flight', more a temporary tactical manoeuvre. And it didn't have all that many earls; recent research has questioned the idea that the ship was laden with Gaelic nobility. The crew made up at least two-thirds of the vessel's complement.

Lamented by Irish bards, the event has been presented, in hindsight, as an emotionally charged final farewell by a man who knew he would never return, and whose departure marked the passing of the Gaelic Order. Yet it wasn't seen that way at the time. O'Neill had high hopes of drumming up support in mainland Europe and of returning at the head of a foreign force. This was not a goodbye, more of an *au revoir*.

Bad weather diverted his ship to northern France. His ensuing trip through Europe was far more like a modern tub-thumping election campaign tour, combined with sightseeing trips, than a sad, forlorn journey to oblivion. At Louvain, Nancy and Lucerne he was hosted with sumptuous receptions. As cheering citizens lined the streets, he wrote to Felipe III demanding aid for another invasion. But Spain and England had declared peace, and O'Neill had become an embarrassment to the King.

Crossing a bridge in the Alps, O'Neill suffered a huge setback when a horse carrying his personal savings fell into the gorge. Within an instant, he was broke.

In the Vatican he received a warm welcome from the Pope, but his hopes for Spanish aid were dashed when Felipe ordered him to remain in Rome.

Years passed. In 1615, at the age of sixty-five, O'Neill was still plotting to return home before 'the English completely conquer our provinces'. It was not to be. He died in Rome in 1616. Four hundred years later, his role in history is still the subject of contention. No one can question his brilliance as a military tactician and as a negotiator. But was he a ruthless operator who cared only to advance his own power? Or an international statesman, a sophisticate years ahead of his time, a visionary who truly appreciated and exploited the pan-European dimension to Irish politics? Experts have come up with both conclusions, and more. Analysing O'Neill is like looking for images in clouds: you will see what you want to see.

In much the same way, some historians view the Flight of the Earls as a logical move, and others as a huge tactical error – because by abandoning his followers, O'Neill left them vulnerable to what came next.

And what came next was the Ulster Plantation. Determined to subdue the Gaelic north of Ireland, the English confiscated O'Neill's and O'Donnell's territories and planted six counties with English and Scots settlers. Boosted by later waves of economic migrants, these newcomers transformed the face of the northern counties and altered the course of history. But that is another, and much longer, story.

As to the others in our tale:

ON THE IRISH SIDE ...

After Kinsale, **FR JAMES ARCHER** accompanied Donal Cam O'Sullivan Beare to Dunboy. There, to Águila's fury, he threatened the local Spanish commander and announced that the Irish would hold the castle for Felipe. (Águila was supposedly so incensed that he offered to reclaim it himself.) After a narrow shave in which his servant was captured, the 'light-footed' Archer escaped to Spain. There he survived both an official inquiry and a black-propaganda campaign involving a forged letter. The Irish Jesuits objected to his plans to return home – his presence was too provocative. He died in 1620, and his lasting legacy was the Irish College at Salamanca.

One fascinating but evidence-weak theory encountered by this author is that Fr Archer was actually a deep-cover *agent provocateur* planted by the Queen's spymasters. Archer was, after all, a man from a solid Old English Establishment background who secretly despised the Irish as 'barbarians'. In this theory of events, the entire plot to kill Elizabeth was a fabrication by the Queen's spymasters designed to establish Archer's credentials and to smoke out Irish conspirators, and the English depiction of him as a super-nimble, supernatural force was an attempt to explain his all-too-convenient narrow escapes. Archer mysteriously turns up everywhere, from the Yellow Ford and Kinsale to Dunboy, and always gets away. And it was Archer, remember, who was most vociferous in urging the Spanish to sally out from Kinsale in response to what Águila believed was an English trick. It is an intriguing hypothesis – but there doesn't seem to be any real evidence to back it up.

While on the subject of spies, **ANDREW LYNCH**, whose boat was supposedly requisitioned, has recently been revealed as an Irish insurgent sympathiser who encouraged the Spanish to invade Ireland. And O'Neill's envoy

RICHARD OWEN, who had confidently assured the Spanish they wouldn't need horses, was suspected by Águila of being a double agent.

BROTHER DOMINIC COLLINS, the Jesuit chaplain, remained at Dunboy when Archer left. He was captured and taken to his native Youghal for propaganda purposes. There he was tortured and hanged. In 1992 he was beatified by Rome.

DONAL CAM O'SULLIVAN BEARE finally lost his beloved Dunboy Castle when Carew captured it in June. O'Sullivan and a thousand refugees set off on a midwinter trek to Leitrim. Only thirty-five arrived there. Donal Cam sailed south, settled in Spain, and founded an important Irish dynasty.

ON THE SPANISH SIDE …

The decade that started with Kinsale effectively ended Spain's role as self-appointed religious policeman of Europe. The Spanish never sent another armada to Ireland. In 1604 the peace treaty that Águila and Blount had dreamed of finally became a reality. Five years later, Spain also agreed a truce in the Netherlands. On one level, this was heartbreaking for Felipe III, who had promised his father he would continue his religious wars. However, it meant the English privateers would no longer plague his bullion fleets.

Felipe partied on, spending a fortune on his children's christenings. The Duke of Lerma continued corruptly dispensing knighthoods. The shifting of the capital from Madrid had ruined that city, so it was expensively shifted back again. As one writer put it: '[Felipe] hunted, danced, prayed and trifled, while the country was dragged from misery to misery.'

In 1605 the silver fleet failed to arrive, and the Italian banks refused to lend more money. Humiliated and exhausted, Spain suspended the religious struggle in northern Europe. It was the beginning of the end. Spain's slow decline from power began as England built up its naval might.

In the 1500s, Spain's celebrated infantry had been perceived as invincible. Whatever the truth, this reputation was shattered in Ireland in 1601. It never recovered, and by the mid-1600s its troops would suffer a morale-sapping defeat at the Battle of Rocroi. The glory days of the *tercios* were well and truly over.

THE DUKE OF LERMA continued to badger England, seeking to improve Spain's negotiating position, until finally agreeing peace in 1604. He achieved short-term profit and popularity in 1607 by expelling 300,000 Spanish Moors. He gained all their property but lost the tax contributions of a hardworking population. Only later was this recognised as a huge mistake. In 1618, Lerma was deposed in a palace plot organised by his own son. He retired to become a cardinal. When Felipe III died, Lerma was forced to repay much of his corruptly acquired wealth. He died in 1625.

FELIPE III ruled until 1621. As a monarch, he was undoubtedly weak, indecisive, spendthrift and economically challenged. Yet modern revisionists point out that the peace agreements negotiated during his reign actually left the country stronger than it had been in the final years of his powerful father's rule.

His wife, **QUEEN MARGARET,** continued to challenge the dictatorial Lerma, and in 1606 nailed him for appointing a corrupt financial committee. As a result, two of Lerma's associates were prosecuted and the Duke left court for a while. However, Margaret died in childbirth in 1611, aged twenty-six, without the satisfaction of seeing her great rival ousted seven years later. Her husband never remarried. The indomitable Margaret had borne eight children, including the heir, Felipe IV. She probably played a major role in persuading her husband to send the Last Armada to Ireland, but just how influential she was in this historic decision, we may never know.

PEDRO DE ZUBIAUR was put on trial for, among other things, sailing home and abandoning his comrades in Kinsale after the September storm. After three years imprisoned on remand he was convicted on only one of the four charges. He was freed in view of his thirty-seven years' service, but died that same year, in 1605.

DIEGO DE BROCHERO was under the protection of Lerma and was never censured for his behaviour after the landing at Kinsale. Brochero went on to enjoy a long and illustrious career as Spain's leading naval expert and ship designer. He died in 1625.

PEDRO LOPEZ DE SOTO, the quartermaster at Castlehaven, was convicted on charges arising out of his failure to support Águila and O'Neill. He lost his job for four years and was exiled from the court for two.

MATEO DE OVIEDO was cleared, but banished from court. He never returned to his second home of Ireland. Yet he behaved as though he were Archbishop of Dublin in practice. He appointed two successive 'vicars general' to administer the See in Ireland. Both were arrested; one died in jail, the other was executed. The Anglo-Spanish peace deal shattered all his hopes of another armada. He died in Valladolid in 1610.

ON THE ENGLISH SIDE …

QUEEN ELIZABETH died in March 1603 – without ever having realised her dream of subjugating Hugh O'Neill and controlling Ireland. The cost of fighting those wars had almost ruined her: £1,255,000 over the past four years alone, a figure that exceeded her nation's revenue by more than 33 percent.

Oviedo's Kinsale proclamation – which she attributed to Águila – had infuriated Elizabeth. It led to a major clampdown on all Catholic priests, even those loyal to her. 'Don Juan published a warrant from Rome to deprive us of our crown, and declare his master [Felipe] lord,' she fumed. Oviedo had hoped to help the Catholics, but his blundering had made their plight immeasurably worse.

Early in 1603 Elizabeth was 'seized with a dangerous illness'. But although she was well aware of the national agitation over her successor, the matter remained dangerously unresolved.

ROBERT CECIL was the man who averted a possible civil war. The Secretary had been thought to favour the Spanish Infanta Isabella as the next queen, and his denials had only fuelled the rumours. But it had all been a smokescreen. No one ever knew what Cecil was really thinking. In actuality, he had been negotiating covertly with James of Scotland. (One time, Elizabeth had stumbled upon one of the secret letters but Cecil bluffed it out, telling her it smelled foul from the messenger's satchel and needed to be aired.)

The transition of power was remarkably smooth. James became King long before most Londoners even realised that the Queen had died. The irony, of course, is that Cecil and his great rival Essex had both wanted the same thing. The plots that cost Essex his head, and endangered Charles Blount's career, had been totally unnecessary.

CHARLES BLOUNT became a national hero in England. Carew's attempt to win the glory through Richard Boyle's epic trip to London proved unsuccessful: the injured Henry Danvers achieved much greater impact when he arrived with Blount's version of events. 'His wounds prove his loyal service,' Carew had to admit.

Blount became a celebrity. Poets sang his praise. A poster for a play named *England's Joy* depicted the Spanish as tyrants attacking 'a beautiful lady, whom they mangle and wound' before being defeated 'by the wisdom and valour of Lord Mountjoy'. One poem declared he was chosen by Jehovah.

After O'Neill's submission in 1603, Blount made a triumphant entry to London with the 'arch-traitor' in tow. A grateful King James gave Blount the title of Earl of Devonshire and rewarded him with huge expanses of land. (It wasn't his only reward. In an intriguing letter of 1602, Blount talked of 'the thousand pounds of Spanish money from Kinsale' and asked Carew to send him 'my share in the Spanish spoils'. There were wild rumours that Blount had put a hoard of Spanish gold onto a ship that was wrecked at Wexford.)

Blount helped negotiate the peace with Spain. Interestingly, Oviedo's proclamation threatened to scupper those talks, too. 'Here they resent the fact that Águila, when he landed in Ireland, proclaimed his master King,' the Venetian Secretary in England wrote during the negotiations. However, a deal was finally hammered out. And in another strange historical twist, as a recognition of Blount's contribution to the peace effort, King Felipe III granted a generous Spanish pension of £1,000 a year to the very same English commander who had frustrated his attempt to invade Ireland at Kinsale.

Peace in the Atlantic benefited England as well as Spain. It enabled the English to colonise Virginia. If it hadn't been for Kinsale and the resulting peace, modern America might have been a very different place.

Blount was riding high when it all went terribly wrong. His longtime lover, Penelope Rich, was divorced in a Church-law separation that did not allow her to remarry. However, Blount managed to get a cleric to perform the ceremony anyway.

This innocent, if technically illegal, marriage scandalised the country. King James described it as 'a flagrant crime' and said Blount had won 'a fair woman with a black soul'. Blount tried to convince him with complex Biblical arguments. But he found 'an alteration in the King's countenance'. It didn't really help that James loathed tobacco and Blount smoked heavily.

Three months later, in April 1606, Blount took ill 'of a burning fever and putrefaction of his lungs' and died. Since his children were all born outside wedlock, the ancient line of Mountjoy died with him.

Blount was a brilliant – although ruthless – military strategist whose icy efficiency at crushing O'Neill's rebellion changed the course of history. His methods were harsh and pitiless. Judged by today's standards, the scorched-earth policies used by Blount and Chichester (and indeed by O'Neill and O'Donnell) are inexcusable. But the most unfair accusation against him is that he waged genocide. Genocide is the systematic attempt to kill everyone of a particular national or ethnic background. Had Blount really wanted to wipe out all the Irish, he would have had to kill his best commanders and half his own army. During his campaigns, he often tried to clear Irish non-combatants out of a target area. At Kinsale, for instance, he endured ridicule because he wanted the Irish women and children removed from danger before the bombardment. That said, however, he did play a crucial role in a centuries-long process that aimed to eradicate Irish culture and the Gaelic Order.

PENELOPE RICH was devastated by Blount's death. Three years earlier, she had stepped out of the shade of Elizabeth's displeasure and into the sunshine of her friend King James's affections. She was chosen to escort the new Queen from Scotland, and joined her in lavish plays at court.

When Blount returned home, it seemed that the future held nothing but happiness. However, the remarriage scandal, followed so soon by Blount's death, turned her world grey and bleak. Aged forty-four, she died just fifteen months after her husband.

Penelope was a remarkable and complex woman, centuries ahead of her era. You sense she would have felt perfectly at home in the revolutionary 1970s. She was obviously very beautiful; she was the caring mother of two parallel families; and yet she was as tough as ship-nails. She stood up to Queen Elizabeth as though she were her equal. Like Homer's Penelope, she used every trick and strategy available to her to outwit the powerful male courtiers. Her quick wit, charm and persuasive ability ensured her survival. If she was manipulative and Machiavellian, it was because she needed to be. Still, Philip Sidney was right – she could be poison to the men who fell for her.

GEORGE CAREW was elevated to Earl of Totnes. When he returned to Ireland in 1611 to inspect the Ulster Plantation, he concocted a plan to gerrymander election districts to ensure a Protestant majority – an abuse that continued as late as the 1960s. He died in 1629. His journals, although self-serving, provide an invaluable historical source.

DONOUGH O'BRIEN, the Earl of Thomond, helped to crush O'Sullivan Beare's last stand. When Dunboy Castle fell, he executed nearly sixty survivors. His legacy includes upgrading a minor fort – Bunratty – into a castle which is now internationally famous. He died in 1624.

RICHARD WINGFIELD, Blount's marshal, was granted a thirteenth-century castle in Wicklow and given its name as a title – 'Viscount Powerscourt'. It now forms the centre of the world-famous Powerscourt Gardens.

FYNES MORYSON received a pension from Charles Blount. He used it to write his masterwork, the massive *Itinerary*, which offered tips and warnings to travellers doing Europe. Moryson, who died in 1630, was the spiritual father of Lonely Planet and the Rough Guides.

JOSIAH BODLEY (1550–1618) surveyed Ulster for the Plantation. When the English officers funded a library to commemorate the fallen at Kinsale, Josiah's brother Thomas Bodley, the Oxford librarian, worked to acquire the best books for both collections. And so, wrote one historian, 'the famous Bodleian Library at Oxford and that of [Trinity College] Dublin began together'.

RICHARD BOYLE (1566–1643), Carew's messenger to London, became Earl of Cork. His son, Robert Boyle, became a scientific pioneer. Richard's purchase of Walter Raleigh's Irish estates made him fabulously rich. Yet in 1631, he refused to ransom 107 Baltimore villagers who were kidnapped by Algerine pirates and sold into slavery in Africa.

RICHARD DE BURGH, the Irish Earl of Clanrickard, was a hero to the English after Kinsale. He married his lover, Essex's widow, Frances Walsingham, but continued to write love poems to Elizabeth. The Queen held him in 'special grace', partly because of his resemblance to Essex. He remained an uncompromising Catholic, for which two successive kings gave him legal immunity. As a powerful figure in his native County Galway, he fought fiercely to prevent an Ulster-style English plantation there. He died in 1635, but his bloodline lives on. He and Frances were the ten-times great-grandparents of Diana, Princess of Wales, and the eleven-times great-grandparents of today's Prince William, the future King of England.

CHAPTER THIRTY-EIGHT

LEGACY

Great was this victory [at Kinsale] ... the Queen's authority was
restored; the insolency of wicked persons restrained; the hearts of
honest men were cheered up and confirmed; and a perfect and solid
peace afterwards established in all parts of the island.
— William Camden, historian, 1551–1623

CAMDEN could not have been more mistaken. Like a slow-burning fuse on an infantryman's musket, the legacy of Kinsale smouldered acridly and malevolently for many years. Eventually, inevitably, it touched a powerfully volatile mixture of pent-up hatred and resentment and exploded with terrifying force ... in 1641, in 1916 in 1968, and at many times in between.

Most Irish people are familiar with the narrative. The defeat at Kinsale and the exit of the Spanish resulted in Ireland's Gaelic nobility departing to the Continent, first at Castlehaven and then in the 'Flight of the Earls', and this in turn resulted in the long, slow decline of the Gaelic Order that once dominated politics and culture in Ireland. It left the already-depopulated north open to King James's large-scale plantations of Protestant settlers from England and Scotland. The inevitable tensions between dispossessed locals and assertive newcomers resulted in a massive blow-up in 1641. Irish Catholics rose in rebellion. The cold-blooded massacre of thousands of Protestant settlers in Ulster and the equally ruthless butchery of the Irish by Oliver Cromwell in 1649 created the template for centuries of mistrust and violence. The atavistic memory of these atrocities sank deep into the national psyche. In the late 1960s, the simmering tensions erupted in the thirty years of conflict known as The Troubles.

In broad-brush terms, that picture of events is accurate, although the finer details are as complex as everything else in history. Yet, as shorthand terms for the defeat of Gaelic Ireland and the departure of its hierarchy to the Continent, Kinsale and the Flight of the Earls still generally hold true. All these epic processes began near a small County Cork town on Christmas Eve, 1601.

But first, let's look at the international repercussions.

Kinsale put an end to Spain's long-cherished dream of conquering England. The Spanish had several times tried to invade England directly by sea: that had failed. Elizabeth had blocked them in northern Europe. The most promising route – the hop, skip and jump up the coast of Brittany which was so brilliantly road-tested by Juan del Águila in Cornwall – had been taken away from them. All that remained was the back-door route through Ireland. But that had made huge demands of their Irish hosts, the insurgents, and the debacle of the battle made it crystal clear that O'Neill had neither the unity nor the resources to facilitate an invasion. At Kinsale, the 'King of Spain's bridge into England' collapsed forever.

Spain had no option but to suspend its religious wars and accept peace with England – a process made easier by the amicable contacts developed in post-siege Kinsale and accelerated by the death of Elizabeth, for whom the war was a fiercely personal matter. The resultant treaty altered not only the map of Europe, but of the globe – for instance, peace in the Atlantic enabled the English to move into a whole new world in North America and to build up their naval power.

However, the financial strain of fighting the Irish and Spanish had pushed England almost into bankruptcy. The Crown became increasingly dependent upon Parliament, creating the great power clashes that resulted in the English Civil War and, ultimately, the drift towards democracy.

Within Ireland, the effect of Kinsale was cataclysmic for the Gaels. For centuries England had been trying unsuccessfully to assert control over its first colony. The O'Neill rebellion presented Ireland's greatest opportunity to defeat the intruders. But since the country was deeply divided – and since O'Neill failed to achieve unity through persuasion, force or religious edict – he depended upon outside help. He got it in 1601, but the defeat at Kinsale, and the departure of O'Donnell immediately afterwards, tore the heart out of the chieftains' alliance and effectively ended the insurgency as a nationwide movement. The peace deal between Spain and England meant O'Neill would never have another chance.

His departure in the Flight of the Earls left Gaelic Ireland bereft, although the decline would resemble a long and slow twilight rather than an instant plunge into darkness. Eventually even the pro-English Gaelic lords were left powerless. The old political structure was steadily dismantled, and a centuries-old culture with a rich legacy of laws, social structure, poetry and literature began to wither and die.

'There was not lost in any defeat ... so much as was lost [at Kinsale],' lamented Ludhaigh O'Cleary. He said the Gaelic nobles had been 'robbed of their patrimony and their noble land which they left to their enemies in defeat. There was lost besides nobility and honour, generosity and great deeds, hospitality and kindliness, courtesy and noble birth ... [and] the authority and sovereignty of the Gaels of Ireland to the end of time.'

The plantation that followed the English conquest was shamelessly politically and religiously motivated. Almost 1.5 million hectares of land was confiscated and only a fifth of it went back to the Irish. Yet this process was far from clear-cut. There were several attempts at plantations: the most radical followed a regional, post-O'Neill, rebellion in 1608 which hardened attitudes on all sides. The six counties that were planted were not the ones you might expect – for instance, Donegal and Cavan were included, but Down and Antrim were not part of the official plantation.

The idea that the 'Gaels' of the north were ousted by 'Sasanachs' or Saxons does not stand up to scrutiny. More than 80 percent of the settlers were Scots, and many of them were fellow Gaels – in fact, quite a few spoke the Gaelic language. To complicate things further, Ireland is so close to Scotland that the two populations have always intermingled and interbred. Large numbers of Scots families fled to Ireland in the 1630s and late 1600s to escape farming famines (in the same way as Irish people fled west to America in the 1800s). Today, in most cases, it's pretty much impossible to distinguish between those people of Scots descent whose forebears were planters, and those whose ancestors were 'natural' migrants – or even starving refugees seeking nothing more than basic survival.

The greater truth is that the small island of Ireland has always been a mishmash of bloodlines – Celt, Viking, Norman, Spanish, and so on to infinity. Our diversity is worth celebrating. It is more fascinating, by far, than the discredited old notion of a land neatly divided between pure-bred Gaels and foreign usurpers.

Before we leave this saga, let's indulge in a bit of 'what-if' speculation.

What if the Gaelic Order had been left intact and even allowed to thrive? This is a fascinating question. Over the ensuing centuries, the Gaelic culture would have had to change and evolve anyway. In its original form, it could not have survived the great social pressures that followed – large-scale international trade, the rise of the middle classes, the great agricultural and industrial revolutions, the worldwide hunger for democracy.

We can imagine a twenty-first-century Gaelic culture that would enrich the world with its music, poetry and literature, while offering some imaginative alternatives to traditional western ideas on family life and childrearing. Politically it might have turned its patchwork of fiefdoms into a Swiss-style canton democracy. Who knows?

Second 'what-if': What might have happened if the Spanish invasion had succeeded? It is commonly, and counter-intuitively, assumed that being conquered by Spain would have advanced the cause of Irish freedom. Yet the Last Armada was a mission to colonise, with the Irish chieftains clearly declared as vassals. The idea that the new Spanish overlords would have sympathetically nurtured the Gaelic Order and cherished the Irish language is a rather large assumption. The slightest glance at Spain's treatment of its conquered peoples – whether in northern Europe, Peru or the hellish silver mines of Bolivia – shows a far from rosy picture.

Anyway, as we know from Venetian intelligence, a Spanish victory would have brought rival French troops into Ireland. Rather than becoming a haven of peace, Ireland might have become one more bloodstained theatre of war in a protracted European conflict.

We will never know. The important thing is not to gaze into alternative universes, but to learn lessons from our experience of history in the real world. We cannot change the past, but we can work to alter the future.

In the votes following the Good Friday Agreement, the people of the island voted overwhelmingly to put the past behind them and accept each other's right to co-exist in peace. It has been a long road from Kinsale … but perhaps the worst of that journey is over. From that icebound winter of 1601, Ireland may yet emerge into a brighter, happier and more harmonious springtime.

Acknowledgements

They say a journalist is someone who doesn't know anything about anything, but knows someone who does. During my researches for *The Last Armada* I got to know lots of people who know things – things about history, geography, psychology, artillery, tidal currents and the difference between a galleon and a galleass. They helped me immeasurably with this book and they have my gratitude.

First of all, a heartfelt thank you to a group of people whom, in most cases, I have never met: the many readers who turned my previous true-life history book *The Stolen Village* into a success, mostly through word-of-mouth recommendation. I wrote that saga of pirates, captives and Irish–African culture-clash mainly for my own enjoyment, and because my journalistic instincts told me it was a ripping good yarn – but no-one was more astonished than me when my publishers said it had become a bestseller. Without the steady build-up of support from readers, booksellers, reviewers, and book club members, it would never have made the breakthrough, and *The Last Armada* might never have been written.

Thanks to Michael O'Brien of The O'Brien Press for recognising that book's potential, and for encouraging me to follow it up with *Armada*. It took me a long time but, like King Felipe III, Michael had the attitude that 'all difficulties must be overcome'. To my wise and insightful editor Íde ní Laoghaire for expertly shaping the book into its present form – every time I work with Íde, I emerge as a better writer. To Ivan O'Brien for his enthusiastic backing, to designer Emma Byrne for going the extra sea-mile with her inspired artwork, and to everyone else at O'Brien Press who helped along the way.

My deep appreciation to the ever-helpful staff at the National Library of Ireland. Thanks, too, to the custodians of the Irish Collection at the Dublin City Library and Archive; to the Libraries at Trinity College Dublin; to the British Library; to the UK National Archives at Kew; and to the Archivo General de Simancas. Especially warm thanks to Catherine Giltrap, Curator of Art Collections at Trinity College Dublin, and to Francisca Caracuel García and Jose Luis Herrero at the Diputación de Málaga.

I'd also like to pay tribute to those historians who have tackled this subject before me (see Bibliography for more details). Their writings lit up my way as I stumbled through the labyrinth of original sources, and I cannot praise them enough.

Thanks to Diana Eugenia González Grandett, to Georgina Roche, and to my good friends Peter and Marian Humphries, whose help in separate areas was much appreciated.

During my years at the *Sunday World*, I was fortunate to be surrounded by gifted and positive writers. It was a very special environment that nurtured many successful authors. So, thanks to all my former colleagues for their morale-boosting encouragement.

Without the solid foundation of my family's support, this book would certainly never have been possible. So thanks to Chris, Sarah and Gráinne for their practical help, their can-do attitude, and their unflagging encouragement; to my brother and sister; and most of all, to my wife, Sally, who was and remains my rock. Any good bits in this book are as much hers as mine. As a qualified psychologist, she must secretly wince at my attempts to understand the actions of my historical figures through modern psychology, but, then again, it was always useful to have a psychologist handy when I returned to the real world after spending too much time amongst those crazy mixed-up Elizabethans. Which is my way of saying: thanks for being so patient.

As for the helpful people I mentioned in the first paragraph, there are far too many to list individually. But they are People who Know Things, and so, of course, they know who they are. Thank you.

Des Ekin

BIBLIOGRAPHY AND RECOMMENDED READING

Someone asked me why I chose to write a book about Kinsale 1601 when there are already so many books on the subject. My answer was: Because there aren't. The main library catalogues show only three English-language history books whose main subject is the Spanish invasion, the siege and the battle at Kinsale. This seems surprising, given the importance of the event. And of all the English-language books that I have read, none devotes more than a few paragraphs to the background, career and extraordinary personality of Juan del Águila.

John Silke's groundbreaking 1970 book, *Kinsale: The Spanish Intervention...* , is an acknowledged masterwork – the first serious attempt to study the topic from a Spanish viewpoint and in a European context. I found it indispensible. However, with the actual period of the invasion taking up only around 45 pages of a 175-page book, the reader – while highly impressed – is left hungry for more on the core subject of the Spaniards in Ireland.

This is equally true of Nora Hickey's slim 1985 volume, *The Battle of Kinsale* – it contains twenty pages in total and, given her obvious expertise, I would have loved to have read 200 or even more.

The Battle of Kinsale (2004), edited by Hiram Morgan, is a scholarly volume containing 21 wide-ranging academic articles and is the definitive work. I found the sections by Morgan, Morales, O'Scea, O'Connor and Shiels particularly helpful.

A fourth book is mostly in Spanish and came a little too late for me. By the time Enrique García Hernán's *The Battle of Kinsale* was published in 2013, my own book was essentially complete. However, I have referenced it in these notes because his 630 pages of '*Documents from the Spanish Archives*' (transcribed in Spanish) have now made this material readily accessible to future scholars and researchers. His introductory 'Study' (40 pages in English) also contained many perceptive insights and helped to steer me clear of some errors. Enrique García Hernán's book – compiled in collaboration with Ciaran Brady and Declan M Downey – is a momentous contribution to knowledge of the period and will prove an invaluable source.

I am aware of, but have not read, three other books in Spanish: *Irlanda y la Monarquia Hispanica: Kinsale 1601-2001*, edited by Enrique García Hernán et al (Universidad de Alcalá, 2002); *El Socorro de Irlanda en 1601 y la Contribución del Ejército a la Integración Social de Los Irlandeses en Espana*, by Óscar Recio Morales (Defence Ministry, 2002); and *La Batalla de Kinsale: La Expedición de Juan del Águila a Irlanda 1601-1602*, by Alberto Raúl Esteban Ribas and Tomás San Clemente de Mingo (Zarazoga: HRM Ediciones 2013).

Of course, many more works deal with Kinsale 1601 as part of a wider study – usually of the entire O'Neill insurgency (RTÉ's documentary *The Battle of Kinsale* is a good example), or of Kinsale's history, or of Irish history in general.

The academic journals contain many scholarly articles on various aspects of Kinsale 1601. Some are referenced below.

For my own book, *The Last Armada,* I concentrated on primary sources and near-contemporary accounts. However, my advice to any new researcher is to begin with Hiram Morgan's wonderfully comprehensive 45-page article, 'Disaster at Kinsale', in Morgan (ed) *The Battle of Kinsale*. This is a thorough, forensic and yet highly readable study in which Morgan – the leading expert on the subject – expertly slices through all the layers of myth and misinformation to reveal the underlying truth. I do not always agree with his conclusions, but throughout my researches whenever I became lost, 'Disaster' was always my road map.

Next, my imaginary researcher should enjoy Bagwell's chapter 'The Spaniards in Munster' in his history, *Ireland under the Tudors*. It may date from 1890, but Bagwell's fresh and enthusiastic style makes it a cracking good read. Talking of prose stylists, Sean O'Faolain's *The Great O'Neill* is enjoyable enough to qualify as holiday reading, although he dispenses with Kinsale – the climactic episode in O'Neill's life – in just 20 pages.

Fourthly, she should read Gerard Hayes-McCoy's expert military account of the confrontation in the relevant chapter of *Irish Battles*.

After that pleasant introduction, she will need to dig deep into those primary sources. Moryson's *History* and *Itinerary* remain the most objective of the English records. I am aware that *Pacata Hibernia* and the *Calendar of State Papers Ireland* have their limitations – the former is shamelessly self-serving and the *CSPI* has flaws that would ideally require every page to be checked against the originals at Kew – but they remain invaluable sources. O'Grady's version of *Pacata* gives good footnotes. The *Calendar of Carew Manuscripts* and the Cecil–Carew letters are also essential.

On the Irish side, it is vital to read the relevant bits of O'Sullivan Beare's *History*; of O'Cleary's *Life of Red Hugh*; and the *Annals of the Four Masters*.

The documents from the Simancas Archives reproduced in Martin Hume's *CSPS* (now available online) provide the most accessible of the Spanish primary sources. Zubiaur's despatches from the war front have been published in the *Epistolario*. The main Spanish source is the vast Archivo General de Simancas (AGS). Two categories are of particular interest: foreign affairs (Secretarias del Consejo de Estado) and war (Secretarias del Consejo de Guerra). The National Library of Ireland has a large collection of Simancas documents on microfilm, and now García Hernán has helpfully provided key transcripts in Spanish. More are appearing online with each passing year. Valuable letters from Oviedo, Archer and Mansoni have been published by F. M. Jones and by Patrick McBride. Águila's career can be pieced together from references in the AGS, CSPS, CSPI, CSPV, Córdoba,

G. Gonzales Davila, H.C. Davila, Duro, Famien Strada, Lainez, Rayon & Zabalbura, and Silke.

Ciaran O'Scea performed a great service to historians by publishing *A Newly Discovered Account of the Battle of Kinsale* (in Morgan *BoK* p366) which is Bustamante's memoir. For my own book, I worked from a copy of Bustamante's original Spanish document.

In 1950s Ireland, when Águila's name was being vilified, historian Henry Mangan single-handedly worked to rescue his reputation. Mangan's courageous cries in the wilderness are well worth searching out. His intellectual sparring partner F. M. Jones also provided expert analysis, especially with his *Spaniards in Kinsale* and *Destination*.

Other favoured sources will be obvious from my Bibliography and Source Notes.

BIBLIOGRAPHY

The abbreviations used in source notes appear in square brackets.

[a4m] Annals of the Four Masters (1630s) Donegal: Franciscan Friary. English translation by
    Owen Connellan (1846)

Bagwell, Richard (1890) *Ireland Under the Tudors* Vol 3 London: Longmans, Green

Berleth, Richard (1977) *The Twilight Lords* London: Allen Lane

Brady, Ciaran and Gillespie, Raymond (1975) (eds) *Natives and Newcomers*... Dublin: Irish
    Academic Press

Bruce, John (ed) (1861) *Correspondence of King James VI of Scotland with Sir Robert Cecil*...
    Westminster: Camden Society

[*Bust.*] Bustamante, Alférez [first name unknown] (c1602) *A True Account of Events in the
    Town of Kinsale* Paris: Archive of Ministry of Foreign Affairs. Copy in National Library
    of Ireland, Dublin. First discovered by Ciaran O'Scea, whose translation appears in
    Morgan, *BoK*. (I worked directly from the original ms.)

Byrchensha, Ralph (1602) *A Discourse Occasioned upon the Late Defeat [at Kinsale]*...London:
    "M.L."

+*CalCarew*] Calendar of Carew Manuscripts. Full ref: Brewer, J. S. and Bullen W. (eds)
    (1870) *Calendar of the Carew Manuscripts* London: Longman

Camden, William (1688) *The History of...Princess Elizabeth* London: Bentley

Camden, William (1625) *Annales* Leiden

Carleton, George (1630) *A Thankful Remembrance of God's Mercy* London: Mylbourne & Robinson

Colles, Ramsay (1919) *The History of Ulster* Vol 1 London: Gresham

Connolly, SJ (2007) *Contested Island* Oxford: OUP

Coombes, J and Ware, Niall (eds) (1978) *The Letter Book of General de Zubiaur: A Calendar of the 'Irish' Letters* Journal of the Cork Historical and Archaelogical Society 83 (1978) pp 50-58

Córdoba, Luis Cabrera de (1857) *Relaciones de la Cosas Sucedidas en la Corte de Espana 1599-1614* Madrid: Alegria

Corporation of Kinsale (1652-1800) and Caulfield, Richard (1879) (ed) *Annals of Kinsale* from *The Council Book... of Kinsale* Guildford: Surrey

Cox, Richard (1689) *Hibernia Anglicana*

Craik, George Lillie (1849) *The Romance of the Peerage Vol 1* London: Chapman & Hall

[*CSP Dom.*] *Calendar of State Papers, Domestic, 1601-1603.* Full ref: Green, Mary A. E. (ed) (1870) Calendar of State Papers, Domestic Series, 1601-1603 London: Longman

[*CSPI*] *Calendar of the State Papers Ireland 1601-1603.* Full ref: Mahaffy, Robert P (1912) (ed) *Calendar of the State Papers Relating to Ireland 1601-1603* London: HMSO

[*CSPS*] *Calendar of State Papers (Simancas) 1587-1603.* Full ref: Hume, Martin (1899) (ed) *Calendar of Letters and State Papers... [in the] ...Archives of Simancas Vol IV 1587-1603* London: HMSO

[*CSPV*] *Calendar of State Papers, Venice, 1592-1603.* Full ref: Brown, Horatio (ed) (1897) Calendar of State Papers...Venice, Vol IX, 1592-1603 London: HMSO

Curry, John (1775) *Review of the Civil Wars in Ireland* Dublin: Burnet & Morris

Cusack, Mary Francis (1868) *An Illustrated History of Ireland* Kerry: Kenmare Convent

D'Alton, Edward (1906) *History of Ireland... Vol 2* London: Kegan Paul

Davila, Gil Gonzales (1771) *Monarquia de Espana... Felipe III* Volume 3 Madrid: Ibarra

Davila, Henrico Caterino (1678) *The History of the Civil Wars in France Vol 1* London: Herringman

Desiderata Curiosa Hibernica Vol 1 (1772) Dublin: Hay

Dictionary of National Biography (1885 onwards) London: Smith, Elder

Dictionary of Irish Biography (2009 and online) Dublin, UCD and RIA, Cambridge University Press

Duro, Cesáreo Fernandez (1830-1908) (1972 edition) *Armada Espanola Vol 3* Madrid: Instituto de Historia y Cultura

[*Epistolario*] Epistolario del General Zubiaur. Full ref: Polentinos, Conde de (ed) (1946) *Epistolario del General Zubiaur (1568-1605)* Madrid: Instituto Histórico de Marina

Falls, Cyril (1950) *Elizabeth's Irish Wars* Syracuse: Syracuse University Press

Falls, Cyril (1955) *Mountjoy: Elizabethan General* London: Odhams Press

Famien Strada, R. P., (1739) *Histoire de la Guerre des Pays-Bas Vol 4*, Brussels: Fricx

Farmer, William (c1615) *Chronicles of Ireland 1594-1613*

Gainsford, Thomas (1619) *History of the Earl of Tyrone* London: Rownthwaite

García González, Francisco and Oviedo, E. O. I. (1992) *Mateo de Oviedo, Perhaps Ireland's Greatest Spanish Friend of All Time* in Fernández-Corugedo, S. G. (ed) (1992) *Proceedings of SEDERI II*, University of Oviedo.

García Hernán, Enrique (2013) *The Battle of Kinsale: Study and Documents from the Spanish Archives* Valencia: Albatros Ediciones and Ministerio de Defensa

Gibson, Charles (1861) *History of Cork* London: Newby

González de León, Fernando (2009) *The Road to Rocroi* Leiden: Brill

Grose, Francis (1801) *Military Antiquities* London: Egerton

Hamilton, Ernest (1919) *Elizabethan Ulster* London: Hurst & Blackett

Hayes-McCoy, Gerard (1980) *Irish Battles* Dublin: Gill & MacMillan

Hickey, Nora M. (1987) *The Battle of Kinsale* Kinsale: Heritage Society

Hogan, Rev Edmund (1894) *Distinguished Irishmen of the Sixteenth Century* London: Burns & Oates

Hull, Eleanor (1926) *A History of Ireland and Her People* London: Harrap

Hume, Martin (1899) *Spain, its Greatness and Decay* Cambridge: University Press

Hume, Martin (1906) *Philip II of Spain* London: MacMillan

Hume, Martin (1907) *Spain under Philip III* in *Cambridge Modern History*

Hume, Martin (1908) *Treason and Plot* London: Eveleigh Nash

'I.E.' (full name unknown) (1602) *A Letter From A Soldier... [at The Battle of Kinsale]* London: Waterson

Jones, Archer (2001) *The Art of War in the Western World* Illinois: University of Illinois

Jones, Frederick M (1944-45) *The Spaniards and Kinsale 1601* in *Journal of the Galway Archaeological and Historical Society vol XXI*, pp 1-43

Jones, Frederick M (1954), *The Destination of Don Juan del Aguila in 1601* in *The Irish Sword v2 no 5* pp 29-32

Jones, Frederick M (1955) *An Indictment of Don Juan del Aguila* in *The Irish Sword v2 no 7* pp 217-223, with comments by Mangan

Lainez, Fernando Martinez and Toca, José Maria Sánchez (2006) *Tercios de Espana* Madrid: EDAF

Lawless, Emily (1896) *The Story of Ireland* London: Fisher Unwin

Leland, Thomas (1773) *The History of Ireland from the Invasion of Henry II* London: Nourse **etc**

Leland, Thomas (1784) *The History of Ireland from the Earliest Authentic Accounts* Dublin: Luke White

Lennon, Colm (1995) *Sixteenth Century Ireland, the Incomplete Conquest* Dublin: St Martin's

McBride, Patrick P (ed) (1955-1956) *Some Unpublished Letters of Mateo de Oviedo, Archbishop of Dublin* in *Reportorium Novum* Vol 1 No 1

McCavitt, John (2005) *The Flight of the Earls* Dublin: Gill & MacMillan

McGurk, John (1997) *The Elizabethan Conquest of Ireland* Manchester: University Press

Maclean, John (ed) (1864) *Letters from Sir Robert Cecil to Sir George Carew* London: Camden Soc

Mangan, Henry (1951-52) *Del Aguila's Defence of Kinsale* in *The Irish Sword* Vol 1 no 3 pp 218-224

Mangan, Henry (1953) *The 'Trial' of Don Juan del Águila* in *The Irish Independent*, Feb 13 and 14, 1953 [note: this is JdA's 'trial' by modern historians, not the inquiry in Spain]

Mangan, Henry (1956) *A Vindication of Don Juan del Águila* in *The Irish Sword, v2 no 9* pp343-351

Mitchel, John (1845) *The Life and Times of Aodh O'Neill* Dublin: Duffy.

[*Monson*] Sir William Monson's Naval Tracts. Full ref: Oppenheim, M (1902) *The Naval Tracts of Sir William Monson Vols 1 and 2* London: Navy Records Society

Morales, Óscar Recio (2004) *Spanish Army Attitudes to the Irish at Kinsale* in Morgan, Hiram (ed) *The Battle of Kinsale* Bray: Wordwell

Moran, Rev Dr (1864) *History of the Catholic Archbishops of Dublin Vol 1* Dublin: James Duffy

Moreau, Jean (1836) *Histoire des Guerres de la Ligue en Bretagne* Brest: Come et Bonetbeau

Morgan, Hiram (1994) *Faith and Fatherland or Queen and Country? Dúiche Néill* journal

Morgan, Hiram (1999) *Tyrone's Rebellion* London: Boydell Press

Morgan, Hiram (2001) *Spanish Armadas and Ireland* in Francois, L. and Isaacs, A.K. (eds) *The Sea in European History* Pisa: University of Pisa

Morgan, Hiram (2004) (ed) *The Battle of Kinsale* [my abbreviation in notes: *BoK*] Bray: Wordwell

[*Mor. Hist.*] Moryson, Fynes (1735) *An History of Ireland Vol 1* Dublin: Ewing.

[*Mor. Itin.*] Moryson, Fynes (1908) *An Itinerary Vol 3* Glasgow: MacLehose

Morrissey, Thomas J (1979) *James Archer of Kilkenny* Dublin: Studies Special Publications

Moryson, Fynes (c1602) *The Commonwealth of Ireland*

Muller, John (1757) *The Attac and Defence of Fortified Places* London: Millan

Ó Cianáin, Tadgh (1607-1608) *The Flight of the Earls* translated by Walsh, Paul (1916) Maynooth: Gill

O'Cleary, Lughaidh (1620s) *Beatha Aodha Ruaidh Uí Dhomhnaill* (Life of Red Hugh O'Donnell) translated by Murphy, Denis (1895). Alternative translation by Paul Walsh, *Archivium Hibernicum* vol 7

O'Conor, Matthew (1845) *Military History of the Irish Nation* Dublin: Hodges & Smith

O'Faolain, Sean (1970) *The Great O'Neill* Cork: Mercier

O'Mahony, Edward (2001) *The Battle of Castlehaven* (transcript of lecture at Castlehaven Commemoration Committee)

[*OSB*] O'Sullivan Beare, Philip (1621) *Historiae Catholicae Iberniae Compendium [A Catholic History of Ireland]* Lisbon

O'Scea, Ciaran (2003) *The Significance and Legacy of Spanish Intervention in West Munster...* in O'Connor, T and Lyons, M A (eds) *Irish Migrants in Europe after Kinsale*. Dublin

O'Scea, Ciaran (2004) *A Newly Discovered Account of the Battle of Kinsale* in Morgan, Hiram (ed) *The Battle of Kinsale* Bray: Wordwell

O'Sullivan, Florence (1905) *Kinsale* in *Cork Historical and Archaelogical Society Journal* Vol XI No 65, Jan-Mar 1905

O'Sullivan, Florence (1916) *History of Kinsale* Dublin: Duffy

Oxford Dictionary of National Biography (2004) Oxford: Oxford University Press.

[*Pac 1810 ed*] *Pacata Hibernia* 1810 edition (orig. London 1633). Full ref: Stafford, Thomas (ed) (1810) *Pacata Hibernia Vols 1 and 2* Dublin: Hibernia Press

[*Pac O'G v2*] *Pacata Hibernia*, O'Grady edition, Vol 2. Full ref: O'Grady, Standish (1896) (ed) *Pacata Hibernia... Vol 2* London: Downey

Parker, Geoffrey (2004) *The Army of Flanders and the Spanish Road* 1567-1659 Cambridge: University Press

Philalethes, Andreas (1602) *An Answer Made by One of Our Brethren*

Prynne, William (1641) *The Antipathy of the English Lordly Prelacy*

Ranke, Leopold von (1843) *The Ottoman and Spanish Empires in the 16th and 17th Centuries* (translated by Walter Kelly) London: Whittaker

Rawson, Maud Stepney (1911) *Penelope Rich and her Circle* London: Hutchinson

Rayon, José Sancho and Zabalbura, Francisco de (1879) *Los Sucesos de Flandes y Francia* vols 72-74 Madrid: Miguel Ginesta

Rickman, Johanna (2008) *Love, Lust and Licence in Early Modern England* Aldershot: Ashgate Publishing

Ross, Alexander (1652) *The History of the World*

Sánchez, Magdalena S. (1996) *Melancholy and Female Illness: Habsburg Women and Politics at the Court of Philip III* in *Journal of Women's History* Vol 8 No 2 Baltimore: Johns Hopkins

Sánchez, Magdalena S and Saint-Saens, Alain (eds) (1996) *Spanish Women in the Golden Age: Images and Realities* Westport: Greenwood

Silke, John J (2000) *Kinsale, the Spanish Intervention in Ireland...* Dublin: Four Courts

Spedding, James (1862) *The Letters and The Life of Francis Bacon Vol II* London: Longmans

Speed, John (1612) *The Theatre of the Empire of Great Britain*

Stow, John (1605) *Annals of England*

Strachey, Lytton (1928) *Elizabeth and Essex* York: Harcourt Brace

Taaffe, Denis (1911) *Impartial History of Ireland Vol 2* Dublin: Christie

Thuillier, John (1987) *History of Kinsale, a Field Study Approach* Kinsale: Frank Hurley

Verstraete, Emile (1866) *Histoire Militaire du Territoire Actuel de la Belgique, Vol 4*, Brussels: Muquardt

Walsh, Micheline Kerney (1986) *Destruction by Peace* Monaghan: Cumann Seanchais Ard Mhacha

Ward, Robert (1639) *Animadversions of War* London: Dawson

Wills, J (1840) *Lives of Illustrious and Distinguished Irishmen, Vol 2*. Dublin: Macgregor Polson.

Wilson, Violet A. (1924) *Society Women of Shakespeare's Time* London: John Lane

Wraxall, Nathaniel (1796) *The History of France Vol 3* Dublin: Wogan

TELEVISION

RTÉ 1: *The Battle of Kinsale 1601* (Sept 22 2001)

BBC1: *Flight of the Earls* (Sept 16 2007)

BBC and RTÉ: *The Story of Ireland* (Feb 20 2011)

SOURCE NOTES

The main sources for this book are the original 17th Century documents, ranging from primary eyewitness accounts and contemporary despatches to histories written within a couple of decades of the event. However, in these notes I also use the abbreviation *'rec'* which usually refers to more modern works and means 'recommended reading' on a particular topic. It does not necessarily mean that the writer agrees with my interpretation.

To save space, regularly cited sources such as a4m, CSPI, CSPS, Pac., etc are abbreviated. These are listed alphabetically in the Bibliography with full references. The main characters are referred to by their initials: JdA, CB, Ho'N and so on. For brevity, many of the Spanish documents are referenced simply by writer, recipient and date rather than the formal AGS *Legajo* citations, although I have all of those. Spanish documents are dated in New Style.

Quotes in the text that are clearly attributed to Bustamante, Farmer, Gainsford, Philip O'Sullivan **Beare**, and 'the Irish annalist' [Annals of the Four Masters] are all taken from their respective works listed in the Bibliography and will not be further referenced below.

TITLE 'The Last Armada'

I am using the word Armada (literally, any 'navy' or 'fleet') in the popular English-language sense of the great Spanish war flotillas that set out to invade England during the Elizabethan era. I am aware of later naval expeditions. (Years after I had chosen this title for my upcoming book, I discovered that the same title had coincidentally been used by historian John Thuillier in an article for *World of Hibernia* magazine (Sept 22, 2001). I am happy to acknowledge this.)

Subtitle '100 days': JdA defended Kinsale in hostile territory from Sep 22 until hostilities ceased on Dec 31. You could argue that the full-scale military investment began a bit later and ended a bit later.

JdA's 'devil' quote: CSPI p292; another version appears in Bacon, Francis (1629) *Miscellancy*

Preface

All these topics are thoroughly described and referenced in later chapters. 'Brilliant example of combined pluck' is from Standish O'Grady (1893) *The Bog of Stars* London: Fisher Unwin p107

Chapter 1: Tinker, Tailor ... Soldier

Richard Boyle's account of his epic trip appears in *The Earl of Cork's True Remembrances* (1632, Ms) and is quoted in Bagwell pp 414-415

His route, timings, and credibility: Townshend, Dorothea (1904) *The Life and Letters of the Great Earl of Cork* London: Duckworth, p27; Lee, Sidney and Onions, C.T. (eds) (1916) *Shakespeare's England vol 1* Oxford: Clarendon p202; Bagwell pp 414-415; Jones, Frederick (1958) *Mountjoy 1563-1606* Dublin: Clonmore & Reynolds p218

Posting, speeds, used by Shakespeare: Mor Itin v3 p479 (10 mph); St Clare Byrne, M (1925) *Elizabethan Life* London: Methuen p111 (70 miles a day); Lee & Onions, *op. cit.,* p202

Carew, Cecil clique and rivals: Bruce pp xv-xvii; Maclean p85 and footnote; rec, Bucholz, Robert and Newton, Key (2009) *Early Modern England 1485-1714* Chichester: Wiley pp 154-156

Important who brought news first: My analysis; Townshend, *op. cit.* pp 27-28; rec, Jones *Mountjoy, op. cit.* p218; rec, Morgan, *BoK*, pp 379-381; see Mor Itin v3 p108

Stench, 3rd largest, population, 450 acres: rec, Bryson, Bill (2007) *Shakespeare* London: Harper Press pp 44-50

Boyle's intrigues: Townshend, *op. cit.* pp15-16

Globe, Hamlet: *The Register of the Stationers' Company* said in 1602 that Hamlet was 'lately acted' by the LC Men. A 1601 date is most likely.

Mansion on Strand: Boyle, *Remembrances*; Ravenscroft, Dennis (1914) *The House of Cecil* London: Constable p40

Cecil stature, appearance, 'pigmy', 'Toad', lampoons: Ravenscroft, Dennis (1914) *The Cecil Family* Harvard: Houghton Mifflin Chapter 8; Bruce, page xiii; rec, Brimacombe, Peter (2000) *All the Queen's Men* Stroud: Sutton pp 67-69

Cecil's Machiavellian control: rec, Brimacombe, op. cit., pp 67-68; 'not even the Queen', see Chapter 37

Over supper... defeat: Summary of story told in greater depth later.

Cecil worried: As evidenced by his letters to Carew. See Chapter 34

2 am: Boyle, *Remembrances*.

Essex plot: *A Declaration Touching the Treasons* [etc] in Camden *Annales*; Camden, *History...* v4 pp604-612; Spedding v4 pp244+

Hundreds of nobles, moles: In Camden, *History* p606, Essex estimates 'about 120 earls, barons, knights and gentlemen' secretly supported him. Spedding, p209 says '300 gentlemen' were involved; also see letter CB-James VI 1599 in Spedding pp 168-170; CB entry in *Ox. Dict. Nat. Biog*; Strachey pp 228-230

'A leprosy…', 'The dregs…': *A Declaration, op. cit.*; Spedding p247

Suppressed: Bruce page xviii; Maclean pp 90-91 footnote

Danvers declaration: Hatfield Mss vol lxxxiii no 108, reproduced in Birch p100+; also in Spedding p333+. Extracts and analysis, Spedding pp 168-171; Strachey pp167-171.

This military figure… the plot: Explained in depth later.

Could cut deal with Ho'N: Mooted in Confession of Thomas Lee, Feb 14, see Spedding p214

Deal with Spanish: See chapter 32. English fears over Sp. deal, see CalCarew p216

Cecil's worries about CB: See his letter in Maclean pp 90-91 and footnote

Cecil-Carew codes; CalCarew pp124-125; decoded in Maclean pp 90-91

'How far…' and 'domestic fortune': CalCarew pp 124-125

'He is either…': CSPI p85

'Domestic fortune' is Penelope: Maclean p91 footnote

At 38 years… under interrogation: All explained in depth with sources in Chapter 19 and Chapter 34. Sidney quotes, *Astrophil and Stella*. Essex quotes from Letter to CB from Nottingham 31/5/1601 cited in Spedding pp 236-237

Macbeth: Written around 1603-1606, just after PR's fall from grace

PR as dark lady: See footnote 193.21 to Oxford University Press 1998 edition of Joyce's *Ulysses*. Dedalus quote, p142 and p193 (comparison with Hathaway)

Now it was… for Blount's sake: All explained in depth with sources in Chapter 19 and Chapter 34

Campion quote from *Umbra* (1619), line 316

'I made a speedy…' and 'By seven…': Boyle, *op.cit.*

Similar journeys: Townshend, *op. cit.* p27 and Lee, Sidney *op. cit.* pp 201-202

Description palace: Hurault, André, Sieur de Maisse (c1599), *A Journal…*; rec, Hibbert, Christopher (2010) *The Virgin Queen* London: Tauris Parke pp 249-251

Bedchamber, Essex: Boyle, *op. cit.*; Camden, *History…* p574

The reality… tiny black eyes: Hurault, *op. cit.* p55; and Hentzner, Paul (1598) cited in Rye, William B. (1865) *England as Seen by Foreigners…* London: Smith, p 103+

Hand kiss, Queen's quote, request for details: Boyle, *op. cit.*

BIBLIOGRAPHY AND RECOMMENDED READING

Chapter 2: 'Haste, Haste for Your Life'

Saxey's role, 100 men, 60 volunteers: CSPI p91. The overall commander at Kinsale was Sir Richard Percy (Camden, *Annales*, 71)

Reports of 55 ships: Meade to Blount, CSPI p81

Early guesses of troop numbers: CSPI p83, p89, p90

Kinsale vulnerable to attack, size of walls, two mills, ovens: JdA *Discourse* quoted in pac (1810 ed) p341; O'Sullivan, Florence (1905) *Kinsale* in Cork Historical & Archaelogical Society Journal Vol XI No 65; *Information from Jordan Roche* (Nov 7 1601) in AGS GA 3143, reproduced in Morgan BoK pp 356-357 and in García Hernán pp 170-171

'The town is…:' Visitor, 1790, cited in (rec) Hickey, Nora (1985) *Kinsale, Glimpses of a Town* Kinsale: Hickey p17

Standard arrangement: As explained by Antonia Fraser (2011) in her *Cromwell* (Hachette e-book)

Smerwick: More details in chapter 12

Arrived Matthew's Day: CSPI p83

Mnemonic: cited in Spicer, Dorothy Gladys (1954) *Yearbook of English Festivals* New York: H. W. Wilson.

'The air is laden…': Cited in (rec) O'Sullivan, Florence (1916) *The History of Kinsale* Dublin: Duffy p3

'There are perpetual…' and 'One of the finest…': cited in Hickey, *Kinsale…*

Famousest: Boate, Gerard (1657) *Ireland's Natural History*, ch 2

'Headland of the sea' or 'smooth basin': both *Lewis's Topographical Dictionary* (1837)

Tidal flow: To author by local mariner

'Picturesquely nestled…': A Mrs Woods (1863) cited in Hickey, *Kinsale*

Links with Spain, exports, imports: rec, O'Sullivan, F., *op. cit.* p12; Falls, *Eliz…* p20; for more on Irish trade, rec, 'Imports and Exports' in Keenan, Desmond (2010) *Ireland 1170-1509* USA: Xlibris

Such connections… olive groves: My observations

'With black hair… swollen': Cited in Hickey, *Kinsale* p22. The SW Irish professed kinship with Spanish: see *The Book of Invasions* and pac O'G v2 p48. DNA research has supported this: see RTE 2009 documentary *Blood of the Irish*

200 houses, population: O'Sullivan, F, *op. cit.* p40; rec, Morgan, *BoK* p355

'Fairly good fish': Cited in Hickey *Kinsale*, p17

'All our men…': O'Sullivan, F, *op. cit.* p20

1594 blaze: *Lewis's Topographical Dictionary* (1837)

In imagining… 400 years old: I compared modern maps with the pac map, TCD picture map and others, and checked dates of buildings.

Friary: rec, S. M. Hession (2010) *A Short History of the Carmelite Friary, Kinsale* p2-3

Preparing to flee, mayor welcome: See notes to Chapter 6

Meade letter: CSPI p81

Steene testimony and 'old man': CSPI p89

Chapter 3: The Man Born without Fear

JdA in prison cell and reasons: CSPI p238, confirmed by diary of Córdoba p70. Also see Duro p218. Many reasons have been advanced, some highly imaginative, as critically demonstrated by Mangan in *'Trial'*

Offered command of expedition: Davila GG p246

Invasion plan as outlined to JdA: This is a fair paraphrase of the Spanish authorities' complacent and insanely optimistic attitude to the invasion, as outlined in the Simancas letters and reports. They really did regard Ireland as a pushover. The expedition would be 'easy and safe' (CSPS 840 f687); it had 'ease and cheapness' (*ibid*, f703); and once in Ireland, the King could 'do as you liked in England' (*ibid*, f686)

6,000 fighters: CSPS 840 f699, f675 and f685

Irish 'welcome': CSPS 840 f675 April 24, 1601; and 840 f685 July 1, 1601; and 840 f703, undated 1601. Also see CSPS 839 f634, May 1596: Spanish will have 'the whole country in their power'

1600 horses, needed saddles: CSPI p105; pac (1810 ed) p352; Mor Hist v2 p316, who says this figure is more accurate than other estimates of 400. It's open to debate, but there were certainly hundreds.

No destination yet: CSPS 840 f699. More in Chapter 5

Oviedo and Smerwick: Explained in depth in Chapter 12

Ho'N and Ho'D control of Ireland, up to 20,000 force: CSPS 839 f641 May 1596, claiming total unity; CSPS 839 f634, May 1596, claiming 28,000 insurgents; CSPS 840 f685, July 1, 1600, claiming 16,000

Replaced by Catholic monarch: See notes on 'Isabella' below

Prelude to invading England: CSPS 840 f686; Mor Hist v2 p316, citing Spanish sources; CSPI p277, Carew quoting JdA; CSPI p438; *Pac O'G v2* p95; rec Silke p94; for a general overview of Sp plans to invade England via Ireland, rec, Morgan, *Spanish armadas...*

Irish approaches to JdA in Brittany, letters: rec, Lyons, Mary Ann (2004) *French Reaction...* in Morgan, *BoK*, pp 241-245; rec, Mangan, Henry *Vindication...* p349; rec, García Hernán, p17; rec, Silke p27

JdA scepticism about mission: Based on his letters to King, see refs at end of this chapter's notes; and his stated views about Ireland post-siege, eg CSPI p642; also rec, García Hernán p29

Irish 'kinship': *Book of Invasions;* eg Donal Cam O'Sullivan Beare letter, *pac O'G v2* p48; rec, Morgan, *Spanish armadas, op. cit.*

Attacked Armada survivors: eg, *Captain Cuellar's Adventures* in www.ucc.ie/celt and, rec, O'Faolain p104, Morales pp 93-95

No unity, warring clans: According to an official survey (in Wills p308) there were traditionally 90 statelets, some very small, ruled by 'kings' or chieftains, each 'making war and peace for himself'. Also see Cuellar, *op. cit.*; Hull, Battle of Kinsale chapter; CSPI Preface page lxxviii; rec O'Faolain pp 172-173; rec, Lennon p58 and pp 51-55

Pledges before Smerwick: See Chapter 12

Ho'N, Ho'D did not control towns, large areas: CSPS 839 f634, May 1596; also rec, Lennon p325

Most Catholic clergy against Ho'N: Thomas Leland (1773), *History of Ireland vol 2*, p306, footnote; OSB, p117; Hull, in 'Battle of Kinsale' chapter; rec, Connolly p246-9; rec Lennon p325; rec, Silke, pp118-9: rec, par 4 in O'Connor, Thomas, *Diplomatic Preparations for Kinsale.* Madrid: Universidad de Alcalá; also rec O'Faolain p176

Zuniga rejection: CSPI p238

Held out at Lorient: See Chapter 22

Should have attacked more cities: eg, Davila, A. C.; Monson v1 pp 306-307; Moreau pp197-198; Mitchel pp 201-202

Near suicide-mission to hold fort until Queen's death, similar role to Blavet: Venetian analysis by Cavalli, CSPV f1025, Nov 12 1601 and Soranzo, CSPV f1009, Aug 22; Preface to CSPV Jan 1592-1603; CSPS 840, f686, July 11 1600; CSPS 840 f697, f698; rec, Silke p97, who says mission needed a 'miracle' to succeed

Isabella candidate: CSPS 840, f686, f684, f697 and f698; also see f733

James mistrusted, 'shifty': CSPS 840 f733; but also see f696 and CSPV f1001 July 28 1601

'Those who say...": Córdoba p108

Long, venerable career: Davila, GG, pp 246-247; Duro ch 5 and 6, note p69; Rayon & Zabalbura pp 46-133; pp139-307, multiple references; Corbett, Julian (1916) *The Successors of Drake* London: Longmans p323

Brittany campaign, motive, true motive, Lorient, Brest: See Ch 22

Cornwall: See Ch 32

Born El Barraco: Duro pp 69-70; Davila GG p75 and p246

Bequest: He put this in his will — see Ch 35

Landscape, area: Avila tourism, www.turismoavila.com

Early portrait: See JdA portrait and picture credits in this book

Men went to war, women convents: Davila, GG, p247; Carramolino, Juan (1872) *Historia de Avila* v1, Madrid: Libreria Espanola

Nuno, Dona Elvira, and St Teresa: rec, Bilinkoff, Jodi (1989) *The Avila of Saint Teresa* Ithaca: Cornell University pp41-42; rec, Alvarez, Tomas and Kavanaugh, Kieran (2011) *St Teresa of Avila* Washington: ICS pp 97-98; Gilí, Gustavo (ed) (1908) *Vida de Santa Teresa* Barcelona; *Historia de Avila* v1, *op. cit.* pp540-541

JdA early career: Duro pp 69-76 and Davila GG ch 6; Famien Strada, R. P., (1739) *Histoire de la Guerre des Pays-Bas Vol 4*, Brussels: Fricx, pp 84, 90, 139, 158, 159, 162, 181, 182, 276, 280, 295, 338, 333; Rayon & Zabalbura vol 73 pp 46-133; pp139-307, multiple references rec, Silke pp 96-97

Guarding galleons: *Cecil Papers* v4 April 10-20 1591

'Signalise themselves': Bentivoglio, Guido (1654) *Complete History of the Wars in Flanders* Antwerp: rec, González de Leon p57 footnote

Mutinies: See Ch 22

Spanish Fury: *Hume, Spain, Its...* p164

One story... while fighting: CSPI p164

'Without fear' quote: Fernando de Toledo, cited in Davila, GG, p246

Lined up for 1588 Armada: Lainez p217

Role in 1597 Armada: rec, Silke p32

Ibarra quote: CSPI p294

'High opinion': CSPS 840 f714, King to JdA, Jan 30 1602

Luminary: Dávila, GG, p246

Venetian references to JdA: CSPV f999 July 15 1601; f1025, Nov 12 1601

'Wise man...': ie, Florence MacCarthy, letter to Cecil, August 1602

Blount, Carew tributes: Mor Hist v2 p320; CSPI p139

'To answer some...': CSPI p238

Unjust advantage: Córdoba p70

Yet the arrests... reputation: My analysis. Also rec Mangan, *The 'Trial'...*

Wife, 'house of sheriff': Córdoba p70

Eminent historian: rec, Corbett, Julian *op. cit.* p323

'Conceived great hopes': Carleton, George (1624) *A Thankful Remembrance*

Lisbon famine, plague, 'wilderness': Hume, *Spain Under...* chapter XVI

Archer personal priest, 'very fervent...': Hogan p339

He was actually high... fighters: See Ch 12

'Of the priests…:' CSPI p160

When Águila… expedition: Letter JdA to King, Aug 1601; summarised in (rec) Morales (2004) p93; also rec, García Hernán pp 128-130; also JdA letter Sep 1601, summarised in (rec) Silke p106; rec, García Hernán pp 137-139. Also see CSPI p467, '12,000' men needed. For JdA general unease, rec Silke p106, Morales p93, García Hernán p24 and p29.

King's motives: See Ch 4

Chapter 4: 'For God, All Difficulties Must Be Overcome'

Queen's drinking ritual: Ranke p53

King's and Queen's ages: Felipe born 14/4/78, Margaret 25/12/84

Scale of empire: rec, BBC *A History of the World*, episode 80

Inca was largest, swallowed: rec, BBC *A History of the World*, episode 73

Economic disaster, farming, corruption: Hume, *Spain Under…*; Watson, Robert and Thomson, William (1742) *The History of the Reign of Philip III Vol 1* Basel: Tourneisen pp 6-10; Beaumont, A (1809) *The History of Spain* London: Oddy p317

10pc 'noble', clerics 20pc of land: *Philip III and Spain's Economy* on www.historyteacher. net

Bankrupt third time, El Escorial: rec, Woodward, Geoffrey (2013) *Philip II* Oxford: Routledge p38 and p32

Bullion fleets, 35m ducats: Hume, *Spain Its…* p200

Ten trillion dollars: Estimate given in BBC (2012) *Andrew Marr's History of the World*

Spent on cathedrals and wars: My interpretation. Rec, Woodward, *op. cit.* p34

Degrade coins, beg door to door: Hume, *Spain Its…* p201; Watson *op. cit.* pp 7-8

Poor because rich: Cited in BBC *A History of the World*, episode 80

Bankers, too big to fail: My interpretation. Rec, Woodward, *op. cit.* p38

King's appearance: My description based on contemporary portraits

Father's dominance, wife choice story: Watson, *op.cit.* Book 1 p3; Beaumont, *op. cit.* p316

'Ah, I fear…': Hume, *Spain Its…* p197; rec, Silke p33

Lerma, passed papers: Hume, *Spain Its…* pp197-198

Real monarch, two decades, 'He has helped' and 'I order…': rec, Watson, *op. cit.* p4; Ranke p55; rec, Feros, Antonio (2003) *Twin Souls* in Kagan, Richard L and Parker, Geoffrey (eds) (2003) *Spain, Europe and the Atlantic* Cambridge: University Press p38

Everything to Lerma: Watson, op. cit., p4; Ranke p51; rec, Feros, *op. cit.* p38

More knighthoods, wedding tour: Hume, *Spain Its…* pp198-199; Watson *op. cit.* p9

Hunting, parties: *Hume, Spain Its…* p199; rec, Feros, Antonio (2006) *Kingship and Favoritism in the Spain of Philip III* Cambridge: University Press p90

Pious: Philip III entry in *Encyclopaedia Brittanica*.

Needed grand gesture: CSPI p119

'King of Spain's bridge…': Carew in CSPI p277; also see CSPI p438, 'a fair step into England'

Prophesy: Philalethes, Andreas (1602) *An Answer Made by One of Our Brethren*

1588 Armada for Ireland: BBC Radio 4, *In Our Time: The Spanish Armada*, broadcast Oct 7 2010

Old king convinced: Hume, *Spain Under…*

Oviedo and cause: See Ch 7

Other factions, Scots, English, Infanta: CSPS 840 f686, July 11 1600; Hume, *Spain Its…* p202

Two Armadas, deathbed, Yellow Ford, new fleet created: Hume, *Spain Under…*

Felipe's promise: Watson *op. cit.* pp 11–12

Ho'N to yield crown: CSPS 840 f685 July 1 1600; letter from Alonso Cobos May 15 1596; rec, Silke p28

Invasion order, Council objection, Felipe 'glory of God': CSPS 840 f688, July 23 1600

'This is the first…': CSPI p119

True affection: Quote cited in (rec), Sánchez, *Spanish…* pp 94–95

Lerma saw Margaret as challenge: Ranke p51; rec, Sánchez *Melancholy* p83

Astute, resolute: rec, Sánchez, *Spanish…* p93

'She is capable…': Ottoviano Bon (Dec 21 1602) cited in (rec) Sánchez *Melancholy* p90

Troika of Margaret, Empress and nun, zealots, alternative court: rec Sánchez *Melancholy* p83; and *Spanish…* p97

Lerma's priorities: Ranke p54; rec, Paas, John Roger (1985) *The German Political Broadsheet 1600-1700 Vol 1* Wiesbaden: Harrossowitz p85; rec, Sánchez, *Melancholy* p85

Lerma clash with Margaret, threat, sicknesses, move to Valladolid: Ranke p51; Hume, *Spain Its…* p200; rec, Sánchez *Melancholy* p84 and *Spanish…* p98–99

Despatch: See 'opportunity' note below

Lerma wanted out of Low Countries war: Ranke p53 and p54; Paas, *op. cit.* p85; rec, Sánchez, *Melancholy* p85

Old allies, marriages, Felipe II rebuilt English navy: rec BBC *In Our Time*, op. cit.

King's County: *Irish Place-Names* in Mills, A. D. (2003) *Dictionary of British Place-Names* Oxford: University Press

Protect bullion fleet, stronger negotiating position, act when Eliz died: CSPS 840 f687, July 13 1600; also 840 f679 Dec 2 1600

Opportunity, shift, fleet not needed: Preface to CSPS 840 f699, 1601; Hume, *Spain Its…*

p203 and, rec, Silke pp89-90. (Troops bound for Flanders by sea would now travel overland from Italy.)

Chapter 5: Sailing to God or the Devil

John Edie's experiences and quotes, galleons, all from *The Examination of John Edye*, CSPI p86. According to Spanish, *Felipe* was 700 tons and *Pedro* 1,000 tons.

Brochero slave: Goodman, David (1997) *Spanish Naval Power 1589-1665* Cambridge: University Press p32

33 ships, 20 State, 4,464 men, companies, seamen: CSPS 840 f712 Dec 17 1601, *Memorandum of all that has occurred*; also see Pedroso report Sept 6 1601; but cf CSPI p86; CSPI p128; CSPI p125; and pac (1810 ed) p323 and p325. Also rec García Hernán p23, and cf Silke (p104) who says 4,432 men

Common practice, sailing formation: BBC *In Our Time, The Spanish Armada, op. cit.*

One witness: ie Silvester Steene, CSPI p89

Andrew Lynch: CSPI p128

Dates, times of leaving: Sep 3 NS=Aug 24 OS: rec, Silke p104; but cf CSPI p89

'Some of them…': CSPI p89

Treasure: CSPI p87 and p89; 165,000 escudos, rec Silke p105, and García Hernán p23.

Crew problems, Brochero's grumbles: Brochero to King, Nov 6 1601; Brochero to Ibarra; pac (1810 ed) p324; rec, Silke p93 and p104

'Barefoot, unclothed…': Luis Fajardo, cited in Goodman, op. cit. p189

Lynch's overheard conversation: CSPI p128

Oviedo and Cerda trip April 1600: CSPS 840 f675, April 24 1601, Oviedo to King; CSPS 840 f685, July 1 1600, Cl of State to King; CSPS 840 f699, undated 1600; CSPS 840 f 706, Feb 9 1601; rec, Silke pp 69-70 and pp73-78.

O'Neill background: See Ch 26

Ho'D background, Dublin Castle, escape: O'Cleary pp15-17

Ho'D's hair: As described by poet Giolla Brighde Ua hEóghusa; temper, CSPI 1600-1601 pp 152-153

Ho'D one ambition: My interpretation; CSPI 1600-1601 pp 152-153 makes it clear that he was banking everything on Spanish intervention; rec O'Faolain p171

Destination controversy (in general): This is a horrendously complex subject. The best analyses are Silke *Kinsale* pp 98-103 and pp 108-109; Jones, *Destination*; García Hernán p20 and pp 24-28; Silke, John J (1963) *Why Aguila Landed at Kinsale* in *Irish Historical Studies* v13, no 51 pp236-245; and Silke, John (1964) *Where Was Obemdub?* in *Irish Sword* v6 pp276-282

Owen's advice: CSPS 840 f696, Pac O'G v2 p95. Oviedo's new formula: Ov-King

Aug 17 1601

Second summit Feb 1601: pac (1810 ed) pp 281-283 and pp 302-303; Moran pp 209-210

Spanish report, 'difference of opinion': CSPS 840 f699; also note Carew's intelligence, pac (1810 ed) pp 318-321

Brochero's views: Broch-War Council Aug 17 1601; rec, Silke pp 99-100; rec, García Hernán p22

JdA preferred…: JdA-King, Aug 18 1601; rec, Silke pp 99-100; rec García Hernán p27

Oviedo, Cerda choice: Ov-King, Aug 17 1601; rec, silke p101; rec García Hernán p25; also CSPI p159

1800s writer: O'Conor p23

Sandoval, Ho'D's new plan: Letter Ho'D to King from Sligo, Aug 6 1601; rec Jones *Destination* p 30 and p32; rec Silke p103

Spanish authorities' U-turn: rec Jones *Destination* p29-31; rec silke p102

JdA objects to Cork, dual option: rec Silke p103. (García Hernán, pp 27-28, shows evidence that an Irishman named Dominic Brown may have promoted Kinsale as a destination.)

Anthony Wells: CSPI p115

'Thirty leagues…': Brochero-Ibarra April 14 1602; rec Jones *Destination*; rec Silke p108

Meeting on *San Andres* and JdA-Oviedo dispute: rec Silke pp 108-109

Dermot MacCarthy quote: CSPI p159. (Though MacCarthy wrongly stated that the destination was altered after news of the dissident chieftains' arrests.)

'It is nonsensical…': 'Report of Mateo de Oviedo to the King' Jan 27 1602; rec McBride pp 115-116

'With everyone…': Broch-Ibarra April 14 1602; rec, Jones, *Destination*, p31

Storm, fleet scattered: CSPS 840 f712 *Memorandum*… Dec 17 1601

'God or the Devil': CSPI p58

Chapter 6: The Invasion

Weather: Zubiaur's experience shows that the storm continued unabated.

A mile out: 'A half league' precisely. Broch-Ibarra April 14 1602. Rec Silke pp 103-104

25 flags: pac (1810 ed) p337

Formed ranks, parade around town: *Bust*

1700 troops: See below; and rec Silke p110

JdA offer to townsfolk, Stafford quote: pac (1810 ed) pp 337-338

Smerwick: More details in Ch 12

19th C historian: ie Standish O'Grady (1893) *The Bog of Stars* London: Fisher Unwin p107

'The Spaniards, on asking…': Testimony of Kingman and Bruen, CSPI pp 90-91

Troop numbers: 1700, later 3,400: Brochero-King, Nov 6, 1601. Plus 300 stranded along coast = 3,700. Cf pac (1810 ed) (pp 354-355) which says 3,500. Also rec, Silke p110

Oxen, Steene: CSPI p89

Edie quote: CSPI p86

Rider quote: Rider, J (1601), *The Copy of a Letter...* London: Thomas Man

Gould, Meade quote: CSPI p87 and p88

Planned colony: Watson, Robert (1787) *History of the Reign of Philip III* vol 1 Basel: Tourneisen p92; for another perspective, rec García Hernán pp 1-2

Left before surprise: CSPI p83

Not worth preserving: CSPI p82

Better sort; could leave with possessions: pac (1810 ed) p341; CSPI p124

Sovereign with rod, Stafford quote: pac (1810 ed) p338

Desmond Castle: Oral tradition in Kinsale says this was JdA's early HQ, later turned into an arsenal (Mor Itin v3 p45). Also see entry for Kinsale in Irish Tourist Board (2000) *Ireland Guide* Dublin: Gill & MacMillan; and *Frommer's Ireland* p311; also see website www.kinsale.ie accessed 20.9.2013; description, from visit by author

Wilmot quotes: CSPI p82

Annalist from *Annals of the Four Masters*: Henceforth known as 'the Irish annalist'

Wine cellars as bomb shelters: CSPI p276 and p199

'No surety made': Geoffrey Fenton's report in CSPI 1586-1588 p192

'Distinguished men': *A4M*

Important to link with Irish; 20k troops: CSPS 840 f685, July 1 1600

The 1600 horses: pac (1810 ed) p352; CSPI p105; Mor Hist v2 p316

Expected meat: CSPI p86; also Preface to CSPI page xv

Importance of MacCarthy, FitzGerald: CSPI pp 159-160 and p244; CSPI p7, p28, p37, p84, p124, p127, p236, and Preface page xvi

MacCarthys on expedition: eg CSPI p82, p236; Dermot, p157, p89, p129, p159, p160, p235; 'Carlos' pp160-161, p235

Exchange with Sov through interpreter: CSPI p84 (2 refs); pac (1810 ed) p351; and CSPV f1601, f1036, Cavalli, Dec 24

Locked up: pac (1810 ed) p283-284; CSPI p4, p6, p7, p27, p37, p127, pp159-160, p244, p258

Chapter 7: 'I Will Never See My Homeland Again'

Zubiaur's storm-buffeted voyage, arrival El Ferrol: Soto-War Council, Oct 22 1601; PdZ to King, Oct 22, 23 and 24 1601; Council of State to King, CSPS 840 f713; rec *Epistolario* pp 70-72

His anxiety; lengthy repairs needed: PdZ report, Oct 23 1601; rec *Epistolario* p72

'When the King…': Monson, William (1682) *Megalopsychy*

Venetian report, 'disturbed': CSPV f1036, Marin Cavalli, Dec 24 1601

Carew spy at meeting: pac (1810 ed) pp 281-283 and pp 302-303

'Surprise Cork': pac (1810 ed) p319

Arrested MacCarthy: pac (1810 ed) p283-284

'Many fathoms': Hull, chapter on Florence MacCarthy Reagh

'Man much deceived': Carleton; also see CSPV *op. cit.*

'State desperate': CSPI pp 159-160

Shut in, deprived: CSPV *op. cit.*

Weak at first landing: CSPI p634

Scant and miserable: Mor Itin v3 p7

JdA letter to King, deceived, 'punish', homeland: CSPV *op. cit.*

Oviedo's optimistic attitude: as reflected in reports from Council of State to King on July 1 and Nov 28 1600, CSPS 840 f685 and f696; also Oviedo to King Dec 1600, CSPS 840 f675; and also report 840 f699 in 1601

Service to God, holy enterprise, tyranny: Moran p207; rec, McBride p92

'O immortal God': In proclamation written by Oviedo, pac (1810 ed) p357; Moran pp 212-213

Money, five chains: Council of State to King, July 1 1600, CSPS 840 f685; Oviedo to King, April 24 1600, CSPS 840 f675; rec McBride pp 95-96, Oct 1599

Money… actions: Oviedo letter to King, Oct 28 1599; rec, McBride p98

Oviedo early life, career: Moran p193-217; also, rec, García González & Oviedo

Distinctive approach: My analysis based on Smerwick (see notes to Ch 12) and pre-expedition correspondence.

Grisly torture: eg, Moran p203 and footnote

Wanted title, no clout: Moran pp 207-208; rec McBride p98, p103

Made Archbishop; reason why merely 'Archbishop-elect': Moran pp 207-208 and 218 with footnote

Christ Church Cathedral: Although Anglican in practice, this was then (and is still) regarded by the Vatican as the Catholic Archbishop's seat

English descriptions, 'called himself': pac (1810 ed) p281; CSPI p89 and p124

Not enough money: Ov-Ibarra Mar 24 1600, rec McBride p108

Sailboat, laughing stock: Ov to Lerma Dec 5 1600, rec McBride p109

Chapter 8: Trust in God and Keep Your Powder Wet

General note: JdA's assessment of Kinsale and quotes: pac (1810 ed) p341; Report of Juan del Albornoz to War Council, Nov 1601; and *Memorandum of all that has occurred...* dated Dec 17 1601 in CSPS 840, f712

Walls: In 1587 they were described as 'ruined' and in 1598 'decayed'. See O'Sullivan, Florence (1905) *Kinsale* in Cork Hist. and Arch. Soc. Journal vol 11 no 65

Hole: *'un hoyo cercado de padrastros'* in Albornoz, *op. cit.;* rec, O'Sullivan, F (1905) *op. cit.*

English expert: Capt William Yelverton, CSPI p634

Brochero's impatience, arguments, food dumped, boat trips, munitions in ooze: Brochero-King, Nov 6 1601; JdA report in pac (1810 ed) pp 342-343; Hume, *Treason and Plot* p455; Hume, *Spain Under...*; rec, Silke pp 112-114

Twenty guns: According to Archer (letter to Fr James Whyte, Jan 15 1602, rec Jones *Indictment* p218). However, CSPS 840 f712 lists only six big guns

Liability, four guns unloaded, JdA explains why only four: pac (1810 ed) p342; but note, a later inquiry document claimed only two guns were unloaded (April 1 1603)

Demi-cannon technicalities: rec, Manucy, Albert (1949) *Artillery Through the Ages* Washington: US Govt

Archer confrontation: In letter to Fr Whyte, *op. cit.;* rec Mangan *Vindication* p349; rec Jones *Indictment* p218

Brochero left after 8 days: *Bust.*

Latecomers: Brochero-King, Nov 6 1601

Troop numbers: 3,400, Brochero-King, Nov 6, 1601; 4,000 according to CSPI p328 and Mor Hist p320; 4,300 according to CSPI p328

Two thirds Spanish, 1,000 Italian, some English, 'poor slaves': CSPI p87 and p88; 'picked body' CSPV f1027 Nov 17 1601, Mocenigo to Doge; 200 Irish, CSPI p328

Blount 'ancient men': Mor Hist p320

JdA on inexperienced troops: pac (1810 ed) p345

Half boys: ie, Zubiaur in letter Dec 22 1601; rec *Epistolario* p89

Two missing: ie, Francisco de Padilla sick, Antonio Centeno with PdZ; see Dec 17 *Memorandum, op. cit.*

Sickness: CSPI p634

Carpenters, smiths, no medics: pac (1810 ed) p346; also *Bust*

Oysterhaven, Knockrobin, Ardmartin: My analysis based on map in pac (1810 ed), on later events, and on visits to scene. JdA later earmarked Ardmartin as a key point for his allies to occupy

Mills, farmhouses, cattle, JdA quotes on meat shortage, no local help, his food needs: pac

(1810 ed) p344

Beeves: CSPI p634

Rider: Rider, J (1601), *The Copy of a Letter…* London: Thomas Man

Wheat: Archer to Fr Whyte, *op. cit.;* rec Jones *Indictment* p218

50-60 days: Dec 17 *Memorandum, op. cit.;* two months according to pac (1810 ed) p346

Rider, 1,000 hobs: Rider, *op. cit.*

1,600 saddles: CSPI p105; pac (1810 ed) p352; Mor Hist v2 p316

R Owen: CSPS 840 f696, Council of State to King, Nov 28 1600

Six shillings, Moryson quote: Mor Itin v3 p7

Andrew Lynch: CSPI p29

Irish horses, cavalry techniques, JdA 'small horses': JdA in pac (1810 ed) p345; Moryson *Commonwealth*; Hogan pp 320-321; rec Lennon p57; rec Hayes-McCoy pp82-83; rec O'Faolain pp 162-163

Harassment after two days: CSPV f1029, Cavalli to Venice, Nov 25 1601

Pattern, Spanish powerless: It happened 'every day', JdA says in pac (1810 ed) p344

One month undisturbed: According to Fr Mansoni (report March 9 1602); rec Jones *Indictment* p219, citing *Archivum Hibernicum XVII* pp36-39

Within 24 hours, Slingsby: pac (1810 ed) p346

Far away: JdA said Ho'N was '75 leagues' away, pac (1810 ed) p343

JdA notified Ho'N and Ho'D: He said he notified them as soon as he lodged in Kinsale (pac 1810 ed, p343). Ho'N later claimed he hadn't been informed.

Latin message, JdA contribution: pac (1810 ed) p353

Chapter 9: '*Iacta Est Alea* – The Die Is Cast'

Queen's letter October 4; handwritten, signed: Mor Hist v1, pp349-351

Warm winter box, Richmond Palace history: www.richmond.gov.uk, Local History, 'Richmond Palace'; 'Queen Elizabeth I and Richmond'

'Taffety of silver…': Scaramelli report Feb 10 1603 cited in Preface to CSPV 1592-1603

Tilbury speech: Letter by Dr Leonel Sharp to the Duke of Buckingham, 1623

Soldiers weakened: Mor Hist p332

Planning to flee: Mor Hist p205

Could change after Queen's death: compare Walter Raleigh, arrested soon after Elizabeth died

Blount family background; first meets Queen; his appearance; dinner conversation; fine garb; jousting, chess gift, Essex duel, 'teach manners': all Naunton, Sir Robert (c1628) *Fragmenta Regalia* London, Cassell

'Grandmother she may be' etc: Letter from Thomas Morgan to Mary Queen of Scots, in 'Elizabeth' in Strickland, Agnes (1843) *Lives of the Queens of England* London, Colburn

Under Penelope's spell: her 'maddening influence' according to Bruce page xxi

By October 4: Timeline from Mor Hist. Obviously he didn't receive the letter until later.

Blount in Cork: Mor Hist p331

Worst/best location: Mor Hist p321

Confirmation, dilemma, conversation with Carew: Mor Hist 314-6; pac (1810 ed) pp 347-349; Camden, 1601

Halters quote: Mor Hist p314

It was never hard... in great excess: Mor Hist p104–107

Moryson biog: rec, FM entry in *Dictionary of National Biography*

His leg grazed: Mor Hist p113

Blount didn't believe... he jibed: Mor Hist p107

Four in the morning patrol: Mor Hist p368

Historian 'eminent in courage...': William Camden

Blount's close shaves, tactics, garrisons, secrecy: Mor Hist p113

O'Neill's need for a retreat: Moryson *Commonwealth* p287; rec O'Faolain pp154–155 and p159

Blount views Kinsale, a good wall: Mor Hist p317 and p355

Few ships left, advantage in horses, oats; shopping list of arms, transport problems: Mor Hist pp 316-319

Battle plan, Cork hospital: Farmer

Bad weather, first camps, little powder: Mor Hist p328; pac (1810 ed) Ch 12

'It rained...': Mor Hist p339

Layout of Knockrobin camp, mill, estuary crossing: map in *Pacata Hiberna*

Caesar quote: Mor Hist p338

Chapter 10: Curses Like Thunderbolts

JdA had a manual on fortifications: *pac O'G v2p249*

In similar situations: His service in Flanders and Brittany, all covered later.

Over the past... almost impregnable: See Ward, Muller. Rec, Jones, Archer, pp194-195. For a readable guide to this subject, I highly recommend *Siege Warfare 1494-1648* on the website www.syler.com

Machiavelli quote: Machiavelli, Niccolo: *Discourses on the First Decade of Titus Livius*

Brittany fort: ie, Blavet, covered later

'Kinsale is... fortification': CSPS 840 f712, *Memorandum of All That Has Occurred...*

Dec 17 1601

Defensive trenches, sallies: See later chapters

Roger Boyle quote: Boyle, Roger (c1640) *A Treatise on the Art of War*

'Upon a hill…': pac (1810 ed) p362

'They set…': O'Cleary p295

Lynch and Clerk, CSPI pp129-130

Sakers: From description of contemporary bronze saker in National Army Museum, London

'There has never…' and colourful dress: rec, Parker p138

JdA quote, naked, unused to war: JdA-King, Oct 31 1601; rec, García Hernán p162

Tercio, Spanish Square: *Encyclopaedia Brittanica*; rec, Jones, Archer pp191-194

Troops in a…7000: rec, González de Leon p57

Zubiaur in Spain: Letters from PdZ on Oct 22, 23 and 31, 1601; Brochero to Castel Rodrigo Nov 5 1601; and King to PdZ Oct 31, Nov 5 and Nov 27 1601; rec, *Epistolario* pp 72-76. Rec, Silke p117

'They are content…' CSPV f1035, Cavalli to Doge, Dec 24 1601

Águila's position: CSPI xii

'14 days' promise: CSPI p126

Three messengers: CSPI p118

'They are far…': Mor Hist pp 326-327; *Memorandum*, CSPS 840 f712 Dec 17 1601

'Nobody worth…' CSPI p119

'The Irish…' CSPI p126

Food for 18 months: Mor Hist p327

'What they have…' CSPI p119

'Neither rice…' etc., CSPI pp126-127

Herd of cattle: Mor Hist p339

'By Day Twenty…': *Bust*

Townsfolk held, 'Some English…': CSPI p124

Edie escape: CSPI p86

'No persecution': O'Sullivan Beare, Philip (1903) *Ireland Under Elizabeth* p55

Catholic clery urged loyalty: Thomas Leland (1773), *History of Ireland vol 2*, p306, footnote; OSB, p117; Hull, in 'Battle of Kinsale' chapter; rec, Connolly p246-9; rec, Silke, pp118-9: rec, par 4 in O'Connor, Thomas, *Diplomatic Preparations for Kinsale*. Madrid: Universidad de Alcalá

Oviedo's and Blount's proclamations: pac (1810 ed) p357; Moran pp212-213

'deprived of her…': Prynne, William (1641) *The Antipathy of the English Lordly Prelacy*

Previous Bulls: McCaffrey, James, *The Church in Ireland During the Reigns of Mary and Eliza-*

beth; rec, p4 in Morgan, Hiram (1994) *Faith and Fatherland*; rec, par 4 in O'Connor *op.cit.;* rec Jones *The Spaniards...* p20

Clement's diplomacy: rec, par 4 in O'Connor, *op. cit.;* rec, Silke p117

'In Venice...', repercussions, CSPV f1036, Cavalli to Doge, Dec 24 1601; Hume, Martin (1907), *Spain Under Philip III, in Cambridge Modern History*; rec, Knecht, Robert, the French Religious Wars, Silke p118, Jones *The Spaniards...* p20

Thunderbolts: Speed (1612)

Dysentery: CSPI p124, p139; CSPV f1034, Mocenigo to Doge, Dec 22 1601

More deaths than English: rec, Duro p221

Offer of 2k troops: See next chapter

Chapter 11: The Lord of Beara and Bantry

Donal Cam's offer, JdA's rejection: OSB

Donal Cam's appearance: his portrait, now in Maynooth

'His face... haughtiness': From *The Last Lord of Beara* in The Cork Magazine [19th Century], vols 1-2

Nickname made him stronger: His own writings in *pac O'G v2* p121; rec, Somers, Dermot (2005) *Endurance* Dublin: O'Brien Press, p83

'These merciless...': *pac O'G v2* p124

But after... inhabitants: See footnotes to *pac O'G v2* p19, p124, p150; and Éigse, vol 6, issue 4, p314

Oviedo complaint: Ov-Lerma Jan 26 1602; rec McBride p113

By mid-Oct... six days: Mor Hist p326; CSPI preface xiv

Troops at Barnstaple etc: pac (1810 ed) p383

Conscripting system, 'either old...', dead-pays, 'ensure they...': CSPI p30; CSPI p507; Cecil Papers, May 1602, 16-21; rec, Connolly p253; rec, O'Faolain pp 156-157, and 160-161; rec, Roberts, Keith (2002) *Matchlock Musketeer 1588-1688* Oxford: Osprey, pp11-12.

Set sail, skilled workers: pac (1810 ed) p383

'God send...': Mor Hist p338

Needed westerly wind: pac (1810 ed) p382; pp385-386

Misconception: eg Mitchel p24 and p26

Sallying: Muller

The night of Oct 19... first engagement: pac (1810 ed) p361; Mor Hist p329

McDermot aided JdA, horse gift: CSPI pp160-161

McDermot charge, Godolphin rescue, 'marvel of all': Mor Hist p330, pac (1810 ed) p362

Strike force, entry through gate: Mor Hist p339; pac (1810 ed) p364

Chapter 12: Confessions and Conspiracies

JdA-captains dispute: OSB

Oviedo prickly: As evident from his letters before and after the mission

Fell out with King, excommunication threat: rec, García Hernán pp36-37 and footnote; disliked Archer, rec, García Hernán p28, citing Ov-Ibarra July 7 1601

From a loyal officer: (ie, Pedro de Colmenares) house visits, treason claims: Declaración de Pedro de Colmenares [to Inquiry], 1602. Rec, Silke p128 and p164

Oviedo was carefully... land and sea: See McBride, multiple examples in letters. 'Failure' and 'Entire country' quotes, Ov-Lerma Jan 24 1602, and Ov-Lerma Jan 26; rec McBride pp 112-113; also rec García Hernán p292

Smerwick episode (generally): a4m, and footnotes to p506 of Owen Connellan edition; Cusack Ch 27; Moran pp197-205; Church, Richard William (1879) *Edmund Spenser: A Study* London: Macmillan pp 56-60; Ryan, John (1900) *Ireland From AD 800 to AD 1600* Dublin: Browne, Nolan, pp199-200; rec Benvenuta, M (1969) *The Geraldine War* in *Proceedings of the Irish Catholic Historical Society 1963-68* Dublin: Browne, Nolan; rec Shiels, Damian (2008) *Dun an Óir* in Pollard, Tony and Banks, Iain (eds) (2008) *Scorched Earth* Leiden: Brill

'That yoke...': Moran p198

'To bring that isle...': rec, Garcia Gonzales p122

A quarter of...: Report to Rome via Nicholas Sanders, Oct 10 1579; see Moran p196

'Principal promoter...': Cusack, ch 27

San Giuseppe: a.k.a. San José. Moran p198; Cusack ch 27

Indulgences: Moran pp198-199; Cusack ch 27

Oviedo-San Giuseppe dispute: Facts, Moran p199, Ryan p199-200, my interpretation. 'In disgust', 'retired...', Ryan p199. Alternative interpretation to Ryan's: rec, Mangan *Vindication...* pp 349-351

Ov sails home to plead: Moran p200

Ov takes best ships: rec, Mangan *A Vindication, op. cit.*

Fighting and surrender: a4m and footnote as above; Moran pp202

Impression that lives spared: Ryan p199-200; Moran pp203-204

Grey's version of terms: CSPI 1574-1585, reproduced in Church *op.cit.* p58-59

'Lord Grey decided...': Speed, John (1612) *The Theatre of the Empire of Great Britain*

'Morning came... 600 slain': CSPI 1574-1585; Church, *op.cit.* p59

San Giuseppe in Spain: Moran p204

'However, another source...': rec, Mangan *A Vindication, op. cit.*

Officers not receiving promotions: rec, Silke p120

Alba's methods; died with him; logjam of officers: rec, Leon *Rocroi* pp 55-59 and pp72-78;

jousting story, p77

Freedom to dress, uniforms: rec, Parker p138

Beef short, maggots: CSPI pp126-127

Clerk on cattle: CSPI p130; also see jdA quote, pac (1810 ed) p344

Illness, hospital overflow: CSPI p124

JdA quote on tortillas, sickness, conditions: JdA-King Oct 31 1601; rec, García Hernán p162-163

O'Sullivan on winter: Florence O'Sullivan (1905) *Kinsale* in *Journal of the Cork Historical and Archaeological Society Vol XI no 65*

Chapter 13 'Crested Plumes and Silken Sashes'

Distant appearance: See *Pacata Hibernia* map

Troop numbers: Mor Hist p344; CSPI xiv; CSPI p154 reckons 3,500 Spanish in town

Pikes, pikemen: John Derrick (1581) *The Image of Ireland;* pictures in pac; rec, Falls, *Eliz...* p44-45

O'Sullivan quote: O'Sullivan, Philip, (1903) *Chapters Towards A History of Ireland...* ch 5

Contemporary illustration: From Derrick, *Sidney on the March*

Clothing: Based on John Harrington's specs for winter clothing for army in Ireland in 1599 in Grose, Francis (1801) *Military Antiquities* Vol. 2 London: Egerton

Archers vs. musketeers: rec, Roberts *op. cit.* p7; armour, rec, Falls, *Eliz...* p40; however, Bagwell (p234, etc) cites isolated instances of arrow attacks in the 1590s

Reason for red: Grose, *op.cit.*, quoting Julius Ferretus

Chester: *Calendar of Cecil Papers* Vol 11, November 4 1601, Mayor of Chester to Privy Council.

'Very deficient...': Mor Hist p344

'Our soldiers are...': CSPI p124

By Oct 26... entrenching equipment: Mor Hist p339 and p344; pac (1810 ed) pp 364-366

Chapter 14: Digging for Victory

Bodley, trenchmaster, career: Mor Itin v3 p15, p38, p54; CSPI p210; *Dict Nat Biog*

Double height of a man: CSPS 840, f714, committee report, Jan 29 1602

'The camp was... perfected': Mor Itin v3 p15

Description of camp: map in pac v2

Fourpence extra: Bagwell p375

Bodley's pay: CalCarew p152

Muller's quotes: Muller p45 etc

Ward's quotes: Ward p98 etc

Farmer quote: Farmer p120

As high as lances etc: CSPS 840 f714, Jan 29 1602; rec, Silke p136

'The great strength…': O'Cleary p311

Chapter 15: The Taking of Rinjora Castle

All references to Sgt Heredia in this chapter are from his own testimony in Carew Ms. 607, p203, April 1 1618

Clavijo commander: *pac O'G v2* p5

Rincorran's setting: My description

Warping up, pinnace Moon: CSPI p155

Culverins: *pac O'G v2* p2-3

Culverin's properties: Sturmy, Capt. Samuel (1669) *Sturmy's Mathematical and Practical Arts* London: Harlock; also Luis Collado (1590s) cited in (rec) Manucy, Albert (1949) *Artillery Through the Ages* Washington: US Govt

One English official: Geoffrey Fenton, Oct 31 1586, in *Annals of Kinsale* xxii

150 men, support: *pac O'G v2* p2

Commander's leg injury, thirty Irish: *Bust*; also rec, Silke p180

Don Dermutio: See Ch 6

Don D. in Rincorran: *Bust*; Heredia's testimony, *op.cit.;* CSPI p159

'Great multitude…': CSPI p348

Contreras: *pac O'G v2* p5; Farmer

Boat relief attempt foiled; two culverins broken: *pac O'G v2* p2; Mor Itin v3 p15

Spanish gun attack: *pac O'G v2* p2; Mor Itin v3 p16; 'killing the vivo', rec, Manucy *op. cit.*

By the morning… all wrong: *pac O'G v2* pp2-3

Carew hated Ireland, 'virgin bride': Stafford in pac Book 3, ch 20; Hull 'Battle of Kinsale' chapter; Bagwell p433; Gibson p423; rec GC entry in *Ox. Dict. Nat. Biog.*

Witches, priests and foul weather, CalCarew p243, CSPI p396

Dublin murder: Hull; Carew entry in Oxford Dict Nat Biog

'Drew a draft': Carew entry in (1878) *Compendium of Irish Biography*

Familiar, 'nothing hidden': *pac O'G v2* p131

Aiming high, shots in spikes, range checks: *pac O'G v2* pp2-3

Secret guild: Manucy, *op. cit.,* p5

Quadrant, staff, point blank, elevation tables: Ward pp 125-127

Adjusting range: Collado cited in Manucy, *op. cit.*

'One lighted': *pac O'G v2* p3

'Every shot…': Ward p80

Eight rounds an hour etc.: Manucy, *op. cit.*

'Without intermission': Mor Hist p346

Feint, battle Oct 31: pac v2, pp3-5; Mor Hist pp346-347

Wingfield and Contreras: Farmer

Two sections 'The culverin snake… might make it' and 'Back in the English… upon his knees': *pac O'G v2* pp5-7; Mor Hist pp347-349; Harvey quote and pillage castle, CSPI pp158-159

Ransom offer and reply: CSPI p182

Dermutio's interrogation, Archer: CSPI pp158-159

Chapter 16: 'The Most Bloody and Treacherous Traitor'

Poison, great service, CSPI 1603-06, v1, p76; A the traitor, CSPI 1603-1606 vol 1 p72 and Hogan p345; tall, CSPI 1603-1606 vl 1 p83

Archduke, *Journal of the Royal Society of Antiquities of Ireland*, v1

'Principal plotter': CSPI 1603-1606 v1 p76

Plot, Cahill: CSP *Domestic* 1591-1594 p442, Feb 25 1594

Destestable: Letter to Walsingham cited in Hogan p319

'Bloody and treacherous', 'absolute', 'gainsay': CSPI 1603-1606 v1 p82

Archer would sail… witchcraft: CSPI 1603-1606 p82; Hogan p207, p347, p324

Description from sketch: Walker engraving in Planché, James (1836) *History of British Costume* London: C Knight p371

Nov 15 meeting, riders, Archer plan, Roche house: Mor Itin v3 p45

Sent messengers: CSPI pp 141-142

Priest messenger: CSPI p185

Would withdraw, CSPI p142

Rough encounters, fight with soldier: Hogan pp 351-353; p168; p326

'Englished': Hogan p356

Uncultivated, barbarous: Hogan p325

Choleric, melancholic: rec Morrissey, p5

Bipolar disorder, Jamison quote: Jamison, Kay Redfield (1994) *Touched with Fire* New York: Simon & Schuster p18

Pharaoh, Moses quote: CSPI pp 394-395

Endangered own flock: rec McCoog, Thomas (2010) *Persons the Peacemaker*, lecture in Rome April 15 2010

Plea to stay away, 'he has made…': Hogan pp 349-350

'Detestable enemy': President of Munster to Walsingham, 1577

Chapter 17: 'There Will Be No Retreat'

Gate notice: Mor Itin v3 p32

Weakened: ie, by Carew's departure, dealt with in Ch 20

Decoy unit and battle: Mor Itin v3 p34; CalCarew p159

Shame upon… posted; 108 deaths; 'moan' over captain: Mor Itin v3 p32 and p45

Warships, new troops: Mor Itin v3 pp 36–37; names, Monson, William (1682) *Megalopsychy*

The Spanish were… in his face: CSPI p182; Mor Itin v3 p37

Another 1,000 and 140: CSPI p182

O'Brien background: rec, entry in *Dict. Nat. Biog.*

O'Brien–Archer incident: CSPI 1600 p101; CalCarew 1589–1600 p381; OSB

Blown west: Mor Itin v3 p31

Sick troops, many died: CalCarew p181 and p186

CB had 9,700 and 575: CSPI p200

Flying column: Mor Itin v3 p42

'God be thanked…': Mor Hist p362

Small force: See next chapter

Chapter 18: Cold as Stone, Dark as Pitch

33 men and a boy: ie, 17 men and a boy died at C Park and 16 survived; see Mor Itin v3 pp44–45

The battle for Castle Park (generally): Mor Itin v3 p37–38 and pp43–44; *pac O'G v2* pp 22-27; CSPI p199 and p209

Coronation Day present: Mor Itin v3 p38; *pac O'G v2* p22; CSPI p209

C Park description, 'small fort': sketch in *pac O'G v2* p25

Storm, pickaxes: Mor Itin v3 pp 37–38

'The sow' and its fate: Mor Itin v3 p38; *pac O'G v2* p22 and footnote (includes Sligo incident); rec, Gravett, Christopher (1990) *Mediaeval Siege Warfare* Oxford: Osprey (includes 'farrowed' story, p32); rec, Young, Peter (2003) *Tortoise* London: Reaktion (includes Humpty Dumpty, p90)

C Park surrenders: Mor Itin v3 p43–44; *pac O'G v2* pp 26-27; commanders, *pac O'G v2* p27

Sixteen survivors: Mor Itin v3 p44; but *pac O'G v2* p26 says 17

Weather, see Ch 27

Weather as weapon: Mor Itin v3 pp38–39

Forty a day: CSPI p208

'The difficulties… and watching': Mor Itin v3 p35

Irish experts: Moryson *Commonwealth* and *pac O'G v2* p24 footnote

'Our approaches...': Mor Itin v3 p28

'It groweth...': Mor Itin v3 p36

Chapter 19: Stella and the Centaur

Coronation Day jousts, now a knight, one with horse, wore Penelope's colours: Peele, George (1590) *Polyhymnia, Describing the Honourable Triumph at Tylt*; also rec, Wall, Alison (2004) *Rich, Penelope* in *Ox. Dict. Nat. Biog* and Falls, *Mountjoy*

Penelope age: b 1563, rec Wall *op. cit.*

Sidney sonnet: Sidney, Philip (1591) *Astrophil and Stella*. For detailed study of Penelope references in poem, see Craik vol 1 pp85-96; encounter after her marriage, see discussion on dates in Craik p90

Poem dedication: Barnfield, Richard (1594) *The Affectionate Shepherd* London: John Danter.

First met, ages, later relationship: Craik pp 81-85; Rawson p36; see Rich, Penelope and Sidney, Philip entries in *Dictionary of National Biography 1885-1900*

Wed Robert Rich, 'dour', 'boorish': Heylin, Peter (1671) *Life and Death of Archbishop Laud* p53; Rawson p59; For his biog, see Robert Rich entry in www.historyofparliamentonline.org

Protest at ceremony, kept hanging on, PS married Frances: Rawson p59 and ch 5, especially p78, p84; see Rich, P and Sidney entries in *Dictionary of National Biography 1885-1900*

CB military career: CB entry in *Dictionary of National Biography 1885-1900*

Rainbow at Gravelines: rec Falls, *Mountjoy*, p 40+; CB entry in *Ox. Dict. Nat. Biog.*

'Graces of beauty...' and 'Long had she...': Heylin, *op. cit.* Also see Rawson p136 citing Alexander Croke

Number of children: Sources differ. See Rawson p183, p191, p299 and pp 304-306, but compare, rec, Wall *op. cit.* and Rickman p114, p117

Conversion bid: autobiography of Fr John Gerard cited in (rec) Falls, *Mountjoy* pp 64-65; also rec Rickman p117

New Lord, positions, *Dict. Nat. Biog.*

Brittany, Queen's order: Naunton, Robert (1641, then 1892) *Fragmenta Regalia* London: Cassell

Chapter 20: That Wondrous Winter March

Carew's encounter with O'Donnell is detailed in *pac O'G v2* pp 9-14; CSPI pp 158-159, p186, p216; CalCarew p162; Mor Itin v3 p31, p33, p48; O'Cleary pp 303-305; and OSB

Carew's discomfiture: Evident from exchange between GC and CB, CalCarew pp 161-163; also see footnote to *pac O'G v2* pp10-11

His fear of Irish 'witches': CalCarew pp 242-243

Council decision, CB's belief: CSPI p153

Ho'N still home on Nov 7: He left around Nov 9, see CSPI p168; this broadly confirmed by a4m

Joined by St Lawrence: *pac O'G v2* p10

St Lawrence biog: Entry in *Dict. Nat. Biog.* Lord Grey story from Camden; rec O'Faolain p219

4,500 and 500, outnumbering Ho'N: OSB, who says Ho'N had 2,600 and 400 then.

Fear of retreat cut off: CalCarew p163

Feared he'd meet 6,000: CSPI p158

'In good faith…' and 'steal by you': CalCarew p161

In one letter… covet': CalCarew pp 163-164

Long, weary, Ardmayle: *pac O'G v2* p10

When he had… reclaim it later: O'Cleary p299

3,000 troops: OSB

Oct 22: O'Cleary pp 301-303, adjusted from NS

Tyrrell's deal: rec, Morgan, *BoK*, p166; rec, García Hernán p17

'Many a river…', 'past quaking…': from De Vere, Aubrey (1814-1902) *The March to Kinsale*

It's hard… colourfully: O'Cleary pp303-305

Ho'D camp details: *pac O'G v2* pp 10-11

Quagmire, frost, night march, jettisoned bags: *pac O'G v2* pp 11-12; CalCarew p165; Mor Itin v3 p48; O'Cleary p305

'He marched…': O'Cleary p305

At Croom, 70 km: *pac O'G v2* p12. March was 60-70 km depending on route.

Carew was stunned… it is true: *pac O'G v2* p12; CalCarew p165

Ho'D headed SW: *pac O'G v2* p12; O'Cleary pp 305-307

Met de Burgh: *pac O'G v2* p13

Clanrickard warcry: CSPI p683

Hubbub origin: *The Oxford Dictionary*

50 + 150 men: CSPI p72, p201

For de Burgh family and Richard generally, see Lodge, John (1692-1774) *The Peerage of Ireland* Dublin: Moore, pp 117-134

De Burgh biog, education, defiant in religion: rec. Lennon, Colm, entry for Burke, Richard, in *Ox Dict Nat Biog*; Lodge, John, *op. cit.,* pp 131-134; Cokayne, George E (1887-98) *The Complete Peerage* London: Bell, Pollard pp230-231

Resembled Essex: *pac O'G v2* p294, footnote

Frances his lover: rec, Morrill, John, entry for Robert Devereux in *Ox Dict Nat Biog;* rec, *The English Journal* (1953) p523

De Burgh poem: *Of The Last Queen,* cited in (rec) Carpenter, Andrew (2003) *Verse in English from Tudor and Stuart Ireland* Cork: University Press

Most ancient: 'Clanricarde' in *Debrett's Peerage*

With Normans, became Irish: Cokayne, *op. cit.*

In 1576... inhabitants: Camden, William *The History of Elizabeth Book* II p218; Hume, David (1854) *The History of England* v4 London: Bell p304

'From bush... hill': *Carew Manuscripts* Lambeth, vol II, document 621

'Served the Queen... faithfully': Lodge, *op. cit.,* p132

Resented rise: rec, *Dictionary of Irish National Biography* vol 2; also see letter from John Chamberlain to Dudley Carleton after his marriage

Innocency, unfainedly loved: CSPI p286

Queen's orders: *pac O'G v2* pp 293-295

JdA escape at Empel: Verstraete pp 291-295; Famien Strada pp 136-143; today's parades, Spanish Ministry of Defence website, accessed December 9 2011

Chapter 21: A Direct Hit on Don Juan

JdA's council: CSPI p199

Report to Rome: By Nuncio Fr Mansoni, March 9 1602. It can be read in (rec) Jones, *Indictment* p219. (Mansoni's figure of 16 at C. Park is *sic.*, although true figure was 34.)

Archer's outburst: Archer to Whyte, Jan 12 1602; rec, Jones *Indictment* p217.

CB's ringfort, frost etc: Mor Itin v3 p44; demi-cannon, deserters, aim, CSPI p199

Direct hit, Patrick Strange quotes: CSPI p199; CalCarew p187; Spanish sentry, Mor Itin v3 p44

Parma lunch: O'Connell, Robert L (1989) *Of Arms and Men* Oxford: University Press pp 118-119

Carlos's Irish company: CSPI p160 and footnote

Grace 'journal'; women, children: Mor Itin v3 pp 44-46

Market deaths: Mor Itin v3 p46; CalCarew p187

Hill camp, St Lawrence: Mor Itin v3 pp 47-49

Carew volunteers: CSPI p191

The English weren't... silenced: Mor Itin v3 pp46-49

Strange's 'celebration': CSPI p199

CB 'fortunate': CSPI p191

'It may please God...': CalCarew p167

CB offer, Nov 28, JdA reply: CalCarew p188

'I had hoped...': CSPI p203

JdA's attitude: My assessment, based on his reply and his later defiant quotes in CalCarew p195

Final two sentences: See notes to next chapter

Chapter 22: Hell at Spaniards' Point

Generally: The full story of JdA in Brittany, Blavet, and El Leon can be found in Davila, H.C. pp 656-658; Moreau chapters 25-28 and (especially) chs 30-31; Duro p73 and pp87-92; Wraxall p139 and pp 143-144; also among the correspondence in CSPV

English associated Kinsale with Blavet and El Leon: CSPI p131, p243

Águila had built... seagulls: See later notes. Death toll, Davila, HC, p658

'The blood of man...': Camden *Annales* p433

Eleven years... king: Hume, Martin (1906) *Philip II* p245; *Monson v1* p252; Davila, H.C. p656; Duro, p87; Wraxall p139; Camden *Annales* p393

Own agenda: rec, Brigham Young University website article *Letters of Philip II, King of Spain* in https://lib.byu.edu accessed 14.04.2010; rec, Goodman, David (2003) *Spanish Naval Power 1589-1665* Cambridge: University Press, p14

The Breton... mistrust: Wraxall p143; Hume, Philip II, p246; Monson v1, p252, p306; Mézeray, Francois (1690) *Abrégé Chronologique...* vol 3 Paris: Thierry etc, p350-351; Davila, H.C. p656

'This new...': CSPI p131

But they had... Águila: rec, History of Port Louis (16th C) at http://www.port-louis.org/en/ citadel.html accessed Jan 29 2014; also, rec, Lepage, Jean-Denis (2010) *Vauban and the French Military...* Jefferson: McFarland pp160-161

Brochero: Duro p83; Monson v1 p323

At Hennebont: CSPV 1590, f1013 Contarini to Doge, Feb 15 1590

At Craon: Duro p84

Morlaix dialogue: A free translation based on Moreau pp197-198 (sources differ on precise words); tensions and split at Morlaix, Mézeray *op. cit.* pp 350-351; Wraxall p143; Monson v1, p307

Crozon, El Leon, Praxede: Davila, H.C. pp 656-657; Moreau chs 30-31; Wraxall p143; Monson v1 p307; Duro pp 87-88

Virtually impregnable: Davila, H.C. p656; Monson v1 p308

Dangerous threat: Hume *Philip II* p245

400 Spanish: Camden *Annales* p433; Monson v1 p308

14 to one: ie, 5,700 against 400, see Monson v1 p308

Like wildcats: Wraxall p143; Monson v1 pp 303-304; Davila, H.C. p657

Battle for El Leon: Davila, H.C. pp 656-658; Moreau pp 243-256; Camden *Annales* p433;

Back in Blavet... enemy cavalry: Davila, H.C. pp 657-658; Monson v1 p308; Moreau p248

Blocked at Plomodiern: Moreau pp 250-251; Monson v1 p308; Davila, H.C. p658

'Being overcome...': Davila, H.C. p658

Frobisher died: Camden *Annales* p433; Wraxall p143

Writers of that era... reach El Leon: Camden *Annales*, p433; Davila, H.C. p658; Oppenheim sourcing Monson (v1, p308), says JdA 'had not been idle' in the relief but was let down by a vengeful Mercoeur

'Perchance...': Davila, H.C. p658

However, later...helped them: Davila's words were twisted by Matthew O'Conor (*Military History...* p21) who was then cited as the main authority for anti-Águila rants – that word is no exaggeration – by Edward d'Alton, John O'Donovan, John Mitchel and others

The truth... them aid; Leon levelled: Camden *Annales* p433; Monson v1 p308; Wraxall p144

Dialogue with 13 survivors: Moreau pp 251-252; Duro p91

Commando raid on England: See Ch 32

Conditions at Blavet, mutiny, 'want of pay': CSPV f591, June 1597, Nani to Spain, June 29; also rec, Lopez, Ignacio (2012) *The Spanish Tercios 1536-1704* Oxford: Osprey

Wave of desertions, 'one historian': ie, (rec) Parker, Geoffrey (2004) *The Army of Flanders...* Cambridge: University Press, chapter 8

Held back pay: rec, Jones, Archer (2001) *The Art of War in the Western World* Illinois: University of Illinois Press p200

Eventually... achievement: Wraxall p144; Hume, *Philip II*, p248; Preface to CSPV 1592-1603

Back in... the walls: CSPI p139

Buried in earth: CSPI p220

By nightfall... waiting for them: Mor Itin v3 pp 49-50

The battering... and repelled: Mor Itin v3 pp 50-51; *pac* O'G *v2* pp 30-32

Spanish more confident: CalCarew p182

Zubiaur: CSPS 840 f714 Jan 29 1602

Chapter 23: 'Let Us Settle This in Single Combat'

Zubiaur, nine ships, 800-1,000: Ocampo in CSPI p237; CSPS 840, f712, Dec 17, *Memo-*

randum of all that has occurred…; also CSPS, 840, f714, Jan 29 1602 (PdZ's fleet originally consisted of ten ships, but one didn't make it out of port.)

Many nations: PdZ-King, Dec 19 and Dec 17 1601; CSPI p205; Mor Itin v3 p60; rec *Epistolario* p77-81 and p83

Collins: Moran p215; rec, entry in www.jesuit.org

David High: Mor Itin v3 pp58-60

Poor state of ships and troops, jailbirds: Mor Itin v3 p60

'Raising companies… own eyes': PdZ-King Jan 15 1602; rec, *Epistolario* p101

Fleet separated: CSPS 840, f718, Feb 21 1602; also CSPS 840, f714, Jan 29 1602

Storm kept PdZ from Kinsale, mercy of God: Council of State to King, Jan 29, as above.

Later Spanish account: CSPS 840, f718, Feb 21 1602, statement of Council of State; also Mor Itin v3 p58-61

High's escape: fastened hatches, CSPI p221; 'Whatever…peacefully', Mor Itin v3 p58-61.

Dermot O'Driscoll reaction and support: OSB; PdZ-King, Dec 19 1601; rec, *Epistolario* p77; also see footnote to *pac O'G v2* pp40-41

'A Catholic and… Majesty': CSPS 840, f718, Feb 21 1602

'Ships may come… clear and clean': Boate, Gerard (1657) *Ireland's Natural History*

Ocampo role: CSPI p237, Mor Itin v3 p60

Ocampo on troops: CSPI p237; Cal Carew p205; but CSPS 840, f718, Feb 21 1602, says 650 men

Entire section 'Back in Kinsale' to 'not for a minute': Mor Itin v3 pp56-58

'In Castlehaven…Brochero's orders': CSPS 840, f712, Dec 17 1601; CSPI pp237-238; calCarew pp204-206

Many Irish chieftains, Fineen O'Driscoll: Pac v2 pp 40-41; also footnote to p41

PdZ disinformation: rec, *Epistolario* Appendix 4, pp123-129

Donal Cam quote: CSPS 849, f717, Feb 16 1602, in letter to Count of Caracena

'The lords… his Majesty': CSPS 840, f718, Feb 21 1602

'Spanish garrisons… owners': CSPS 840, f714, Jan 29 1602

'Inaccessible… artillery': CSPI 1586-1588 p192

'But it was Baltimore… *Sasanach*: PdZ-King, Dec 19; rec *Epistolario* p79

Single combat, Blount reply: Mor Itin v3 p57

John Norreys: Nolan, John S (1997) *Sir John Norreys and the Elizabethan Military World.* Exeter: University of Exeter Press, p188

Leveson's orders, departure: Pac v2 p39; CSPI p211

Boost, 'took heart': Mor Itin v3 p61; calCarew p182

Battle of December 2 (generally): *pac O'G v2* pp33-36; Mor Itin v3 pp52-55; CSPI pp

197, 198, 219, 220

Probably largest: The Battle of Kinsale featured only around 200 Spaniards; also compare Águila's 1595 Cornish raid and the 1719 Battle of Glen Shiel in Scotland, which each involved about 200 Spanish

Thousands engaged: Mor Itin v3 p53, *pac O'G v2* p34

'Although… the insurgents': See *pac O'G v2* p38 footnote. (Also see p36 footnote on importance of engagement.)

Time, rainy weather, 2,000 men, 'exceeding fury', spikes: *pac O'G v2* p34

Stones to block: a4m

'They seized…' etc: Mor Itin v3 p53

Boyle quote: CSPI p197

Bowlton quote: CSPI p219

'Blount's marshal… towards the town': *pac O'G v2* p34-35

De Burgh's 30 men, push of pike, held trench, much honour: CSPI p220

'Next day's… another attack': CSPI p220; Mor Itin v3 p55; farmer p122; *pac O'G v2* pp34-36

Spells, STDs: Mor Itin v3 p55

Boyle, 200 killed: CSPI pp197-198

Lost 40, 100: CSPI p219, CSPI p220

Guns back in action: Farmer p122

'The revival…sealed off': Mor Itin v3 pp61-62

PdZ describes land: PdZ-King, Dec 19, 1601; rec *Epistolario* p80; also PdZ-King Dec 24; rec *Epistolario* p91

Great friendship, young stags, courageous, etc: PdZ-King, Dec 20 1601; rec, *Epistolario* p85 and p86

'From Lisbon…': PdZ-King, Dec 24 1601; rec, *Epistolario* p91

His sailors' behaviour: PdZ-King, Dec 19 1601; rec, *Epistolario* p83

'Over dinner… onslaught': OSB; PdZ Dec 19 letter as above; rec *Epistolario* p77

Chapter 24: The Battle of Castlehaven

In this chapter, all quotes from Leveson are *pac O'G v2* p44

All quotes from Preston are CSPI p205

'Sir Richard…': Monson, William (1682) *Megalopsychy*. Also see Monson's *Naval Tracts v2* p124

'Thanks to the…': Council of State report Feb 21 1602, CSPS 840 f718

'Sank flagship': CSPS 840 f714, Jan 29 1602

'In this battle': OSB

PdZ 'victory': PdZ-King, Dec 19 1601; rec *Epistolario* pp82–84; rec, Coombes and Ware p54

'Leveson arrived': CalCarew p190

Guns heard in K.: CalCarew p189

'Lady of Heaven' quote: Gainsford

PdZ's flagship on rocks: OSB, CalCarew p190

'Two other...': CalCarew p190

Maria F, Cisne: PdZ-King, Dec 19 1601; rec *Epistolario* p83

Landing craft, Donal Cam's arrival: OSB

Cut cables, towed out: OSB

209 holes: Farmer. (John Lennon allusion is to the celebrated counting of 4,000 holes in the Beatles' *A Day in the Life*)

'English reports...the port': CSPI p211

Lost eight men: Monson *Megalopsychy*

Spanish assessment of losses: Anywhere between 20 (according to CSPS 840 f714, Jan 29 1602) and 40 (rec Jones, *The Spaniards...* p31, citing Zubiaur). Amias Preston also says 40 (CSPI p205)

'575' claimed by some Spanish: *OSB*

Chapter 25: 'Send Us Home Some Greyhounds'

Jeronimo's letter: CalCarew p206

Silence since JdA letter Oct 21: (ie Oct 31 NS) CSPS 840 f712 Dec 17 1601

'Don Juan...': CSPS as above

Swift ship: CalCarew p204

Lerma letter and 'confidence in your care': CSPI p293

CB's 7,000: Mor Itin v3 p40 says 6,900 at Kinsale

Ibarra letter, 220 men, and 'heart lightened': CSPI p294

'The reality was...reprisal raids': See CSPS 1601-1602 *passim*

Padilla letter: CSPS 840 f710, letter to Felipe, Dec 10 1601 NS

PdZ 'like flies' etc: PdZ letter Dec 22 1601; rec *Epistolario* p89

Council of State report, Fourth Wave: CSPS 840 f711 Dec 11 1601

Origin of troops: CSPS 840 f712 *Memorandum...* Dec 17 1601

Ibarra, levies: CSPI p294

From Flanders: CSPS 840 f713, end Dec 1601

'By mid-Dec...in the New Year': CSPS 840 f713, end Dec 1601

'The most important...': CSPI p293

'If they have not...' and 'hold out'; God's aid, constant prayer: CSPS 840 f713 end Dec

Ho'N in heartland: i.e., Tipperary. CSPI p190

Slow: My interpretation based on the dates. The 1800s historian Standish O'Grady also described it as 'slow' and 'leisurely' (*The Bog of Stars p107*)

Heard early Oct: That is, Oct 2, or Oct 12 NS – rec García Hernán, p30, citing Ho'N letter to JdA on that date. Morgan (*BoK*, p103) says news would have reached Ho'N within a week of landing

Reached Carrickfergus: On Oct 8. CSPI pp110-112

Left Nov 9: CSPI p168, rough date confirmed by a4m

Burning and looting, Oct 7 report: CSPI p118 and p127

'Spoiled 22 villages... swine'; 7 villages, beggars: CSPI p135

Wife and 16 women: CSPI p188, p135

'The English wondered': CSPI pp 107, 134, 141, 156, 235; 'dangerous', CSPI p134; also see Leland v2 pp371-381

'Some believe... others state': For a sample of the opposing viewpoints, rec CSPI Preface xviii to xx; and Hamilton ch 34 (on the one hand); and O'Faolain pp 247-249 and Jones *The Spanish...* pp 24-25 (on the other). The debate continues

O'Cleary, 'waited', p307. Also see a4m

'In Gaelic society... adjacent territories' etc: *Captain Cuellar's Adventures*; Hull; rec Lennon p58 and pp51-55; rec Falls *Elizabeth's...* p29

Poet wrote: i.e., Blind Tadhg O'Higgin, see Hull

Culture of Honour: I first encountered this term in Malcolm Gladwell's 2008 book *Outliers* London: Allen Lane (ch 6) and was intrigued to see how this mainly Irish and Scots border phenomenon explained some of the mysteries about Kinsale – as we'll see later. Sean O'Faolain anticipated the concept with what he called the 'border raiders' mentality (p171). For more, rec Nisbett, Richard E and Cohen, Dov (1996) *Culture of Honor...* Oxford: Westview Press; and Cohen, D, Nisbett R et al (1996) *Insult and Aggression...* in Journal of Personality and Social Psychology Vol 70 No 5 945-960

Shepherd's first quarrel: Campbell, J K (1966) *Honour and the Devil* in Peristiany, J. G. (ed) Honour and Shame... London: Weidenfeld & Nicholson pp 139-170

'I am sent...': CSPI p163

'The Spanish mislike': CSPI p186

Ho'N 3,000; joined Ho'D: CSPI p188; O'Cleary p309, Mor Itin v3 p62.

Farmer: p122

'The Spaniard curseth': Rider, J (1601), *The Copy of a Letter...* London: Thomas Man

Archer demanded, letters torn up: rec, Jones *Indictment* p218 and pp219-220

JdA letter mid-Dec: pac v2, pp45-46

JdA's blunt letter: CSPI p238

Oviedo's meetings, desperate straits: *Bust*

CB returned letters: See numerous examples in current book

CB narrow escape: *pac O'G v2* p33

JdA wounded in face: CSPI p235

'These poor people... love of God': PdZ-King, Dec 20; rec *Epistolario* p88

500 cloaks: PdZ-King, Jan 15 1602; rec, *Epistolario* p101

'It is pitiful...' PdZ-King, Dec 20 1601; rec, *Epistolario* p85

'Cannot brag...': CalCarew p204

Ocampo and de Soto quotes: CalCarew pp205-206

PdZ on Baltimore: PdZ-King, Jan 2 1602; rec *Epistolario* p96.

PdZ sent 120, then 80: CalCarew pp204-206; CSPI p238, p235; CSPS 840 f714, Jan 29 1602; CSPS 840 f718, Feb 21 1602; PdZ-King, Dec 19, 20 and Dec 24 1601, rec *Epistolario* pp 82-84 and p90; cf OSB, who says 300 sent

Ocampo, 'The cause...': CalCarew p205

PdZ armed 700 Irish, six flags, armour: CSPS 840 f714, Jan 29 1602; CSPI 235-236; CalCarew p205

PdZ send 100 to Bearhaven: CSPI p235; OSB; CalCarew, p206

'By Dec 13...': CSPI p217; Mor Itin v3 p62; O'Cleary p309

'Towards night' [on Dec 21]: *pac O'G v2* p50

Ho'N 6,000: CSPI p141, and rec Morgan *BoK* p1; but estimates vary. See Morgan *BoK* p118; Connolly p251, footnote; Silke p126-127

Variety of Irish troops: CSPI pp 665-666; CSPI p284; Moryson *Commonwealth*; Rec, Falls, *Elizabeth's...* ch 4; rec, Lennon pp 57-58

'Kingdom lost': Ho'D entry in *Nat Dict Biog*, citing AGS GA 3144; rec Silke, John (2001) *Kinsale Reconsidered in Studies, An Irish Quarterly Review*, v90, no 360

Chapter 26: The Great Persuader

Blacksmith grandfather: Testimony of kinsman Shane O'Neill in Camden *History* p62; Mor Hist v1 p16; Gainsford; Wills p96; Hull; rec Lennon p62

Mean stature, etc: Mor Hist v1 p16

Victorian fantasy: rec Morgan *BoK* p110, caption

1620s drawings: Carleton *A Thankful...*

Puppet, puppeteer, childhood, 'a creature...': Gainsford, Hull. Rec, Morgan, *Tyrone's Rebel-*

lion p85, p93, p214

Liquidated, elderly cousin, land division, O'Donnells: Mor Hist v1 p17; Hull

Ho'N strangled Graveloch: Gainsford, Hull, CSPI 1600-1601 p127-136; but rec Lennon p293 and O'Faolain p110

For seven years… nobles: Hull; Armada, rec, Morgan *Tyrone's…* p106

Ho'D jailed, land grab, wife Mabel: Gainsford; Lawless p198; Hull

'Affable' etc: Mor Hist v1 p17

Tears for Judge: CSPI 1592-1596 p225

'Mortal enemy': CSPI 1596-1597 Preface

'Infinite capacity': Connolly p235; also see Wills pp 104-105

Some claim…: e.g., in RTÉ *The Battle of Kinsale*

Against interests: My interpretation; but rec, O'Faolain p151 and p283 (13)

Troops, arms build-up: Cox, Hibernia Anglicana; Gainsford; Hull; Leland (1784) p182; rec, Lennon p295

Given the gun: rec, Hayes–McCoy p111

Lead: Cox ; Hull

Red coats etc: rec, Hayes–McCoy p96

'Craving…': Hull

Yellow Ford: Hull

Essex's experience: Camden p569-571; Leland (1784) pp193-194

Promised control of Ireland, Ho'N governor: Evidence of Thomas Wood and James Knowd, Spedding pp 292-293; CSPS 840, f685, July 1 1600; rec, Silke pp 61-62 who says Ho'N offered Essex 'the kingdom of Ireland'; rec O'Faolain pp 219-220

To an Austrian and two Spaniards: Ho'N and Ho'D declared themselves 'faithful vassals' of the Spanish monarchs in 1596, 'begging' that Albert of Austria be made their Prince. Report from Alonso Cobos May 15 and 16 1596, CSPS f635 and f638

To James VI: Colles ; also p48 of Walsh, Paul (ed) (1930) *The Will and Family of Hugh O'Neill* Dublin: Colm O Lochlainn

Bigger game, Spain: Gainsford; suited him, rec, Lennon pp 300-301

Not overly devout: Lawless p199; rec, O'Faolain p175

'Thou carest…': Wills p114; Lawless p200

Catholic crusade, etc: Leland, Thomas (1773) *History of Ireland* v2, pp354-367 and footnote; rec, Lennon p326 and Connolly pp 245-247

'Chiefly…intentions': O'Neill's manifesto Nov 15 1599 NS. See Leland, as above

This was an… today: Author's opinion, but rec Leland; Lennon pp326-327 and conclusion of RTE *The Battle of Kinsale*

We were Catholics…: rec, Connolly p245

Like Fr Archer: Hogan p325

Slashed faces of priests' spouses: Lombard, Peter (1600) *Commentarius* p156, cited in O'Connor, Thomas, *Diplomatic Preparations for Kinsale*. Madrid: Universidad de Alcalá. Also rec, O'Connor, Thomas, in Morgan (ed) *BoK* pp60-66. Rec, Connolly pp 245-246. For comparisons elsewhere: rec, Janelle Werner (2009) *Priests and Concubines in England 1375-1549*

Águila's forebear: See Ch 3

Catherine beaten: Colles p152

Lap of honour: Leland (1773) v2 pp366-368

'Win the horse': CSPI p235

Chapter 27: 'They Died by Dozens on a Heap'

Monson quote: *Megalopsychy*

40 men a day: Ormond in CSPI p208

Dying by dozens: Mor Itin v3 p62

'Dysentery…': CSPV f1034, Dec 22 1601

Soldier's gear: See note in ch 13

'In a hard winter…': Moryson *Commonwealth*

Trench ladder: CSPS 840 f714 Jan 29 1602; rec Silke p136

Up to knees, PdZ to King, Dec 24 1601; rec *Epistolario* p91; filled, Mor Itin v3 p28.

Fuse cord: Kellie, Thomas (1627) *Pallas Armata*

Sentries frozen in position: Mor Itin v3 p66

'The winter…': Farmer

'Some are…': Mor Itin v3 p66

Camp layout: Map in pac v2

'Our horses…': CSPI p236

'So bad is…': Mor Itin v3 p81

'The fear they…': O'Cleary p309

'Our force grows…': CSPI p221

'A great part…': Mor Itin v3 p65

According to… plague: CSPI p216, p234

Bowlton: CSPI p220

D'Otthen career: Farmer and D'Otthen's monument in St Clement Dane's

Whip-round: Mor Itin v3 p66

'They died…': Moryson *Commonwealth* p293-294

'Not ten…': CSPI p154

Henry Danvers: refs in CSPI and Mor Itin v3; rec, entry in *Dictionary of National Biography*

'The weather…': CSPI p212

'It seems…of heart': CSPI p216

Carew has touched… end of a rope: Mor Itin v3 p66; had gallows, CalCarew p159

Severely punished: CSPI p216

'The misery…': Mor Itin p66

'In intolerable straits…': O'Cleary p309

Bacon quote: P 526 of Bacon, Francis (1824 edition) *The Works of Francis Bacon* v3. London: Baynes

'Houses so torn' and 'hard to make any….': CSPI p276

Feet visible: rec, Silke p169

JdA 'The enemy…' and 'now with him 1800 men': CSPS 840 f714 Jan 29 1602

Lost a thousand: CSPI p216

Tatters, unclad: OSB.

Sentries dying: *Bust*, PdZ

'Endure infinite…': CSPI p235

'Their best…': CSPI p191

'In want of fish… mid March': CSPS 840 f714

To New Year: *Bust*.; CSPI p641

'The Spaniards…': O'Cleary p309

Oviedo confirms…: Ov–Lerma Jan 26 1602; rec, McBride p113 and García Hernán p292.

Miseries incredible: CSPI p236

Chapter 28: A Meeting in the Fastness of Wood and Water

Most of this chapter is based on Bustamante's *True Account,* except:

'So trustworthy…': CSPS 840 f714, Jan 29 1602

Weather, storm: Mor Itin v3 p74; CalCarew p190

'Fastness…': *pac O'G v2* p50

Plashings: *pac O'G v2* p11

Variety of Irish troops: Rec, Falls, *Elizabeth's…* ch 4

Mantles as cabins: Moryson, *Commonwealth*

But Águila himself…be well': CSPI pp642–643

Mansoni's report: rec Jones *Indictment* pp 219–220

'concentrate and…': CSPS 840 f714, Jan 29 1602

'The Earls themselves…': CSPI pp642–643

Bustamante uneasy, Irish had no intention: See *Bust* dialogue with JdA later, his quotes in

Ch 30 and War Council findings in Chapter 36

O'Cleary quotes: O'Cleary pp 311-313. His hidden agenda: Author's view. Rec Morgan *BoK* p15, citing scholarship of Micheál MacCraith; also rec, Ho'D entry in *Dictionary of Irish Biography* (again by Morgan)

Most of CB's Irish loyal, gung-ho: See Ch 30

In any case... sea approaches: Author's view

Christmas feast: O'Cleary p311

McMahon: *pac O'G v2* pp54-55; 'bad limb' on footnote

Whiskey and warning: *pac O'G v2* p55; Mor Itin v3 p76

Cast doubt: 'must be discounted', Morgan, *BoK*, p124; 'fabrication', Silke p142; also rec Hayes-McCoy p161.

F. M. Jones says...: rec, Jones, *The Spaniards...* p37

Standish...: See footnote in *pac O'G v2* pp54-55

I believe... fool history: Author's view

CB had many sources; 'very strong guards': Mor Itin v3 p74

'Blount was worried... meet them halfway': CalCarew pp191-192

Three-division formation: Mor Itin v3 p78, OSB, a4m; two divisions, *Bust*. Rec, Ciaran O'Scea's analysis in Morgan *BoK* p367

200 Spanish with Ho'N: This is according to most sources, eg CSPS 840 f714, Jan 1602 and CSPI p235 and p240; however CSPI pp237-238 citing Ocampo says 180; *Bust* says 159; and *OSB* and Captain Dutton in *CSP Dom* p142 both say 300

Papal banners: Byrchensha, Ralph (1602) *A Discourse...* London: 'M.L.'

Went in order and array: O'Cleary p313

Chapter 29: 'My Lord, It Is Time to Arm'

Speed quote: Speed, John (1612) *The Theatre...*

Pinpoints of light: CalCarew, p192

'Flames' on lances: Mor Itin v3 p76

St Elmo's, spirit candles: Page 3 of Trevelyan, Marie (1909) *Folklore and Folk Stories of Wales.* London: Elliot Stock

Fuses: Kellie, Thomas (1627) *Pallas Armata*

He had honoured... at dawn: *Bust*; CSPI pp642-643

Ho'N left at midnight: *Bust*.

'By the darkness...' GC to Cecil, CSPI p240

Hardly rings true: Author's view. Hayes-McCoy says O'N was familiar with Kinsale, having camped there before

Modern historians tend to dismiss: eg: Hayes-McCoy p162

Irish 'dragged feet': rec Morgan, *BoK*, p126, citing Albornoz

'Not the desire for battle…': O'Cleary p313

CB heard news; 'some accident': Mor Itin v3 p76

Cavalryman's words: *pac O'G v2* p56

Power's version: CSPI p242

CB implements plan: Mor Itin v3 p77

CB took 1,200 foot and 300-400 horse: official Journal in CalCarew p193; report from I.E., who also says CB took all horses; but Power in CSPI p242 and Carew in CSPI p240 both say 1000 and 300-400, and *Bust* agrees; CB despatch of Dec 26, says 2000 and 300-400; and Dutton in *CSP Dom* p142 says 1,500 and 700

Wingfield… of battle: *ibid*

Power holds line: Mor Itin v3 p77

Halt advance: I.E.

Hugh O'Neill… old nemesis Blount: Mor Itin v3 p77; CSPI p242; Gainsford. Black tempest: I.E.

Ho'N reached spot on time; his troop numbers: *Bust* says he had around 6,000 foot and 500 horse overall; IE and Dutton in CSP Dom p143 agree, but Power says 5,000; on hilltop, *Bust* says Ho'N had 2,000 Ulstermen plus 400 Leinstermen and Ocampo's Spanish

Ho'N retreated: CalCarew p192; Mor Itin v3 p78; CSPI p242

Another English officer…: Edward Wingfield, CSPI p239

Ocampo 'embattle': CalCarew p192

One Spanish captain…: Pedro Sandoval, cited in (rec) Morgan *BoK* p126

'They tried to go…': O'Cleary p315

Blount agreed… close: CalCarew p192

The main reason… to react: CSPI p240, p242

Disadvantages of retreat: e.g., Battle of Turnhout. Rec, Jones, Archer (2001) *The Art of War in the Western World* Illinois: University of Illinois pp202-205

Thunderstorm: I.E.

The weather… the rear: Pac v2 p57

Blount decided… another ford: *Bust*; CSPI p242; CalCarew p193

At least four to one: that is, Ho'N's 6,500 vs CB's 1,600 (or 1,400), see earlier note.

Henry Power's… distant: CSPI p242

CB-scout dialogue: Pac v2 p58

Follow them and attack: I.E.

Arranged square: CSPI p242

Flying attack, 'in swiftness': Quote cited in Hogan p320-321; Moryson *Commonwealth*; JdA in pac (1810 ed) p345; also rec, Hayes-McCoy pp82-83; and rec, Lennon p57

Meanwhile, O'Neill's… part of it: Shane Sheale in CSPI p285

Both sides… in reserve: *Bust*; CalCarew p192-193; CSPI p242

O'Donnell… believe: CSPI p285; rec, Hayes McCoy, p164

Resolution to fight, ground of advantage: CalCarew p193

Chapter 30: 'The Day of Trial': The Battle of Kinsale

General note: The 'contemporary painting' is TCD's *The Battle of Kinsale* (see picture credits).

Monson quote, London earthquake, omen: Monson, William (1682) *Megalopsychy*

At the standoff…: William Farmer: *pac O'G v2* pp58-59; Mor Itin v3 p78-79; CSPI p268; CalCarew p193; Farmer; I.E; O'Cleary quote, p315

De Burgh escapes: Mor Itin v3 p81

Wingfield's 250: one cavalry officer: Capt. Dutton in CSP *Domestic* 1601-1603 p141-142

Wingfield and de Burgh… O'Neill has won: I.E.; CalCarew p193

'Great shout': CSPI p242

Just first move: rec, Hayes McCoy p165

500-600 horsemen; elite: Mor Itin v3 p80

Carew may confirm: CSPI p240

'In an instant': CSPI p240

The Irish horsemen… their horse fled and their foot brake: Moryson *Commonwealth*; *Bust*; CSPI p240; OSB; rec, Ciaran O'Scea's analysis in Morgan *BoK* p367

Shane Sheale 'our horsemen…': CSPI pp284-285

Watching incredulously… shifted for themselves: CalCarew p193; Power, CSPI p242. Note that accounts of this phase of battle differ fundamentally, with some English sources insisting that the Irish breakup and retreat was caused by an English charge. Rec, Ciaran O'Scea's analysis in Morgan *BoK* p367

If we had not… admit: CSPI p285

3,000 weapons: Farmer

'The execution… field': CSPI p269

'In each dike… moan': Byrchensha, *A Discourse*…

'Make no… revenge': CSPI p269; CalCarew p194

Sheale, 'butt end': CSPI p284

CB 'Had not the weather…': CB despatch to Council of Dublin, Dec 26

Irish three units, Tyrrell actions: *Bust*; rec, Hayes McCoy pp 166-167

Ho'D whereabouts: O'Cleary pp315-317; Sheale, CSPI p285

'The Spaniards, like…' : CSPI p269

Lopez De Soto 140: rec, García Hernán p34

Pikeman's capture: CSPI 1615-1626 p551; National Library of Ireland ms (1636) *Copy of Certificates and Evidence as to Capture of Alonso de Campo…* Ms 2, pp 28-29. Note, Ocampo capture also claimed by Dutton and Godolphin

JdA waiting at gate, watchmen posted: AGS, Report of Council of War to Felipe III, July 12 1603.

At one stage Fr Archer… triumph: Archer to Whyte, Jan 15 1602; rec, Jones *Indictment* p218 and Mangan's comments on that, p221

Scouts' report, proclamation: Ov-King Jan 27 1602; rec, McBride p115; also see War Council's report July 12 1603

Then: a furious explosion… closed once more: Mor Itin v3 p82; CSPI p239

De Burgh knighted: CalCarew p193, Gainsford. CB's words are a composite of reports in CalCarew and Farmer.

'Disordered and routed by…': Carleton, George (1624) *A Thankful Remembrance*

'Great harm': rec, García Hernán p17

Jealousy of de Burgh: rec, *Dictionary of Irish National Biography* vol 2

Irish deaths: '500', Ho'N to King Jan 16 1602, rec García Hernán pp 8-9; Power, CSPI p242; CB 1,000 in despatch to Council of Dublin; Carew 1,200, *pac O'G v2* p61; CB 1,200 in CalCarew p194; Moryson in Mor Itin v3 p80; O'Cleary 'many' in p317. However, CSPI p275 says 1,600 dead

The figures reported… slain, 1995: Mor Itin v3 p82

English deaths: D'Otthen cited in Morgan *BoK* p130; Dutton, CSP *Domestic* 1601-1603 p142; Cox, Richard (1689) in *Hibernia Anglicana*; Bacon, *op. cit.* p526

Ford of Slaughter: F. O'Sullivan *History*

Pushed into Kinsale: rec, Silke p146

The Irish insurgents… of Kinsale: Mor Itin v3 p101; Pac v2 p62; CalCarew p194; I.E.

'With sound of trumpet…': Farmer

Chapter 31: Wondering Why

'God did not…': Ov-Ibarra, Jan 24 1601; rec McBride p111 and rec, García Hernán p287

PdZ quote: PdZ-King, Jan 15 1601; rec *Epistolario* p99

'It was not the will…': O'Cleary p317

'God cast…': CSPI p240

'There appeared…': Bacon, *op. cit.* p526

'They think it no shame…:' and 'At Kinsale, when…': Moryson *Commonwealth*

1800s writers: e.g., D'Alton, Mitchel, O'Conor

The idea that… overruled them: Archer quote from letter to Whyte, rec, Jones *Indictment* pp 221-222; heard but ignored, *ibid* p222 and Oviedo-King Jan 27, rec McBride p115

Mangan: rec, *Vindication* p343+

Hayes-McCoy: rec, Hayes-McCoy p168

Weather foul: CB despatch to Council of Dublin, *op. cit.*

'Wind blew…:' Camden *Annales* p76

Multiple Error Theory: PdZ criticisms from PdZ-King, Jan 15, 1602; rec *Epistolario* p99. Rest, rec Hayes-McCoy, pp 168-170

Stirrups Theory: rec, Morgan *BoK* p141; Moryson Commonwealth; RTE1 *The Story of Ireland*, episode 2, 54 mins; Morgan *BoK* p131

Treachery: Mansoni, rec Jones, *Indictment* p220; Oviedo, Ov-Lerma Jan 26 1602 and Ov-King Jan 27; rec, McBride pp 113-115; 'English gold', Moran p214; rec García Hernán p8; rec Hayes-McCoy p169

The word 'panic'…: e.g., OSB; D'Alton p179; McGregor, John James (1829), *True Stories from the History of Ireland* Dublin: William Curry. p386

'Ran confusedly' etc: CSPI p269

However, recent… each other: e.g., Cocking, Chris, Drury, John and Reicher, Steve (2008) *The Mass Psychology of Disasters and Emergency Evacuations* (Presentation in Dublin 2/4/2008); McPhail, Clark (1991) *The Myth of the Madding Crowd* New York: De Gruyter

In my view…: My theory based on research by Perkins, Fruin, etc (see below)

Bend railings: rec, Perkins, Larry B. (2005) *Crowd Safety and Survival* USA: Lulu Press p140

John J. Fruin: rec, Fruin, JJ (1993) *The Causes and Prevention of Crowd Disasters* in Smith, R.A., Dickie, J. F. (eds) *Engineering for Crowd Safety* Amsterdam: Elsevier

Culture of Honour: My view. For more on C of H, see notes to Ch 25; dispute over precedence, *A4M*

Soon after… the prediction: Mor Itin v3 p82; *pac O'G v2* pp62-63

Nora Hickey quote: Hickey p19

Of course… last stand: rec silke p144; rec, Thuiller Hist. of Kinsale p29; rec Hayes-McCoy p147 and p164

In 1916…: Slaughter: F. O'Sullivan, *History*, pp67-70

Damian Shiels: Shiels, Damian, (2007) *The Kinsale Battlefield Project*, in IPMAG newsletter, Vol VI, Winter 2007

Chapter 32: 'Honourable Terms, or a Thousand Deaths'

In a two-hour sortie... big guns: Mor Itin v3 p83 and p110

'a volley...': Mor Itin v3 p83

Zubiaur reported...: CSPS 840 f714, Jan 29 1602

Blount wasn't...: CalCarew p195

Ho'N had 4,000-5000: My rough estimate, based on original force of 6,200 to 6,500 less Kinsale deaths and deserters. No-one knows for sure

Return to your...: CSPI p284

Ho'N switching: *pac O'G v2* p96

'Ill luck...': O'Cleary p317

'Many very brave...': PdZ-King, Jan 15 1602; rec, *Epistolario* p99

Led by Donal Cam: OSB.

Honour sacrifice, guard territories: O'Cleary p321

My brother... : OSB

'Rage and anger...': O'Cleary p321

Survivor Guilt: See DSM-IV, 'Associated Features and Disorders [of PTSD]' which refers to 'painful guilt feelings about surviving when others did not survive...' Also rec, Neeb, Kathryn (2005) *Fundamentals of Mental Health Nursing* Philadelphia: FA Davis, p191; Valent, P (2007) *Survivor Guilt* in Fink George (ed) (2010) *Stress of War, Conflict and Disaster* Oxford: Academic Press p623-625; and Leys, Ruth (2007) *From Guilt to Shame* Princeton: Princeton University Press pp 100-106. For symptoms, see UK National Health website www.ncbi. nlm.nih.gov/pubmedhealth/PMH0001923

accessed 30/01/2014

When O'Donnell finally... Innishannon: All O'Cleary p321 and a4m

Returning with 20,000, CSPI p284.

'With reluctance': a4m, also see *pac O'G v2* p96

Ho'D at Castlehaven: CSPS 840 f718, Feb 21 1602; *pac O'G v2* p64

PdZ 'encouraged them' etc: PdZ to King, Jan 15 1601; rec *Epistolario* p99; rec, Silke p148

Donal Cam 'courage': OSB

Ho'N's bid to submit, CB's reaction: *pac O'G v2* p96 and pp98-100; also rec, Silke p147; I am willing, *pac O'G v2* p96

Meanwhile George... he ordered: My analysis. Report with Boyle, see ch 1

March home, Sheale: CSPI p285

Rivers in flood: Mor Itin v3 p103

'A troop...': CSPI p275

Five days after... force us out: All *Bust*. Oviedo concedes that hunger was the greatest killer in Kinsale (letter to King, Jan 27). However, García Hernán (p8) believes the evidence shows that the Spanish did not have a problem with provisions.

900 sick, wounded: CSPS 840 f718, Feb 21 1602

'They rail...': CSPI p240

'The poor Spaniards...': Philalethes, Andreas (1602) *An Answer Made By One Of Our Brethren*

Águila asked, etc.: *Bust*; supported by CSPI pp 641-642; CalCarew pp 195-196

'I pray...': CSPI p272

Godolphin had excelled...: Stow, John (1631), *Annals*, cited in Gibson p86

Cornish raid: CSP *Domestic*, 1595-97 pp 78-81; *Monson Vol 1* p313, pp 323-324; Duro pp 92-93; rec, Rowse, A. L. (1941) *Tudor Cornwall* London: Jonathan Cape; rec, Ward, Alastair (2004) *Espana Brittania* Shepheard-Walwyn p83+; rec, BBC Radio 4 documentary, *Things We Forgot To Remember*, rec, website www.west-penwith.org.uk/raid.htm, accessed 29/12/2013

JdA's, CB's quotes in negotiation: CalCarew pp195-197; CSPI pp641-642; Mor Itin v3 pp 88-92

JdA had 1,800 effectives: CSPS 840 f714, Jan 29 1602 (but CalCarew p197 says 2,000). Insurgent force now <5,000: See earlier note in this chapter

He had been deserted...negotiations: CSPI p642

It was important... in the town: Mor Itin v3 pp109-110; CalCarew p195 footnote

Weak, indefensible: CSPI pp641-642, and *Bust*; like Blavet, CSPI p243

Despite all... miserable town: *pac* O'G *v2* pp83-84; CSPI p276

One week later... own expense: Mor Itin v3 p95; *pac* O'G *v2* p91

Cecil reaction to deal: CalCarew p216

Oviedo reaction: Ov-King, Jan 26; rec, McBride pp113-114

1,800 and 5,000: See earlier note in this chapter

Archer, Mansoni reactions: Archer to Whyte in Jones *Indictment* p218; Mansoni Report, *ibid* p223

Donal Cam quotes: CSPS 840 f717 Feb 16 1602; CSPI pp 301-302

Chapter 33: 'A Barbarous Nation for Which Christ Never Died'

An officer named... in their flesh: CSPS 840 f714, Jan 29 1602 NS

Young King... and thanks: CSPS 840 f715, Jan 30 1602 NS

Venetian report: CSPV f1048 and f1049, Jan 22 1602 NS

French invasion: CSPV f1035, Dec 24 1601, Marin Cavalli to Doge; CSPS 840 f713, end Dec 1601

As O'Donnell... relieve Don Juan: *pac* O'G *v2* 84-85; CSPS 840 f718, Feb 21 1602 NS

'Good friends': *pac O'G v2* pp 84–85

'Kind friendship': CSPI p272

'Truly… worse place': CSPI p292; also Bacon, *op.cit.*, p527. For more on JdA's disenchantment see CSPI p438 and p642

Maudling quote: BBC News website www.bbc.co.uk , (Jan 6 2006) *The Politics of Drinking in Power.* Accessed Dec 29 2013

JdA suggests peace: Mor Itin v3 p139

Stolen letters episode: All *pac O'G v2* pp101–103; CSPI p643

'Don Diegos': CSPI p276

Morejón's roots: Mor Itin v3 p134

Gold chain: rec, Morgan *BoK* p130

Harvey-Lopez de Soto: *pac O'G v2* pp129–134

Cecil doubted it: CalCarew p272

Gift of book: *pac O'G v2* pp 248–249

Bullets in mouths: e.g., see Davis, Edward (1619) *England's Trainings*, in Gleig, George (1832) *Eminent British Military Commanders* London: Longman

It was Feb 20… entire ordeal: CSPI p328; Mor Itin v3 p141; *pac O'G v2* p136

Separate tally: Carew in CSPI p300

60-70 pc: My estimate. Original force was 4464 (CSPS 840 f712 Dec 17 1601) Returning survivors: 1400 or 1880 in Feb + 1200 in March = 2,600 to 3080. Separately, Silke (p156) estimates 2,200 + 440 = 2660 returned. Report by Spanish Council (CSPS 840 f714 Jan29 1602) says JdA had 1800 + 900 sick = 2,700 in January

Ho'N lost…: See note 'Irish deaths' to Ch 30

Spanish deaths: OSB reckons 500 and Oviedo (Jan 27 to King) says 400-500, but see my statistics above. More dying daily, CSPI p297

English deaths: OSB reckons 8,000; 'eminent historian' reckoning 10,000 is Standish O'Grady, see footnote to *pac O'G v2* p256; PdZ reckons 3,000–4,000 'killed' as opposed to died (CSPS 840 f714)

Carew was… winter siege: *pac O'G v2* p256

Chapter 34: Dossier of Treason

CB under suspicion (generally): See p lxxiii of J. S. Brewer's Introduction to CalCarew; CalCarew p221; Spedding, numerous references (see CB listing in Index) especially pp 170–171; CSPI Introduction pp xi–xii; CSPI p220; Mor Itin Volume Two pp354–355; Maclean *Letters* p85 footnote; and pp90–91; Bruce, multiple references, especially page xviii, and xxi to xxv (also see CSPI Preface lxxiii)

Essex-Ho'N truce: Camden *History…* p571-574

Carleton letter: CSP *Domestic* 1601-1603 pp134-135

Lords' criticism: Mor Itin v3 p97

Even Secretary… heartbeat: CalCarew p216

CB negotiations with HO'N: *pac O'G v2* p96 and pp98-100

CB bared soul: Letter to Cecil Feb 15 1602 in Mor Itin v3 p120

The childless Elizabeth… once and for all: Camden *Annales* (1635); threat to Cecils from James, rec Connolly p241

Penelope wrote to James: rec, Wilson p108; rec, Rickman p119

Blount firmly… Privy Council: rec, CB entry in *Oxford Dictionary of National Biography*

'We that… negligence': Rare letter printed in p330 of (1663) *Cabala, Sive Scrinia Sacra* London: Bedell and Collins

Halfway… claim: Spedding, p168-170; rec, Strachey pp 228-229; rec, CB entry in *Oxford Dict. Nat. Biog.*

Essex in Queen's chamber, disgraced: Camden *History…* p574; rec, Strachey pp137-138

Vanished to Portsmouth: CSPI pp368-369

Blount who was… business ended: Declaration of Charles Danvers reproduced in pp333-337 of Spedding v2 Also see Spedding's damning comment pp170-171

Penelope at court: rec, Wilson pp99-100; rec, Falls *Mountjoy* p114; 'violating' Camden *Annales* p535; courtiers fawning, rec, Rickman p119

Penelope letter, power of press: From *Proceedings of the Earl of Essex* (1601) in p178 of Spedding. Also see p199. Quotes, letter reproduced in (rec) Rawson p226 and Wilson pp101-107

This stuff… little finger: rec, Wilson pp 101-106; rec, Rickman p119; rec, P Rich entry in *Oxford Dict. Nat. Biog.*

Southampton visit to CB; 'utterly rejected': Testimony of C. Danvers; Spedding v2 pp171-2 and p171 footnote; Strachey pp229-230; rec, Falls, *Mountjoy*, p135.

Foppish etc: rec, pp 85-86 of Bryson, Bill (2007) *Shakespeare* London: Harper; 'fair youth', rec, Boyd, William (2005) *Two Loves Have I* in The Guardian newspaper 19/11/2005; courageous soldier, rec, Falls, *Mountjoy* p135

Essex's financial plight: Letter from Essex to Elizabeth 22/9/1600; going mad, journal of Sir John Harington, cited in (rec) Dawson, Ian (1993) *The Tudor Century* Cheltenham: Nelson

Essex revolt: *A Declaration Touching The Treasons* [etc] in 1601; Camden *Annales*; Camden, *History…* v4 pp604-612; Spedding v4 pp244+

'Stood for a while…': Ross (1652)

Penelope dined with ringleaders, vacillating nobleman: rec, Rawson p244; rec, Wilson p112; rec, Rickman p119; rec, P Rich entry in *Ox. Dict. Nat. Biog.* Rawson (p222) says she was probably aware of CB's 'troops to Scotland' plot too

'Coward' quote: Letter to CB from Nottingham 31/5/1601 cited in p17 of Goodman, Godfrey (1839) *The Court of James I* v2; also see Spedding pp236-237; and Wilson ch 9

'Slave than sister': Letter to Nottingham from P. Rich cited in Goodman p18 and Rawson pp 252-253

Before his execution... design: Ross; Camden *Annales* p35; Goodman p17; rec, Falls *Mountjoy* p153; rec, Rickman p121

CB mentioned, damning parts suppressed: Spedding v2 pp 291-292 and footnote; and pp325

On Feb 22... he admitted privately: Mor Itin v3 pp353-355

'Dissembled, concealed': Camden *Annales* p35

'Lord Mountjoy... of the matter': Camden, *History*... v4 p629

'I am confident... this conspiracy': Letter CB to Cecil Feb 24, *CSPI 1600-1601*

Private cook, beddings: rec Rickman p121; rec, Falls *Mountjoy*, p155

Fortunately... black eyes: Letter to CB from Nottingham, *op. cit.*

By March... by Essex: Mor Itin volume two pp356-357

Conspire and collude: See first ref in this chapter; also following refs

Dark allusions: Maclean *Letters* p90 footnote

'Unworthy friends': Letter Cecil-Carew Aug 13 1601 in CalCarew p124

Gentleman or devil: CSPI p85

'It is sad... at home': CSPI introduction, page xii

'Kitchenmaid': *Calendar of the Carew Manuscripts* 1589-1600 item 494, from Lambeth Palace Dec 3 1600; she uses the nickname again in July 1602 (Qu-CB letter from Greenwich 15/7/1602)

Wreck peace deal: CalCarew p215

Scandalous, Portsmouth: CSPI pp368-369

'The emulation... removed': CSPI p279

Chapter 35: A Dead Juan Walking

Irish schoolbook: i.e., Gwynn, Stephen Lucius, Mrs. (1904) *Stories from Irish History, told for Children* Dublin: Browne & Nolan. Thanks to (rec) Morgan's *BoK*, p30 for drawing this to my attention

Pleasant passage, March 21: CSPI p363; *pac O'G v2* pp247-248

His return to Coruña: Duro p221, Cordoba p140

Águila stepped... turn at Ireland: CalCarew p217; CSPI p363

Cordoba diary: Cordoba p140

Merchant claimed: CSPI p362

Venetian report: CSPV f1068, March 28 1602. Also see Coroba p136–137 and Duro p221

Mightily railed, great credit: CSP *Domestic* 1601–1603 p176

Carew intelligence: CalCarew p225

Men dying, dead: CalCarew p249; *pac O'G v2* pp252–253; CalCarew pp324–325. Separately, JdA's report to King in April said he returned with 1,500 fit soldiers and 700 sick (= 2,200) plus Lopez de Soto's 400 foot soldiers = 2,600

'Some few'…: CalCarew p217

End of Irish-bound Armadas: Historical fact. Also, rec, Silke (p161) who says Ireland was 'written off' in mid-1602

Two months beforehand… as a Spanish colony: O'Cleary p323; a4m; CSPS 840 f716, Feb 13 1602. 'As colony', also see Watson, Robert and Thompson, William (1792) *The History of the Reign of Philip III Vol 1* Basle: Tourneisen, p92

5K, 10K, 13K troops: CalCarew p289; CSPI pp439–440; other port, CalCarew p324

Cecil reaction: CalCarew p272 and p324

Biron plot: Mor Itin v3 p174; background, rec, Biron entry in *Encyclopaedia Brittanica*

'Another report… desperate': CSPS 840 f732, Florence Conroy to King, Jan 13 1603

Ho'D's anguish, death: O'Cleary p327

Blake: CalCarew p241 and pp350–351

'Serpent': CalCarew p370

10k ducats: CSPS 840 f730, Nov 2 1602

The Duke… move on: My analysis; see notes to Ch 4; also rec, Silke on Lerma's attitude, p158 and pp170–171

'These people… may be': CSPS 840 f732 Jan 13 1603

'I would… Majesty': Count de Olivares in CSPS 840 f735 March 2 1603

Mansoni claim: Report to Rome, rec, Jones, *Indictment* p219

The Spanish had… depositions: CalCarew p220; rec, Silke p158

'To say the truth…': *pac O'G v2* pp247–248

Flung into prison as some histories assert: eg, D'Alton p182. This is a persistent myth. JdA was merely 'restrained in his lodgings' pending inquiries (CSPI 1603–1606 p8). He wrote letters from his home near Avila – see AGS E 3145 and AGS GA Leg 3145, both March 1603 (rec, García Hernán pp532–533). Also, rec, Silke p167

Águila was not… to the King: Monson letter to Cecil Oct 4 1602 in p417 of (1910) *Calendar of Ms of Robert Cecil* London: HM Stationery Office. Also (rec) James Archer entry by C. J. Woods in *Dictionary of Irish Biography* (2009) Cambridge: Cambridge University Press;

Archer's criticisms, rec, Jones *Indictment* and Mangan *Comment*

'God many times…': Mor Itin v3 p144

Gifts, JdA letter: *pac O'G v2* pp247-248

CB illness: Mor Itin p142; *pac O'G v2* p139

Carew wanted share: CalCarew p243

'The bearer… sending': CalCarew p248

Carew was not…kindness: CSPI p427

I render… myself: *pac O'G v2* pp217-218

'By Don… dream': Mor Itin p140

Edney episode and his quotes about trial: CalCarew p333, p356; *pac O'G v2* pp248-249 and pp251-252; CSPI pp 643-644

Chapter 36: The Trial

General note: An entire book could be written on the JdA trial alone: there are reams of complex accusations and rebuttals. I have tried to summarise the main charges based on the following documents, in order of importance: (1) Cristobal de Moura to War Council, April 1, 1603, listing 12 counts; (2) Ibarra to War Council, Sept 2 1602, listing five unanswered questions; and (3) Oviedo's complaints to Ibarra on August 6 1602. JdA's main defence is in his letter to the King on January 18, 1602. Silke (rec) presents a good brief analysis on p163; also rec García Hernán, p534, p498, p495 and p275. I have also incorporated Oviedo's, Archer's and Mansoni's accusations from other sources and included relevant documents from CSPI, *pac O'G v2* and CalCarew

The five topics: Ibarra-War Council, Sept 2 1602

Failure to capture Cork: also see CSPI p442

Failure to defend, cowardice: also see Archer letter to Whyte and Mansoni Report, rec Jones *Indictment* pp 217-220; Oviedo letters, rec McBride pp111-116

The twelve charges: de Moura-War Council, April 1 1603

JdA's defence document, great bravery: JdA to Ibarra from Avila, March 29 1603; JdA to King, Jan 18 1602

PdZ 'worst place': PdZ-King, Jan 15; rec *Epistolario* p99

Destination: War Council ruling July 12 1603. Also, rec, Silke p171

If Águila had marched…: CSPI p442

JdA hadn't enough men: CSPS 840 f712, Dec 17 1601; also see CSPI p467, '12,000 needed'

Shoreline: pac (1810 ed) pp 342-343

'The Irish… saddles': CalCarew p263

'Harnesses… horses': CSPS 840 f696 Nov 28 1600

Oviedo quote: Ov-King, Jan 27; rec McBride p115

Archer quote: Letter to Whyte *op. cit.*

JdA's quotes in defence: JdA-King, Jan 18 1602

Dereliction of duty: War Council ruling, April 12 1603. Also see Cordoba p137, CSPS 840 f719 Feb 22 1602.

Donal Cam letter: CSPS 840 f719

Lopez de Soto, timing: CSPI p441

'I waited… to escape': CSPI p641

'One puff': Quoted in Carleton, George (1624) *A Thankful Remembrance*

Ho'N explanation: In letter to King, Jan 16 1602; rec, García Hernán p37

Council verdict, JdA exonerated, minority opinion: War Council ruling from Valladolid, July 12 1603, with five points and a summary. Rec, García Hernán p564. Also see CSPI p573; Mor Itin v3 p313; CalCarew p316, p249; rec, Silke pp 171-173

PdZ was accused… he had trained: CSPI p573; CSPS 840 f714 Jan 29 1602; War Council report to King, Aug 3 1602; rec, *Epistolario* p104

Heredia: Carew ms, Lambeth Palace Library, MS 607 p203

'Don Juan… of the King': CSPI p573

Leading another mission: Mor Itin v3 p313; CalCarew p316 and p249; rec, Silke p172

Retired to El Barraco; quotes from Gil Gonzáles Dávila (1578-1658) pp 246-247; and Duro p221

He died: Gonzáles Dávila p247; Duro p221; 'of grief': *pac O'G v2* p251

'August 1602': This date seems based on *pac O'G v2* p251 and is probably a misunderstanding of 'shortly after'

English records: eg, Mor Itin v3 p313

Writing letters: eg JdA to Ibarra from Avila, March 29 1603

JdA funeral, interment, chapel and bequests, 'Juana': Gonzáles Dávila p247. I am also grateful to (rec) Professor Juan Carlos Bermejo de la Cruz, who reproduces JdA's Will in his website http://bermejoyclio.blogspot.ie (Accessed 01/01/2014). Summary and interpretation mine

Writers' verdicts, sources listed by name:

O'Conor (p21); Mitchel (p202); Gibson (vol 1, p369); D'Alton (pp 172-173 and 181-182)

Archer: from Letter to Whyte, *op. cit.*

Cecil: rec, Mangan *The Trial…* citing HMC Cecil Mss xi p526

Bacon, Francis (1670) *Certain Miscellany Works* London: Rawley

Carew, George: *pac O'G v2* pp217-218 and pp248-249

Blount, Charles: Mor Hist Book 2 p320

Leveson: From Mangan *The Trial...* citing HMC 5th Report p137

O'Sullivan: OSB

Toledo: Gil Gonzáles Dávila, p246

Ibarra: CSPI p294

Felipe III: CSPS 840 f715 Jan 30 1602

Gil Gonzáles Dávila: in p246

Hume: In p455 of Hume, Martin (1908) *Treason and Plot* London: Eveleigh Nash

O'Grady, Standish: *pac O'G v2* p251 footnote and *The Bog of Stars* p111

Chapter 37: The Aftermath

'Iron hot': Letter to CB July 15 1602

'We have killed...:' CSPI vol CCVIII Part two p91, cited in Falls *Eliz* p277

'Multitudes... nettles' and cannabalism: Mor Itin v3 pp281-283

Ho'N ravages: See notes to Ch 25

Ho'D plundering: O'Cleary p303

Ho'N held out...to Blount: Mor Itin v3 pp298-301

Ho'N terms: Mor Itin v3 p302; see preface p vii to Ó Cianáin

'I went near... peace': Colles p141.

CB was Ho'N's protector: Colles, *op. cit.*; also rec, Canny, Nicholas (2004) O'Neill entry in *Ox Dict Nat Biog*

Dogged by spies: Colles pp151-152

London warning: rec, Canny, Ho'N entry in *Ox Dict Nat Biog*

Plotting: Wills p324-325; rec, *The Flight of the Earls* summary in BBC History website in www.bbc.co.uk/history/british/plantation/ Accessed Jan 3 2014.

Breton ship sailed Sep 14: Ó Cianáin p9

Not a flight: This is hotly debated. See Gainsford; Colles pp153-154, Canny Ho'N entry in *Ox Dict Nat Biog* and the BBC History website *op. cit.* For another perspective, see John McGurk quoted in Irish Times *The Flight of the Earls Was More A 'Strategic Regrouping'*, Aug 20 2007

Not many earls: Two (O'Neill and Ruairi O'Donnell), plus a baron, a countess and some minor chiefs. See a4m and Preface to Ó Cianáin. Rec, BBC History article *op. cit.*: 'not so jam packed with the Gaelic nobility after all'

Lamented by Bards: e.g., Mac an Bhaird and Fear Flatha O Gnímh

Ho'N's high hopes: Rec, McGurk in Irish Times *op. cit.*

Sightseeing: eg, Ó Cianáin p67, p69, p71

Louvain, Nancy, Lucerne: Ó Cianáin pp51-59; p77; p87

Wrote to Felipe: rec, Canny, Ho'N entry in *Ox Dic Nat Biog*

Horse fell: Ó Cianáin pp88-89

Rome experience: Ó Cianáin pp169+

'The English completely...': Letter to Andres Velasquez, May 1615

Died in Rome: Ho'N entry in *Ox Dic Nat Biog*

Pan-European visionary: eg, rec, O'Faolain, pp 277-279

Tactical error, vulnerable: See a4m, 'Woe to the heart...'; rec, Morgan, Hiram, final two pars in Ho'N entry in *Dictionary of Irish National Biography;* and Canny, Nicholas (1970) *Hugh O'Neill... and the Changing Face of Gaelic Ulster* Studia Hibernica No 10 pp7-35, who says the 'ill-advised' flight led to the extinction of the Gaelic way of life

Plantation, economic migrants: See notes to Ch 38

Archer in Dunboy: O'Halloran, W (1916) *Early Irish History...* ch 16; Hogan p339

JdA's threat to re-take Dunboy: *pac O'G v2* p120

Archer's narrow shave: *pac O'G v2* pp181-182

Inquiry, forged letter: CSPI 1603-1606 p8; Hogan p340

Jesuits objected: Hogan pp349-350

Death, legacy: Hogan, assessment of JA

Archer 'English agent' hypothesis: Merely an interesting thought experiment. As I say, the evidence is purely circumstantial.

Lynch: Dual role revealed by Morgan, rec *BoK* pp353-354.

Owen: Rec, García Hernán p37

Dominic Collins: *pac O'G v2* p572, pp577-578; CSPI p437, p439-440; rec, www.jesuit. org biog of Dominic Collins, accessed 04/01/2014

Donal Cam: D'Alton pp182-187

Spanish side:

General aftermath in Spain; Lerma, Felipe III paragraphs: My analysis based on facts in Hume *Spain, Its...* and Hume, Martin (1907) *Spain Under Philip III* in *Cambridge Modern History.* 'Hunted, danced' quote from the latter

Decline of *tercios*: My analysis, but rec, Israel, Jonathan (1997) *Conflicts of Empires* London: Hambledon, p90 and rec González de Leon (2009)

Felipe left country stronger: For insights into both viewpoints, see Feros, Antonio (2000) *Kingship and Favoritism in the Spain of Philip III* Cambridge: University Press, pp2-3, and Parker, Geoffrey (1984) *Europe in Crisis* London: Fontana

Margaret's 1606 clash with Lerma: p93 of Sanchez, Magdalena S (1996) *Melancholy and*

Female Illness... at the Court of Philip III in Journal of Women's History Vol 8 No 2; also Hume, *Spain Its...* pp219-220; her children, her death: Hume *Spain Its...* p216

Zubiaur and Lopez de Soto trials: War Council report to King, May 12 1605; rec *Epistolario* pp109-110. Also rec, Silke p174 and pp160-161 and Coombes and Ware p57

Brochero: Under protection, rec, Silke p170; career and death, Goodman, David (2003) *Spanish Naval Power 1589-1665* Cambridge: University Press, p32 and p189

Oviedo's later life: Moran pp217-236; rec, Silke pp174-175; rec García Hernán pp36-37

English side:

Cost of wars: CSP *Domestic* 1601-03 pp244-245; Bagwell v3 p439; Colles p137

'Don Juan...lord': CSP *Domestic* 1601-1603 pp260-261

Seized with illness: Ranke, Leopold (1875) *A History of England Vol III* Oxford: Clarendon p352

Cecil and smooth succession: generally, Bruce, Introduction; his supposed support for Infanta and denials, Bruce pp31-33; satchel story, Bruce p34; Also rec, BBC Radio 4 (2009) *In Our Time: The Death of Elizabeth I*, broadcast Oct 15 2009

Carew's attempt... admit: CSPI p244; rec, Morgan *BoK* p139

Poets sang: eg Byrchensha, *A Discourse*, which invoked Jehovah; Ford, John, *Fame's Memorial*

Play: *England's Joy*, poster for The Swan theatre Nov 6 1602

Earl Devonshire, lands, peace commission: Lee, Sidney, CB entry in *Dictionary of National Biography* 1885-1900 vol 5l; Craik, p268

Spanish spoils etc: CalCarew p231

Venetian report: CSPV late 1603, f147, Oct 22 1603

CB's Spanish pension: Hull ch 19; rec, Lee, Sidney, *op. cit.*

Virginia, America: rec, Morgan *BoK* p3

Divorce, remarriage: Heylin, Peter (1671) *Life and Death of Archbishop Laud* p53; alteration in King, *ibid* p53-54; Craik, p273

'Flagrant crime', 'black soul': Craik pp274-275 and p277; Rawson p287

Burning fever, CB death, line died with him: Rawson p287, p288, p299; Craik pp282-283

'Genocide' unfair: My view. Tried to clear: rec, Connolly p268. Evacuated women and children from Kinsale: Mor Itin v3 pp44-46 and p57. Also, CB's letter to London, 1602, pleading for tolerance and an understanding of Irish fears (in Curry, pp 19-20) clearly refutes this myth

Penelope's revival under James: Craik pp268-272; Rawson pp 267-277

Remarriage scandal, PR disgraced: Craik pp273-277; Rawson p287

World grey, PR's death: rec Rawson p310; Wall, Alison, P Rich entry in *Ox Dict Nat Biog*

Carew aftermath: Entry in *Ox Dict Nat Biog,* my comments

O'Brien aftermath: Entry in *Dict Nat Biog*

Wingfield aftermath: Dict Nat Biog; website www.powerscourt.ie Accessed 06/01/2014

Moryson aftermath: Mor *Itin; Dict Nat Biog*

Bodley aftermath: Entry in Dict Nat Biog; quote, Parr, Richard (1686) *The Life of James Usher*

Boyle aftermath: Entry in *Dict Nat Biog*; 1631 incident, see Ekin, Des (2006) *The Stolen Village* Dublin: O'Brien

De Burgh aftermath: Hero, see *pac O'G v2* pp293-295 and notes to Ch 30

Married lover Frances, see Morrill, John, entry for Robert Devereux in *Ox Dict Nat Biog*

Poems to Queen, 'special grace', see Carpenter, Andrew (2003) *Verse in English from Tudor and Stuart Ireland* Cork: University Press, citing RdB's 1602 poem and John Massingham's 1602 diary

Immunity for his beliefs, resisted Galway plantation: Lennon, Colm, entry for Burke, Richard, in *Ox Dict Nat Biog*

Ancestors of Diana and William: Author's genealogical research. Also rec Evans, Richard K (2007) *Ancestry of Diana, Princess of Wales* New England Historic Genealogical Society

Chapter 38: Legacy

Camden quote: from Camden *Annales* (1635) p170

Smouldered: See *Long Term Consequences* in www.bbc.co.uk/history/british/plantation/ Accessed 11/12/2013

Exploded in 1641, 1916, 1968: i.e., 1641 Rebellion; the Easter Rising of 1916 (following the Home Rule Crisis of 1912-1914); first year of Troubles in 1968. Many more dates could be added

Flight, Plantation: See notes later in this chapter

1641 massacres, Cromwell butchery: Colles, Ramsay (1919) *The History of Ulster* Vol 3. London: Gresham Publishing, pp 1-148; rec, Stewart, A. T. Q. (1989) *The Narrow Ground* Belfast: Blackstaff Press, p51-52; also see *1641 Rebellion* and McCavitt, John, *The Plantation Provoked the 1641 Rebellion* both in www.bbc.co.uk/history/british/plantation/ Accessed 11/12/2013. For more on Cromwell, rec Micheál Ó Siochrú (2008) *God's Executioner.* London: Faber & Faber.

Kinsale put… wither and die: My analysis

Death of Gaelic Order: a4m; rec, Canny, Nicholas (1970) *Hugh O'Neill… and the Changing Face of Gaelic Ulster* Studia Hibernica No 10 pp7-35. Canny says the Flight of the Earls made the extinction of the Gaelic way of life 'inevitable'. Wills's 1840 viewpoint (pp 321-323) speaks volumes about colonial attitudes

1.5 million hectares: Lenihan, *op. cit.*, p 45, says 4 million acres = 1.6m hectares

A fifth to Irish: See Hunter, R. J., (2009) *Settlement Map* (transcript) in BBC History link above; also Lenihan, *op. cit.*, p 47

1608 Rising: Colles, Ramsay (1919) *The History of Ulster* Vol 2. London: Gresham Publishing, chs 22-23; rec, Lenihan, Padraig (2008) *Consolidating Conquest*. Harlow: Pearson Education, p 44.

Six counties: Colles, *op. cit.*, vol 2, p177

80pc Scots: Actually 83pc (100,000 Scots to 20,000 English in 1641.) See Montgomery, Michael (2009) *The Linguistic History of Ulster* in www.bbc.co.uk/history/british/plantation/ Accessed 11/12/2013

Spoke Gaelic: rec Roger Blaney in *Presbyterians and the Irish Language* (Ulster Historical Foundation, 2012)

Always intermingled: rec Fitzgerald, Patrick, *The 17th Century Irish Connection* in Devine, T.M., Wormald, Jenny (eds) (2012) *The Oxford Handbook of Modern Scottish History*. Oxford: Oxford University Press. Also rec, Stewart, *op. cit.*, p 39; and Lennon pp 268-269

Scots fled farming famines: See *Economic Background of the Settlers* and *Settlers Were Poor People Who Came to Ulster to Prosper* via BBC History link above. Also rec, Fitzgerald, *op. cit*, pp 297-8

Two 'What ifs'...: author's speculation

French troops: CSPV f1035, Dec 24 1601, Marin Cavalli to Doge; CSPS 840 f713, Council of State to King, end Dec 1601

DES EKIN is a journalist and the author of four books. Born in County Down, Northern Ireland, he began his career as a reporter at age sixteen and rose to become Deputy Editor of the Belfast *Sunday News* before moving to his current home in Dublin. He worked as a journalist, columnist, Assistant Editor and finally a Political Correspondent for the *Sunday World* from 1982 until 2012. He has written two crime novels, *Stone Heart* and *Single Obsession*. His true-life history book, *The Stolen Village* (2006), was shortlisted for the Argosy Irish Nonfiction Book of the Year Award and Book of the Decade in the Bord Gáis Energy Irish Book Awards 2010. He is married with a son and two daughters.